Discovering
the
Moscow Countryside

Discovering
the
Moscow Countryside

A TRAVEL GUIDE TO THE HEART OF RUSSIA

Kathleen Berton Murrell

I.B.Tauris *Publishers*
LONDON • NEW YORK

Published in 2001 by I.B.Tauris & Co Ltd
6 Salem Road, London W2 4BU
175 Fifth Avenue, New York NY 10010
www.ibtauris.com

In the United States of America and in Canada distributed by
St Martin's Press, 175 Fifth Avenue, New York NY 10010

ISBN 1 86064 673 5

A full CIP record for this book is available from the British Library
A full CIP record for this book is available from the Library of Congress

Library of Congress catalog card: available

Typeset in Times Roman (Monotype) by The Midlands Book
Typesetting Company, Loughborough
Printed and bound in Great Britain by MPG Books Ltd, Bodmin, Cornwall

CONTENTS

For my dear friend, Mary Escombe, the most delightful and resourceful companion on so many of my journeys in the Moscow countryside, with deep affection and gratitude.

ACKNOWLEDGEMENTS

In addition to Mary Escombe, to whom this book is dedicated, I would like to thank sincerely those who generously provided help and companionship in my travels. Central to the project were my husband Geoffrey Murrell, Sergei Romaniuk (whose original suggestion gave birth to this book), Kate Cook (companion in many adventures), Delmar Fall (the best navigator), Galina Romaniuk, Margaret Potter, Sarah Murrell, Nikita Vvedenskaya, Mark Frankland, Natasha Razgon, Eleanor Carpenter. Other kind friends who took part in the excursions were Gila Andreev, John and Verabelle Berton, Kathy Bond, John and Jenny Bowan, Jill and Rodric Braithwaite, Paula and Annick Charousset, Tim Colton, Virginia Crowe, Ellen Dahrendorf, Stephanie Early, Jim Escombe, Frances Green, Myra Green, Jane Banfield Haynes, Natasha Hritzuk, Lindsey Hughes, Nina Iovleva, Jane Karch, Jack Lancere, Jennifer Louis, Tatiana Mallinson, Karina Migranyan, Olga Morel, Alec Murrell, Alice Murrell, Vera Nanivskaya, Raili and Martin Nicolson, Andrei Petrov, Catherine Philips, Wendy Ramsell, Eleanor Randolph, Alexei Rogachev, Natasha Semenova, Dmitry and Katya Shvidkovsky, Ruth Steele, Jeanne Sutherland, Terri Tollemache, Olga Trifonova, Joanna Woods, Vasily Zhuravlev.

Kathleen Berton Murrell supplied all the photographs except the portrait of Abramtsevo church, caption 25, by the Russian photographer, Igor Palmin. Pamela Goodwin kindly drew the maps.

GLOSSARY

apse - semicircular or faceted eastern extension of a church, containing the altar.

balki - beams, in wooden churches often decorated.

bargeboards - decorated boards on the gabled front of wooden houses which hide the ends of the roof timbers.

begunets - traditional horizontal triangular design on the upper part of a facade.

belvedere - a small look-out tower, usually on the roof of a house.

betonka - a road of concrete blocks; also the formerly closed A-107 and A-108 ring roads in the Moscow Oblast.

bochka - ogee-shaped roof gable.

boyar - the aristocracy before Peter the Great.

Cheka- Soviet secret police 1918-22.

cour d'honneur - the enclosed front courtyard of a mansion or palace where carriages can draw up.

cupola/dome - derived from Byzantine architecture. In Russia the early helmet-shaped domes soon evolved into the familiar onion shape.

Decembrists - young officers of the nobility who took part in the uprising against Tsar Nicholas I in December 1925. Most of them were sentenced to hard labour or exile in Siberia.

D.O. - *dom otdykha,* house of rest.

dumny dyak - fourth rank in the Muscovy (pre-Petrine) Boyars' Duma (Council).

dumny dvoryanin - third rank in the Muscovy Boyars' Duma.

Empire - an expressive, decorated form of the severe classical style popular from about 1800 to 1830.

fresco - wall and ceiling paintings on fresh, wet plaster which are very durable.

GAI - *Gosudarstvennaya Avtomobilnaya Inspektsiya,* State Automobile Inspectorate (transport police), now changed to GIBDD (State Road Safety Inspectorate) but the acronym GAI is still employed by motorists.

grotto - artificial rustic caverns for pleasant retreats in the grounds of large houses.

gulbishche - an open gallery usually elevated surrounding three sides of a church.

iconostasis - the screen of icons separating the chancel from the main church, which developed in the 14th century (see p.15).

icons - venerated images of saints and religious scenes painted on wooden panels.

inscribed cross or cross in square - a square church cross-vaulted and centrally domed (quincunx).

KGB - Soviet secret police 1953-91.

kokoshniki - non-structural decorative gables, round, triangular or ogee-shaped (see *zakomary*).

kottedzhi - 'cottages' - large modern mansions in fanciful designs built by new Russians.

Lavra - title of the most important Russian Orthodox monasteries.

lemekhi - roof shingles of aspen wood carved and slotted to fit the curves of cupolas.

lopatki - pilasters without base or capital which divide a wall.

lucarne - a small window in an attic or spire.

MGB - Soviet secret police 1946-53.

MKAD - acronym for the major highway that circles Moscow.

nebo - literally sky or heaven. It refers to the ceiling in wooden tent-shaped churches divided into wedges and painted with saints and archangels.

NKVD - Soviet secret police 1934-46.

nomenklatura - the ruling elite, holders of the most important Party posts in Soviet times.

Oblast - the region around Moscow.

ogee - a double curved concave and convex line like an S. Describes the onion-shaped Russian cupolas and *bochki* gables.

P.L. - *pionersky lager*, pioneers' camp for children aged 7-14.

palatka - small tent-shaped building.

papert - church porch.

parterre - level formal garden on the French pattern.

pilaster - a shallow pier in one of the classical orders projecting slightly from a wall.

pogost - enclosed country cemetery with one or two churches (winter and summer) and bell tower, which was the social centre for far-flung communities.

porebrik - traditional brick horizontal design on the upper part of a facade.

pritvor - entrance lobby of a church.

quatrefoil - describes a building in the form of four lobes or cusps.

refectory - the dining room of a monastery.

shatrovy - tent-shaped - describes the octagonal tower churches of the 16th and 17th centuries derived from the wooden architecture of the north.

skit - hermitage.

summer church - the larger of a pair of churches without heating facilities.

trapeza - means 'refectory' but also in church architecture the first, western hall or vestibule where traditionally meals could be taken during long services.

tyablo - shelf of icons.

ulitsa - street.

verst - Russian measurement of distance equivalent to 1.06 km.

v lapu - walls of logs so fitted that the corner ends do not protrude, i.e. by the use of mortice and tenon joints.

v oblo - the commonest method used in wooden buildings whereby the log joints meet through semicircular notches allowing the overlapping ends to project.

winter church - the smaller of a pair of churches, provided with heating.

Yedinoverie - (single faith), the movement to bridge Old Believer and Orthodox beliefs which began in 1800.

zakomary - roof gables, round or pointed, reflecting the interior vaulting.

zek - abbreviation of *zaklyuchenny*, a prisoner in the Soviet concentration camp system.

LIST OF MAPS

INTRODUCTION

One of the benefits of the collapse of the Soviet Union was the removal of the barriers to travel, particularly for foreigners, in October 1992. The hitherto largely closed Moscow Oblast (Region) that surrounds the city in a great circle at a radius of 100 to 150 kilometres, was thus thrown wide open to the curious. For four years I made trips two or three times a week winter and summer along the major routes beginning, as in the book, with the Minsk/Mozhaisk road. Later, after my husband and I left Moscow, I returned often, borrowing cars from kind friends and checking and double checking the places described. An essential companion was the formerly 'secret' map of the Oblast which was put on general sale in 1993. My main reference, a gift from my daughter, was the two-volume *Pamyatniki Arkhitektury Moskovskoi Oblasti* published in 1975 under the editorship of E. Podyapolskaya and now in the process of republishing in an expanded, six-volume version. Its one defect is that it describes the main buildings in strictly architectural terms never alluding to their surroundings or present use. Thus the object of the search might turn out to be a dilapidated church unexpectedly concealed behind the high walls of an army base (the kind soldier on duty would sometimes allow a glimpse). Or I would travel long distances to a former monastery to find it in use as an insane asylum (now gradually being closed). But more often the old estates are sanatoria or houses of rest where no-one seems to mind inquisitive visitors. There were also many interesting buildings not mentioned in the exclusive Podyapolskaya volumes. Thus driving down the road to Yegorevsk through the Gzhel villages I was astonished to see the soaring Old Believer Church of St George, a brilliant Art Nouveau adaptation of traditional tower churches. Of course most of the churches so imposingly designated 'monuments of architecture' were in appalling condition, their cupolas leaning at rakish angles or gone altogether, huge cracks or holes in the fabric, bell towers turned into stumps, the interiors completely vandalised filled only with pigeons. I am conscious that the words 'ruined', 'dilapidation', 'neglected', recur all too frequently in this book. But there is also much evidence of restoration and renewal. With the renaissance of the Russian church even some of the worst have begun to be taken under the care of parishioners who in spite of their frugal means are slowly embarking on expensive repairs. It was a heartening sight to enter a church where only a dirt floor remained to find the priest in a corner baptising a group of noisy children or, on another occasion, to happen upon a rededication service packed with people in flickering candlelight without an iconostasis and against bare brick walls.

Encounters with people were one of the delights of these travels. The many new priests I met, hastily recruited to the reopened churches, came unlike the traditional Orthodox priests, from all walks of life, e.g. a former scientist, journalist, naval officer. I came upon artists in their studios, such as Andrei Volkov mentioned below, a group of archeologists whose only means of funding their dig was to make it an educational project by including children, several excellent self-appointed local historians, and, most unexpectedly, many people pleased with the new conditions after the demise of the Soviet Union. In all my journeys in the Moscow countryside I saw no sign of the lawless, violent post-Communist Russia portrayed in the Western press. On the contrary I found kindness and helpfulness everywhere, pride and the usual Russian tendency to pour out their troubles at the slightest prompting. Neither did I see terrible poverty; indeed judging by the shops and general look of the villages where new building is going on apace (including the ugly red brick *kottedzhi* of the new Russians) life has definitely begun to improve after the stagnation of the Soviet years.

I travelled by Russian Zhiguli (Lada) which proved very reliable suffering no more than the odd flat tyre. The roads are on the whole remarkably good although there was the occasional impassable track. I never stayed overnight as even the most distant places are accessible within a day, although now there are many houses of rest happy to have customers. Petrol was a problem in the early 1990s when I had to take a spare canister but nowadays there are plenty of petrol stations especially outside the larger towns. Picnics are advisable as cafes are still few and far between except in the towns. I occasionally travelled by suburban railway, the *elektrichka*, which with connecting bus routes covers most of the area, but there are large parts of the countryside where there is poor service. I have kept to strict transliteration for place names to make it a little easier for drivers to recognise signs in Cyrillic.

I can truly say that the research and travel undertaken in the course of preparing this book was always a fulfilling and exciting experience. In the Moscow countryside you never know what lies round the next corner but you can be sure it is always intriguing.

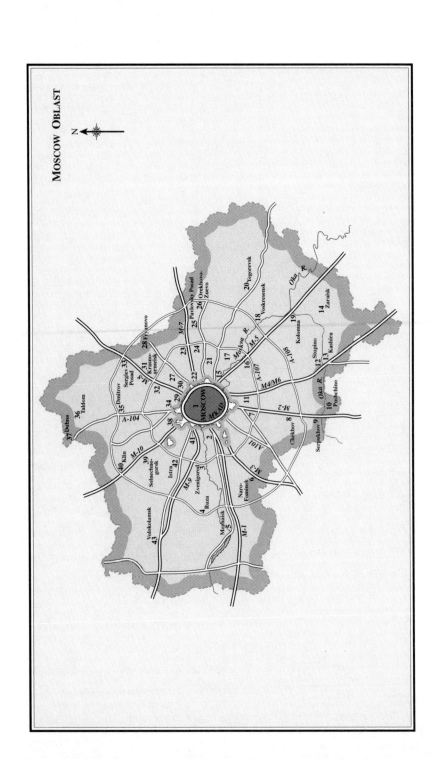

MOSCOW OBLAST

N

MOSCOW OBLAST

1. MOSCOW
2. ODINTSOVO
3. ZVENIGOROD
4. RUZA
5. MOZHAISK
6. NARO-FOMINSK
7. PODOLSK
8. CHEKHOV
9. SERPUKHOV
10. PUSHCHINO
11. DOMODEDOVO TOWN
12. STUPINO
13. KASHIRA
14. ZARAISK
15. LYUBERTSY
16. BRONNITSY
17. RAMENSKOE
18. VOSKRESENSK
19. KOLOMNA
20. YEGOREVSK
21. ZHELEZNODOROZHNY
22. BALASHIKHA
23. NOGINSK
24. ELEKTROSTAL
25. PAVLOVSKY POSAD
26. OREKHOVO-ZUEVO
27. SHCHELKOVO
28. FRYANOVO
29. MYTISHCHI
30. KOROLEV
31. KRASNOARMEISK
32. PUSHKINO
33. SERGIEV POSAD
34. DOLGOPRUDNY
35. DMITROV
36. TALDOM
37. DUBNA
38. KHIMKI
39. SOLNECHNOGORSK
40. KLIN
41. KRASNOGORSK
42. ISTRA
43. VOLOKOLAMSK

Road 1   MINSK-MOZHAISK HIGHWAY M-1: ZVENIGOROD AND BORODINO

The old southwest Mozhaisk Road (the modern Minsk Highway M-1 runs parallel) was in the 16th and 17th centuries the main road to Poland and western Europe. The magnificent church of Tsar Boris Godunov's estate survives from this time as does the great monastery at Zvenigorod. French and Russian soldiers confronted each other along this road culminating in the Battle of Borodino. Among the many former stately homes are modern dacha settlements like the writers' village at Peredelkino.

Leave Moscow on the Mozhaiskoe Shosse going southwest past dull tower blocks to cross the MKAD and join the Minsk Highway M-1 where green watered fields and tall birch forests soon appear.

THE MOZHAISK ROAD

On the M-1 a few hundred metres beyond the MKAD take the first paved road to the right. It soon crosses the busy railway line into the dacha village of **NEMCHINOVKA**. Although so close to the capital, the village of small wooden houses feels light years away. Before and after the revolution it was a popular place for summer visitors including Moscow's leading Art Nouveau architect, Fedor Shekhtel, and the film director, Sergei Eisenstein. Kazimir Malevich, the leading avant-garde artist, also spent his summers here in the early 1900s in the dacha of his in-laws. To find it turn left immediately after the railway and then left and right onto Borodinskaya Street to No 18. Here he wrote his definitive *On New Systems in Art* published in 1919 (his enthusiasm was so great for the new art that he called his daughter Una after Unovis, the society he founded). By 1935 when he died his art had been rejected for socialist realism, the style imposed by the Party and Government. His ashes were quietly brought to Nemchinovka and buried deep in the woods nearby. A cube made from a huge log of pine was sculpted by his friend, Nikolai Suetin, and placed over the grave but was lost during the war. In the *perestroika* years devotees erected a memorial stone to the artist and placed a new cube at the edge of the woods just beyond the village. Malevich admirers meet here every year on May 15, the anniversary of his death, to celebrate his genius.

2

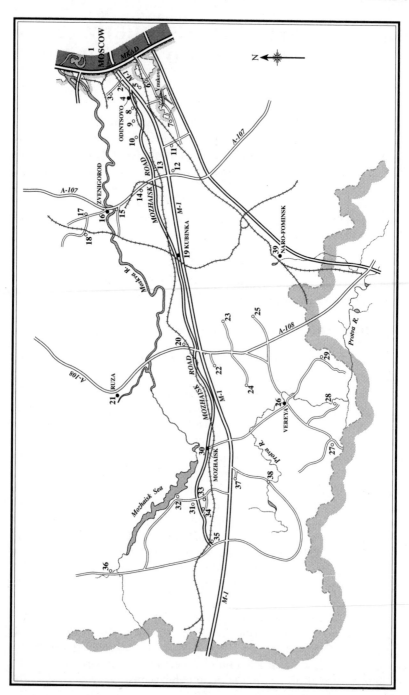

ROAD 1
ZVENIGOROD AND BORODINO

1. MOSCOW
2. Nemchinovka
3. Romashkovo
4. ODINTSOVO
5. Peredelkino
6. Fedosino
7. Izvarino
8. Akulovo
9. Yudino
10. Perkhushkovo
11. Krekshino
12. Sidorovskoe
13. Bolshie Vyazemy
14. Zakharovo
15. Vvedenskoe
16. ZVENIGOROD
17. Yershovo
18. Koralovo
19. KUBINKA
20. Dorokhovo
21. RUZA
22. Petrishchevo
23. Arkhangelskoe
24. Bogorodskoe
25. Slepushkino
26. VEREYA
27. Subbotino
28. Vyshgorod
29. Spas Kositsy
30. MOZHAISK
31. Borodino
32. Staroe Selo
33. Semenovskoe
34. Shevardino
35. Kolotskoe
36. Poreche
37. Sivkovo
38. Troparevo
39. NARO-FOMINSK

Continue west passing, right, a self-important institution sprouting commu-
nications discs and surrounded by ugly peeling apartment blocks. Known
as Nemchinovka-1, it is the Scientific Research Institute of Agriculture
founded in 1931 to discover new strains of hardy grains, a harbinger of the
era of the quack biologist, Trofim Lysenko, with his theory of the inheri-
tance of acquired characteristics. **ROMASHKOVO** *is 7 km.*

Ahead is the Uspenskoe area and the summer villas used by Stalin and
the other Party bosses. On the right is the Romashkovo railway station
on the spur line that served the Soviet leaders' dachas at Zhukovka and
Usovo.

At the end of the 16th century Romashkovo belonged to **Ksenya**
Romanova, the mother of Mikhail, the first Romanov Tsar. Boris
Godunov, determined to forestall rival claims to the throne, sent
Ksenya to a nunnery and forced Mikhail's father, Fedor, to become a
monk. In 1613 eight years after Godunov's death and at the end of the
Time of Troubles, 16-year-old Mikhail was proclaimed Tsar and his
mother, now Sister Marfa, became his chief advisor. But Mikhail's
father, now the monk Filaret, became Patriarch and soon ousted
Ksenya from her position of influence. Romashkovo remained a royal
property until the liberation of the serfs in 1861. In the 1930s a huge
collective farm, *Stalin*, was organised there (renamed *Druzhba*, Friend-
ship, in 1960). The brick **Church of St Nicholas** was built in pseudo-
Russian style in 1867 by the elderly Petr Zavyalov. In 1940 the church
was closed, the iconostasis and icons were burned, and the building was
used to store grain and then documentary films. In the spring of 1990
the decaying church was restored and reopened. **Stalin's daughter**,
Svetlana, liked to walk to Romashkovo from her father's dacha, and
refers to it in this touching excerpt from her memoirs:

> And when I die let them bury me in the ground here in Romash-
> kovo, in the graveyard by the station, on the little hill. There's a
> feeling of space there; there are fields and sky. There's a nice old
> church on the hill. True, it's not used any more and it's falling
> down and the trees have grown up rank in the enclosure around it,
> but it stands splendid in the dense greenery and goes on all the
> same serving the cause of everlasting good on earth. Let them bury
> me there.

Return to Nemchinovka and rejoin the Minsk Highway. After 5 km where
the road divides take the lesser, Mozhaisk Road on the right signed

*ODINTSOVO and follow it 20 km to Bolshie Vyazemy. All the churches
are now functioning.* At **Odintsovo** are the classical **Church of the Grebnev
Icon of the Virgin,** *Grebnevskoi Bogomateri,* built in 1802, the fine Art
Nouveau **Railway Station** of 1900 by Lev Kekushev, and the former
offices of Yakunchikov, the brick manufacturer, now the local museum.
At **Akulovo,** 2 km right is the classical **Church of the Intercession,** *Pokrova,*
built in 1807 with a fine iconostasis, all that remains of Countess Varvara
Razumovskaya's estate. At **Yudino** go 4 km right across the railway
for the **Church of the Transfiguration,** *Spasa Preobrazheniya,* built in
1724 in Moscow baroque as a memorial to the drowned Prince
Cherkassky. Some 4 km on at **Perkhushkovo** is the **Church of the Intercession,** *Pokrova,* built in 1756 in baroque style with a 19th century bell
tower and *trapeza* and the 18th/19th century **wooden house** of Alexander
Herzen's father and uncles which Herzen called the 'Radcliffe castle'
after Ann Radcliffe, author of the Gothic novel *Mysteries of Udolfo.*

On the Mozhaisk Road **BOLSHIE VYAZEMY** *is 10 km beyond
Perkhushkovo. On the Minsk Highway M-1 travel to Golitsyno, turn right
signed ZVENIGOROD 3 km to the Mozhaisk Road and turn left to
Bolshie Vyazemy and left again at the war memorial, then right to the*
Church of the Transfiguration, *Spasa Preobrazheniya, and the attractive
classical* **mansion** *on the Vyazemka River.*

The estate at Bolshie Vyazemy is remarkable not only for its beautiful
architecture but also for the fascinating historical associations. The
church and house at various times sheltered the ill-fated Tsar Boris
Godunov, Napoleon and his officers at the head of the invading French
army, and the remarkable Golitsyn family whose princes owned the
property from the time of Peter the Great to the Bolshevik Revolution.

In the late 16th century **Boris Godunov**, the most powerful boyar in
Muscovy, acquired the estate. Godunov, regent to the sickly Tsar Fedor
who was married to Godunov's sister, was well placed when Fedor died
in 1598 to manipulate the elections in his favour. Although illiterate and
of obscure ancestry, Boris proved a clever and skilled ruler but his weak
claim to the throne, the widespread famine which followed his accession
and the Polish intervention proved his undoing. Of his splendid estate
established at Bolshie Vyazemy it is only the remarkable **Church of the
Trinity** built in the 1590s and later renamed the **Transfiguration** which
has survived.

Royal churches of this antiquity are rare in the Moscow region. The

massive cube rises high from the broad terrace and is crowned by picturesque gables, round drums and seven hemispherical domes (predecessors
of onion domes) topped by tall gold crosses. It is built of white
limestone up to the double cornice and then of brick. The three main
facades are divided into three bays articulated by pilasters, *lopatki*, and
surmounted by round gables, *zakomary*, in the manner of the Archangel
Cathedral in the Kremlin. The two side chapels that close off the
eastern end of the open terrace display three rows of decorative gables,
kokoshniki. The five round apses at the east end of the church which jut
outwards in a deeply satisfying rhythm relate to the three altars of the
main church and the two side chapels. On the north side is an unusual
sight; a *zvonnitsa* or medieval belfry of which only a few are still extant
in Russia. Like the church it is divided into three vertical sections with
two horizontal tiers in which there are three arched openings for the
bells. In 1993 after a lapse of 60 years, bells once more hung in their
proper place.

The original **iconostasis** and **frescoes** were plundered many times. At the
end of the Godunov reign the Polish army under the pretender, False
Dmitry, with his bride, Marina Mniszek, passed this way, burning the
palace and desecrating the church. Two centuries later the French Army
under Napoleon left some interesting graffiti on its walls. The church
suffered again when it was closed in 1936 and the late 17th century
iconostasis was lost although some of the icons were removed to the
Tretyakov Gallery. However, **Soviet restorers** are to be thanked for their
careful restoration of the church and belfry which included the demolition of a late and ungainly bell tower. In 1993 this spectacular assem-
blage was returned to the Orthodox Church and religious services were
restarted in the basement (winter) chapel.

As a child the great poet, **Alexander Pushkin** visited his grandmother's
estate every summer at nearby Zakharovo (on the way to Zvenigorod –
only the park survives) and attended church at Bolshie Vyazemy. The
grave of his little brother, Nikolai, who died at the age of seven, can still
be seen behind the apse. Perhaps Pushkin's childhood memories of
Bolshie Vyazemy are reflected in his fine verse drama *Boris Godunov*.

In 1694 the estate of Bolshie Vyazemy was granted to **Boris Golitsyn**,
Peter the Great's tutor and companion (see Dubrovitsy). As a compli-
ment to the Tsar, Boris renamed the church, then the Trinity, the **Transfiguration** in honour of the village Preobrazhenskoe in eastern Moscow
where Peter grew up. Although undoubtedly intelligent and able, he

reputedly drank heavily. In later years he took the tonsure and died in 1713 as a monk.

Boris's son, Vasily, who should have inherited the estate died at a dinner in Moscow when the ceiling fell in crushing all present. Mikhail, grandson of Boris, therefore acquired Vyazemy at the age of 7 but it was his son, Nikolai, a bachelor and Marshal of the Nobility, who built the estate house which still stands today; the first wing in 1771, the second in 1772 and the main house, its date still visible, in 1784. The property passed to his brother, Alexander, in 1800 but he died soon after and was succeeded by his nephew, Boris, whose mother was the model for the old Countess in Pushkin's story, *The Queen of Spades*. Prince Boris Golitsyn, although an Old Believer, was also a Francophile who took part in the storming of the Paris Bastille in 1789. But such is the whim of fate that he died in 1812, from wounds, defending Russia against the French. The estate then passed to Boris' brother, Dmitry, the Governor-General of Moscow, who was notorious for his poor command of Russian. His grandson, also Dmitry, owned the house until 1917.

Kutuzov's army, retreating after the **Battle of Borodino**, rested on September 11 at Vyazemy. The very next day, after the Russian general left, **Napoleon** and his entourage arrived and in their turn occupied the estate. Their brief stay was long enough for Napoleon's secretary to describe the house to a correspondent as very fine, 'as if one was in a salon in Paris'.

The two-storey **mansion** from the courtyard where the avenues and plantings of the park are still discernible, has the severe facade of the neo-classical style. It is softened by pilasters which delineate the central shallow bay, by the large windows and associated panelling, the round upper blind window, and the balustrade and belvedere of the roof. At the back an attractive bay and balcony overlook the bridge on the Vyazemka River with its 18th century dam and old piles. This harmony is not reflected in the ravaged interior which since the revolution has lost all the furniture and works of art including wall and ceiling paintings. Even the room in which Kutuzov and Napoleon stayed was not protected and the library of rare books on the first floor has long been pillaged. However, a museum of the history of the estate reopened in the house in June 1999 (*closed Mondays and Tuesdays*). A hospital uses the service buildings while the local music school is located in the small Soviet classical building behind and to the left.

WRITERS AND RELIGION

Leave Moscow on the Mozhaisk Road and cross the MKAD to the Minsk Highway. After 7 km turn left signed **PEREDELKINO** *and travel 2 km through woods and across a pond to the writers' colony of pleasant wooden houses.*

Until the 1930s Peredelki, as it was known then, and the noble estates of Izmalkovo and Lukino were surrounded by thick forests. In 1934 by special decree of Stalin the woods were cleared to build a dacha colony exclusively for writers, a carrot to go with the stick of tightening state control. The disposition of these highly desirable country houses was within the competence of the Union of Writers which rewarded those who wrote on acceptable 'socialist' themes as well as the more deserving. Thus writers of the stature of Pasternak rubbed shoulders with now forgotten hacks. It was well understood that the dachas did not belong to the persons using them and could be taken back should the occupants fall foul of the regime. Beyond the park of Izmalkovo, Peredelkino is divided tidily like a distant city suburb into a regular grid of wooden houses, each in its own garden, along streets named for prominent Russian writers. The dachas have hot and cold running water, electricity and central heating, services rarely available in ordinary villages.

Immediately after crossing the bridge, park the car on the right by the gate to the former estate of **Izmalkovo**, *now a children's hospital.*

The mature park of oak, birch, larch and sycamore is beautiful at all times of year but particularly in autumn when the leaves turn golden. Through the trees on the right is a large two-storey house in yellowish ochre. The facade, an elegant portico of six Doric columns supporting a balcony and broad pediment, faces the pond through recently planted larches. Built in the first half of the 19th century in the prevailing classical style, the house is actually of wood construction under the stucco. Nothing of the interior remains except for the arrangement of the rooms. Lions which once guarded the porch were removed by officious Ministry of Culture officials for 'safe-keeping' and are theoretically on view at Arkhangelskoe. The foundations of the Church of Dimitry Rostovsky, built in the 1750s and demolished in the 1930s, are to the right of the house.

This was the home of the Samarin/Komarovsky family who were prominent in 19th century intellectual circles. Yury Samarin was a prominent

Slavophile, those who idealised the national character of Russia and opposed Westernisation. However he took an active part in the discussions that led to the liberation of serfs in 1861. The family had hoped to set up a museum in honour of their illustrious relation after his death but the tsarist government refused to give approval and the Soviet government was even less enthusiastic. Many of the Samarin relatives, including the Osorgins featured in the book *Echoes of a Native Land* by their descendant, Serge Schmemann, came to live in Izmalkovo after they were obliged to leave their country estates in 1918. In 1923 they were once again forced to move on.

Many prominent Russian writers had dachas in Peredelkino but the best known was the lyric poet **Boris Pasternak**. Pasternak spent from the 1930s to his death in 1960, at his attractive dacha at No 3 Pavlenko Street, now a part-time museum (*from the main road turn left at the yellow brick transformer building*). He wrote to his father when he moved into the brown frame house in 1939 '...this is exactly what one dreams of all one's life.' Pasternak, although never arrested, suffered much harassment by the Soviet authorities. His mistress, Olga Ivinskaya, was imprisoned in the late 1940s and again after Pasternak's death, and he was viciously attacked when his novel *Dr Zhivago* was published in the west in 1957. When the Nobel Prize was awarded him a year later, Pasternak was obliged to return it and he was expelled from the Writers' Union. His neighbour, Konstantin Fedin, then secretary of the Writers' Union and a vociferous critic, did not even go to his funeral.

The vendetta against Pasternak continued into the 1980s when the Writers' Union allocated the dacha, where his family had continued to live, to another writer, Chingiz Aitmatov. Aitmatov, to his credit, refused the offer but the bailiffs came anyway and threw out Pasternak's belongings. Eventually, in response to public outrage the authorities established a **museum** to the writer which can be visited four days a week (*10-4 Thursday, Friday, Saturday and Sunday*). It is particularly moving to see the plain, simple interiors, the table on which Pasternak wrote, and the family photographs.

Admirers of the poet can also visit his grave at the **cemetery** across the fields. In the despotic period of Khrushchev's early rule, Pasternak's funeral in 1960 was a sensational event. He had become a symbol of free speech and of hope and his death caused a kind of hysterical despair. Hand-written notices of the funeral were put up all over

Moscow and thousands came streaming out to Peredelkino and a great crowd accompanied the body from the house to the cemetery. As the lid of the coffin was closed, the bells of the nearby Church of the Transfiguration happened to ring out, an apparently unintentional salute to the great man. On May 30, the anniversary of his death, people still make the pilgrimage.

The cemetery can be reached by continuing along the main road to the entrance, left. For **Pasternak's grave** turn left along the boundary fence at the top of the hill, bearing left where the fence turns right. At three birches turn left and then right at the next row to Pasternak's grave, where two of the famous three lone pines are still standing. His sons, Leonid and Adrian, and second wife Zinaida are also buried in this plot. Kornei Chukovsky's grave is nearby, a little to the west and north, and the grave of Arseny Tarkovsky, the poet and father of the film maker, Andre Tarkovsky, is farther down the hill.

The colourful cemetery church, the **Transfiguration**, *Spasa Preobrazheniya*, was first built in 1819 by Countess Razumovskaya in the classical style – a rotunda with a tiered bell tower. Its appearance was greatly altered in the 1870s when the Bode-Kolychev family added a bizarre touch by grafting on to its classical core a squat new porch with bright tiles in 17th century style and encircling the rotunda with a group of fretted and vividly coloured cupolas reminiscent of St Basil's in Red Square. The church, closed in the 1930s, was allowed to reopen in 1949 and has links with the Patriarch's residence in the old estate of **Lukino** next door.

On the other side of the high wall Baron Mikhail Bode-Kolychev assisted by Academician Fedor Solntsev, the restorer of the old Kremlin palaces, had created a wonderful fantasy in the 1860s based on 17th century Muscovite architecture. The picturesque house burned down in the 1920s and only the main gate, the entrance to the rebuilt house, and some of the towers survive. Bode-Kolychev was descended on his mother's side from the Kolychevs, an ancient boyar family who claimed kinship with the Romanov Tsars. It seems entirely appropriate that Lukino should now be the home of the Patriarch for the most famous Kolychev was Metropolitan Philip, head of the Russian Church when he was murdered in 1569 for opposing Ivan the Terrible. The Bode ancestor as the name implies was French – Baron Bode fled the French Revolution to settle in Russia where his son married the last Kolychev heiress and his grandson built Lukino.

Across the river from Lukino in Choboti is the dilapidated Art Nouveau **Levenson Dacha** built in 1900 by the outstanding architect, Fedor Shekhtel. Near Peredelkino on the Borovsk Road by Vnukovo Airport is **Izvarino** and the **Church of St Elijah**, *Ilii*, with its huge dome built in 1904. Long a film depository, it is now functioning again and has been repaired. At **Fedosino** (*from Choboti right on Borovskoe Shosse to Fedosino Street right*) encircled by high-rise apartment blocks is the diminutive **Church of the Annunciation**, *Blagoveshcheniya*, built in 1854 in the late classical style. In 1991 on our first visit the scene was completely desolate – the ruined church lacked even a roof and industrial garbage including a sad heap of discarded gravestones was strewn about. When the apartment blocks were being planned in the 1980s the church had been slated for demolition. But in 1992 it was returned to the parishioners who set out to repair the ruin and only two years later the roof was in place, a neat fence had been built around the church, and the bell tower was under repair.

Turn left from the M-1 at Golitsyno at the GAI and traffic lights and left again to **Sidorovskoe** *avoiding the Krasnoznamensk 'Spetsgorod' military town to see the* **Church of the Bogolyubskaya Virgin**, *1689 and 1895. From the Minsk Highway, M-1, travelling towards Moscow turn right (left if coming from Moscow) at traffic lights 5 km from Golitsyno signed* KREKSHINO. After 3 km passing Dachy on an avenue of birch trees turn right onto a paved but unmarked road towards a farm at **KREKSHINO**. In 200 metres, opposite the bus-stop, is a strange house out of place among the haphazard buildings that make up the farm. Its proper milieu would be among the late Victorian houses built in their thousands in England at the end of the last century. The large **house** on two floors has pointed gables, tall chimneys and bay windows, and even a touch of the Tudor in the painted timbers. It does indeed have a curious connection with England.

In an indirect way the house is linked to the English nobleman, Lord Radstock, who visited Russia in the 1870s as a missionary for the evangelical movement. Among his mainly upper-class converts was Colonel V.A. Pashkov of the Guards Regiment who built this extraordinary house for his family in the English pseudo-Tudor style.

A relative of the Pashkovs, Madame Chertkova, whose husband was aide-de-camp to the Tsar, was, with her son, Vladimir, another of Lord Radstock's converts. Vladimir began reading Tolstoy and became even more enthused by the Tolstoyan ideas of a new christianity than he was about evangelism. He met and so admired Tolstoy, who was equally taken by the young proselyte, that his alarmed mother sent him to England. But the correspondence with Tolstoy did not cease and soon Chertkov returned to Russia, renewed his close relationship with Tolstoy, and began to publish Tolstoy's religious tracts.

In 1897 Chertkov again fled to England with his wife and children. He had dared to publish a pamphlet that offended the authorities about the plight of the Dukhobors. (Eventually, the Dukhobors, a religious sect persecuted by the authorities for refusing military service, went to Canada financed by proceeds from Tolstoy's last novel, *Resurrection*, where the good Englishman with his Bible making the rounds of the prison cells may have been based on Lord Radstock.) In England, Chertkov founded a printing house to publish works by Tolstoy forbidden in Russia.

After Chertkov's return from England in 1907 he was not allowed to live near Tolstoy in Yasnaya Polyana so he settled in this house of his Aunt Pashkova. Tolstoy came to visit him here several times. In September 1909, although Chertkov and Tolstoy's wife, Sophia Andreevna, were deeply suspicious of one another, her name day was splendidly celebrated in this house. The daughter of one of the musicians who played for the guests described the house: 'With its sharply pointed ingenious roofs under red tiles, all intertwined with thick braiding of wild grape vines or ivy ... the house was like a castle from the tale of Puss in Boots.'

During one of Tolstoy's last visits to this house Chertkov helped him draw up his will by which his youngest daughter, Alexandra, would be the sole beneficiary of his literary estate on the understanding that she would reject the copyright and turn it over 'to the people'. The struggle between Chertkov and Sophia Andreevna over control of Tolstoy's manuscripts, which had been going on for some time, was thus not resolved. However, in 1928 under Chertkov's editorship the standard 90 volume edition of Tolstoy was at last published.

ZVENIGOROD

Zvenigorod can be approached three ways: via the Minsk Highway M-1, 45 km to Golitsyno then turn right 3 km to the Mozhaisk Road, turn left then turn right on the A-107 signed ZVENIGOROD for 17 km past several unguarded level crossings to the town across the Moskva River; via the Uspenskoe Road through Nikolina-Gora and Akulina to Zvenigorod;

via the Volokolamsk Highway, M-9, turn left (south) at the 68 km post signed ZVENIGOROD reached in 12 km.

Zvenigorod, population 15,000, on the winding Moskva River means a settlement (*gorod*) with an alarm bell (*zvon*). In the 14th and 15th centuries deeply involved in the princely internecine wars, it later became an ordinary provincial centre with a hospital and other amenities serving the countryside. The writer Anton Chekhov worked here in 1884 and again 1886-7 at the small hospital (10 Lermontovskaya Street, right of the main road), his first post after he finished his medical training as a doctor. Zvenigorod's beautiful countryside, proximity to Moscow and easy access by rail make it ideal for dachas and sanatoria and in summer its population is greatly enlarged.

Follow the main road to the river and the steep cliff, right, where there is a holy well and sign GORODOK. Climb up the steps to a miniature street of wooden houses closed at the end by a breathtakingly beautiful white church, the **Cathedral of the Assumption of the Virgin**, *Uspeniya na Gorodke*, the sole survivor with the earthen ramparts of the old **KREMLIN**. Built in 1399-1400, it is one of the oldest buildings in the Moscow region. *Enquire at the last cottage on the right as you face the church for the key if it is closed.* In 1389 Prince Yury Dmitrievich, younger son of Dmitry Donskoy, Grand Prince of Moscow, inherited the principality of Zvenigorod and set out to create a power base from which he hoped to oust the Moscow ruler, Vasily, who was also his older brother. Prince Yury embarked on a major building programme intent on rivalling Moscow. With the construction of the cathedral and the Zvenigorod Kremlin, he more than succeeded.

In 1425 when Prince Yury's brother, Vasily, died, the Principality of Moscow was inherited by Vasily's ten-year-old son, Vasily II, in defiance of the will of Prince Yury's father, Dmitry Donskoy. The infuriated Yury took up arms and with his two sons drove Vasily II out of Moscow and took for himself the title of Moscow Grand Prince. Eventually Yury was killed in battle and a bloody civil war ensued that lasted for twenty years ending only with the deaths or mutilation of all concerned: Yury's son, Vasily the Cross-eyed, was blinded by Vasily II; Dmitry Shemyak, Yury's second son, in return blinded Vasily II, and was himself poisoned. To top it all the Tatars took advantage of the turbulence to invade Moscow laying waste to everything in their path. Peace was only imposed when Ivan III, the son of Vasily II and creator of the Moscow Kremlin as we know it today, took the throne.

Inspired by the 12th century churches of Vladimir, the cathedral is a simple and striking cube, its plain stone walls enlivened by a triple-band frieze that encircles it on three sides, dividing it horizontally. A similar frieze is found under the eaves of the apse on the fourth, eastern side. Each of the facades except for the east is divided vertically into three by slim pilasters, *lopatki*, and the north and south facades are further enhanced by grand portals of receding pointed arches. The ogee-shaped gables, *kokoshniki*, which originally clustered around the powerful drum, were removed in the 17th century. The drum with its slit windows and frieze supports the helmet-shaped cupola and elaborate gold cross. On the west side the squat open bell tower was added in the 19th century. Unfortunately only traces remain inside of the early 14th century frescoes on the pillars within the altar which were painted by Andrei Rublev, who was relatively unknown when commissioned by the prescient Prince Yury. The beauty of the lost iconostasis is obvious from the three magnificent paintings by Rublev, the *Saviour*, the *Archangel Michael* and *St Paul*, discovered in a shed in the Monastery of St Savva Storozhevsky in 1918. Remarkably, this ancient cathedral remained open, although with a tiny congregation, throughout the Soviet period.

Yury's second building spree involved the construction of the magnificent **ST SAVVA STOROZHEVSKY MONASTERY**. **St Savva**, the first head of the new monastery, was a pupil of the great Sergius Radonezh, Yury's godfather and founder of the Trinity-St Sergius Monastery. Rectangular in shape, the monastery is situated high above the confluence of two rivers – the Moskva and Storozhki – in wooded uplands. (This countryside is so hilly that it has acquired the hyperbolic sobriquet of the Russian Switzerland.) *One km along the embankment at the sign for the Ministry of Defence sanatorium leave the car and walk up the track past the Krasny Gate to the north entrance. There is a charge for the monastery and a small charge for photography (closed Mondays).*

Sacked and pillaged by the Poles at the beginning of the 17th century, new buildings were constructed in the 1650s in the reign of **Tsar Alexei Mikhailovich**, including his own palace along the west wall. The picturesque Tsaritsa palace for Alexei's first wife, Mariya Miloslavskaya, was built along the east wall in 1654. With the removal of the capital to St Petersburg, St Savva's Monastery lost its royal connections, although from time to time it played host to reigning monarchs. In 1760 it withstood a peasants' revolt but was sacked and pillaged in the invasions of the French in 1812 and the German Army in December 1941. In 1919 the monastery was closed and placed under the military authorities. After the Second World War, it opened as a museum.

Nativity Cathedral, *Rozhdestvensky Sobor*, built in the lifetime of St Savva (who died in 1406), was probably finished about 1405. It has in some ways survived better than the lonely Assumption Cathedral for its *zakomary* roof gables are in place and some early 15th century frescoes by artists of the Rublev school have survived in the altar. Frescoes in the main church were painted in the 17th century as was the splendid **iconostasis**. It complies with the traditional scheme: above the lower row of local icons and the nativity is the *deesis* tier of Christ flanked by Mary and John the Baptist, and other saints, above them is the small row of festivals of the church, above that a line of solemn Old Testament prophets, and finally overlooking all, are the Ancient of Days flanked by Old Testament patriarchs. Although the church follows the same design as the Cathedral of the Assumption – a cube with walls divided horizontally by decorative bands and vertically by pilasters, topped by a heavy drum and cupola – it is squatter and less elegant. The southern chapel was added in the 17th century to house Savva's remains; the porch at the western end in the 19th century. The gilded cupola on its powerful drum eclipses the tiny dome that distinguishes the tomb of St Savva. After the revolution, in spite of furious protests by priests a Soviet commission opened Savva's coffin to prove that the saint's remains, a skeleton, was that of an ordinary person. Predictably this evidence failed to convince believers.

Other buildings of note in the ensemble include the **refectory** with the **Church of the Transfiguration** and **bell tower** on the left of the north gate. It was donated by the Tsarevna Sophia in the 1680s and altered in the 18th and 19th centuries when the upper floor was removed and the colourful clock tower added. Over the powerful **Krasny Gate** is the plump form of the Trinity Church built in 1652. The **monks' cells** also built in the mid 17th century are located along the south wall. Six of the seven original towers of the monastery walls survive.

The wealthy monastery in the decade before the revolution built three hotels outside the north gate for pilgrims and, in Moscow, a luxurious apartment building, the **Savvinskoe Podvore**, on Tverskaya. At the end of the 19th century a rich merchant, P. Tsurikov, built a **skit** (hermitage) a little to the north in the ravine near St Savva's cave. Services are again being held in the Nativity Cathedral and at the hermitage. Meanwhile,

the museum continues to operate. One of its delights is the view from
the tall bell tower.

VVEDENSKOE *is across the river from Zvenigorod. On approaching the
town from Golitsyno turn left onto a narrow road after the railway station
to the estate, right. Parking is to the left.*

Vvedenskoe is a special place with its beautiful classical mansion and
elegant church high on the steep escarpment of the Moskva River. It is
pleasant to find the buildings and park much as they were before the
revolution, where the rich foliage and the winding river make the perfect
setting for Zvenigorod's ancient churches. In the late 1790s **Paul I**
presented this village to the Lopukhin family, relatives of the young
Anna Lopukhina. She had caught his attention at the coronation of 1797
and became his *favoritka* (mistress), bestowing her favours even the
night before the unfortunate Tsar was murdered. Anna's father, Prince
Petr Lopukhin, chose one of St Petersburg's most fashionable architects
of the day, **Nikolai Lvov,** for the grand house he was intent on building
at Vvedenskoe. Although not formally trained, Lvov was highly
regarded and had designed many stately buildings for Catherine II and
Paul I. He was a man of many parts, a poet, artist and lithographer, a
collector of folk songs, an economist and something of an agronomist.
In a letter to Prince Lopukhin in 1798 he extolled the wonders of the
landscape of Vvedenskoe even though he first saw it in winter in 24
degrees of frost.

Lvov's classical **house** in wood was of two storeys with a circular porch
of Corinthian columns facing the courtyard and a portico of six
columns, also of the Corinthian Order, facing the river. The detached
wings flanking the house were similarly embellished with porches and
columns. In 1912 the increasingly fragile mansion was dismantled and
the central part faithfully rebuilt of brick and stucco. A false note,
however, crept in when the rebuilt wings were attached to the house by
galleries which block the view of the river from the front garden, now a
formal parterre. In 1928 a second floor was built on to the wings and on
the west side the original open porch with columns was enclosed.
Within the main house, something of the original has been retained in
the painted ceilings, round and oval rooms, vases and balustrades.

The tranquil **Church of the Presentation**, *Vvedeniya*, set a little apart
south of the main house, was built in 1812 also to the designs of Lvov.
Its oval form decorated with pilasters and pediments is offset on the

west by the round bell tower which originally stood alone, and at the roof level by the finely tapered spire.

As so frequently happened in Russia the estate changed hands many times. In the 1880s it was purchased by rich merchants, the **Yakunchikovs**, manufacturers of textiles and brick, who had become involved in the resurgence of arts and crafts sponsored by Savva and Elizaveta Mamontov at Abramtsevo.

Vasily Yakunchikov's wife, Zinaida, was first cousin of Savva Mamontov, his daughter-in-law, Mariya Fedorovna, looked after the Abramtsevo crafts and pottery stores in Moscow and one of the Yakunchikov daughters, Natalya, married the leading artist, Vasily Polenov, who was also closely associated with Abramtsevo. It is not surprising then that his youngest daughter, **Mariya**, became an artist. As a child she loved the beautiful house and wild landscape and her painting of Vvedenskoe, *From the Window of the Old House. Vvedenskoe, 1897*, juxtaposes the nobility of the architecture with the natural beauty of the surrounding countryside. The leading symbolist artist, **Viktor Borisov-Musatov**, was also inspired by Vvedenskoe and painted the estate in three important works of 1903-4, *Ghosts, In the Light of the Setting Sun*, and *House at Vvedenskoe*. Mariya Yakunchikova suffered from tuberculosis and was sent to Paris where she was treated by Dr Weber whom she later married. She was upset to learn in 1884 that the estate had been sold to Count Sergei Sheremetiev. The count gave it to his daughter as dowry when she married **Count Gudovich** and it remained in the latter's family until the revolution.

Between 1918 and 1923 Vvedenskoe was a museum, then an orphanage, part of a state farm and a Communist Party school. In 1933 it became a sanatorium for the **Moscow City Party bosses** who continued to use it until 1991. In the 1980s a huge modern addition to the sanatorium was tactfully built on the edge of the ravine beyond the church where it does not interfere with the view of the house. Recently, the house and church, which for so long were firmly shut to visitors, have been open to the public. The sanatorium continues to function on a commercial basis.

For two estates north of Zvenigorod turn right in the town signed VOLOKOLAMSKOE SHOSSE. In just over a kilometre take the left fork, a bus route, and turn right at a T-junction signed **YERSHOVO** *to the rest house on the right.*

Count Vasily Olsufyev, the civil governor of Moscow and Marshal of

the Court of the Tsarevich Alexander (later Alexander II), built the 19th
century estate which remained in his family until just before the revolution. In 1928 Yershovo became a holiday retreat and a number of
Soviet-style buildings were added back of the old mansion. The
landscaping in the natural English manner makes for delightful walks in
the grounds. Among the amenities offered by the sanatorium is horse
riding.

The Olsufyev estate was designed by some of the best architects of the
early 19th century. The main house painted white with tall arched
windows and a portico faces the avenue, ponds and landscaped park. It
was built in 1837 by Afanasy Grigoriev, the architect born a serf, who
helped reconstruct Moscow in the Empire style after the fire of 1812.
Note the curious triangles above the capitals and the coat of arms, a
circle with sun rays emerging, evidence of the fascination of the Russian
nobility with masonic emblems. The mansion was damaged during the
short German occupation in 1941 when the village was fired (of 106
houses only 11 survived). It has since been restored with some alterations.

It is impossible to miss a short distance from the estate, right, the
elegant **Church of the Trinity 'Under the Bells'**, *Troitsy pod Zvonom*. This
too was designed by Grigoriev, the only church to be authenticated as
his and one of the loveliest of the Empire churches. However, in
December 1941 German forces locked 90 wounded soldiers and 40 villagers inside the church and blew it up killing all inside. In February 1998
the Prefect of the Zvenigorod region inaugurated the reconstruction of
the 1829 church, which proceeded so rapidly it was completed in six
months. Although 14 metres from the original site (by the war
memorial) it is a faithful copy of Grigoriev's church. Strictly symmetrical it is a cube from which the semicircular apse on the east is offset
by the entrance on the west while Doric porticoes embellish north and
south. But its most impressive feature is the soaring cylindrical bell
tower at the centre, crowned by the dome and tall cross. The names of
those who died in the 1941 atrocity are inscribed within.

Three km past Yershovo is **Koralovo**. On the left is the small circular
Church of the Tolgsky Virgin, like a garden pavilion, facing the main
estate across the small Storozhka River. Originally built in 1863, it was
totally destroyed in Soviet times but reconstructed in the mid 1990s.
Prince Alexander Vasilchikov, from 1879 to 1888 the energetic director
of the Hermitage Museum in St Petersburg, who owned Koralovo,

embellished the house with a fine library and rare works of Italian art, of which a few survive in the Zvenigorod local museum. Vasilchikov sold the estate to Count Grabbe in the early 1900s. Damaged in the Second World War, the house was totally rebuilt afterwards as a Soviet holiday home, a function it still fulfills on a commercial basis. Within the grounds is an ancient grassy lane flanked by birches, once the direct road to the Monastery of St Savva 4 km away.

ON THE WAY TO VEREYA

Leave Moscow by the Minsk Highway M-1 and travel 87 km on the straight road to the GAI post. Turn left signed VEREYA onto the A-108 road by the statue of Zoya Kosmodemyanskaya, a heroine of the Second World War.

At **PETRISHCHEVO** 3 km to the right, is a museum to 18-year-old *partizanka* **Zoya Kosmodemyanskaya**, executed there in 1941 for sabotage by the German army. Two km farther is the unsigned road left 3 km to **ARKHANGELSKOE** where Osip Bove, the architect who rebuilt Moscow after 1812, lived with his wife, Princess Trubetskaya, in her country estate. The rotunda **Church of Michael the Archangel**, built by Bove in 1822, is in poor condition but services have recommenced and repairs are underway. Three km farther on the A-108 is the right turn 9 km to **BOGORODSKOE**, the former estate of Count Dmitry Gurev, Finance Minister to Alexander I, whose wife was related to Princess Trubetskaya above. The main house perished in the war but the **Church of the Intercession**, *Pokrova*, built in 1807 and long used as a cafe-bar for a holiday home, has been reconsecrated under Father Boris of Mozhaisk. The **stables**, now used as accommodation, also survive. Farther on at the fork past Kolodkino turn left towards Naro-Fominsk to Slepushkino to see the ruined early classical **Church of the Transfiguration**, *Spasa Preobrazheniya*, built in 1804.

At Kolodkino take the right fork for Simbukhovo, then at the T-junction right again for Vereya, 27 km from the Minsk Highway.

VEREYA enjoyed a brief period as an independent princedom from 1432 to 1486 until it was caught in Muscovy's spreading tentacles. It was ruled from 1519 to 1567 by the powerful Staritsky princes whose pretensions to the throne of Moscow are vividly portrayed in the Eisenstein film, *Ivan the Terrible*. Over its long history, Vereya has been attacked and occupied by Tatars, Poles, French, and in this century,

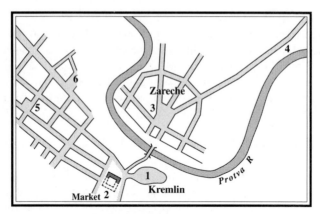

VEREYA 1. Kremlin, 2. Market Place, 3. Zareche, 4. Krasnaya
Sloboda, 5. Sovietskaya, 6. Bolnichnaya

Germans. The fever of 19th century railway building bypassed the old
town which thus was spared hasty industrial expansion and has
preserved a timeless, provincial air. The main industry, the sewing
factory, is still as it was in the 19th century and the population remains
small at around 5,500. Although depressed economically, Vereya is
attractively situated, its small almost identical wooden houses with their
elaborately carved barge-boards punctuated by tall striking churches,
are set along straight streets which, for both lower and upper towns,
end abruptly at the steep ravine of the Protva River.

The splendid 17th century church in Krasnaya Sloboda, **Entry into
Jerusalem**, *Vkhodoierusalimskaya*, is on the far left when entering
Vereya from the A-108. On the way to the church note the sad
memorial in the form of a triangle to the Belyaev family who were killed
here by the German army in 1941. The picturesque church situated on
the high bank of the Protva with fine views to the Vereya Kremlin, was
built 1667-79 as the cathedral of the Saviour Monastery but became a
parish church when the monastery was dissolved. A tent-shaped bell
tower stands on the left of the delightful, peaked western porch; similar
porches once decorated the north and south sides of the church but
were removed, one in the 19th century, the other in Soviet times. The
voluptuous cupolas are made of wooden shingles, *lemekhi*, but they like
the rest of the building are in a lamentable state with no sign of
imminent improvement.

Farther on is the **lower town**. Where the main road forks left, take the dirt road straight on to the tall **Church of the Epiphany**, *Bogoyavleniya*, in Zareche, built in 1777 in a restrained baroque style by a local merchant, M.E. Sedelnikov. On closer inspection it is shocking to find the apse has been turned into the local grocery store and shoppers hang around the steps gossiping, like a local club. Although its paint is peeling, the roof of the church is intact and could be restored but Vereya already has a functioning church and it seems unlikely more will be opened. It is located on a pleasant square of little wooden houses with, in the distance on the other side of the river, a view of the St Elijah Church (see below), its gold cupolas sparkling in the sun, and, nearer to hand, the ramparts and tall bell tower of the Kremlin.

Take the pedestrian bridge over the river and climb to the upper town or by car take the main road over the bridge to the spacious **market place**, right. Of the arcaded 19th century trading rows which formed a square the south side was destroyed in fighting in 1941 and rebuilt later as a plain wall. Standing by itself with the Russian flag flying is a Soviet classical style building, formerly Communist Party headquarters and now the mayor's office. On the north side is an impressive late 18th century two-storey building with a corner rotunda, the former district school, now the local museum *open Wednesdays and Saturdays*.

Beyond the market place across a causeway earthen ramparts encircle the old Kremlin comprising the tall bell tower, the crumbling **Cathedral of the Nativity of Christ**, *Rozhdestva Khristova*, and the classical government building, *prisutstvennye mesta*. The ruined cathedral first built in 1552 by Prince Vladimir Staritsky was rebuilt in the late 17th and early 18th centuries in a provincial version of the baroque. To the right in front of the bell tower is a figure sheltering a child, a memorial to the Second World War. On the left placed on the ramparts overlooking the river are three rather diverse monuments through which Vereya's more recent history can be read. The nearest is an **obelisk** with the names of those who died in WWII. Just beyond that on the brow of a hill is the figure of young **General Dorokhov**, the partisan hero of the Napoleonic war and liberator of Vereya, cockily brandishing a recently renewed sword. His statue which was first erected in 1912 was destroyed in 1918 during the revolution but was rebuilt in 1957 during the post-Stalin 'thaw'. The last memorial is to **three good communists** (including a policeman) who were killed putting down the so-called kulak revolt of 1918 when the peasants of the area refused to accept Soviet rule.

There are several other churches in the old town west of the main square. Here on the left is a church of the Old Believers (see p.54), the **Intercession**, *Pokrova*, now in spic and span order. Turn right three blocks on, onto Sovietskaya St to see among low wooden houses the large dilapidated red brick baroque church, **Sts Constantine and Helen**, *Konstantina i Eleny*, built in 1798 by the wealthy Zanegin merchants. Two blocks farther along Sovietskaya turn right onto Bolnichnaya St to the **Church of St Elijah**, *Ilii*, with its tall facade and five small green and white cupolas built in 1803 in the early classical style. This, the only working Orthodox church in Vereya, is in the care of a young priest, Father Vladimir, who seems to be thoroughly disenchanted with the changes in Russia particularly the high price of building work.

South of Vereya are three very different **ELIZABETHAN CHURCHES** all built in the same year, 1761, the last year of the reign of Elizabeth, Peter the Great's daughter and patroness of the flamboyant baroque style of Rastrelli. Turn left coming from the Kremlin onto Kaluzhskaya Street and take the road south 15 km to **Subbotino** and the ruined **St Nicholas**, built 1761-4 in highly florid baroque. Take the same road from Vereya and turn left at Veselevo 10 km on a hard dirt road to **Vyshgorod**, the old fortress. Where before the revolution there were nine churches, today only the derelict **Assumption**, *Uspeniye*, stands left, across the river by a footbridge, large and severely plain like a monastery church. (At **Dubrovo** on the high bank opposite is a rare monument to **Alexander II**, the Tsar Liberator responsible in 1861 for freeing the serfs.) For the third Elizabethan church at **Spas Kositsy** travel southeast from Vereya 14 km to Ustye and turn right 2 km to the splendid baroque **Church of the Transfiguration**, *Preobrazheniya*. Built for Count Alexander Shuvalov it hints at the forthcoming classical style.

MOZHAISK

Travel 96 km on the reasonably fast Minsk Highway (very crowded on holidays and summer weekends) turning right to the Mozhaisk Road at the GAI post and Yak-3 airplane monument signed BORODINO 26 km. Mozhaisk is in 8 km across the busy mainline level crossing. Past modern tower blocks is the old core of the city, small wooden houses interspersed with shops of brick and stucco. Mozhaisk, with a population of 32,000, has apart from a big printing plant, few industries although there is a modern **Cash and Carry** (clean toilets) on the right.

Mozhaisk's golden age was nearly half a millennium ago, in the 15th and 16th centuries, when it was one of the most holy places in Russia

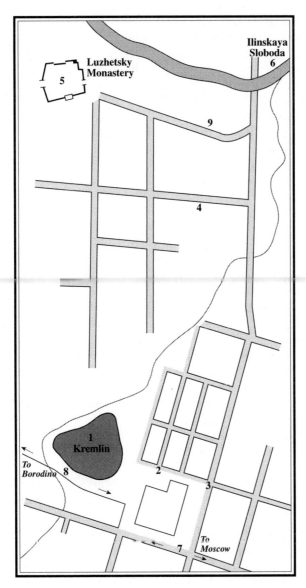

MOZHAISK   1. Kremlin, 2. Krupskaya, 3. Klementevskaya,
4. Kozhany, 5. Luzhetsky Monastery, 6. Ilinskaya
Sloboda, 7. To Moscow 8. To Borodino,
9. Gerasimov

attracting floods of pilgrims. Although the Orthodox Church favoured painted icons and disapproved of sculptural forms, in the provinces away from the centre of Orthodoxy carvings of saints in the favourite medium, wood, were quite common. The wooden statue of St Nicholas of Myra, a fourth century Byzantine saint, carved in Mozhaisk in the early 15th century, was kept in the old cathedral in the Kremlin and quickly became a cult object around which a popular pilgrimage grew up. The tsars too liked to display their veneration of Nikolai Mozhaisky and came so often on pilgrimage that a special palace was built for them. Anastasiya, Ivan the Terrible's first and most beloved wife, became ill on one such visit to Mozhaisk and died on the return journey; her untimely death was undoubtedly a factor in turning the young ruler into the 'terrible' Tsar.

Because of the pilgrims, the number of churches and monasteries in Mozhaisk grew rapidly until by the middle of the 16th century there were 75 churches and 16 monasteries for only 12,000 inhabitants. But this prosperity did not last. In the late 16th century probably because of the crowds of pilgrims the plague struck, greatly reducing the population. In 1613 and again in 1618 the town suffered devastating Polish raids from which it never properly recovered when many of the churches and monasteries, the majority of which were of wood, were destroyed. When in 1712 the capital moved to St Petersburg Mozhaisk lost its strategic importance. It was further affected by the closures of the monasteries under Catherine II. In 1917, when the population was about 5,000, only six churches and one monastery were functioning. Nowadays for a population of 30,000 there are four church buildings (3 functioning) and the Luzhetsky Monastery which reopened in 1993.

The Mozhaisk **KREMLIN**, like the town, suffered a lengthy decline long before the revolution when its old walls and buildings were progressively dismantled for other uses. It was further impoverished in the Soviet period and is now more like the barren Kremlin in Vereya than the glorious fortresses of Moscow or Kolomna.

Past a war memorial of a soldier brandishing his gun, turn right into Komsomolskaya Square and enter the Kremlin from Borodinskaya Street through red and white gates across an old bridge over the former moat. The Kremlin occupies a triangular high plateau overlooking the steep ravine of the narrow Mozhaika River on the north and west. Its stout brick walls were demolished in the early 19th century and all that now remain are earthen ramparts and two red and white churches, one large and one small, or the old and the new, although the 'old' is actually younger than the 'new'. The impressive 'new' **St Nicholas Cathedral**, stands tall and pinnacled in vividly coloured Gothic dress of white stone on a red brick background, and with four smaller towers at each corner. Beside it the 'old' **Nikolsky Cathedral**, renamed Peter and Paul, appears tiny, like a small child next to an elaborately decked out matron.

The new St Nicholas Cathedral was built over a long period, 1779-1812, using the materials from the demolished Kremlin walls. Its Gothic style is executed with great delicacy probably by an architect from the circle of Matvei Kazakov. Unusually, it is all of a piece; the bell tower at the western end with its slim spire is not divided from the main church nor is there an obvious *trapeza* section although there is an anteroom at the western end. Built over the former main gate it incorporates part of the old 17th century gate church in the upper south chapel where heavy columns and low vaulting belie the spaciousness suggested by the church's exterior. The later west chapel, which from the outside has the same dimensions as the south, is much more airy. The new Nikolsky Cathedral vies with the Bazhenov churches at Podzhigorodovo and Bykovo (see p.142, 293) for the expressive Gothic style.

The cathedral was closed in the 1930s and has served various secular functions since, most recently a workshop for making men's ties. On our visit we found scraps of bright tie material still sitting on the floor but the cathedral was at long last being tidied up and repaired in preparation for a return to worship. It has structural problems that must be overcome; the north wall of the cathedral suffered considerable damage when waste water from the tie factory was allowed to collect in pools and flow freely alongside it on its way downhill.

The **Old St Nicholas Cathedral**, *Staro-Nikolsky*, modestly stands next to its richly garbed neighbour. Originally built in the 14th/15th century, a new church was constructed in 1849 by Fedor Shestakov over the ruins of the old white-stone foundations, hence the new and old sobriquet. Shestakov intended to copy the earlier church but the pointed gables that stop short of the roof and the inappropriate dome are a self-conscious imitation of the early style, an early example of the pseudo-Russian style of Nicholas I. Shestakov was more successful however in recreating the lovely medieval-style portals. The local museum is now housed within the former cathedral and its knowledgeable assistants are eager to help visitors.

From the main Komsomolskaya Square turn left (north) down Krupskaya Street, the second street from the Kremlin ravine. Here among
the small wooden houses is the striking peach and white **Church of
Sts Joachim and Anna**, *Ioakima i Anny*, built in the 1880s, and open
for services. But more interesting is the small brick church nestled
next to it topped by the domed bell tower. Part of its south wall in
limestone is all that remains of the original Sts Joachim and Anna,
the oldest church in Mozhaisk. It was built in the 1390s as a convent
but was closed in the 17th century following a bad fire. Later, in the
1770s, the church was rebuilt from the ruins as a parish church but in
the middle of the 19th century most of this, second, church was
demolished leaving only the north chapel dedicated to St Leonty. This
north chapel became the south wall of the small church we can see
today, the only survival of the original, 14th century church, giving
few clues to the many rebuilding processes through which it has gone.
The colourful 19th century Sts Joachim and Anna presides trium-
phantly over this remnant of Mozhaisk's time of glory.

For the **LUZHETSKY NATIVITY of the VIRGIN MONASTERY**,
*Monastyr Rozhdestva Bogoroditsy, turn left onto Klementevskaya Street,
the fourth parallel street to the Kremlin ravine, and go north down the hill
and across a bridge over the Mozhaika River which is nearly at its confluence with the Moskva River. (Across the Moskva in Ilinskaya Sloboda is
the green and white pseudo-Russian cemetery church of* **St Elijah**, *Ilii.)
Ignore the bridge across the Moskva by turning immediately left on
Kozhany Street, turn right at the sports stadium and the Luzhetsky
Monastery is soon reached.* It stands within low brick walls on a bank
overlooking the winding Moskva River with two gates, four round
towers at each corner and one square tower where the river wall makes
a zig-zag. Founded in 1408 by Ferapont of Belozersk it was the most
important of Mozhaisk's many monasteries and the only one to survive
into the 20th century. Polish and Lithuanian invaders wrought havoc
here in the 17th century and in 1812 it was turned into a convenient
base for Napoleon's Westphalian regiment. In the 20th century it
suffered both from Soviet depredations – the church in honour of the
founder, St Ferapont, was demolished in the 1930s – and from German
occupation in the autumn and winter of 1941-2. The old track of the
busy Smolensk road which once ran alongside the river below the
monastery has long gone, there is very little river traffic, and it is now a
serene place set among the meadows, *luga*, from which it derives its
name.

The impressive **Cathedral of the Nativity of the Virgin**, *Rozhdestva Bogoroditsy*, opposite the central gate built in mid 16th century is typical of the severely plain but majestic monastery architecture of the time (ask in the monks' cells for permission to enter). It consists of a high basement, and tall triple-bayed walls interrupted at intervals by narrow windows and recessed portals culminating in round-headed gables over which tall drums support helmet-shaped cupolas of wooden shingles. A gallery once surrounded it. During the French invasion of 1812 the original iconostasis was destroyed by fire so that, combined with neglect in the Soviet period, only fragments remain of the interior decor.

Near the cathedral is a delightful triple-tiered bell tower built 1673-92 which once held a clock. Behind at the river wall stands the refectory with its **Church of the Presentation**, *Vvedeniya*, originally constructed in the 16th century but heavily rebuilt in the 18th. Monks' cells were contained in the long 17th-19th century building west of the cathedral. The monastery is functioning once more.

Nearby, east of the monastery on Gerasimova Street, is the caramel-coloured wooden house, now the **museum of Sergei Gerasimov**, the First Secretary of the Union of Artists under Khrushchev. He was one of the best known Socialist Realist artists whose favourite subjects were collective farms and studies of the revolution (he should not be confused with the more notorious – and unrelated – Alexander Gerasimov who in the 1930s painted Stalin and other Soviet leaders in heroic poses). During the Soviet era art historians despised his paintings but they are now fashionable and in demand in Russia and elsewhere. Gerasimov erected this delightful dacha for himself near his parents' small house on the banks of the Moskva. Of two storeys, the upper part is a light, airy studio. Photographs of Gerasimov show him hard and unsmiling, the tough secretary of the Union of Artists, who enjoyed many privileges including the most prized: permission to travel abroad in the 1940s and 50s. Nevertheless, he served his locality well for he helped save the historic battlefield at Borodino from collective farm expansion.

SOUTH OF MOZHAISK. *Cross the railway line and then the M-1, 3 km to Bolshie Parfenki by a lake, left, and a small dam, right. (Or from the M-1, turning left at the 113 km post signed VAULINO.) Turn right and cross the dam then follow the rough dirt track through the woods 2.5 km to* **Sivkovo**.

The red brick romantic ruin, the only sizeable building in the tiny hamlet, well repays the bumpy ride. The **Church of the Transfiguration**, *Spasa Preobrazheniya*, was built in 1685-87 for **Patriarch Joachim** on the country estate of his brother, T.P. Savelov. Joachim was Patriarch 1673-90 through the three reigns of Alexei, Sophia and Peter. A supporter of Peter in his struggle with his half-sister, Sophia, he was nevertheless a notorious conservative who tried to prevent foreigners of different religions, especially Jesuits, from establishing churches in Russia and proselytising their faith. Here special arrangements to accommodate the Patriarch were his own seat (*lozha*) built into the thick western wall of the church, like a box in a theatre, and a patriarchal room above the south chapel where he could change and meditate.

The Transfiguration resembles other small 17th century parish churches by its decoration – the pointed window architraves, the clutches of columns at the corners – and the lack of symmetry. It is a cube with separate extruding apse, south chapel and traces of the gables, *kokoshniki*, that supported the tall, windowless drum. The classical bell tower was added about 1828 by **Dormidont Grigoriev**, brother of the more famous Afanasy, for the then owner of the estate, **Prince Petr Nikolaevich Kropotkin**, grandfather of Prince Peter Alekseevich Kropotkin, the famous geographer and anarchist. Nothing has survived of the other estate buildings and only a few wooden dachas relieve its lonely situation.

Continue south 7 km to **Troparevo**. The elegant **Church of the Intercession**, *Pokrova*, on the meandering Protva River, was built by N.P. Korkodinov in 1713 in Moscow baroque style. The cube is surmounted by two elongated octagons, the second serving as the bell tower, that culminate in a slim drum and onion dome. Although only twenty years later than the patriarchal church at Sivkovo, the complex window frames and long slim silhouette make it entirely different.

Troparevo also has revolutionary associations. The Armfeldts, who had an estate here, entertained members of the terrorist **People's Will** including Andrei Zhelyabov and his lover, Sophia Perovskaya, both of whom were executed for their involvement in the assassination of Alexander II in 1881. At the Orfano mill at Vaulino by the Protva the disaffected law student, **Dmitry Karakozov**, found temporary employment as an accountant. A fanatical member of a secret revolutionary society called 'The Organisation' and its inner group 'Hell', he attempted to murder Alexander II in 1866 in the Summer Gardens in St

Petersburg. He missed, apparently because his arm was jogged by a loyal bystander, a peasant from Kostroma. The peasant was raised to the nobility for being in the right place at the right time but died of drink celebrating his elevation. Karakozov was hanged.

BORODINO

Leave Mozhaisk on the old Smolensk Road alongside the Kremlin across the Mozhaika River 12 km to Borodino.

On the way note the old verst (slightly more than a kilometre) markers. At **Gorki** Kutuzov and his officers on September 7 (August 26 old style) 1812, set up a post where they could easily view a large part of the terrain to the south and west. An impressive **obelisk** erected in 1912 for the centenary of the battle stands at the high spot chosen by Kutuzov. At the side of the road the layout of the battle can be ascertained from a somewhat threadbare **map**. Next to it a second, more modern but equally poignant, war memorial commemorates the soldiers who died fighting the Germans in 1941/2 in the same fields as those fought over in 1812

Cross the narrow Koloch River and turn right to **BORODINO VILLAGE** after which the battle of 1812 was named. Immediately on the left, next to the local hospital, stands the **Nativity of Christ**, *Rozhdestva Khristova*, built in 1697-1701 by Petr Savelov, courtier and owner of the village. Unlike some Moscow baroque churches which soar upwards it has a marked horizontal line traced from the peaked-roof porch and steep covered steps through the bell tower and *trapeza* to the central church and apse. A rare feature is the open wooden gallery supported on brick piers that flanks the church on north and south. In 1812 the bell tower over the western entrance became a convenient Russian lookout post but return fire from the French damaged the main cupola. The French moved forward forcing the Russians to retreat, took the village and in the ensuing fire the old iconostasis was destroyed. After the war Nicholas I purchased the church and decreed that the new cupola should be painted darker to show where French fire had holed the original, and that the old, damaged cupola be kept as a trophy (it seems to have disappeared). The new iconostasis was displaced in 1839 by the iconostasis from the historic Alekseev Convent in Moscow, demolished to clear the site for the gigantic Christ the Saviour (demolished in turn, now rebuilt). However, this iconostasis too did not survive the combined forces of the Bolshevik revolution and the German invasion. Finally in the 1960s the

church was repaired and since 1990 is functioning normally with yet
another, entirely new iconostasis.

In the early 19th century Borodino was owned by the aristocratic
Davydov family. Denis Davydov, an officer and poet notorious for his
satirical verses targeting the Tsar, knew the local terrain intimately as he
had grown up in Borodino. His group of partisans formed in 1812 were
legendary for their daring exploits behind French lines.

Although **THE BATTLE** spread five km north of Borodino as far as
Staroe Selo, now on the long reservoir known as the Mozhaisk Sea, the
main battle was fought southeast of Borodino. Its tragic heroism has
been made famous in Tolstoy's novel, *War and Peace*, where the scene
comes alive through the eyes of the horrified Pierre. Once a year on the
first Sunday in September, the battle is re-enacted in the fields by young
men dressed in the uniforms of both armies. Today, by good fortune
and design, the meadows, as they sweep away to the south and west in
an undulating expanse of green in summer or white in winter, are interrupted only by the memorials and those small hamlets that experienced
the battle nearly two hundred years ago. Electric cables have even been
placed underground to preserve the authenticity of the view. But this
was not always so for after the revolution scant regard was paid to
reminders of Borodino.

Judging by the large number of **memorials** the regiments competed
fiercely to record their moment of glory. The first and most spectacular
was erected in 1839 at the **Raevsky Battery** where the body of Prince
Bagration was reinterred. For the 1912 centenary over 30 more were
placed at particular battle points. Many of the memorials, usually in the
shape of obelisks surmounted by eagles, were sponsored by the
regiments or were the gift of descendants. The French government too
donated a memorial-obelisk at Shevardino, to the southeast, where
Napoleon was stationed.

At first the Bolsheviks dismissed the war of 1812 as the 'War of the
Tsar's Generals', and Borodino was neglected and vandalised. Typical
of the time was the slogan painted on the wall of the convent at the
Bagration fleches: *Down with the Heritage of the Slave Past!* In 1932 the
1839 monument on the Raevsky battery was dismantled for scrap and
the burial place of Prince Bagration plundered. But in the mid 1930s as
the threat from Germany increased Russian history was re-evaluated
and once again Borodino and the War of 1812 were honoured in the

history books. The battlefield was tidied up and the neglected monuments renovated. No sooner did this happen than the Germans invaded, reaching Borodino in October 1941, and fighting resumed on the old battlefield.

In 1812 the armies were fairly equally matched in numbers – 133,000 on the French side and 154,00 on the Russian side (the Russians in spite of their heavier guns, were less experienced and included some 20,000 hastily formed Moscow volunteers). In the end the battle was a stand-off in which neither side won outright. Although it only lasted 15 hours on September 7 (August 26 old style) casualties were huge – 45,000 Russians and more than 30,000 of Napoleon's forces. Napoleon called it 'the most terrible of all my battles'. The heavy losses persuaded the cautious Kutuzov to withdraw his forces that very night enabling the French to take Moscow unopposed. But it was a Pyrrhic victory. Moscow, its population gone, was soon burned to the ground and the French, without supplies, were forced to withdraw in the face of an early, harsh winter.

The line of battle ran roughly north-south cutting across the Smolensk Road down which the French hoped to gain access to Moscow. The Russian line ran from north of Borodino and Gorki to Utitsy (south of the present railway line), while the French army was drawn up in a broad line facing the Russians from north of Valuevo – where Napoleon had his bivouac – to a point just west of Utitsy.

For the battlefield turn left at Borodino towards Semenovskoe and cross the Koloch River. The small **museum** in 1 km with car park and toilet at the back is by the famous Raevsky battery. *Open 10 to 6 daily except Monday and the last Friday of the month.* First opened to the public in 1912 it is based on collections of Borodino veterans and includes fascinating objects like Napoleon's field bed and Kutuzov's carriage. But it is the hilly landscape and 34 memorials which really stir the imagination and repay long walks. The **Raevsky battery**, where the French and Russians battled all day long until the French finally withdrew, is marked by the black granite **obelisk** unveiled in 1839 in the presence of Nicholas I (dismantled in 1932, it was rebuilt in 1987). It is topped by a strange, stylised cupola in the form of a spiky gold ball surmounted by a plain cross. In the bays of the lower octagon are inscribed the numbers of Russians who died in each regiment. Nearby is the renewed gravestone of the great hero of the battle, Prince Petr Bagration.

From here continue on the paved road to **Semenovskoe** *and turn right towards Shevardino.* The high point on the left, now taken up by a convent, was where Prince Bagration's Second Army fought against the fierce onslaughts of the French until they were finally defeated at the end of that long day. Among the many dead was **General Alexander Tuchkov** whose inconsolable widow, Margarita, searched long and hard among the thousands of dead and dying before she found her husband's body. Margarita could not bear to be separated from her adored husband and accompanied him on all his marches and battles. In 1818-1820 on the place she had found him she built the church, the **Saviour Untouched by Hand**, *Spasa Nerukotvornovo*, as his mausoleum. It stood majestically alone for nearly twenty years, a simple domed classical building with portico of Doric columns, looking out over the field of battle, until Margarita built the **Saviour Borodinsky Convent** around it. She and their son are also buried there.

The colourful conventual buildings, in red brick with white detailing, are almost shocking against the white simplicity of the mausoleum. They were designed by the leading architect of the day, **Mikhail Bykovsky**, and expressed the newly fashionable pseudo-Russian style, appropriate to the national sentiment aroused by Borodino. The large five-domed cathedral, **St Vladimir**, rests on a high sub-basement, its facade distinguished by the recessed quadrangles and white stone detailing of 17th century Russian architecture. The convent was closed after the revolution to become a school, hospital, and workshops but has returned to the church. Within the grounds there are more memorials of 1812 including arrow-shaped earthen defences of the Bagration fleches, an obelisk to Konovitsyn's 3rd Infantry, and the grave of an unknown soldier. Next to the convent entrance is the guest house where Lev Tolstoy stayed in September 1867 when visiting the scene of the battle for his novel, *War and Peace*.

Continue west towards **Shevardino**, *the high point captured by French troops before the battle.* The French obelisk stands just behind the village and in front of the place where Napoleon and his officers stationed themselves during the battle. Again, like the Russian monuments, an eagle spreads its wings ready to fly off. It bears the laconic inscription: 'Aux morts de la Grande Armee 5-7 Septembre 1812'.

Another interesting walk is south from Semenovskoe to the railway line and across to **Utitsy**, where another clutch of monuments commemorates the Polish regiment under **Poniatowski** which fought on the French side.

KOLOTSKOE lies another 12 km beyond Borodino in the direction of Uvarovka. Beyond the railway line **Kolochevsky Uspensky Monastery** presents at first a desolate picture, especially in winter, as no walls survive to link the few remaining towers. A closer look, however, reveals the attractive **Cathedral of the Assumption**, *Uspeniya*, hiding behind the tall gate/bell tower. Originally erected in 1626 it was heavily rebuilt in baroque style in the early 18th century. In the distance a little tower stands alone among the trees. Behind the cathedral former monks' cells, used as communal housing, are being prepared for the reopening of the monastery.

Kolotskoe, like Borodino and Mozhaisk, also felt the full force of the **French and German invasions**. Kutuzov, retreating before Napoleon's army as it flowed towards Moscow from Smolensk and Vyazma, stopped there on September 1 and departed September 2 for Borodino. Napoleon was close behind. On September 4 Konovitsyn, with his guard, made a stand at the monastery walls against the approaching French, but then withdrew to Shevardino. The next day Napoleon arrived on his charger (optimistically named *Moscow*) and the monastery, now behind French lines, became the main French hospital during and after the battle of Borodino. Six weeks later, however, the situation was reversed when, on October 19, the retreating Napoleon was forced to abandon Kolotskoe in the face of attacks by Platov's cossacks.

More than a century later, in the autumn of 1941, Kolotskoe was occupied by the German Army. After they were pushed back, in January 1942, a Soviet military hospital opened there – graves of Soviet soldiers can be seen in the grounds. A plaque on the tower mentions these events and also the skirmishes of Denis Davydov, the partisan leader in 1812.

THE MOZHAISK SEA

The dam on the Moskva River, creating the 'Mozhaisk Sea', the long reservoir northwest of Mozhaisk, was completed in 1960 at the village of Marfin Brod. It not only provides electric power for Mozhaisk and the area but a huge recreation area some twenty kilometres long for the many houses of rest and dacha settlements that have grown up along its banks. Not far away to the west, where the Moskva River flows

naturally before being forced into the configurations of the reservoir, is
Poreche, a once glorious estate famous for its archeological collection
and botanical garden.

*Turn right from the Minsk Highway, 139 km from Moscow, onto the R-
90 and 32 km on through Uvarovka is* **PORECHE**. The **Church of the
Nativity of the Virgin**, *Rozhdestva Bogoroditsy*, now functioning, stands
in the centre of the scruffy village. Begun in 1804 it was not completed
because of the French invasion until 1819 but kept the severe classical
line in the giant Tuscan columns and noble pediments, repeated in the
tall arched windows of the elongated drum, and resolved in the small
belvedere at the top. The architect is unknown although some suggest
he might have been a member of the Kazakov school.

The first owner of Poreche, in 1742, was **Alexei Razumovsky**, the
handsome Ukrainian choir boy who became the 'favourite' and
probably secret husband of Grand Duchess, later Empress, Elizabeth.
Poreche remained in the Razumovsky family until 1824 when it was
acquired through marriage by **Sergei Uvarov**. The Paris educated
Uvarov was Minister of Education and a notorious reactionary – it was
he who devised the slogan reflecting the ideology of Nicholas I's reign:
Orthodoxy, Autocracy and Nationalism.

It was left to Uvarov's son, **Alexei**, to give Poreche its most vivid stamp.
He was an ardent enthusiast in the early days of Russian archeology,
organising at his own expense excavations all over the country. He
founded the Moscow Archeological Society, helped create the History
Museum, and pioneered architectural preservation. At his death in 1884
his remarkable wife, **Praskovya**, became president of the Archeological
Society in turn although in her husband's lifetime she had not even been
allowed membership. She added greatly to the Uvarov collection of old
Russian manuscripts and archeological finds and displayed them at
Poreche, allowing anyone who wished to see them. During the First
World War she gave a large part of the Poreche library and collection
to the History Museum. Among visitors to the estate in the 19th century
was the poet Vasily Zhukovsky, a contemporary of Pushkin, and tutor
to the future Alexander II. The Uvarovs so admired Zhukovsky that
after his death in 1852 they turned his cottage into a memorial and
raised a statue to him (not extant).

*To see the main house turn left at the sign P.L. ELEKTRON, park the
car and walk down the avenue of limes.* Perched on a hill overlooking the

valley of the winding Inoch River the **mansion**, with two flanking wings bearing Tuscan porticoes, presents a strange sight. Rising out of the roof is a large glazed structure, the lighting for the Uvarov archeological collection which was located in the great hall below. The Razumovskys' original wooden house burned down in 1812 and was rebuilt in brick in 1838. In the 1870s a third storey was added and at some time the roof was made to accommodate the huge glass cylinder. Although badly damaged in World War II, the house has been restored more or less as it was. After the revolution when the Uvarovs left, over 400 boxes of books and archeological finds which had remained in the family were handed over to the History Museum. But the fine furniture and other valuables including a classical sarcophagus and statues by Canova remained at Poreche. By the mid 1920s the estate was in use as a forestry institute and over the years, as different Soviet organisations came and went, and German troops arrived, these valuables disappeared. Recently Poreche has been a house of rest for the trades unions.

Other buildings of the estate are in worse condition. To the left (facing the main house) is the stable **courtyard** with one of the tall end buildings still standing. Beyond that is the heavily rebuilt **forge** and on the same path to the right the old **carriage house**. Walk beyond the carriage house towards the extensive neglected park, where about 90 varieties of rare trees can still be found, to see what is left of the vast **greenhouse**. Botanical gardens, inspired by the Tsarskoe Selo landscaped park designed by English gardeners for Empress Catherine, had become very fashionable at the beginning of the 19th century in Russia and Poreche under the Razumovskys, who also owned the impressive garden at Gorenki, had one of the greatest. The greenhouse was enlarged in the 1830s by the Moscow architect, Domenico Gilardi, and again in the 1870s when it was further strengthened by a metal carcase enabling it to contain several thousand exotic plants including tall palm trees. Now the huge metal frame is exposed to the weather and will surely in time disintegrate completely.

KIEV HIGHWAY M-3:
VALUEVO TO VORONOVO

The Kiev Highway M-3 and parallel Kaluga Road A-101, like the Minsk and Mozhaisk Roads, have echoes of Napoleon's hasty retreat and the rapid German advance in 1941. Former estates of court grandees, an Art Nouveau dacha, a tiny convent lost in the woods, an ancient church, and the stunning town of Borovsk are also highlights of these roads.

ON MOSCOW'S DOORSTEP

From Leninsky Prospekt join the MKAD going east to the intersection with the Kaluga Road, A-101. Turn right and immediately double back on a minor road that leads to Mosrentgen, the X-Ray Institute. The area of **TEPLY STAN** is nowadays cut in two by the busy MKAD ring road. All that is left of the former estate, **Troitskoe**, on the outer side of the MKAD, is the small **Church of the Trinity**, *Troitsy*, the only building of interest in this thoroughly Soviet suburb. An octagonal on a cube, it was built in 1686 by Avtamon Ivanov, an influential *Dumny Dyak* (court secretary) under Peter the Great and head of both the Foreign Office and Estates Office. It was rebuilt in 1823 in the popular Empire style by a later owner, Ivan Tyutchev, father of the poet, Fedor Tyutchev. The white apse and lower bell tower are of the 17th century while the ochre tint of the central cube and octagonal tier indicate modifications of 1823. The church began functioning again in the early 1990s.

Take Leninsky Prospekt from Kaluzhskaya Square going southwest and cross under the MKAD to join the Kiev Highway M-3. Two kilometres from the MKAD turn left (unsigned) then left again to the centre of the attractive village of **SOLAREVO**. A civic-minded inhabitant has commemorated **Napoleon's departure** by erecting the small cross marked simply 1812 . It stands next to the **war memorial** of 1941-5 near the site of the village church, demolished in 1973.

In mid October 1812 the dusty Kiev road was crowded with the retreating French army, struggling to carry away the spoils of Moscow. The fire which had destroyed most of the city had also consumed Napoleon's winter supplies and there was nothing for it but to beat an ignominious retreat and count on finding food and fodder in the as yet untouched lands around Kaluga. In this the French were to be disappointed: Russian troops under Kutuzov stole out of Moscow by the parallel Kaluga Road and stationed themselves at Tarutino at the end of the Kiev road blocking the French. Napoleon then headed southwest for Maloyaroslavets to obtain another route to Kaluga but Kutuzov made another flanking movement and met and engaged the French there. Although technically Napoleon won the battle of Maloyaroslavets, in fact he lost the war for again Russian troops were able to close the road to the south decisively cutting off access to vital supplies. The French were forced to flee Russia west through Smolensk and the lands they had despoiled only two months earlier. The troops suffered terribly from the early onset of winter, insufficient supplies and constant harassment. The humiliated army managed to cross the Beresina and leave Russia in late November but with only 40,000 men, one-tenth of its original strength.

From the Kiev Highway 5 km beyond Solarevo (8 km from the MKAD) turn left at traffic lights signed MOSKOVSKY SOVKHOZ. Four kilometres on through the industrial sprawl of the state farm and a little wood is the former estate of **VALUEVO**. *Enter through the lesser gate, left of the main entrance, and cross over to the courtyard.*

Valuevo was inherited by Yekaterina Volkonskaya in 1763. Her husband, the noted scholar, **Count Alexei Musin-Pushkin**, in 1795 discovered in Yaroslavl the 16th century manuscript copy of the priceless 12th century *Lay of Igor's Campaign*, the first epic poem in the Russian language. Although the precious manuscript perished in the Moscow fire of 1812, Musin-Pushkin had fortuitously made copies.

The estate of Valuevo was shaped by Musin-Pushkin at the turn of the 18th into the 19th centuries when, as elsewhere in Europe, the classical style was in full flower. Valuevo is unusual in that although the church and the orangerie were unceremoniously demolished in 1965 during the Khrushchev anti-religious campaign, it has changed little from its original conception. In particular it retains the harmonious composition of the main courtyard and the attractive park which descends gently to the little Likovka River.

The Musin-Pushkins owned the estate until the middle of the 19th century when it was acquired by the **Princes Svyatopolk-Chetvertinsky** and then from 1863 by the wealthy textile merchant and philanthropist, **Dmitry Lepeshkin**. After the revolution Valuevo became the summer

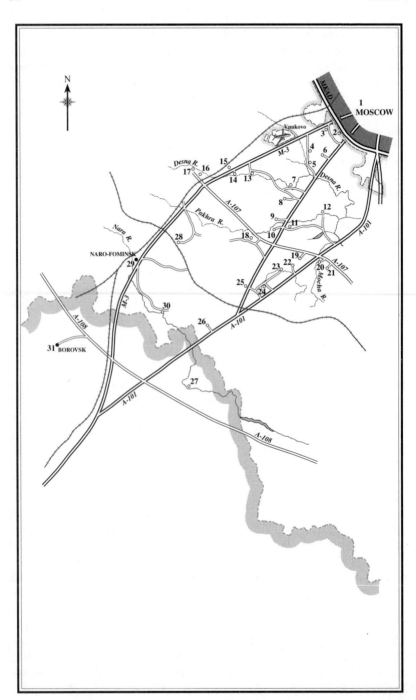

ROAD 2
VALUEVO TO VORONOVO

1. MOSCOW
2. Teply Stan
3. Solarevo
4. Valuevo
5. Filimonki
6. Letovo
7. Vatutinki
8. Puchkovo
9. Bylovo
10. Varvarino
11. Krasnoe
12. Polivanovo
13. Staroe-Nikolskoe
14. Afineevo
15. Aprelevka
16. Petrovskoe Alabino
17. Burtsevo
18. Mikhailovskoe
19. Satino-Russkoe
20. Fillipov Dacha
21. Nikulino
22. Tovarishchevo
23. Vorsino
24. Pokrovskoe
25. Voronovo
26. Vasyunino
27. Tarutino
28. Zosima Pustyn
29. NARO-FOMINSK
30. Kamenskoe
31. BOROVSK

home for senior Party leaders like **Alexei Rykov** who was shot in 1938. Later a clinic for the nearby Vnukovo airport, it is now a holiday home for building industry employees of *Glavmosstroi*. Members of the public are free to enjoy the grounds.

At the main gates instead of the usual sleepy lions slim deer stand trembling on the posts as if ready to leap away at the slightest sound. The two-storey **main house**, of wood under plaster with Ionic porticoes and tall belvedere on the roof, was built 1810-11 by an unknown architect. It is attached by galleries to two-storey wings, one serving as the kitchen, the other the serf theatre. Within, furnishings and paintings have long since disappeared and only heavy 19th century plasterwork survives. The mansion is flanked by miniature classical houses which served as **stables** for horses and cattle and which complete the three sides of a cour d'honneur facing the main gate.

The wooded park follows a cascade of ponds, right, to the Likovka River. A tall **water tower** and **grotto** stand by the upper right pond while further on the left, are three **priest's houses** near the site of the demolished church. The larger central house was for the priest himself, the smaller ones on either side for the deacon and priest's assistant. At the river's edge overlooking the steep bank is the delightful temple-like **pavilion** or hunting lodge built in the 18th century. Tall arched windows peek through the jutting portico of Tuscan columns and pediment. Set into the bank beneath is a second rustic **grotto** which beautifully offsets the smooth perfection of the pavilion above. The views over the river are very attractive. In the distance on the left can be seen the tall bell tower of the former convent at Filimonki.

From Valuevo turn right across the Likovka River and continue for 1 km until on the left woods and buildings appear. At this point turn left down an unmarked paved road and follow it across a ditch to **FILIMONKI**. Here are the grandiose ruins of the 19th century **Convent of Prince Vladimir**. They stand within the territory of a mental hospital but the inmates, although they may beg for cigarettes, are not aggressive. The tall bell tower, 50 metres high, can be seen from a long way off and the four high Gothic arches of the church, almost as tall as the tower, are, even in their ruined roofless state, enormously impressive. In the 1960s, according to local lore, soldiers arrived to pull the convent buildings down. When one was struck by a falling brick and died, the others refused to continue working. So, by an act of God so to speak, it is still standing in all its lean and gaunt beauty.

The convent has connections with a small estate on the other side of the river. Cross the river by the bridge beyond the old convent and turn immediately left on a narrow road to a classical **house** with belvedere high on the river bank. At the beginning of the 19th century the house was rebuilt of wood on a stone foundation by the then owner, Lachinov, although it has since been much altered. In the 1820s it was acquired by Prince Boris Svyatopolk-Chetvertinsky whose son, Vladimir, purchased the neighbouring Valuevo estate.

Prince Vladimir's pious wife, Olga, found a lovely position across the river at Filimonki where she wished to build a church but she died before it could be realised. Her husband took over the task but he too died. Finally his sister, Princess Vera, completed the church in 1862 and organised the burial there of Princess Olga and Prince Vladimir and other relatives. In 1891 this family mausoleum together with a second church and bell tower became the centre of the now ruined **Convent of Prince Vladimir** above.

Meanwhile return to the deserted **house**. According to an obliging local resident, after the revolution it became a school then, in the 1980s, Vasily Konotop, first party secretary for Moscow Oblast, fancied it as his dacha. But his wish was never realised for just after the house had been adapted to his use, Mikhail Gorbachev took power and Konotop was ousted and no longer entitled to such privileges. Since then it has been unoccupied although a caretaker looks after it.

Return to the M-3 or continue on to join the Kaluga Road, the A-101.

BY THE BANKS OF THE DESNA

From Moscow take Profsoyuznaya under the MKAD where it becomes the Kaluga Road A-101. Six km on at Sosenki, turn right 4 km for **Letovo** *clinging to the valley of the little Sosenka.* The ruined **rotunda Church of St Nicholas**, built 1778-83 for P.I. Bibikov has an attractive egg-shaped dome pierced with lucarne windows. 12 km farther along the A-101 (36 km post) through the dacha village DESNA-1, right, is **Stanislavl** and the interesting truncated **Church of St Michael the Archangel**, 1696. Five km past Desna-1 (41 km post) turn right signed VATUTINKI and go through the gates of this Writers' Village where Yury Trifonov who so vividly depicted the life of Muscovites in the 1960s and 1970s had a dacha. The **KRASNAYA PAKHRA HOUSE of REST** is left and then right past a theatre by the River Desna (the

Pakhra River is farther south). Go through the gates to the splendid Soviet 1940s ensemble. The main building in the heavy classical Stalinist style, now a hospital for children with heart diseases, was built as a luxurious house of rest for employees of the Coal Ministry. The large, quiet park on the river, complete with islands, pavilions, narrow bridges, columns and balustrades, resembles a noble estate from the early 19th century. The romantic old lamps come from Yekaterinburg – the name can still be seen on the posts.

A few km farther along the A-101 turn right into Troitsk, where unattractive tower blocks house physics institutes of the Academy of Sciences. Turn left and then right on paved roads and go through a small wood to the hamlet of **PUCHKOVO** and the attractive half baroque, half classical **Church of the Kazan Virgin**, 1791-1806, which has reopened.

From the A-101 take the road west from Troitsk along the Desna R. through Ptichnoe and turn sharp left to Pervomaiskoe. Or on the Kiev Highway M-3 20 km from the MKAD turn left signed PERVOMAISKY SOVKHOZ. At the fork go straight ahead to the unprepossessing dairy and cattle farm on the winding Desna River. Worn out entrance gates into the park hint at the former glory of the **STAROE-NIKOLSKOE ESTATE** but nowadays it seems a miracle that the decrepit buildings are still standing.

Staroe-Nikolskoe has had a large number of owners. Among them in the early 18th century was **General Vasily Rtishchev** (grandson of Fedor Rtishchev, organiser in 1648 of the first school in Russia), who built the church. In 1786 it passed to **Ivan Musin-Pushkin**, relative of the owner of nearby Valuevo, who built the main house and landscaped the park and ponds. In the early 19th century the **Bibikov** owners let a part of the estate to Yakov Yesipov who experimented with extracting sugar from beets. But he died before the project was completed and sugarbeet production, although successful farther south, never became established in the Moscow region. Later owners badly neglected the property.

Through the higgledy-piggledy gates the free-standing **wing** of the house can be seen left of the tree-lined avenue. The dilapidated three-storey **main house** built in the early 19th century stands right, now turned into the local shop. Left derelict in the late 19th century it suffered even more in the Soviet period and the original plasterwork is barely discernible. In the lean winter of 1992 a long queue of despairing men and

women from the farm could be seen waiting patiently outside the shop
with their string bags for a delivery of bread that might or might not
come.

The large brick church located across a small bridge over a ravine, was
built in 1709 by Vasily Rtishchev and is one of the earliest churches to
display the innovative classical style. The **Church of the Holy Spirit**,
Dukha Svyatavo, is set high on a basement, the cube graduating to the
cupola via a rotunda instead of the usual octagon, the first example of
this in Russian architecture. The north facade originally mimicked the
south but in the late 19th century was altered to accommodate the
pseudo-Russian bell tower/chapel with its round apse. The church,
which lost its renowned iconostasis in the 1920s, was further desecrated
when interior walls were removed to facilitate its use as a storehouse. In
1991 it returned to worship and is slowly being restored.

From the church and war memorial continue until the road descends
sharply and turn right into woods. Count V.P. Berg created a complex
summer home here at the beginning of the 20th century incorporating
all the latest technology including an electricity generator, a water
tower, greenhouses, orangerie and stables. The **Berg dacha** seen through
the trees is the pretty blue and white log house with columns and an
overhanging first floor but it too is in a lamentable state. After the
revolution the isolated dacha was sometimes used for meetings of
foreign communist parties – in 1928 the 6th congress of the Chinese
Communist Party and in 1930 the 2nd congress of the Hungarian
Communist Party. The **NKVD** (secret police) also used it as their
holiday home – a good place to relax after interrogating terrorised
prisoners at the Lubyanka. The NKVD officers have long gone as have
also the nursery school children who succeeded them. Berg's brick
pseudo-Gothic carriage house and large stables can be seen to one side
and near them the three-storey wooden house for farm workers.

*On the Kiev Highway towards Aprelevka take the first left after the
Pervomaisky Sovkhoz for* **Afineevo** *signed P.L.TERESHKOVOI (named
after the lady cosmonaut) to* **AFINEEVO**. The striking red and white
church, **St John the Baptist**, *Ioanna Predtechy*, built 1704–9 in the
Moscow baroque style, was in 1800 larded with classical afterthoughts
such as the incongruous portico and spire. Happily the original iconostasis survives in this church which was not closed. In 1913 Alexei
Bakhrushin, the collector of theatrical memorabilia, purchased and
managed to renovate the estate before the First World War and revolu-

tion intervened but now nothing remains except a wood-working yard, some straggling dachas, and the church.

Strange forms like huge lollipops greet the visitor to the town of **APRELEVKA**. They belong to the institute *Teploproekt* (thermal power) of the Academy of Sciences. Aprelevka is also known for its production of records, audiotapes and CDs, offspring of the German firm **Metropole-Record** founded in 1910. The old factory buildings and small museum are on the east side of the railway line, right of the road.

On the Kiev Highway past Aprelevka turn right at the 50 km GAI post onto the A-107 Ring Road. After crossing a railway line and at the confusing sign PRYAMO NALEVO (straight ahead left), turn right again to **PETROVSKOE ALABINO (Knyazhishchevo)**. Three hundred metres on the left is the delapidated **Church of St Peter the Metropolitan** while on the right, in bizarre juxtaposition, is a second church in excellent order. Straight ahead however are the giant columns of a huge, wrecked mansion standing bare to the sky like an ancient Greek ruin.

Petrovskoe was once one of the most splendid of Moscow's country estates. The property was acquired in the 1740s by the Demidov family whose ancestor, **Nikita Demidov**, founded the family fortune as a blacksmith and gun maker in Tula for Peter the Great. His descendants successfully moved into exploitation of the mineral wealth of the Urals and Siberia – Demidov iron became so sought after that it was even exported to England. This unique house was built for Nikita Akinfievich, grandson of the Tula blacksmith and an influential person at the court of Catherine II, by Matvei Kazakov. Some historians still argue that Vasily Bazhenov, Kazakov's mentor, could have been the author of Petrovskoe but the 1776 foundation stone specifically names Kazakov.

Today, it takes a vivid imagination to picture the once majestic **mansion** surmounted by a shallow dome. A cube of two tall floors, the four main facades of Tuscan columns and the four bevelled and angled corners with Ionic porticoes were linked together by the rich cornice. Except for the principal entrance which led to a triple hall, the main facades and the four corners opened onto large rooms linked by corridors to the grand circular salon at the centre of the mansion. The internal plan was thus in the shape of a diagonal, something like a huge X. Outside, the diagonal continued to the four free-standing two-storey houses or wings which face the blunted corners of the main house in a brilliant, geometrical design. Originally these wings were joined together by wrought iron railings that formed an enclosed space around the main house. The garden and large park leading to the Desna River surrounded three sides of this courtyard while the access road provided the fourth. This most sumptuous house was further enhanced by marble statuary and superb iron work from the Demidov factories. Over the cupola stood the iron figure of Catherine II and iron sphinxes embellished the porches. A large figure of Apollo dominated the small hill leading to the Desna River.

The formidable Demidov wealth was squandered by Nikita's son, Nikolai, but was for a time recouped when Nikolai married Elizaveta, daughter of the wealthy Alexander Stroganov. But the succeeding generations proved as feckless and the inheritance was rapidly depleted. Thus in 1852 the estate was sold to **Prince Alexander Meshchersky**, the personal adjutant to Alexander III. He married at the advanced age of 73 and died just before his youngest daughter, Yekaterina, was born. Yekaterina in her memoirs recalled pleasant days at Petrovskoe in the 1910s when grand balls were held in the circular hall and plays staged in the theatre. Then in 1914 a strange incident occured which was to have fortunate repercussions. Three political convicts being escorted by train managed to escape. They unknowingly climbed a high wall into the grounds of Petrovskoe and were brought before the mistress of the house. She took pity on the young students, harbouring them for several months and giving them money and clothes when they left. Years later, in 1933, Yekaterina with her mother was arrested and taken to Lubyanka prison. The interrogator studied her papers and then stared at her intently for a long time. In an ironic twist of fate he turned out to be one of the three escaped convicts. Somehow he managed to have her and her mother released and issued with the essential internal passports. So Yekaterina, born Princess Meshcherskaya, continued to live quietly in the Soviet Union until her death in the 1990s.

The grand house survived the 1917 revolution but in the early 1930s when the local authorities needed bricks for their new farm buildings, it was callously blown up. Only the houses that completed the diagonal have survived and Petrovskoe, arguably Kazakov's best work, is now a romantic ruin. But, astonishingly, the Meshcherskys are back in residence. In the late 1990s a descendant was able to have his claim as owner of the estate accepted, a rare event in Russia, and is now living in one of the houses.

Like the main house, the baroque **Church of St Peter the Metropolitan**, *Petra Mitropolita*, built in 1785-6 and also by Kazakov, is in a sad state although the roof, minus its dome, is still intact. The Demidov tombs which originally stood inside the church are gone and the iconostasis, once sheathed in glittering precious stones from the Demidov mines, was pilfered in the 1920s during the policy of *oblegchenie* (relieving icons of their valuable frames and stones). But the remarkable Father Alexander who has been the priest in the area for 30 years is determined to succeed where the state restorers, who have been timidly attempting repairs, have failed. He has persuaded soldiers of the famous Tamansky division from nearby Naro-Fominsk to give their services free and hopes to completely restore the church.

The round bell tower on the other side of the road opposite the Church of St Peter was also part of the Kazakov ensemble and was originally free-standing. In 1858, the bell tower became part of a new church, the functioning **Intercession of the Virgin**, *Pokrova Bogoroditsy*, built by the Meshcherskys as the mausoleum of a beloved child. However, the family tombs were thrown out when the local collective farm decided to use the cool vaults to store potatoes. It is curious that the apses in both churches face southwest instead of east.

About 1 km north of Alabino towards the Minsk Road is the ruined **Church of the Ascension**, *Vozneseniya*, built 1730–3 in the small village of **Burtsevo**.

IN THE VALLEY OF THE PAKHRA

Take the Kaluga Road A-101 beyond Troitsk to Krasnaya Pakhra, 44 km from Moscow. For **BYLOVO** *descend the hill and take the second right signed MALINSKY LESOPUNKT.* Follow the road 2 km to the pretty, unexpectedly rural village with the charming red and white pseudo-Russian 19th century church, **Michael the Archangel**, standing in a commanding position looking across fields to a dark line of trees. The priest who thoughtfully came out on a frosty day to put cinders on the icy steps, told us that the small attractive cottages which surround it are mostly dachas which are often burgled in the winter.

In Krasnaya Pakhra past the bus-stop turn right opposite a crude statue of a mother and child. A few hundred metres on turn left by some modern flats and follow the road veering right 1 km to **VARVARINO**. At the sign P.L. CHAIKA turn left on a concrete road up a hill to the church now visible. The red brick **Church of the Nativity of Christ**, *Rozhdestva Khristova*, which stands in a cemetery alone among the abandoned buildings of the pioneer camp, was built in 1692 by the Miloslavskys, relations of Tsar Alexei's first wife. Its intriguing design consists of a red brick cube with a tall drum and cupola and an unusual square apse supporting a second tall drum and cupola. The whimsical baroque window frames include downwardly tapering columns of white limestone and pediments broken by white balls. The 19th century *trapeza* and bell tower cleverly repeat the original design.

At Krasnaya Pakhra turn left signed KRASNOE. In 1 km the road turns left across a ravine and rises to the top of the bank. Take the minor left road to the crumbling estate, house, church and park.

KRASNOE belonged in the 17th century first to the Miloslavskys and then in 1685 to the Imeretia (Georgia) heir, Prince Alexander, a close friend of Peter the Great. When Prince Alexander was taken prisoner in the unsuccessful battle of Narva against the Swedes in 1700 Peter agreed to exchange him for 50 Swedish prisoners. But the noble Prince obstinately refused any deal and died in a Swedish prison in 1710. The estate was later acquired by the Saltykovs. In 1812 Kutuzov rested here for five days before setting out for Tarutino and the Battle of Maloyaroslavets. A century later, in 1912, the estate was purchased by Count Sergei Witte, the moderate conservative prime minister who was suddenly dismissed by the Tsar in 1906. He wrote his memoirs here before his death in 1915.

The **Church of St John the Theologian**, *Ioanna Bogoslova*, was built by Prince Alexander's father, Archil, in 1706 during the Prince's imprisonment. Only its general form, an octagonal on a cube, is evidence of its early date, for 19th century additions of Doric columns and pediment to the west front and north chapel have given it a doleful look. Closed and stripped of its belltower and cupola, volunteers are now trying to restore the building but progress is slow. Inside not even the floor survived.

The decaying mansion of the **Krasnoe estate** across the road from the church was first built in the 18th century by the Saltykov family. From the depths of the park of ancient limes in the straight rows of their original planting, the empty, desolate house – largely rebuilt in the middle of the 19th century – with its alternating red brick and white stone stripes is still impressive. Of the two wings, only the right, now a police station, is original. The left wing, built in Soviet times in the classical manner, is now a sanatorium for chronically sick children of the Podolsk area.

At Krasnya Pakhra turn left signed KRASNOE and continue for 10 km past Shaganino then turn left signed POLIVANOVO for 2 km across the Pakhra River. Polivanovo can also be approached from the Varshavskoe Shosse 6 km from Podolsk by turning right to Shchapovo then right again signed POLIVANOVO.

The heavily wooded high bank of the curving Pakhra is here especially wild and beautiful. On the left bank is **POLIVANOVO**, the once splendid estate of Count Kirill Razumovsky which was also closely associated with the Petersburg court. The name is alleged to derive from the words *polit* (to pour) and *Ivan*. As the story goes a 16th century boyar, named Ivan, who was invited to dine with the fearful Tsar, Ivan the Terrible, in the Kremlin, unluckily spilled some of the precious salt on the table. The Tsar sarcastically jeered *polivan* and the name stuck.

The **Razumovsky** family came to prominence through Kirill's brother, Alexei Razumovsky, older than Kirill by 15 years. Alexei was a handsome, sweet-voiced shepherd boy who caught the eye of the Empress Elizabeth, the daughter of Peter the Great, and probably became her unacknowledged husband. Elizabeth was kind to her lover's brother and sent Kirill to study abroad. On his return Elizabeth made him head of the Academy of Sciences at the age of only 18, and three years later made him Hetman of the Ukraine and endowed him with huge estates. Because of his good nature or perhaps his adroit political sense he managed when Elizabeth died to remain on good terms with both Peter III and Catherine I; indeed he played an important part in Catherine's coup against her husband. Although Catherine soon abolished the office of Hetman, he was consoled with the rank of Field Marshal.

As is often the case among venerable country houses, the main house is now a mental hospital. The priest's house, a service wing and the dilapidated church also survive from Razumovsky's time. In view of Count Razumovsky's high rank the designer of both house and church might have been the leading architect, Vasily Bazhenov. The **Church of the Annunciation**, *Blagoveshcheniya*, built 1777–9, sadly dilapidated after suffering two recent fires but once again holding services, is typical of Bazhenov: a well proportioned cube with no protruding apse, rounded rusticated corners, with pilasters and pediments on three sides and a tall spire. In the pediment above the portico is an open bible within a sunburst.

Farther on past an old larch, the classical two-storey **house** built in the 1780s faces the Pakhra. It avoids monotony by the high rusticated ground floor (in brick and stucco) and the round domed towers at each corner, two of which enclosed staircases. At the back is an attractive loggia while the formal entrance on the Pakhra River is marked by a portico of six Ionic columns and a pediment.

The Razumovskys left no heirs and the estate changed hands many times. Mme Davydova, the last and tragic owner, let it to the Troitse-Sergiev Monastery as a teachers' college. After the revolution she was abandoned by her husband who took their only son to America leaving her to disappear in the purges of the 1930s. At first a technical college, then apartments, the mental hospital opened in the 1950s. Patients who enjoy the peaceful grounds can be reminded of the past when they see Kirill (Cyril) Razumovsky's monogram in Latin letters, 'CR', worked into the railings.

From the Kaluga Road A-101 travel to the intersection with the A-107 guarded by the GAI and turn right. Four km on at Shishkin Les turn left at the grocery shop to Mikhailovskoe (sometimes called Novomikhail-ovskoe). After a narrow bridge the road bends right and soon a water tower appears. This is the entrance into the former estate of **MIKHAILOVSKOE** now a rehabilitation centre for heart patients.

The estate of Mikhailovskoe was built at the end of the 18th century for General Mikhail Krechetnikov, the Governor of Tula and Kaluga; his initials 'M.K.' can still be seen in the railings of the house. During Napoleon's retreat regiments of the French army, camped in the grounds of Mikhailovskoe, lit so many fires the peasants feared the woods would catch alight. In the 1820s the **Sheremetiev** family acquired the estate, then sold it to the Musin-Pushkins to pay off debts but, in the 1870s, bought it back. The last owner, the historian Count Sergei Sheremetiev, wrote an interesting monograph on Mikhailovskoe and is responsible for the informative plaque on the main house giving details of ownership. The archives pertaining to the family estates at Vyazemy and Ostafyevo, held at Mikhailovskoe, are now in the Russian State Library.

Of all the many buildings that made up the ensemble in 1917 only two small towers and the main house, now *Korpus No. 1* through the trees on the right, are standing. The large **house** is best viewed from the river side, where extensive parkland and ponds descend to the Pakhra. The central part with the circular hall jutting out towards the park was built between 1776 and 1784 by either Petr Nikitin or Ivan Starov of St Petersburg. Within, the layout has survived in the central section together with some old stoves. The long wings either side of the main house were added at various times during the occupancy of the Sheremetievs; the left wing embellished with pseudo-Russian windows is dated 1903, the right is given as 1890 and 1908. An unusual feature is the **twin two-storey pavilions** in the shape of towers situated either side of the house. The one on the left built in 1794 was the belltower for the Church of the Archangel Michael, which was demolished in the Soviet period and after which the estate was named. The one on the right was used for drying food and as storage – it now serves as a ski base for the sanatorium.

After the revolution Mikhailovskoe became a rest home for former political prisoners of the tsarist regime. At first a privileged group, in the late 1930s they became victims of Stalin's purges and nearly all were arrested and shot.

Continue northwest on the A-107 and turn left onto the Kiev Highway M-3. After 6 km turn left at Yakovlevskoe by the sign 50 YEARS OF THE USSR STATE FARM (SOVKHOZ) (if still there). Continue past the large war memorial at Yakovlevskoe 6 km to Rudnevo and turn right at the top of the hill marked P.L. BEZAKOVO. After about 5 km on the somewhat rough road the woods part for a view of **ZOSIMA PUSTYN**, a romantic walled settlement with pointed towers, a church and tall bell tower. Closer up however the dilapidated state of the buildings destroys the favourable first impression.

In the 19th century new religious communities, *pustyni* (hermitages), sprang up all over Russia. Here nestling in the little valley of a stream that flows into the Sokhna, and thence the Pakhra, is the **Trinity**, *Troitsy*, known more colloquially as **Zosima Pustyn** after its founder. The venerable Zosima Verkhovsky and his wealthy patron, Mariya Bakhmeteva, established this religious community of 22 nuns in 1826 in the depths of the forest not far from the Bakhmetev estate. After Father Zosima and Mariya Bakhmeteva died, the community came under the care of Semen Lepeshkin, a wealthy Moscow merchant (his son was the last owner of Valuevo, p.37) and who in 1855 rebuilt the wooden hermitage in brick. After the revolution, the Pustyn, then under the direction of Afanasiya, Lepeshkin's granddaughter, was obliged to join the local agricultural *artel*. A curious document written in 1922 by a local official, A. Kotov, praises the selfless labour of the sisters of the community, who proved better workers than the farmers. However, their good work did not prevent closure of the convent in 1928 and the exile of Afanasiya. After the war Zosima Pustyn became a summer camp for children but the buildings deteriorated badly. Today, the various small houses and workshops that cluster around the church are inhabited by a trio of amazing crones who with their dogs act as fierce caretakers. But on 7 December 1996 prayers for Zosima, founder of the hermitage, were held in Trinity Church, and the sisters plan to return.

On the Kiev Highway M-3 about 70 km from Moscow turn right signed **NARO-FOMINSK**, *a mill town founded in the 1840s with a population of 60,000 on the banks of the Nara River. (To the left 7 km via Afanasovka is Mogutovo with its fine 17th century Moscow baroque church built in 1693.)*

The immense bright yellow church of **St Nicholas the Wonderworker** in the form of a Greek cross with an outsize cupola overwhelms the town. It was erected in 1862 for the 50th anniversary of the French invasion (Napoleon had bivouacked in Naro-Fominsk during the retreat) on the model of the gigantic Christ the Saviour in Moscow. The German Army held Naro-Fominsk for 66 days in the autumn of 1941 until December 26 when it was freed by Soviet troops.

On the opposite bank are the red brick buildings of the **textile mill** purchased in 1864 by **Vasily Yakunchikov**, the industrialist. Yakunchikov's large house on the Nara (remnants remain off Pogodinskaya Ulitsa by the *Granitnaya Masterskaya*) welcomed Chekhov and his wife, Olga Knipper, in the summer of 1903 when Chekhov was writing the **Cherry Orchard**. Chekhov clearly did not find the company congenial for he wrote: 'Such a hideously empty, stupid and tasteless life as that in the white house it would be difficult to find elsewhere.' Perhaps the theme of his play, the decline of the old order and rise of the brash new world, was inspired by the Yakunchikovs for they too bought up old noble estates and cut down the trees to build railway lines.

On the Kiev Highway M-3 past Naro-Fominsk turn left at the GAI signed ATEPTSEVO. After 13 km a stone pyramid for the state farm,

VOSKHOD, denotes the entry to **KAMENSKOE.** Its urban-looking five-storey blocks of flats popularly called *Khrushchoby* (a pun on *trushchoby* – slums – since they were erected cheaply and quickly in the Khrushchev period) are quite shockingly ugly against the beautiful forests, rolling hills and River Nara that surround the village. But all this is soon forgotten when on the right appears the ancient stone **Church of St Nicholas.** Built in the middle of the 14th century, fifty years earlier than the churches at Zvenigorod, it is the oldest building in the Moscow Oblast.

The early history of the small church is obscure but it was probably built by one of the Moscow princes, perhaps Prince Yury of Zvenigorod (see p.13). Inevitably over the 550 years of its existence, it was greatly altered but was restored to something like its original form in 1958-64 by dedicated Soviet architects. It gives an impression of power and simplicity for the plain walls, undivided into the usual three bays (although there would have been roof *zakomary* gables), are devoid of any kind of decoration apart from the pattern of the white limestone blocks and the lovely recessed portal. The plan is of a cross of equal arms set within a square without the usual free-standing columns – the roof and cupola rest on piers within the walls. On the east, the triple apse protrudes extensively and a tall elegant drum with slit windows and a helmet-shaped cupola complete the picture. The church, still not functioning, is wonderful at any time of the year but seen on a sunny winter day against the pure white of untrammelled snow it is at its best.

BOROVSK

Although Borovsk lies just outside the Moscow Oblast in Kaluga Oblast, it is an easy 80 km from the MKAD on the Kiev Highway M-3. From Naro-Fominsk proceed 22km to the untidy railway junction at Balabanovo. Turn right a little past the GAI post onto the A-108 road signed BOROVSK. At 8 km take the left fork also signed BOROVSK down the hill and with Borovsk straight ahead turn left to **Roshcha** *and the* **Pafnuty Monastery***.*

The main attraction of **ROSHCHA** on the Protva River at the outskirts of Borovsk, is the tall **Church of the Nativity of the Virgin**, *Rozhdestva Bogoroditsy*. The church which remained open was built in 1708, a tiered octagonal on a cube with the delightfully curvaceous window designs of Moscow baroque. The belltower and *trapeza*, added a century later are contemporary with the finely carved five-tier iconostasis. In the 1960s the parishioners were scandalised when the priest was discovered selling church icons and was sent to prison.

The **PAFNUTY MONASTERY of Borovsk**, *Svyato-Pafnutiev Borovsky Monastyr*, lies a little north of Roshcha, across the small stream, Isterma, which circles attractively around the monastery, widening into ponds before flowing into the Protva. **St Pafnuty**, of Tatar origin, founded the ancient monastery in 1444 and ensured that it played an important role in the political history of Russia by immediately siding with the Moscow grand princes. It has survived periodic attack: in 1610 by Polish forces under the second False Dmitry, in 1812 by the French under Napoleon, and again in 1941–2 during the German occupation.

Closed in 1919 after the advent of Soviet power, it served first as a museum, then an orphanage, then an agricultural college. In the course of time the buildings were altered, the silver icon frames melted down and even the icons taken to stoke fires during the fuel crisis. However since the middle of the 1950s, dedicated museum curators and Soviet restorers with limited resources have worked to protect and return the buildings to their original state. In 1991 the monastery was reopened under the energetic Abbot Gavril.

The 17th century fortress-like walls were built by the master stone mason, Trofim Sharutin, from Kashin. The excellent local museum with its exhibition on Borovsk Old Believers continues to occupy the old refectory, centre right, with its **Church of the Nativity of Christ**, *Rozhdestva Khristova*, built in 1511. The 17th century bell tower decorated with tiles by Polubes can be entered via the refectory porch where the old frescoes have grown rather faint. The tall **Cathedral of the Nativity of the Virgin**, *Rozhdestva Bogoroditsy*, to the right, was built 1590-6 in unadorned monumental style crowned by five old-fashioned helmet-shaped cupolas. The first works of the great icon painter, Dionisy, executed here in 1470, were lost in the late 16th century rebuilding; the present frescoes are of 1644. Ahead and to the left along the wall are two functioning churches, the pink **St Mitrofan**, 1680–1763, attached to the abbot's residence, and the infirmary church of **St Elijah**, *Ilii*, built in 1670.

From Roshcha return to the main road where there is a fine view of **BOROVSK TOWN**. Streets and squares of low houses punctuated with the towers and cupolas of churches line the high right bank of the looping Protva River. Climb the north bank to the main thoroughfare,

Kommunisticheskaya. On the left clinging to the escarpment is the reopened **Church of Sts Boris and Gleb**, built in 1704. In a few yards on the right, among the unpromising sprawl of a vehicle service station, *avtobaza No 63*, stands the gigantic **Church of the Intercession**, *Pokrova*, built 1909-12, incongruously a garage for trucks. The massive church, based loosely on the style of 14th century Novgorod churches, is reminiscent of Gornostaev's contemporary Old Believer bell tower at Rogozhskoe in Moscow.

Old Believers *or Schismatics were those Russian Orthodox believers who refused to accept the seemingly minor reforms – changes in the liturgy, the spelling of Jesus' name and the number of fingers used to make the sign of the cross – introduced in the 1650s by Patriarch Nikon. The Old Believers, like the rest of the Russian population largely illiterate, fought a long battle against the Church and the Patriarch, and the Tsar and his representatives. The great Solovetsky Monastery in the White Sea withheld a siege for 8 years; many other Old Believers locked themselves into churches and immolated themselves, or fled to remote parts of Russia. Borovsk at that time was firmly in the hands of Tsar Alexei and Patriarch Nikon and it was there that many leading members of the Old Believers were imprisoned. The great arch priest, Avvakum, the most notable of the opponents of the reforms and author of the first Russian autobiography, was held in the Pafnuty Monastery in Borovsk in 1666-7 before being banished to Siberia where he was eventually burned at the stake. Among his fanatical followers were the highborn* **Feodosiya Morozova**, *widow of a leading boyar, and her sister, Princess Yevdokiya Urusova. Their opposition came to a head when Boyarina Morozova refused to attend the wedding of the Tsar to his new wife, Natalya Naryshkina (mother of Peter the Great). Both sisters were arrested, placed in chains and taken to Borovsk where in 1672 they were starved to death. (There is a famous painting by Surikov of Boyarina Morozova being carried off by sleigh defiantly making the sign of the cross with two fingers instead of three.) The place where the two sisters died soon became a source of pilgrimage for Old Believers who by 1917 formed 70% of the population of Borovsk. After 1905, when the Old Believers were allowed to build their own churches, three were rapidly constructed in Borovsk, all closed during Soviet rule. Today, still a considerable force in the town, they are making a comeback and one of their churches, also the Intercession, on the low bank of the Protva and for 40 years a poultry incubation centre, has reopened.*

Up the hill on the left in another splendidly commanding position is the

Orthodox **Cathedral of the Annunciation**, *Blagoveshcheniya*, with stylised drums and cupolas built at the end of the 18th century. The elegant round bell tower with the spire was added in 1819. On the right are local government offices with the Russian flag flying. The striking aluminium shaft supporting a rocket is a memorial to **Tsiolkovsky**, 1857-1935, the inventor of rocketry, who lived and taught in Borovsk. The large white local court building was constructed in the 1970s over the graves of **Boyarina Morozova** and her sister, deeply offending local Old Believers.

At the top of Kommunisticheskaya in Lenin Square is the war memorial and the obligatory statue of **Lenin** erected in place of a demolished church.

From here long narrow streets follow southwards the contours of the Protva. On Lenin Street to the left of the Annunciation Cathedral is the impressive local art gallery. Unbelievably it was once the Old Believer **Church of All Saints**, *Vsekh Svyatykh*, shorn of its tower and cupola in the 1920s and rebuilt as a club and gallery. Next door, in winter a steep ice slide attracts crowds of screaming children with their sleighs. Farther along the street is a fine wooden merchant's house of the late 19th century.

The ridge of the escarpment, lined with attractive wooden houses and the odd factory, curves around left via Mira Street to the district known as Vysokoe where an especially lovely wooden church stands in the town cemetery. Also bearing the popular name of the **Intercession**, *Pokrova*, it was built at the end of the 17th century and is kept in good repair. From here yet more wonderful views of the town and the Pafnuty monastery can be obtained.

ON THE MOCHA

Within the rough triangle formed by the ring road A-107, the Kaluga Road A-101 and the Varshavskoe Road from Podolsk, are many small villages and at the apex, the great estate at Voronovo. The narrow stream, the Mocha (meaning urine!), winds its way throughout before emptying into the Pakhra. On the Varshavskoe Road, turn left on the A-107 for 3 km then turn right to the sports centre signed PODGOTOVKA OLIMPIADY. Presumably training is carried out here in preparation for the Olympics although it does not seem very busy. Here among other buildings is the country home of the **Fillipov family**, the successful

Moscow bakers of the beginning of the century. Set on a hill
overlooking the Mocha River the house is now the clinic for the sports
centre. A solid, late 19th century building with a picturesque tower it is
in the romantic, historical style of many comfortable houses of this
time. Inside there are brightly painted plaster ceilings.

Two km farther east on the A-107 turn right signed **NIKULINO** *then
right again down a sometimes muddy lane, and stop on the grass in front
of a cottage.* On a mound in the midst of an old graveyard across the
stream, a tributary of the Mocha, stands the tiered **Church of the
Saviour**, *Spasa*, built in the early 18th century in the attractive Moscow
baroque style. The later *trapeza* and the late 18th century bell tower
with spire successfully blend with the earlier church.

*On the A-107 travel 2 km west of the GAI junction with the Varshavskoe
Road. Just after the right turn to Krekshino turn left onto an unsigned
poorly paved road to* **SATINO-RUSSKOE**. On the right is a dacha
village of wooden houses with barn-like roofs placed close together in
orderly lines, like a crowded city suburb. State farms would give city
organisations small plots of land like this where the builders, oblivious
to the spacious country around, would build dachas comfortingly close
to one another. Ahead reflected in the water of a pond are the rounded
forms of the lonely **Church of the Ascension**, *Voznescniya*. The church,
which now has for company only the summer *dachniki*, was built in
1819 in the classical style (the north chapel is a later addition). Coming
closer it is obvious that the walls are beginning to crumble and bricks lie
in desolate heaps on the ground. To the south of the church is a
charming cottage and beyond that nothing but fields and woods.

*On the Kaluga Road A-101 travel 40 km from the MKAD (59 km post)
to Voronovo and turn left signed VORONOVO SOVKHOZ. In 1 km turn
left at a little square passing the squalid buildings of the large Voronovo
beef and dairy farm, and in 2 km take the poor dirt road right to*
POKROVSKOE. A delightful metal footbridge and causeway crosses
the dammed pond of the Mocha to the tall elegant **Church of the Intercession**, *Pokrova*. On our first visit the church was merely a large shell
filled with the whirring sound of birds. Now, under the Patriarch's
patronage, it is being renovated for nuns who have opened a girls'
orphanage here. First built 1722-6 by another of Peter the Great's
courtiers, I.R. Streshnev, it is an interesting example of the new fascination with Europe in the reign of Peter. The main body of the church
and the apse display large windows, Tuscan pilasters, and a pediment

grafted on to the familiar form of an octagonal on a cube while the tall drum reflects the Moscow baroque style. The *trapeza* was added in 1781 and the bell tower a century later. The curious open work 'crown' in place of a cupola like that of Dubrovitsy also hints at western fashion. Small wooden houses surround the church on three sides, while the dreamy pond makes the fourth. A little to the north near the ubiquitous war memorial and hidden in foliage, is the ruin of a wing of the old 18th century Streshnev mansion.

Two km from Pokrovskoe through open country is the small, rundown village of **VORSINO**, *which also belongs to the Voronovo dairy farm.* Ignore the outdated sign telling outsiders not to continue further and proceed on the bumpy local road to the **Church of St Fedor** built in 1834-7, a fine example of the classical, Empire style. Vorsino belonged in the medieval period to the influential Kolychev boyars. A later owner, T.S. Karina, built this unusual church, its arched niches and low dome resembling a park pavilion, incongruous in the unprepossessing village. The bell tower has been thoroughly beheaded and the church, empty and unused, provides marvellous nesting places for birds. Across the fields can be seen the impressive baroque bell tower at **Tovarishchevo.**

The grand estate of **VORONOVO** *is situated to the right of the A-101 opposite the turn to Pokrovskoe.* The sprawling settlement of Khrushchev era five-storey concrete apartment blocks looks distinctly uninviting. But persevere for Voronovo on a small tributary of the Mocha River was one of the most magnificent estates in the Moscow region whose successive owners represented some of the grandest families in Russia. Park along the road or by the church.

Most of the principal buildings survive including the main house (rebuilt), the church, the Dutch house, service buildings – including the corner stables tower, the long pond and park. It now belongs to a house of rest whose more modern buildings are discreetly located across the pond.

The **Voronov-Volynskys** who acquired the estate at the beginning of the 17th century were descended from a boyar at the court of Ivan III nicknamed Vorona (crow). In 1726 Artemy Volynsky, Ambassador to Persia and Governor of Astrakhan and Kazan, inherited the estate. Because of his opposition to the German clique around Empress Anna Ivanovna led by the powerful Biron, he was arrested in 1740 and executed, his family were exiled to Siberia and their property confiscated by the crown. Empress Elizabeth, however, on coming to the throne in 1742, revoked the edict and the Volynskys returned to Voronovo.

In the mid 18th century Voronovo passed through marriage to **Count Ivan Vorontsov**, a high-ranking courtier whose brother was vice-chancellor to Elizabeth. It was during the sojourn of the Vorontsovs that the Dutch House and the splendid church were built. In December 1775 Catherine II visited Voronovo after her long trip to the south. Putting up the Empress in those days was no mean feat. It entailed finding accommodation for the great entourage that accompanied her, feeding them all, illuminating the house, and providing entertainment. On this occasion **Catherine**, who must have been tired, merely played chess and dined. But the honour of a visit by the Empress was such that two pyramids were erected on either side of the entrance and an obelisk was put up on the main avenue – all destroyed after the revolution.

Count Vorontsov's son, Artemy (who was god-father to Pushkin) built a new, magnificent, mansion at Voronovo designed by the leading court architect, **Nikolai Lvov** (see Vvedenskoe). The expensive palace of three storeys with three-storey wings linked by colonnades ruined Artemy who in 1800 was obliged to sell the estate to Count Fedor Rostopchin.

The Rostopchins' sojourn at Voronovo, from 1800 to 1815, was the most glittering in the history of the estate. The Count spent a great deal of time there, sometimes staying all year round. The wonderful parks were so carefully managed that once, when an oak was struck by lightning, it was immediately replaced by a mature oak of approximately the same age (although it took three tries before the new oak struck root). An anglophile, Rostopchin brought from England various specialists, agronomists and others to introduce the latest agricultural methods. He invited the St Petersburg architect, Quarenghi, to design the orangerie (it has not survived). But his main interest was **horse breeding**. With his German veterinary surgeon and English horse manager and jockey he was able to develop an enviable stud of more than 100 Arabian and Persian horses.

Count Rostopchin became military **Governor-General of Moscow** in 1812 and played a vital role in fomenting opposition to the French, even to the sacrifice of his beloved estate. In September 1812, Voronovo was in an untenable position poised between Moscow and the French camp at Tarutino. Rostophchin, accompanied by the British military officer,

General Robert Wilson, bivouacked at Voronovo on 20 September as part of the Russian rearguard. In the grandest of gestures before leaving he set fire to his elegant mansion, burning it to the ground. The people of Moscow nervously awaiting the arrival of the French were immensely impressed by this act of self-sacrifice. The mansion was never to be so splendid again.

Voronovo was purchased in 1856 by the **Sheremetievs** who rebuilt the main house as a grand palace with their coat of arms emblazoned on the pediment. In 1919 Voronovo was confiscated by the Bolsheviks and suffered again from fire. A school for crafts was established there briefly in 1930 only to be closed when the estate became a house of rest for Gosplan, the powerful state planning organisation. In 1949 the **mansion** was totally rebuilt in the heavy Soviet classical style of three storeys with high-pitched roofs and stylised baroque window designs. Nevertheless, it harmonises well with the surviving old buildings. The Sheremetiev coat of arms is even reproduced in relief on the pediment with their motto: Deus Conservat Omnia – God Preserves All.

The most interesting of the old buildings is surely the baroque **Church of the Saviour**, *Spasa*, situated to the left of the house from the main road. Built in brick and stucco about the middle of the 18th century in the reign of Elizabeth and probably designed by Karl Blank, it is in the form of a Greek inscribed cross with rounded corners from which springs a tall octagonal tier supporting the dome. Its rich facade displays pediments, pilasters and paired columns, a strong cornice and curvaceous figured window surrounds. The dome is punctuated by lucarne windows and completed by a baroque cupola. The once magnificent tiered bell tower, much neglected with trees growing out of the roof, is of the same period. With the return to worship of the church a row of bells again hangs from the belfry.

Blank is also responsible for the colourful **Dutch House** of the 1760s situated at the end of the long pond. Its steep tiled roof is supported by volutes and stepped gables with vases on each step. Nowadays expensive cars surround the house where holiday rooms can be rented at considerable cost. The extensive park of limes, pine and birch harbours fine walks and excellent views of the house, the Dutch House and the pond.

On the A-101 Kaluga Road 7 kms south of Voronovo beyond the peculiar L-shaped railway crossing, turn right to **VASYUNINO**. *The* **Church of**

the Trinity, *Troitsy*, stands impressively on the right across a small field. It was built of red brick in three tiers in 1735 for the estate of G.M. Chelishchev and gives the impression of an ascetic version of Moscow baroque. The wide *trapeza* and the bell tower which were added on the west side in the middle of the 19th century are still roofless and in ruins but, since the Trinity reopened for services, the main roof and windows have been replaced and most of this splendid village church is once more in good repair.

Road 3

KHARKOV HIGHWAY M-2: PODOLSK TO SERPUKHOV

The route of the Kharkov Highway M-2 south to Serpukhov traverses well-watered, wooded country passing former mansions, powerful monasteries and two industrial towns: Podolsk, which emerged in the 19th century and Serpukhov, whose heyday was the 18th. The M-2 is a modern three-lane highway providing a rapid road to Podolsk, Chekhov and Serpukhov. The quieter Warsaw (Varshavskoe) Road to Podolsk and then Serpukhov runs parallel linking the old villages.

ON THE WARSAW ROAD

Join the MKAD from Profsoyuznaya and travel east about 6 km past a bridge (note the modern KGB building, right, at Kommunarka, where Beria had his dacha and where the NKVD interrogated and tortured senior Party victims of the Great Purge) and turn right at the mauve-coloured building, BITSA ZONA OTDYKHA. Park by the cafe and take the path, right, parallel to the fence to tall metal gates with the forbidding sign POSTORONNIE ZAPRESHCHENY (Strangers Keep Out). Nothing daunted, turn the round latch on the door, right, disguised within the gate, to see the ochre-coloured mansion of **ZNAMENSKOE-SADKI** *on the dammed Bitsa River, a tributary of the Pakhra.*

The mansion and other buildings were constructed in the mid 18th century by **Prince Dmitry Trubetskoy**. In 1865 Znamenskoe-Sadki became the property of **Mikhail Katkov**, the influential newspaper publisher, whose family remained in ownership until 1918. After the revolution a state farm was set up in the grounds and a children's home in the mansion; it now houses the Scientific Research Institute of the Protection of Nature and National Parks.

The **main house** in the late classical style although altered in the 19th century retains much of the original layout and even some of the interior decoration. The ground floor is brick and the first floor wood under a coat of plaster. The double row of windows in the central bay lights the grand first floor salon which is enhanced by a musicians' gallery and a superb painted ceiling of Apollo driving his chariot. The baroque church of 1756 was demolished in the 1930s.

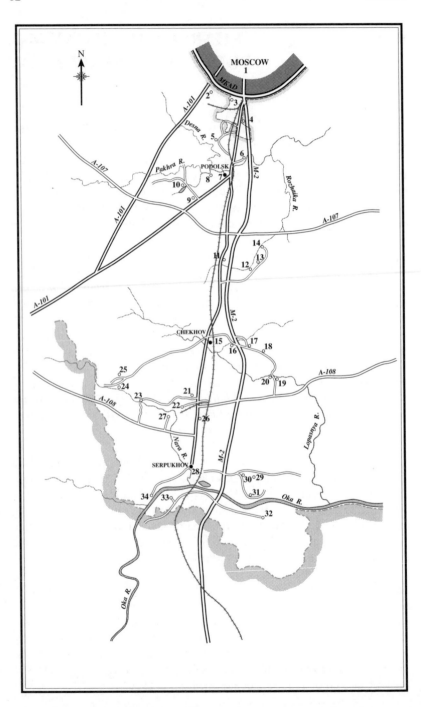

ROAD 3
PODOLSK TO SERPUKHOV

1.	MOSCOW	18.	Melikhovo
2.	Kommunarka	19.	Davidov Monastery
3.	Znamenskoe-Sadki	20.	Stary Spas
4.	Butovo	21.	Starye Kuzmenki
5.	Ostafyevo	22.	Ivanova Gora
6.	Pleshcheevo	23.	Nekhoroshevo
7.	PODOLSK	24.	Spas-Temnya
8.	Dubrovitsy	25.	Vasino
9.	Oznobishino	26.	Vasilievskoe
10.	Shchapovo	27.	Rai-Semenovskoe
11.	Molodi	28.	SERPUKHOV
12.	Otrada	29.	Oka River National Park
13.	Meshcherskoe	30.	Sushki
14.	Skobeevo	31.	Luzhki
15.	CHEKHOV	32.	Pushchino
16.	Novoselki	33.	Podmoklovo
17.	Vaskino	34.	Drakino

Across the dam are romantic **stables** of red brick with white detailing in the popular 19th century Gothic style, most likely by Mikhail Bykovsky. The sense of a picturesque but abandoned park is increased by the profusion of heavily overgrown lime trees, planted in the 18th century. The small pond is well used for fishing both in summer and in winter when it is dotted by black figures huddling over holes in the ice.

Mikhail Katkov, the Anglophile, was a highly conservative but influential political journalist, hostile to the revolutionary movement and the Polish rebellion of 1863. However, he was not afraid to criticise government policies, and the opinions in his newspaper, *Russky Vestnik* (Russian Herald), sometimes influenced the government. Katkov's close friend who frequently stayed at Znamenskoe-Sadki was the slavophile, **Mikhail Pogodin**, son of a peasant who became Professor of Russian History at Moscow University. As a young scholar he visited Nikolai Karamzin, the historian, who lived only a few kilometres away at the Vyazemsky estate, Ostafyevo.

From Znamenskoe-Sadki follow the MKAD east to the intersection with the Warsaw Road (Varshavskoe Shosse). Turn right here to join the old road to Podolsk. At 10 kilometres turn right at Shcherbinka signed ST. SHCHERBINKA (railway station). At the railway line turn left and then immediately right to cross the line and continue 3 kilometres to Ostafyevo. Where the road turns sharply left, the main estate stands on the right and the church on the left.

OSTAFYEVO was purchased in 1792 by **Prince Andrei Vyazemsky**, one of the best educated men of his generation, for the large sum of 26,000 rubles. Prince Andrei, while travelling in Europe in the 1780s met a delightful Irish lady named Jenny O'Reilly who abandoned her French husband and ran away with the Prince to Russia. Despite his parents' sharp displeasure he installed Jenny as his wife and mistress of Ostafyevo. The marriage of Ireland and Russia resulted in the birth of **Petr Vyazemsky**, one of Russia's outstanding poets.

Ostafyevo was also the home of another eminent writer, **Nikolai Karamzin**, the Russian historian. In 1804 after his marriage to Prince Andrei's illegitimate daughter, Yekaterina Kolyvanova, he came to live at Ostafyevo and it was here that eight volumes of his *History of the Russian State* were written. At Prince Andrei's death in 1807, Karamzin became head of the family. He was in this position when in 1812

Napoleon's army marched through the estate but fortunately refrained from plunder.

During the 1820s and 1830s life at Ostafyevo was at its most brilliant. Every summer it was invaded by Prince Petr's friends, the poets and writers of Russia's Golden Age, who were happy to enjoy his generous hospitality and have use of his extensive library. **Alexander Pushkin** came often and wrote many of his poems here. There is a delightful story of a dishevelled Pushkin arriving at the estate in an ancient *drozhky* (carriage) and being refused entrance by the gate-keeper horrified at his appearance. Pushkin stood up in the vehicle and, using the third person for himself, shouted loudly *Ostav'yevo, ostav'yevo!*, a pun on the name Ostafyevo meaning 'leave him'. Many of these young writers died young and by the 1850s they were all in their grave except for Vyazemsky. Aged and alone Prince Petr became increasingly bitter and reactionary. Nevertheless his late verses are considered among his best.

After Prince Petr's death Ostafyevo passed to his granddaughter, Yekaterina, who married the historian, **Count Sergei Sheremetiev** (see Mikhailovskoe). The Sheremetievs loved the old house and enthusiastically embellished it, preserving Karamzin's room and Prince Petr's study. For the centenary of Pushkin's birth in 1899 they opened Russia's first museum to the poet. They also erected statues in 1912–13 to the writers of the Golden Age: Karamzin, Zhukovsky, Vyazemsky and Pushkin, the latter by the leading sculptor, Opekushin. After the revolution Ostafyevo became a museum for which Pavel, the Sheremetievs' son, was appointed curator. In 1929 the museum was closed and its valuables dispersed; the Pushkin memorabilia including Opekushin's statue went to the Pushkin House in Leningrad and the books to the Lenin Library. The Sheremetievs were expelled in 1930 and given rooms in the unheated Naprudny Tower at Novodevichy Convent in Moscow where Pavel and his son eked out a living as artists. Meanwhile, the house and park were transformed into an elite rest home for the **Council of Ministers** and closed to the public. In 1988 with the changes wrought by *perestroika* the Pushkin museum reopened and the public welcomed.

Remarkably, many of the major buildings survive in only slightly altered form. The classical **main house** with its long facade was built in 1801 perhaps by the Petersburg architect, Ivan Starov, although some say it is by Prince Andrei himself who had a penchant for architecture. Its six giant Corinthian columns rise two floors, single-storey wings at either side linked to the centre by an open-columned gallery, now glassed in. On the park side, the marvellous two-storey oval room containing the musicians' gallery (the painted ceiling is lost) projects beyond the facade. Also from the park can be seen the room used by Karamzin – it was on the right on the second floor. In front of the main house are two ancient oak trees grown as legend has it from acorns found at George Washington's grave in America.

By the road across the dam that separates the pond from the little River Molodi is the early classical **Church of Michael the Archangel**, built in the 1780s. It follows Orthodox tenets in the wide dome over the central cube and the western bell tower and *trapeza* but the square cube cleverly conceals the circular inner church while the altar area remains square, turning the usual plan of a square church and round apse upside down. Services restarted in 1992.

On the old Warsaw (Varshavskoe) Road to Podolsk go under the railway line past the turn to VIDNOE, then cross the little Gvozhdyanka River and turn immediately left at a wooden cross (by a petrol station) 800 metres to the **BUTOVO BURIAL GROUND**. *Leave the car by a green wooden fence where the sign reads:* **Burial Place of Victims of Political Repression**, *1937-1953. Open for Visitors on Saturdays and Sundays from 11 to 16 hours.*

This is one of the saddest places in the Moscow countryside. To the right of the entrance is a notice board bearing photographs of members of the **Memorial Society** (devoted to recording the fate of the victims of Stalinist repression) who officially opened this tragic place to the public in the summer of 1993.

On a Sunday in January 1999 several priests and a group of people including about a dozen soldiers mingled around a wooden cross. At a sudden command, six of the soldiers stood in a line facing across the field and fired a salute. Everyone listened fascinated and horrified as a grey-haired man began speaking to the soldiers. The son of a priest executed there, he told how this village, Drozhzhino, became after the revolution a military base for weapons testing, a **Poligon**. When in July 1937 Stalin made his chilling speech calling on all traitors to be weeded out, Drozhzhino, where the local people were accustomed to the noise of firing weapons, became a convenient **execution ground**. In August 1937 the systematic murders began and in the first fourteen months, between August 1937 and October 1938 over 20,000 people were executed including 600 priests. Again in 1939 and in 1941 more mass executions occurred including, on the eve of the Second World War, many leading generals and army officers. The executions only stopped after Stalin's death in 1953 – 100,000 people had been murdered here. Because burial space became quickly used up the victims were buried one on top of the other. In 1992 when Memorial began excavating they found the bodies in three careful layers, with clothes and even the fashionable white shoes of the period among a massive number of bones. Apparently some victims had already been killed when they arrived while others were brought from the railway station at Butovo in sealed vans with *khleb* (bread) painted on the outside. So many *khleb* vans were moving to and fro that the locals began to wonder why the army needed so much bread. Among the victims buried here were Lenin's loyal Latvian troops, members of foreign communist parties, and even NKVD officers when the terror began to devour the executioners themselves.

In the depths of the field is the attractive wooden **Church of the New Martyrs and Confessors of Russia**, *Novomuchenikov i Ispovednikov Rossii*, built in 1994. A line of plaques on the church lists the names of all the priests executed at the Poligon. But even more terrible are the numberless mounds visible through the thick snow.

Take the old Warsaw Road to Podolsk and after crossing the railway line turn first left signed TSEMENTNY ZAVOD (Cement Factory) and criss-cross several railway lines. Turn left at the T-junction and continue through a workers' satellite town down to the Pakhra River with new brick houses on the right. Down the hill at the bottom of the rutted road two obelisks show the entrance to the once grand country house, **PLESHCHEEVO**, where Tchaikovsky was an honoured guest.

But Tchaikovsky would not recognise it today. One of the bays has completely collapsed of the gloomy old house still filled with people living precariously in communal flats. What at first seemed a stable now bears a cupola identifying a new **Cossack church** which seems a little bizarre so far from Cossack country. More pleasing are the remnants of the park and rickety bridge by the river crowded with people on a summer's day.

Nadezhda von Meck, Tchaikovsky's friend and patron of 13 years, was happy in 1884 to give Tchaikovsky, in need of solitude after a summer with his brother's noisy family, the use of her newly acquired house at

Pleshcheevo. His extraordinary relationship with Mme von Meck was conducted on the understanding they were never to meet (although they did once accidentally) so he delayed his arrival until his patron left Pleshcheevo to return to Moscow at the end of the summer. Tchaikovsky lived completely alone there apart from his beloved servant, Alexei, recently released from army service, and the cook loaned by his brother. A terrible quarrel broke out when the estate manager discovered that Alexei was using Mme von Meck's boudoir as a bedroom. Nevertheless Tchaikovsky was able to work well and completed the *Concert Fantasia*, the *Impromptu Caprice* and two of the songs of the *Six Romances*. And the cold, wet summer, turned into a glorious golden autumn. Tchaikovsky wrote enthusiastically to his correspondents about his stay but, strangely, did not mention the cement factory, founded in the 1870s and only a kilometre away, which must surely have disturbed the sensitive composer's peace and quiet.

In the course of their long and at times almost passionate relationship conducted entirely by correspondence, Tchaikovsky and Mme von Meck conceived a plan to unite their two families by marriage. Through adroit manoeuvres they brought together Tchaikovsky's niece, Anna Davydova, and Nadezhda's eldest son, Nikolai. To the delight of their conniving relatives, the two young people fell in love and were married in Moscow in January 1884. To Mme von Meck and Tchaikovsky, the marriage seemed to provide, if only by proxy, the personal link between them that was otherwise impossible. So Tchaikovsky's second visit to Pleshcheevo in August 1885 was to call on the newly-weds in the company of his brothers, the twins Anatoly and Modest; Mme von Meck was of course not present.

Take the second exit from the Kharkov Highway M-2 marked PODOLSK or take the more attractive old Warsaw (Varshavskoe) Road. After 15 km cross the River Pakhra to Podolsk old town.

PODOLSK, its name from *po dol* meaning along the valley of the Pakhra River, is a large industrial town, population 200,000. It grew so rapidly following the emancipation of the serfs and the construction of the railway in 1866 that two remarkable estates, Ivanovskoe and Dubrovitsy, came within its boundaries. Major industries include textiles, paper, cement and brick manufacture, as well as the traditional stone and marble quarrying (quarrying tools are displayed on the town coat of arms). A new power station in the early 20th century persuaded the **Singer Sewing Machine Company**, already a big business in Russia, to set up a large factory which in 1914 employed 5,000 people. Singer was nationalised in 1918 but the factory continues to operate.

Above the River Pakhra is the **old town** of mostly wooden houses and the masonry government offices, *prisutstvennye mesta*, at Sovietskaya Square 7. The **Cathedral of the Trinity**, *Troitsy*, at Karl Marx Square 3, right from Lenin Prospekt, the only church in Podolsk to remain open, was built 1819-32 in the attractive Russian Empire style by the school of Bove.

To get to **Ivanovskoe** turn right from the main square, still named for Lenin whose large statue points the way, and continue on the Warsaw Road. In about a kilometre the impressive shiny aluminium war memorial of heroic defenders, their weapons at the ready, comes into view. On Saturdays newly-weds can often be seen there posing for photographs. Turn right at the memorial and the street ends at a huge stately home resting on the high bank of the Pakhra.

The large **mansion** set back behind iron railings within a courtyard is flanked by wings reaching almost to the gate. The estate was built at the turn into the 19th century by **Senator Count Fedor Tolstoy**, a distant relation of the writer and avid collector of old books and rare manuscripts. His only child, the Countess Agrafena, married Count **Arseny Zakrevsky**, the notoriously reactionary governor of Moscow during the reign of Nicholas I. The lovely Agrafena, known as the Bronze Venus, dallied with Pushkin inspiring some of his poems including *The Portrait*, and was the model for Nina Vronskaya in *Yevgeny Onegin*. She was famous for giving elaborate entertainments in the theatre at Ivanovskoe for the cream of Moscow society.

The grand strictly classical brick and stucco **house** of over 100 rooms has a portico of six giant Corinthian columns which rises from the arched and vaulted ground floor two storeys to the pediment. A central bay on the park side where terraces descend to the Pakhra, contains a similar portico. The main house is joined by low galleries to two-storey wings, in themselves substantial houses with porticoes. Other buildings dot the territory. To the left is a charming park pavilion, the **tea house**. The ruined early 19th century **theatre**, right, is now in the process of being rebuilt; beyond it are brick service buildings. At the back where there is an enchanting view of the Pakhra, a tunnel was built under the river to allow the Zakrevskys to bathe on the better bank opposite.

Although in 1830 Count Zakrevsky was forced to retire as Minister of the Interior, he was recalled in 1848 to serve as Governor-General of Moscow when Nicholas I, frightened by the wave of revolutions in Europe, wanted a strong hand at the helm. But Zakrevsky was again relieved of his duties on the accession of Alexander II in 1855, when his conservative views clashed with the Tsar's, especially over the emancipation of the serfs. By this time, divorced from the Countess, he decided to go abroad and left the estate to his relative, **Sophia Keller**. Mme Keller's extravagant style soon got her in debt and in 1894 she was obliged to hand over the estate in lieu of payment to her chief creditor, the rich merchant firm of **Bakhrushin**. The Bakhrushin brothers, including Alexei, the famous collector of theatre paraphernalia, owned it jointly until in 1903 they agreed to sell it to Vladimir, Alexander's oldest son.

Vladimir Bakhrushin in charge of the trade and manufacturing side of the leather firm, was a photography enthusiast and chairman of the Russian Photographic Society. The family came to Ivanovskoe for the holidays of Shrovetide and Easter as well as the summers. As head of the Pyatnitsky Guardianship for Poor Girls, Vladimir invited his wards to Ivanovskoe to enjoy a taste of the country. One of the girls recalled later that for Vladimir's name day on July 28 a grand ball would be held at which the girls would sing. In 1916 it was decided that the estate was too expensive to keep up and it was given to the Moscow city council as a **children's home** although the Bakhrushins kept a few rooms for their personal use. The big central rooms were divided up into separate floors and cubicles to accommodate the orphans. After the revolution the mansion continued as a home for children then, for a long time, as the Podolsk Palace of Youth and in the mid 1980s the Podolsk museum. Recently the grand hall was restored to its original size when the dividing walls were removed.

On the Warsaw (Varshavskoe) Road 4 km from central Podolsk turn right signed **DUBROVITSY** *and follow the road curving left and then right across the bridge.* Here nearly three centuries ago a boyar founded an estate on the secluded isthmus where the Desna River flows into the Pakhra.

First to be seen is the exceptionally beautiful **Church of the Sign**, *Ikony Bozhiei Materi 'Znamenie'*, built in 1690-1704 in the local white stone by Peter the Great's tutor and friend, **Boris Golitsyn**. Inspired by the exuberance of 17th century Italian churches, it was the first frankly

European baroque building of Peter's reign and perfectly reflects his policy of looking to the West. It is composed of a centrally planned quatrefoil design like some of the Moscow baroque churches, where the protruding apse is indistinguishable from the other three cusps. The traditional drum is here a centrally placed octagonal tower liberally pierced by windows. Completing the structure is the curious open crown, resembling those used in the Orthodox marriage service, surmounted by a tall soaring cross. Richly adorned with carved stone foliage and figures, it is like an elaborate jewel set against the summer green or winter white landscape. The interior is equally sculptured with figures and the finely carved wooden iconostasis and special box for the owner. Splendid baroque scrolls with names of the saints in Latin (replaced in the 19th century with Cyrillic) must have made a huge impression in Peter the Great's Russia. Even today the church exudes a catholic air in comparison with other Orthodox churches. Closed for many decades after the revolution it was not allowed to fall into ruin, and it reopened for services on October 14, 1990.

Dubrovitsy's owner, Boris Golitsyn, was a close companion and tutor to Tsar Peter and later head of the important *Kazansky Prikaz*. He played a vital role in wresting the throne for Peter from his half-sister, the Regent Sophia, even though her lover, Vasily Golitsyn, was a relation. However, he did save Vasily Golitsyn from execution by pleading on his behalf to the Tsar, who sentenced him instead to exile in Siberia.

The church is so splendid that the **main house** standing a little farther away can be easily overlooked but it too has a fascinating history. Originally built in the middle of the 18th century by Boris's grandson, Sergei Golitsyn, and heavily rebuilt later in the classical style, it retains some baroque features. Better preserved are the three (originally four) single-storey service buildings set at each corner of the estate house. These houses were linked by iron fencing and three stone gates making an inner courtyard for the main house, somewhat like the arrangement at Petrovskoe Alabino. The park, as now, was to the west of the main house. There are also interesting 19th century Gothic **stables**.

In 1781 Dubrovitsy was sold to Grigory Potemkin, Empress Catherine's former lover famously responsible for the Potemkin villages, those stage sets which created a false impression of prosperity along her route to the Crimea. In June 1787 Catherine visited Potemkin's beautiful estate at Dubrovitsy and was so impressed she decided to make a present of it to her new lover, the young **Alexander Dmitriev-Mamonov**. Poor

Potemkin, who had to remain in the Crimea as Governor, was obliged
to sell it to the Empress so that she could give it to Mamonov.

But her new lover soon incurred the Empress's disfavour by falling in
love and even marrying one of her ladies-in-waiting, then compounding
the insult by carrying her off to Dubrovitsy. Catherine responded by
spreading rumours that he had gone mad. Alexander, embittered at
losing his position, busied himself redesigning the house, adding a
portico in the front, open terraces at the ends (later filled in) and the
rotunda with columns facing the River Desna. (Strangely, the capitals
were added only in the Soviet period.) Fortunately Alexander did not
alter the church although he did build a bell tower, pulled down in the
1930s.

His son, Matvei, aged 13 inherited the estate in 1803 along with excep-
tional wealth. Brought up by his grandfather, he clothed and armed a
whole division to fight Napoleon in 1812 and emerged from the war a
much decorated hero. He then retired to Dubrovitsy and proceeded to
live an isolated and strange life with minutely detailed orders to his staff
to serve meals and prepare his dress according to a strict timetable.
Impressed by medieval English castles, he had the whole property
surrounded by a fortress wall with battlements (demolished in the
1930s). In 1825, shortly before the uprising of the Decembrists in St
Petersburg, he privately and then publicly challenged the military
Governor of Moscow, Dmitry Golitsyn, to a duel. Rumours abounded
that he was not wholly sane and the authorities descended on Dubrovitsy, tied him up and brought him to Moscow where he was held under
house arrest at his villa, the Mamonov dacha, in the Lenin Hills (now
the Institute of Physics). Here he lived for nearly 40 years until his death
in 1863 from a fire started while lighting his pipe.

The last owner of Dubrovitsy was another **Sergei Golitsyn**. He spent
most of his summers at Kuzminki in Moscow, for he didn't care for
Dubrovitsy tainted by the Dmitriev-Mamonov affair. However, he
found it had its uses when in 1883 he divorced his first wife, leaving
her at Kuzminki, and married a young woman 20 years his junior
whom he installed at Dubrovitsy. It was at this time that the artist
Makovsky did a painting of the Empress Catherine's visit to Dubrovitsy which hung on the stairwell together with the Golitsyn family
tree. The coat of arms of the Dmitriev-Mamonovs on the wall of the
sitting room on the first floor has recently been rediscovered under
layers of whitewash.

1. **Sivkovo.** The lonely Transfiguration Church, now in ruins, was once a refuge for Patriarch Joachim, advocate of Peter the Great during his struggle for power against his half-sister Sophia.

2. ABOVE. **Troparevo.**
Soon after Yeltsin's decree
allowing churches to
reopen, the villagers here
somehow found the means
to revive the abandoned
Intercession Church with
its elegant baroque tower.

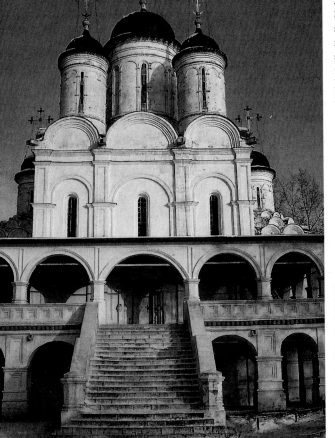

3. LEFT. **Bolshie Vyazemy.**
Desecrated by Polish
then French invaders, and
firmly closed in the Soviet
period, the splendid
Transfiguration Church of
Tsar Boris Godunov has
not only survived but is
once again holding services.

4. ABOVE. **Peredelkino.** Although the writers' colony was always under the watchful eye of Soviet officials, Pasternak's dacha provided a much-needed haven when he was working on *Dr. Zhivago*.

5. BELOW. **Kamenskoe.** Although 14th century St Nicholas, the oldest extant building in the Moscow Oblast, had greatly altered over the centuries Soviet restorers returned it to its original form.

6. ABOVE. **Roshcha.** Since the Moscow baroque church remained open over the Soviet period, its fine iconostasis was not the victim of official vandalism. In the 1960s, however, it was discovered that the priest was selling off the rare icons.

7. BELOW. **Voronovo.** The mansion was rebuilt many times: once after the locals set it on fire in 1812 in the face of the invading French and most recently in 1949 when, remarkably, the crest of the Sheremetiev Counts was retained.

8. ABOVE. **Vasyunino.** The Trinity Church originally part of a small early 18th century estate has reopened for services in spite of severe dilapidation.

9. BELOW. **Ostafyevo.** Prince Petr Vyazemsky provided a hearty welcome at his estate to fellow poets of the Golden Age. Pushkin, who came often, called the beautiful park the Russian Parnassus.

10. OPPOSITE. **Dubrovitsy.** The Church of the Sign, the first truly baroque building of Peter the Great's reign, was built for his friend and tutor Boris Golitsyn.

11. ABOVE. **Melikhovo.** For Chekhov, who purchased this small estate in the 1890s, the greatest pleasure was to be able to fish in the pond below merely by opening his window.

12. RIGHT. **Vasilievskoe.** 17th century St Nicholas, the oldest wooden church in the Moscow area, was built for a courtier of Regent Sophia.

13. LEFT. **Sukhanovo.**
The Temple of Venus is on
the estate of Prince Petr
Volkonsky, the model for
Prince Bolkonsky in
Tolstoy's *War and Peace*.

14. LEFT. **Yekaterinskaya
Pustyn.** Stalin's most
notorious prison was
located in this monastery in
the 1930s and 40s when
the gate church was
employed as its macabre
crematorium.

After the revolution the rich mansion became a museum to which in 1921 much furniture and fine paintings from the Vasilchikov estate in Lopasnya was transferred. At the end of the decade the museum was closed and in the 1930s when it became a hostel a third floor was added. In 1967 the Institute of Animal Husbandry, which is still in situ, took over the premises.

Follow the Warsaw (Varshavskoe) Road south of Podolsk to **Oznobishino** *where the late 19th century church has reopened. Turn right 4 km to* **Shchapovo** *and the small* **Assumption Church**, *built in 1779, and wooden house of I.V. Shchapov, the philanthropic Moscow factory owner. He built schools and a poor house here and willed it all to the Tsarist Government which in gratitude renamed the village Shchapovo.*

AROUND MOLODI

Either continue on the Warsaw Road to Molodi or from Moscow on the wide Kharkov Highway M-2, bypassing Podolsk and at the intersection with the A-107 cross under and turn right (west) on the A-107 for 2 km to the junction with the Warsaw/Serpukhov road. Turn left 8 km to Molodi.

It is hard to imagine in this quiet village the fierce battle of 1572 when Russian forces got their revenge against the Tatars who had ravaged Moscow a year earlier. In more peaceful times **MOLODI**, with its frequent rail link to Moscow, became desirable dacha country where Leonid Pasternak, the artist and father of the poet, Boris, rented a dacha. Where the village rises above the Rozhaika River are the church and buildings of the modest estate of Fedor Golovin, who served as General-Admiral and Chancellor under Peter the Great. Golovin built the **Church of the Resurrection**, *Voskreseniya*, in 1706, an octagonal on a cube. It was largely rebuilt in the late 18th century by the Domashnevs, hence the classical porticoes and the twin bell towers that flank the entrance. The now functioning church served as the dance hall for the local Palace of Culture for which the interior walls were covered in startlingly white plaster tiles. The estate house next to the church was for a time the local school but is now empty. Behind the church stands the late 18th century family tomb of the Domashnevs with its pitched roof. A pretty park with ponds descends to the river behind the house.

Continue south of Molodi for 2 kilometres to Stolbovaya. Turn left near the war memorial onto a road signed P.L. OTRADA, cross over the M-2 and go through the village of Lyubuchany. At Zykeevo take a left turn to join the concrete road which leads within 3 km to the **OTRADA** *pioneer camp at Malvinskoe.*

On the right, past the modern buildings of the camp, is a pleasant wooden house with porch, now used for offices, which may have been the summer dacha of **Vladimir Chertkov**, Tolstoy's loyal disciple at Otrada. The elderly **Tolstoy**, accompanied by his daughter Sasha, his doctor and secretary, spent ten days in June 1910 with Chertkov, only five months before his death. While at Otrada he faithfully kept his diary and even wrote his last short story, *Nechayanno*, The Unexpected. With Chertkov he visited the surrounding country including the innovative mental hospital at Meshcherskoe and was even well enough at the age of 82 to ride 7 km to Troitskoe. This idyll was shattered when he was summoned peremptorily back to Yasnaya Polyana by his wife, Sonya, who had become hysterical in his absence. The camp director has poignant photographs of Tolstoy on his visit to Otrada.

From Stolbovaya as above but ignore the turn to Otrada and go 1 km further to Meshcherskoe. **MESHCHERSKOE** is built around an old and decaying **psychiatric hospital**. Founded by the *Zemstvo* in the late 19th century, it was remarkably advanced for its time and the patients, far from being locked up, were sympathetically treated, allowed to use the hospital grounds, and even entertained by film shows. Tolstoy and his daughter attended one of the films here sitting with the inmates which discomfited Sasha but not Tolstoy. In 1894 Chekhov visited the hospital to attend a medical conference.

The hospital, renamed in Soviet times for Doctor Vladimir Yakovenko, the progressive director who had been dismissed by the Tsarist government in 1906 for left-wing activities, is housed in the pseudo-Russian former estate buildings of **Baron Bode-Kolychev** whose coat of arms can still be seen on the gate house. They include the now functioning church, the priest's house, the gate house and a large two-storey mansion with steeply pitched roof, the main hospital building. The decaying buildings, the white-coated patients wandering the grounds, and the extensive park seem to belong to another era.

Follow a poor road over the Rozhaika River past Prokhorovo where there is a late 19th century Church of the Saviour, 3 km to a group of modern buildings on the left, a branch of the psychiatric hospital. In the 19th century **SKOBEEVO** on the Rozhaika belonged to Vladimir Yershov who let a dacha to Anatoly Tchaikovsky, brother of the composer, in the summer of 1884. Beyond the red brick buildings of the hospital is a faithful copy of this wooden house rebuilt after a fire. **Petr Tchaikovsky** paid a visit to Anatoly and his family that summer but was put in a poor frame of mind when his luggage with the score of the *Concert Fantasia* got mislaid. It was eventually found and Tchaikovsky so recovered his good mood that he had a piano sent out from Moscow and continued composing.

CHEKHOV COUNTRY

Continue south from Molodi on the Serpukhov Road or take the exit signed CHEKHOV from the M-2. Lopasnya, after the river, was renamed **CHEKHOV** in 1954 after the writer whose home was at Melikhovo, 15 km away. Near the station is a charming museum of Chekhov in the old wooden post office he gave to the town. A lanky statue of the writer by A.N. Ukushin (1987) stands in front.

Chekhov, population 60,000, is known for its large printing works and two estates from the time of Catherine the Great positioned on opposite sides of the Lopasnya River. Cross the river to **Lopasnya-Zachatiev-skaya**, right, where the main house and splendid church still stand. The **Vasilchikov** family owned the estate from the 16th century with small interruptions until 1905, when it passed to Nadezhda Goncharova, niece of Alexander Pushkin's wife. Pushkin's widow, Natalya, had married Petr Lanskoy, a first cousin of the Vasilchikovs, and Pushkin's children and grandchildren lived at the estate. In January 1917 a box was discovered in the house containing original Pushkin manuscripts, now in the Pushkin House in Petersburg. The most notorious Vasilchikov was the handsome Alexander, who at the age of 28 caught the eye of Catherine II, then aged 43, and became her lover. Although he did not long remain her favourite, gifts and lands from the Empress amounting to over 1 million roubles, greatly enriched the family. Alexander built the large two-storey Vasilchikov **mansion** with baroque features overlooking the park and ponds of the Lopasnya in the 1770s when he was at the height of his power. A museum to the Vasilchikovs is to be opened here.

The **Church of St Ann**, *Anny Zachatiya*, behind the gate and walls was built 1689-94 in the traditional manner: a cube divided by tripartite bays and arches interspersed with decorative windows, corner columns and five deep blue domes on slim drums. The handsome, classical 1820 *trapeza* and bell tower with the spire make uneasy partners for the old church. Inside, the carved iconostasis is long bare of icons – St Ann was

closed in the early 1960s – but some oil paintings survive. Scattered
around are impressive marble and black granite graves of the Vasilchikov family. Local merchants and **Pushkin descendants** are also buried
there including Pushkin's son, General Alexander Alexandrovich, and
his grandchildren and great grandchildren. Graves of the first
Komsomol heroes in Chekhov lie just outside the cemetery wall, as if
not daring to come closer to the church.

For the remains of the Yeropkin estate at **Sadki** cross back over the
river and turn right past the tank memorial for several hundred metres
parallel with the river, ignoring the main road which turns left, to
6 Rodnikovaya St. The Yeropkins held this property from the 17th to
the first half of the 19th century, when it was acquired by the Ryumins.
One of the more distinguished Yeropkins, Petr, sent to Italy by Peter
the Great to study architecture, designed the new Admiralty district of
Petersburg. But his life ended tragically for he joined the opposition to
the Germans at the court of Empress Anna and in 1740 his tongue was
torn out and he was executed.

On a visit in 1992 the old two-storey **wooden mansion** was still standing
but badly damaged after a fire. Since then it has been pulled down
altogether although there is talk of rebuilding it. But the red brick,
classical **St John the Baptist**, *Ioanna Predtechi*, built in 1771, has on the
contrary reopened and revived. Composed of a heavy rotunda over the
main cube, the windows betray traces of baroque. The *trapeza*, chapel
and upper levels of the bell tower were added in the 19th century.

*From Chekhov turn left (coming from the north) just before the bridge at
traffic lights past the tank memorial following the main road left to the
railway station and past another war memorial. Turn right on a poor
paved road parallel to the railway line and then left across the line signed
MELIKHOVO. After 4 km turn right at the T-junction to NOVOSELKI
(Novosyolki) above the Lyutorka River. Park by the blue wooden schoolhouse built by Chekhov and take the path to the church through allot-
ments.*

The handsome **Church of the Assumption**, *Uspeniya*, which remained
open, forms an imposing figure in the village. Built in 1756 for the
estate of **I.M. Golokhvastov**, it is a fine example of restrained baroque in
the curved eyebrow window designs although the basic form is the traditional octagon resting on the tall cube. What is most appealing is that
the taller bell tower is a slimmer mirror image of the church both in the

windows and in the octagonal tier on the elongated cube; the two
vertical structures are linked by the low *trapeza*. An odd note is struck
by the kitschy gold stars on the blue cupolas.

*Take the exit from the Kharkov Highway M-2, marked MELIKHOVO or
from Chekhov take the road as above and then left at the T-junction for 3
km. Turn left signed DOM OTDYKHA VASKINO and left through the
gate.*

VASKINO (Novorozhdestveno) founded in the early 18th century was
purchased in 1795 by **Prince Dmitry Shcherbatov.** Prince Dmitry, who
had studied philosophy under Immanuel Kant at Konigsberg, disliked
the Petersburg court preferring more intellectual pursuits. His son, Ivan,
a veteran of Borodino who became involved in the budding officers'
movement for reform, fell under suspicion in 1820 and was taken into
custody thereby missing the **Decembrist uprising.** His rank was reduced
to that of an ordinary soldier, and he was sent to the Caucasus where in
1829 he died. Ivan's sister, Natalya, had married another Decembrist,
Fedor Shakhovskoy, 'The Tiger', who was first exiled to Siberia and
then imprisoned in a Suzdal monastery. At the end of the 19th century
when Vaskino belonged to V.N. Semenkovich, nephew of the poet
Afanasy Fet, Chekhov was a frequent visitor. The last owner, the
merchant Kapkanshchikov, remodelled the buildings.

The **Church of the Nativity of the Virgin**, *Rozhdestva Bogoroditsy*, built
in 1700 then rebuilt in Gothic style in 1800, has lost its cupola and
drums and, in use as a garage, can be recognised only by the twin apses.
But the long low single-storey mansion, right, painted brown and
situated above the dammed Lyutorka River, is well preserved. Built
originally of wood in 1825 the brick porches and pediments with Tuscan
columns are additions of the late 19th century when it was extended. In
1969 the remaining wooden walls were rebuilt of brick.

After 1917 the estate was used as a holiday home for the **Communist
University for Workers of the East.** Then in 1927 it was taken over by
Swiss communists under Fritz Platten who organised a successful model
farm. By 1930 it had become a children's home but today it is a house
of rest which sometimes accommodates delegates to Chekhov confer-
ences at Melikhovo.

Return to the main road and continue east from Vaskino 3 km to
MELIKHOVO. The famous residence of **Anton Chekhov**, now a

museum, lies to the left. The writer impulsively purchased the modest house, garden and farmland in 1892 before even setting eyes on it. He lived there with his parents, sister and younger brother (Chekhov did not marry until 1901) until 1899 when his worsening tuberculosis obliged him to move to the Crimea. A statue of Chekhov by Motovilov in 1951, which stands before the inner gate is popular with newly-weds posing for photographs.

The **wooden house** and grounds that now make up the museum are much too modest to be called an 'estate'. Although not beautiful the sprawling house, with its strange à la Russe merlons, window surrounds and stylised cupolas cut into the verandah, is immensely charming. Chekhov described it in a letter to Alexis Kiselev of 7 March 1892:

> The house is good and bad. It is more spacious than the Moscow apartment, it is light and warm and roofed with iron, standing in a nice place, having a terrace and a garden, Italian windows [large windows with shutters] etc. but it's bad in that it is not high enough, not young enough, and outside its appearance is completely stupid and naive...'

In addition to the house there are service buildings, and in the corner by the garden, a small building, the annexe, where Chekhov retreated to write. The house and grounds which Chekhov sold in 1899 in his impractical way to a timber merchant, who reneged on the payments, later passed to a mysterious Baron Stewart. Long neglected, it was pulled down in 1929. When with the revival of Russian history and literature it was decided in 1940 to establish a Chekhov museum at Melikhovo, only the annexe was still standing. Then began the tale of Melikhovo's rebirth. In September 1944 the museum opened and slowly the complicated business of restoring all the buildings from plans, memoirs, letters and photographs was set in train. Fortunately, Chekhov's sister, Mariya, was still alive and other quiet collectors of Chekhoviana came to the rescue – the original dining room furniture and set of china was donated by Chekhov's nephew, his desk and bed came from the house in Yalta. Finally, in January 1960 for the centenary of Chekhov's birth, the museum celebrated the reconstruction and refurnishing of all the buildings. The Melikhovo of today is thus the achievement of amazingly dedicated Chekhov devotees.

The house has low, rather dark rooms in the manner of a dacha. It is furnished as it was in the 1890s even to the wallpaper – a nice touch is

Chekhov's winter coat and hat hanging in the hall. The writer's study is the largest and best room after the sitting room with three windows overlooking the park. On one side of the house is a pond, now rather neglected, but in Chekhov's day it was stocked with carp and tench and it delighted him to think he could go fishing without moving from his window. The big bell which announced the meals prepared under the supervision of Chekhov's mother still hangs by the door. Chekhov, who acted as a benevolent squire of the area, found the money to build schools (one in Melikhovo) and used his skill as a doctor to help the local population especially during the threatened cholera epidemic of 1892. And, in addition to many stories including the dark tale, *Ward No 6*, it was here he wrote the *Seagull*, his first successful play.

When Chekhov first arrived at Melikhovo the rare wooden church, at the back and right, was without a priest and he greatly pleased the villagers by hiring one for the Easter service. The **Church of the Nativity of Christ**, *Rozhdestva Khristova*, built in 1757 in wood on a stone foundation, was sheathed a century later with weatherboarding to protect the old timbers. In 1966 Soviet restorers examined the church, which had been closed in the 1920s, and removed the boards revealing the logs which slot into one another in the age-old Russian fashion. The tower over the cube is a series of decreasing octagonals, each with an overhanging fringed roof, culminating in a small cupola resting on a tall drum like a long neck. The western entrance *trapeza* matches the pentacular apse on the east. Handed back to the parish in 1991, it is served by the hospitable Father Vladimir, who manages well in spite of a paralysed arm and who makes excellent nettle soup. Unfortunately, in December 1994 a fire greatly damaged the church but it has since been repaired.

For Novy Byt return and rejoin the M-2 Kharkov Highway and exit at the next junction signed SEMENOVSKOE to join the A-108 east. After 3 km turn left at the first paved road 2 km to Novy Byt. (Notice, right, the parking place of thousands of Zhiguli cars of the Logovaz firm, an important sponsor of the Davidova Pustyn Monastery.) The **ASCENSION DAVIDOV MONASTERY**, *Voznesenskaya Davidova Pustyn*, is on the right overlooking the valley of the Lopasnya. The interesting late 19th century pseudo-Russian building just outside the gates was the **guest house** for visitors and pilgrims. In 1892 Chekhov asked the abbot for help for the expected cholera epidemic but he was haughtily refused the use of the guest house. Ironically, after the revolution the monastery was closed and the guest house became a hospital named after Chekhov.

The monk **David**, a disciple of Joseph of Volokolamsk, with two acolytes in 1515 discovered this lovely place overlooking the Lopasnya and decided it was ideal for a new hermitage. Eventually it became a monastery under David who is buried in the old cathedral. It suffered some damage in the Polish invasion of the early 17th century but managed to avoid closure under Catherine II's policy of hostility towards the richer monasteries. One of the sources of its wealth was the hiring out of its wonder-working icon of the Saviour.

Directly opposite the new gate with its tall 19th century bell tower is the much mutilated **Cathedral of the Ascension**, *Vozneseniya*, now bereft of its cupolas. Begun under the patronage of Ivan the Terrible it was never completed, and was reconstructed 1676-82 on a high sub-basement. During the 19th century religious revival, the cathedral became encrusted with additions: on the north by the **Church of St Nicholas**, 1804, and on the west by the **Church of the Sign**, '*Znamenie*', 1865-70, containing the sacristy.

Today the monastery still gives a hint of its former power even though, closed in the 1920s and taken over by a community called the New Way of Life, *Novy Byt*, it was allowed to decay. The walls still stand as does the impressive gate bell tower and the buildings within, some huddled along the east wall. Before it was given back to the church in 1995 it was occupied by a local technical college whose students adopted a cavalier attitude to the old buildings. Until recently the former monks' cells were used as the student canteen, *stolovaya no 7*, and posters hung in the central square by the cathedral extolling the virtues of socialism, hard work and exercise. Services have restarted in the massive **Church of the Saviour**, *Spasa*, on the east wall, constructed in 1900, which bears an unbelievably huge cupola.

Past the monastery down the hill and over the bridge take the first left concrete road by some dachas. Recross the Lopasnya River by the swinging wooden footbridge, taking care not to trip on the holes, to the peaceful **Church of the Transfiguration**, *Spasa Preobrazheniya*, at **Stary Spas**, an octagon with a high vaulted roof, bell tower and *trapeza* built in the 18th century.

ON THE NARA

From the Vasilchikov estate in Chekhov follow the road west 7 km to **Dubna** where the classical rotunda **Purification Church**, *Sretenka*, built in 1815, stands left. Turn left here signed *STREMILOVO 6 km to Bulychevo, then turn left 3 km to Merleevo and take the left fork 2 km to* **SPAS-TEMNYA**. The single street lined with pretty houses and a shop is guarded at the end by the impressive but dilapidated baroque *pogost* (cemetery) **Church of the Transfiguration**, *Spasa Preobrazheniya*. Built in 1735, an octagonal on a cube, only the skeleton remains of the cupolas and the interior is empty except for the broken iconostasis frame and some 1915 wall paintings. Its name, Saviour of the Dark, is deserved despite its position on the lovely Nara.

Return to Merleevo and turn left 1 km along the main road across a stream and turn right onto the dirt and concrete road across fields. Follow this nameless betonka (cement road), passable with care, 2 km to **VASINO**. Park near the first house and take the path, right, to a large, decaying **wooden manor house**, a rare example of a summer home of the nobility. It was built in the early 19th century for the Velyaminov family in Empire style of logs covered with weatherboarding bearing a central dome and spires at either end. Two porches face the river but the more formal portico on the south side with six Tuscan columns and pediment, is heavily overgrown and unused. Until 1976 the house was a school but now two old people live there as caretakers, carrying water from the well and complaining that promised repairs never happen.

From Spas-Temnya continue 7 km on a paved road which deteriorates to concrete and then dirt. At Siyanovo-2 do not cross the Nara but turn left and continue on the dusty road 2 km to Lisenki. Turn right and slither down a steep unmade gravel road 1 km to **NEKHOROSHEVO**. *Or approach it from the Serpukhov Road at Starye Kuzmenki 11 km to Lisenki.* The road may be improved by the Russian-American company who are developing the old schoolhouse as a holiday home. In the tiny hamlet on the Nara only one house is occupied but the ruined and splendid **Church of Michael the Archangel** is reason enough for the visit. It was built in 1691 in brick in the traditional style with *kokoshniki* gables, decorative windows, single drum and cupola and the tent-shaped bell tower. The side chapels added in 1860 when Prince N.S. Vyazemsky owned the village are now roofless.

From Chekhov travel 12 km south on the old Serpukhov Road and turn right to **STARYE KUZMENKI** *(Kuzmyonki). Or from the M-2 Kharkov Highway take the exit west onto the A-108 signed SHARAPOVA OKHOTA. Some 8 km on at the junction of the Serpukhov Road with Rodionovka turn right signed MOSCOW 11 km to Kuzmenki and then left.*

The **Church of the Assumption**, *Uspeniya*, built in 1694 for the rich Vysotsky Monastery in Serpukhov is heavily obscured by the 19th century pseudo-Russian *trapeza* and bell tower. Hidden within is the traditional cube, the bulging single apse and richly diverse window frames of a provincial 17th century church whose local builder ignored the new fashion for Moscow baroque. The church was open almost throughout the Soviet period and within its well-kept fencing it has an attractive air of order and neatness so poignantly missing in the numerous abandoned and rotting churches elsewhere. Within, even the old white tiled stove in the *trapeza* that made the church cosy in winter is still in place.

Continue south from Starye Kuzmenki on the old Serpukhov Road and at the end of the village take a right turn on the unmarked paved road just before the GAI post at the junction with the A-108 and Rodionovka. Continue for 2 km to the large village of **Proletarsky** *high above the Nara River.* In the 1870s the Khutarev merchants from Serpukhov opened a textile factory in what was then the village of Gorodenka. In 1897 the mill employed nearly 2,000 workers but in Soviet times production has slumped. On the left are two charming three-storey apartment houses with Doric fluted columns built in 1924 as 'Lenin' apartments for mill workers. The long facade, right, is the old brick mill.

Through the unlikely arch made of giant heating pipes (it is much cheaper to run them above ground than to bury them) turn right down a steep slope, across a stream and left along the bank on a poor road of concrete blocks to an impressively tall **bell tower** at **IVANOVA GORA**. It was built in the pseudo-Russian style in 1895 for Khutarev as his mausoleum by the Moscow architects Mikhail Kulchitsky and Adolf Netyksa. The matching building alongside was the poor house, now a psychiatric hospital. The five-tiered bell tower flanked by two side chapels of alternating white and red brick is, even in its ruined state and bereft of its spire, simply magnificent, lording it over the Nara River valley and visible a long way off. From here are stunning views south-west to woods and the river and the dark cupola of the Kazakov church at Rai-Semenovskoe which latterly also belonged to Khutarev.

On the old Serpukhov Road 3 km south of the A-108 at **VASILIEVSKOE** *turn right signed D.O. SHAKHTEROV 2 km to see the baroque Nativity of Christ, Rozhdestva Khristova, in the miners' holiday home built in 1731 for the Rozhdestveno-Telyatevo estate. For the spectacular wooden church, take a difficult left turn just past the bus-stop where the Serpukhov bypass* *joins the main road going north. Follow the dirt road doubling back for a brief moment parallel with the main road until the dirt road turns right.* Leave the car and walk down the lane with houses on the right and a stream on the left to the small cemetery and wooden church of St Nicholas.

If wooden churches in the Moscow countryside are rare, then **St Nicholas**, one of the oldest, is in a class by itself. It was built in 1689 (the logs of course are constantly renewed) for the estate of Afanasy Soimonov, a courtier of the Regent Sophia. His grandson Fedor Soimonov, born here in 1692, was a noted geographer and explorer of Siberia. The church is an arrangement of two units or cells with a pentacular apse, overhanging fringed roof, and single cupola. The bell tower was demolished years ago and the porches on the north and west were not replaced when it was restored in the 1980s and 90s. Within, are fivesided richly carved and decorated beams, *balki*, common in northern Russia but rare here. Services have restarted conducted by the priest from Rozhdestveno-Telyatevo.

On the old Serpukhov Road, 6 km south of Rodionovka, turn right at the GAI post onto the A-108, west. At 6 km turn right (at the junction with a secondary road to Serpukhov left) on a straight road through Tveritino 3 km to Rai-Semenovskoe.

RAI-SEMENOVSKOE was the grand estate of the **Nashchokin** family from the 17th century to the end of the 19th. In the late 18th century Alexander Nashchokin and his wife named the estate *rai* (heaven) to distinguish it from the Orlovs' *Semenovskoe Otrada* (joy). Rai-Semenovskoe was richly appointed with a huge park, pavilions, ponds, wild goats, natural springs of good quality mineral water and even special deer imported from Britain. Nashchokin, feeling the pinch of constant entertaining, decided to exploit the mineral springs and open a watering-place like the fashionable spas in western Europe. The spa operated from 1803 to 1820 but was not a financial success although well patronised by friends and acquaintances. The Nashchokins sold the estate in 1900 to the Serpukhov factory owner, Khutarev, whose mill at Gorodenka was only 4 km away across the Nara River. Khutarev must have enjoyed the excellent view from Semenovskoe of the tall bell tower at Ivanova Gora that he built.

On closer acquaintance, the formerly elegant estate is brutally disappointing. On the right are ugly apartment blocks for the farm workers.

The main house of the late 18th century, left, is now the *selsoviet* or village offices painted dark grey and white. Inside, the first-floor salon with columns and plasterwork is all that is left. The once splendid **Church of the Saviour**, *Spasa*, completed in 1783 and a masterpiece of the great Matvei Kazakov is in total disarray, its cupola at a rakish angle, its marble iconostasis stripped from its once rich interior, the crenellated wall and gates almost completely obliterated and the tall spire on the bell tower at a precarious angle. The park and ponds are badly overgrown. Goats, sheep and cattle peacefully graze in front of the ruins.

SERPUKHOV AND THE OKA

Serpukhov on the Oka River is 100 km from Moscow. Take the Varshavskoe Shosse in Moscow to the MKAD and then the fast M-2 Kharkov Highway and leave it at the exit signed DANKI and SERPU-KHOV. The slower route is by the old Serpukhov Road.

From the M-2 Kharkov Highway take the exit east signed DANKI to the **OKA RIVER NATIONAL PARK**, *Prioksko-Terrasny Gosudarstvenny Zapovednik, right.* The huge wooded area of 10,000 acres on the left bank of the Oka was founded in 1948 to protect threatened plants, including rare orchids, birds and animals. Among the latter are beaver, European bison and a few buffalo from North America. During the Second World War the bison in the forests of Poland were nearly all wiped out but a small number brought here have successfully bred.

Once in the park turn left towards wooden park offices where officials are happy to organise excursions. Or turn right at the T-junction following the paved road to the **Bison Breeding Station**. The bison are visible in the distance and with the help of a guide, one can get quite close, especially at feeding time.

Just before the road turns left to the bisons, an unsigned dirt road leads to **SUSHKI** which, strictly speaking, is outside the park on the Sushka, a small river that flows into the Oka. In 1752 the Kishkin brothers, Serpukhov manufacturers of sailcloth for the Russian fleet, dammed the river and established paper factories here. The tall, ruined **Church of St Nicholas** built in 1746 by Gerasim Sevastyanov, the Kishkins' prede-cessor and probable relative, is still impressive with its undecorated tall cube crowned by five naked cupolas and one elegant cross. The bell tower is especially forceful with four octagonal tiers, each one narrower than the last, finally culminating in a truncated spire. Even in its ruined

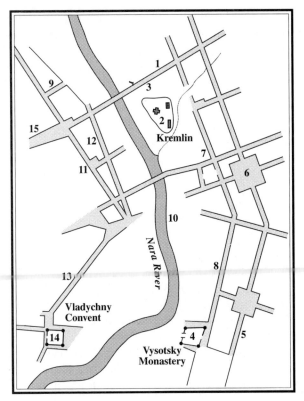

SERPUKHOV 1. Volodarskovo, 2. Kremlin, 3. Sitsenabivnaya Sq,
4. Vysotsky Monastery, 5. Chekhov Street, 6. Lenin
Square, 7. Kaluzhskaya, 8. 2nd Moskovskaya,
9. Engels Lane, 10. Nara River, 11. Karl Marx,
12. Proletarskaya, 13. Oktyabrskaya, 14. Vladychny
Convent, 15. Chernyshevskovo

state it makes a beautiful background to the fields and stream which in
early summer are redolent with wild flowers – wood avens, lady's
bedstraw, speedwell, vetch, hostas.

*From the M-2 Kharkov Highway take the exit marked SERPUKHOV
1 km to Borisovo and turn left signed LUZHKI 6 km. Where the road
turns sharply right continue straight ahead on a bumpy dirt road.* **LUZHKI**
lies just below Sushki almost at the Oka. The two villages not only have

rhyming names and ruined mid 18th century churches but also a shared connection with the Kishkin brothers. The **Church of the Trinity**, *Troitsy*, situated in a meadow looking across to the Oka River, was built in 1756 for Vasily Kishkin. In a reversal of roles the main cube with three tiers of windows towers over the squat tent-shaped bell tower partnering it.

The Moscow Oblast continues across the Oka River for a brief way. *Follow the M-2 Kharkov Highway over the Oka and turn right signed LUKYANOVO. Go through Lipitsy and turn right and then left under the railway and over the River Skniga then, 10 km from the bridge, turn right past greenhouses and where the road turns left go straight ahead on the dirt road, then right and left again towards the Oka.*

All that is left of the grand house of **PODMOKLOVO** is the ruined north wing. But here in this unlikely spot on the shore of the Oka is the stunning **Nativity of the Virgin**, *Rozhdestva Bogoroditsy*, where services are again being held. Built in the reign of Peter the Great, the completely round church in the western baroque style of Peter's new capital was unprecedented in the Moscow region. Thought to have been completed in 1754, the date of its consecration, research by O. Yakubovskaya has established the astonishingly early date of 1714. It was commissioned by a leading statesman of the time, **Prince Grigory Dolgorukov**, who had served three times as ambassador to Poland where Italian architects working there may have been hired to construct this exciting church. Dolgorukov retired from diplomatic life to his Podmoklovo estate but at his death in 1723 the church interior was still incomplete. After the death of Peter II in 1729 the Dolgorukovs' fortunes plummeted which explains why it was not until 1754 under Prince Grigory's grandson, Nikolai, that the church was finally dedicated.

The central rotunda is surrounded by a gallery of 16 arches reopened following recent restoration. An egg-shaped dome with regularly placed lucarne windows rests on the rotunda supporting drum, cupola and cross. The use of sculpture in religious buildings although frowned on by the Orthodox Church was becoming popular in Peter's reign and here figures of the apostles crowned the pilasters of the gallery – they have long been under restoration. A villager, right, keeps the key.

From the M-2 cross the bridge over the Oka and turn left for 11 km. On this right bank of the Oka is the modern town of **PUSHCHINO**, the

Akademgorod, founded in 1959 to provide ideal research and living conditions for top biologists. Nowadays the concept of special research towns is outdated but Pushchino, with boulevards of white and red tower blocks, is not unpleasant. Near the Oka is the former estate of the Pushchins, after whom the town is named.

Turn left from the main boulevard at the sign GOSTINITSA and curve left towards the river to the run-down **estate of the Pushchins** down a steep hill. The huge house with the broad terrace facing the river was originally constructed in classical style for Ivan Pushchin, one of Pushkin's closest friends and a prominent Decembrist. By the end of the 19th century it was in the hands of a nouveau riche merchant, Sergei Perlov, the successful tea entrepreneur whose Chinese-style shop adds such colour to Myasnitskaya Street in Moscow. He rebuilt the house 1900-10 which is now an intriguing mixture of 19th and 20th century classical architecture with touches of Art Nouveau. After the revolution it served as a hospital but is now under the Academy of Sciences who would like to repair it as a conference centre should funds become available.

Take the Kharkov Highway M-2 99 km to the SERPUKHOV exit. Follow the road into Serpukhov to a T-junction (on the right a church has been turned into a radio station and sports a mast instead of a tower). Turn left here and follow the road right which curves to meet the old Moscow road. At traffic lights cross the Moscow road to continue west on Volodarskovo Street.

SERPUKHOV, population 140,000, is an ancient town where the Nara flows into the Oka on its way to join the Volga. Under Prince Vladimir Khrabry (the Brave), Serpukhov joined with Moscow in the battle against the Tatars at Kulikovo in 1380. In 1698 Tsar **Boris Godunov** visited the town in a successful attempt to stave off a Tatar attack and sponsored much new building. By the early 18th century it had become an important centre for the manufacture of sailcloth not only for the Russian fleet but also abroad. Sailcloth gave way a century later to the textile boom which transformed the town.

The old **Konshin textile factory** stands on the right, a row of three churches on the left, and the bridge over the Nara River straight ahead. The Konshin works, renamed *Krasny Tekstilshchik* after the revolution, and now **Serpukhov Textiles**, was founded in 1805 by Maxim Konshin, and became one of the largest in Russia with the most up-to-date equipment employing in 1914 over 11,000 workers. The modern administration building fronts the river near the classical two-storey 18th/19th century former **house** of the Konshin family, who like most factory owners liked to live on top of the factory. It is now the offices of the director and, although much altered, some splendid fireplaces and staircases survive. The rest of the factory is a confused jumble of 19th/20th century red brick buildings with hints of Art Nouveau linked together by the ubiquitous heating pipes that roam around the factory. At the eastern corner are two run-down churches huddled miserably together on the inner side of the boundary wall. The tall, square **Church of the Exaltation of the Cross**, *Vozdvizheniya*, missing its cupolas, was built 1746-55 when Serpukhov was in the middle of its first industrial boom. The second, tiny winter **Church of the Cave**, *Peshcherskaya*, built 1804-9, stands against the north wall of the older church, a simple cube with a large round apse, the Tuscan porticoes mostly gone.

Immediately opposite the factory on **Sitsenabivnaya** (Printed Textile) **Square** is a row of three tall elegant churches. Nearest the Nara River stands the red and white **Assumption**, *Uspeniya*, built in 1854 by the Konshins in the traditional Russian style. It reopened for services in 1988.

Next to it is the tall yellow and white brick **Church of the Prophet Elijah**, *Ilii shto na torgu* (at the market place), built in 1748 by Popov, another of Serpukhov's merchants. It is a cube surmounted by an octagonal tier in the baroque manner with the south chapel of St Catherine, a mirror image of the main church. The unusual shell and flower mouldings were added in the 19th century. Within are wall oil paintings and two brightly patterned stoves of this century. This church which has been functioning for most of the Soviet period, comes under the Vysotsky Monastery. Its priest, Father Alexander, a former journalist and photographer drawn into the priesthood as the churches began to reopen, was ordained after a six-month course.

The third in this attractive row of churches is also the oldest. The **Trinity**, *Troitsy*, built in 1714 is in the pre-Petrine traditional Russian style, a vivid example of the stylistic time-lag in the countryside and a remarkable contrast with the Podmoklovo baroque church across the Oka built in the same year. The tall cube with its *kokoshniki* gables, five cupolas and fine crosses is offset by the pyramid-shaped octagonal bell tower which seems to be leaning. The entrance *trapeza* and five-tier iconostasis are of the 19th century. This church remained open for worship until the 1960s when it was shut under Khrushchev and turned into a musuem.

Behind the three churches is a path up the old hill to the **Kremlin**, the start of a pleasant **circular walk** through the old town. In the early 1930s the walls were cannibalised to build the Moscow metro and only tiny fragments remain. The Kremlin is now a peaceful place, a large open park overlooking the town on one side and the River Nara on the other in which the only buildings are the war memorial and the **Cathedral of the Trinity**, *Troitsy*. The Cathedral, now a museum of the Kremlin, was originally built in 1696 by Archimandrite Fedoty of the Andronikov Monastery in Moscow but almost completely rebuilt in 1837-41 in the Empire style. In the 1960s some of the 17th century forms – the ogee-shaped window designs, the octagon on the cube, and the splendid tent-shaped bell tower – were restored while retaining the broad central dome and the classical portico on the north side.

From the Kremlin cross the little Serpeika stream to the **Vysotsky Monastery** at the southern end of old Serpukhov, its name from the raised, *vysoky*, position above the Nara. On the left note the large red brick neo-Byzantine town prison and across the river the towers of the Vladychny Convent. From this path where the road to Tula once ran, the monastery is entered through the Holy Gate under the church/bell tower of the **Three Saints**, *Trex Svyatitelei*, built in 1840 and reckoned to be the best classical building in Serpukhov.

The monastery is an ancient establishment, founded in 1373 by Prince Vladimir Khrabry and Sergius Radonezh whose follower, Afanasy, became the first abbot. No buildings survive from before the 16th century although there may be traces in the foundations. Its importance as a religious foundation was emphasised by the **seven huge Byzantine icons** acquired by Abbot Afanasy on a visit to Constantinople and in place in the cathedral by 1395 (in 1920 six were removed to the Tretyakov Gallery and one to the Russian Museum). The half figures of the *deesis* row with Christ at the centre flanked by Mary, John the Baptist, the archangels and the disciples Peter and Paul were over 9 metres wide when placed side by side completely filling the building. This early *iconostasis* or screen of icons before the altar greatly influenced the emerging Moscow school of iconography. New building programmes were inaugurated after the Tatar attack in 1571 and visits by Tsars Ivan the Terrible and Boris Godunov. In the mid 17th century under Tsar Alexei the walls and towers were built and at the end of the century St Sergius was erected by the Naryshkins. The monastery was closed in 1920. Some of the buildings were the focus of attention by state restorers in the 1960s and in 1990 the monastery was finally reopened and more energetic repairs undertaken. There are now about 15 resident monks under the abbot, Father Joseph. It is important to ask permission, which is usually granted, not only to enter the monastery but also to take photographs.

Two magnificent towers and half of the walls are still standing. Within the grounds a series of churches and other buildings flank a broad avenue with at the far end the house of the abbot. On the right is a line of service buildings and monks' cells while on the left stands the refectory with its church of the **Intercession of the Virgin**, *Pokrova*, rebuilt in 1835 over an earlier church. Beyond is the majestic **Cathedral of the Immaculate Conception of the Mother of God**, *Zachatiya Bogoroditsy*, on the same axis as the Holy Gate. Built at the end of the 16th century and modelled on Moscow's Assumption Cathedral it is a monumental cube divided into three bays topped by five cupolas, a gallery on three sides and pentagonal apse. It is further complicated by later additions haphazardly attached: a small chapel on the northeast, and at the southeast corner a 17th century building on three floors of which the upper is **St Sergius**, the middle contains the vestry, and the basement the chapel of **St Nicholas**.

Outside the east wall in the former cemetery is the ruined but still impressive **Church of all Saints**, *Vsekh Svyatykh*, which harboured the tomb, now gone, of Nikolai Konshin, the textile factory magnate. It was built in a tent-shape in 1896 in alternating red and white horizontal brick (like Byzantine churches) by the Moscow architect, Roman Klein, who was particularly active in Serpukhov.

At **Chekhov Street**, one block east of the monastery, turn left towards the centre. The **Serpukhov History and Art Museum** is at No 87 in the former home of **Anna Maraeva**, widow of a rich merchant, containing her paintings and furniture. The house was designed, like the Konshin tomb church, by Roman Klein in 1900 in a mixture of classical and renaissance styles with richly panelled interiors and fine plasterwork. After her husband died Anna's brother-in-law took her to court over the inheritance. While waiting for the court decision – eventually in her favour – she spent as much money as possible acquiring a great art collection and building this luxurious house. The museum was further enriched after the revolution by paintings and objects from the Orlov-Davydov estate at Semenovskoe Otrada. Apparently Stalin stayed here once during the civil war and for a long time there was a revered 'Stalin slept here' room.

Next door to the Maraeva estate is a fine red brick **Old Believer** church in pseudo-Russian style, the **Intercession of the Virgin**, *Pokrova*, which has reopened for worship. Anna Maraeva, who like so many of the merchants was of Old Believer stock, built this church in the early 1900s for the Pokrov Community and filled it with icons from her excellent collection, some of which are now on display in the museum. The church, once more functioning, may also have been designed by Roman Klein.

Farther along Chekhov street is the **war memorial**. The old **Sverikov textile factory** built in the 1740s is at No 18. At **Lenin Square** by the turn of the century shopping arcade, turn left to **Kaluzhskaya St** where **Count Vladimir Sollogub**, the 19th century writer lived at No 46. A little south on 2nd Moskovskaya Street No 8/19 within a hospital complex is a two-storey building that housed the famous **Kishkin Brothers sailcloth factory** of the 1740s.

Across from Count Sollogub's house are the remains of the **Crucifixion Monastery**, *Raspyatsky*, entered through the gates of No 38 Kaluzhskaya. The monastery only functioned from 1695 to 1764 when it became a victim of the closures under Catherine II. The odd, single-storey cathedral is still standing as are some of the walls and gate bell tower built in 1718-19 in the daring new European style of Peter the Great's time with a spire and large windows. Its benefactress, Princess Nazareta Gagarina, daughter of the Siberian governor executed in 1721 for corruption, died before the church was finished and only one storey was ever completed. It is now one side of an intimate town courtyard and although the buildings seem to be in precarious state, children tumble in and out, dogs bark and chickens scrabble in the dirt.

Nearby on the same street is the powerful bell tower and church of **St Nicholas the White**, *Nikoly Belovo*. It was built in 1835-57 in the Empire style with a huge dome and Ionic portico. It became a workshop in the Soviet period, but according to legend so many nasty accidents occured on the two feast days of St Nicholas that it closed on those days. From here it is a short walk back to Volodarskovo St

The old town leaps the Nara River to the **right bank** where there is a further group of ruined old churches and the splendid Vladychny Convent. On the right at No 4 Engels Lane is the **Church of the Intercession**, *Pokrova*, built in 1721, the familiar octagonal on a cube. **Nikola-Budki Church** of almost the same date, 1711, is in the parallel street on the corner of Chernyshevskovo. To the left of the bridge is the slightly less derelict **Church of the Purification**, *Sretenskaya*, at 30 Karl Marx St built in 1702 in Moscow Baroque style. At No 27/3 Proletarskaya St closer to the river is the former **Voronin merchant's house** in stuccoed brick, erected in the late 18th century now in multiple occupation and very dilapidated. Finally, at the end of Oktyabrskaya Street, is the majestic **Vladychny Convent**.

This great monastery/fortress, now very dilapidated, has stood here near the confluence of the Nara and the Oka for more than six centuries. Closed in 1927 three of the churches became schools for training fighter pilots, other buildings were used as factories and hostels, as archival deposits and for the storage of vegetables. Restoration attempts in the 1990s were not very successful but since the convent was returned to the church in 1995 some progress is being made.

The monastery, founded in 1360, is older by a decade than the Vysotsky Monastery across the river. With its position on the Oka it proved a vital defence against Tatar attack. In 1598 **Boris Godunov**, made a rare visit to Serpukhov to rally support against the Tatars under Kazy-Girei and at the same time curry favour in his bid for the throne. The Russian forces, lined up along the Oka and Nara Rivers before the Vladychny Monastery, so impressed the Tatars that a peace settlement was quickly negotiated. Godunov expressed his gratitude by initiating much new building at Vladychny. In 1810 its status was changed to that of a convent.

The oldest church, the ruined **Cathedral of the Presentation**, *Vvedeniya*, built anew by Godunov in the early 17th century, of brick covered with stone cladding and with a voluptuously jutting triple apse and five domes, is situated opposite the Holy Gate. It is curiously constructed for the main dome is not at the centre but towards the east, perhaps to balance the large apse. A second row of gables is now hidden by the later roof. Another odd feature is the two drums, one on top of the other. The cone of the central dome is a Soviet alteration and will no doubt soon be changed for the more usual onion shape.

To the left of the entrance into the monastery is the group of buildings that make up the old **refectory and Church of St George**, also erected under Godunov, in 1599. The twin-peaked bell tower was originally a simple frame for holding bells, a *zvonnitsa*, but was rebuilt in its present form in the late 17th century.

Vladychny was extended westward in the middle of the 19th century when the demands of the new convent created a need for more buildings. Along the western wall right of the entrance are nuns' cells and the abbess's Empire-style residence.

Beyond the sign SOVKHOZ BOLSHEVIK on the main Chernyshevskovo Street are the walls, right, of the former *pogost* (cemetery), **Berezina**, for long used as a lumber yard with piles of newly-sawn sweet-smelling timber. In addition to the walls and towers only the almost unrecognisable 17th and 19th century **Church of St Nicholas** survives. The impression of a forgotten place is intensified by a discarded statue of Lenin sitting forlornly in a corner by a shed.

From Berezina continue west 3 km towards Protvino on the paved road and turn left signed DRAKINO 5.3 km. **DRAKINO** is located where the little Protva River, which rises near Mozhaisk and snakes its way, looping and twisting for over 200 km, empties into the Oka. At the village continue past the cemetery and follow the road right to the **war memorial** in the form of a Soviet plane, a MIG-3, on a plinth. The Germans, who came within a hair's breadth of taking Serpukhov in the early winter of 1941-2, were stopped at Drakino.

Just before the memorial, turn right on a dirt lane to the **Church of Sts Boris and Gleb**, a *pogost* or cemetery. The central cube and small cupola survive from the early church of 1684 but the rest is 19th century. Of all the forlorn churches in the Serpukhov area, this one was fortunate in that, from the 1980s to 1995, it has been the studio of the sculptor, **Andrei Volkov**. We stumbled upon the church one miserable, rainy September day in 1992 to be warmly welcomed by Andrei and to find gleaming in the darkness of the apse a row of intriguing metal figures ranged on shelves. Volkov's talent is in composing out of scrap metal gleaned from local factories scenes that capture the essence of Russia – a woman on a bench shelling peas, people hurrying along a street to work, a cyclist repairing his bicycle. Before the advent of the new Russia, Volkov made his living designing Soviet monuments but his real passion is for these evocative figures.

In 1995 when the church was given to the Serpukhov convent, the nuns embarked on repairs and the creation of a garden. Volkov, who loves the village, has built a new house and studio next to the church on the headland overlooking the Protva. Before leaving the church he re-roofed it and impudently added his initials, AV, to the cross.

Road 4 KASHIRA HIGHWAY M-4/M-6: SUKHANOVO TO ZARAISK

Near the Kashira Highway close to Moscow are the magnificent properties of the Volkonskys and the estate where Lenin died. Farther out are the lands once controlled by the powerful Orlov and Sheremetiev families. Three exceptionally rare and beautiful tower churches lie along this road. One hundred kilometres south at Stupino the highway crosses the Oka to Kashira and the ancient fortress of Zaraisk.

PRINCES, PRISONS AND TOWERS

From the Warsaw (Varshavskoe) Road in Moscow cross the MKAD onto the Kharkov Highway M-2 then turn immediately right to the old Warsaw Road to Podolsk. At the 24 km post and traffic lights turn left signed VIDNOE. Pass under the Kharkov Highway and after 4 km where the road turns sharp left continue straight ahead to the gates of Sukhanovo where the car can be left.

The attractive estate of **SUKHANOVO** was acquired in 1769 by Alexei Melgunov whose daughter, Yekaterina, married Prince Dmitry Volkonsky. Childless, she bestowed Sukhanovo on her favourite nephew-by-marriage, Prince Petr Volkonsky, and it remained in the Volkonsky family until the revolution. After 1917 it became a school and a museum but fire in the late 1920s destroyed the interior and in 1934 Sukhanovo, stripped of its fine furniture and paintings, was given to the Union of Architects as their rest home. In 1934–8 Viktor Kokorin remodelled the interiors in the Soviet classical style.

Prince Petr, adjutant to Alexander I, inherited the Tsar's furniture, including his bed, and kept it as a memorial at Sukhanovo where an obelisk to Alexander was also erected. It is no secret that Tolstoy in his great novel, *War and Peace*, based Prince Andrei Bolkonsky on Prince Petr even to the transparent use of the name. Like his fictional prototype, the real Prince Volkonsky fought at the battle of Austerlitz against Napoleon in 1805; he too snatched up the regimental standard and not once but three times led his greatly outnumbered troops against the enemy. Later Prince Petr was put in charge of palace building works and became acquainted with the leading architects of the day – Rossi,

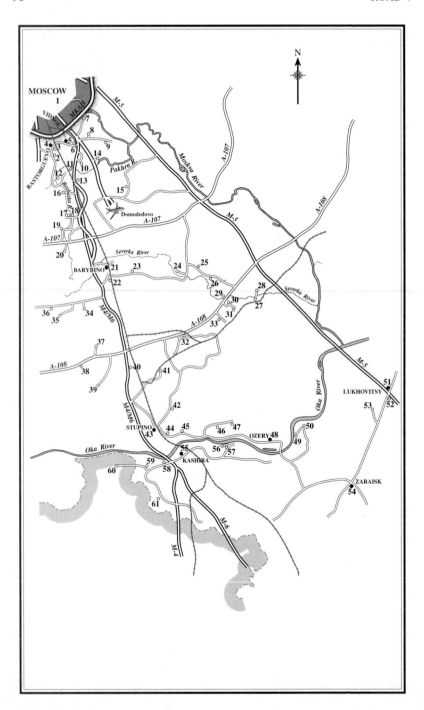

ROAD 4
SUKHANOVO TO ZARAISK

1. MOSCOW
2. Sukhanovo
3. Yekaterinskaya Pustyn
4. RASTORGUEVO
5. VIDNOE
6. Tabolovo
7. Besedy
8. Ostrov
9. Molokovo
10. Gorki-Leninskie
11. *Leninskaya Stn*
12. Domodedovo Village
13. Yam
14. Jerusalem Convent
15. Rozhdestvensky Pogost
16. Konstantinovo
17. Bityagovo
18. Serafimo-Znamensky Skit
19. Odintsovo
20. Dolmatovo
21. BARYBINO
22. Kuzminskoe
23. Lyakhovo
24. Avdotino
25. Troitskoe-Lobanovo
26. Marinka
27. Shkin
28. Prusy
29. Meshcherino
30. Fedorovskoe
31. Gorodnya

32. Malino
33. Chirkino
34. Mikhailovskoe
35. Shcheglyatovo
36. Dobrynikha
37. Ivanovskoe
38. Semenovskoe
39. Khatun
40. Kiyasovo
41. Verzilovo
42. Staraya Sitnya
43. STUPINO
44. Belopesotsky Monastery
45. Staraya Kashira
46. Sukovo
47. Aleshkovo
48. OZERY
49. Sosnovka
50. Sennitsy
51. LUKHOVITSY
52. Sushkovo
53. Troitskie Borki
54. ZARAISK
55. KASHIRA
56. Baskachi
57. Kropotovo
58. Lidy
59. Taraskovo
60. Bogoslovskoe
61. Zlobino

Gilardi, Stasov and Menelaws – some of whom were employed at Sukhanovo.

The usual arrangement whereby the mansion is the main focus of the estate was disregarded at Sukhanovo. Here the stables and guest houses in Gothic style form one group, the main house (together with the church, now destroyed) another and the Volkonsky mausoleum near the river, a third. Although Sukhanovo today is incomplete – some buildings disappeared before the revolution, and the church, most of the pavilions, sphinxes and statues were demolished in the 1930s – yet the house, the stables, the service buildings, mausoleum, and a fine pavilion remain.

The 18th century mansion has undergone much remodelling. The Ionic portico and colonnades linking the wings were introduced about 1816 probably by Adam Menelaws. In the 1840s the right colonnade was removed leaving the south wing free-standing, then the north wing lost its colonnade and the space between was filled in.

The path in front of the mansion leads to a perfect, round **pavilion** with eight Doric columns – the Temple of Venus – on the high bank overlooking the large pond. Over the bridge is the charming, derelict **statue** of a girl with the broken jug, a copy of Pavel Sokolov's famous figure at Tsarskoe Selo (and the inspiration for Pushkin's poem).

The **mausoleum**, the Church of Dimitry Rostovsky, lies just beyond. Built in 1813 at the behest of Yekaterina Volkonskaya to house the body of her husband who died in the flight from Moscow, it is by the classical architect, Domenico Gilardi. The central domed rotunda with six Doric columns now lacks the semicircular colonnade and the bell tower behind. It was disfigured in 1935 by the architect, Nikolai Vinogradov, who linked the wings to the main mausoleum in order to make a dining room, thus destroying the circular form. It was further impoverished by replacing the red brick and white portico with ochre stucco.

In 1993 Sukhanovo was awarded to new businessmen on the understanding repairs would be undertaken. Expensive cars carrying well-dressed young men swept into the drive but no such repairs took place. The Union of Architects protested and in April 1996, after presidential intervention, got back their rest home.

On the road to Vidnoe as above, go past the turn to Sukhanovo through the pleasant streets of small wooden houses of Rastorguevo following the road right and then right again. At the war memorial and sign to the militia training school, turn right to **YEKATERINSKAYA PUSTYN**, *St Catherine's Monastery.* Tsar Alexei founded the monastery in 1658 on this lonely spot where St Catherine came in a vision to him correctly predicting the birth of a royal daughter.

But this is not just another monastery. Closed after the revolution and attached to the architects' home at Sukhanovo, it became in the 1930s the notorious prison, *Sukhanovka.* The architects' home supplied food for the prisoners but each normal meal had to be shared among 12. Solzhenitsyn in his *Gulag Archipelago* describes it thus:

Sukhanovka was the most terrible prison the MGB had. Its very name was used to intimidate prisoners; interrogators would hiss it threateningly. And you would not be able to question those who had been there: either they were insane and talking only disconnected nonsense or they were dead.

During interrogations prisoners were not allowed to sleep for five days and nights – relief came only because the interrogators took weekends off. The top military officers imprisoned there, including generals, were questioned personally by Ryumin, assistant of Abakumov (Beria's deputy), who beat them himself with a rubber truncheon on the sciatic nerve.

This melancholy place after Stalin's death became a police training school but in 1993 was returned to the church. The new monks must find it strange to occupy the same rooms where the notorious interrogations took place. In the centre stands the **Cathedral of St Catherine**, built in the late 18th century, with the later refectory church of **Sts Peter and Paul** adjoining it. The best of the surviving buildings is the south gate-church of **St Dimitry of Rostov**, under the elegant bell tower with brand new bells shining in the belfry. It is hard now to imagine the terrible executions in this church and the smoke wafting upwards at night when it doubled as a crematorium.

Follow the one-way system in Rastorguevo left to cross the railway line at Rastorguevo station. Just before entering Vidnoe note the road, left, to Tarychevo where the beautiful oval **Church of the Nativity of the Virgin**, *Rozhdestva Bogoroditsy, built 1764–5 in baroque style, is all that survives of the Golovin estate.*

VIDNOE is a purely 1930s Soviet town servicing the large gasworks. Located in forested dacha land it was designed as a showpiece by architect Boris Yefimovich and engineer A.M. Ruzsky. Street after street of attractive red brick two- and three-storey houses with white gables and fat columns lead to the huge empty Soviet Square where a grey and white classical palace (former Party headquarters) flanked by two lesser wings focus on the inevitable statue of Lenin. From the main square follow the road right 3 km to the bus terminus at Tabolovo where the lofty **Church of the Assumption**, *Uspeniya*, built in 1705-21, in white limestone, the familiar Moscow baroque octagonal on a cube, is the only survivor from the estate of Count Petr Apraxin, a naval commander and governor under Peter the Great. The separate stone-clad bell tower within the territory of the busy bus terminus served for a time as the ticket office. The church, which closed in 1937, was returned in 1990 and many small icons hang everywhere on the bare stone walls touchingly donated by the new parishioners. One of them related how her mother was christened and married in the church before it closed and lived long enough for it to reopen in time for her funeral.

From the Domodedovo Airport Road, 4 km from the MKAD, turn left signed MOLOKOVO. After 3 kilometres just past Misailovo turn left by a cement fence 3 km to **OSTROV**. *Take the left road past the war memorial to the splendid church high up on the right.*

Ostrov (island), was so named because it is on a prominent mound in the flat Moskva River valley. From here Ivan the Terrible and Alexei Mikhailovich enjoyed hunting expeditions and pilgrimages to the Nikolaevsky-Ugreshsky Monastery on the opposite bank. Catherine II presented Ostrov to Count Alexei Orlov who planted gardens, laid out the park in the English manner, and founded a stud farm in which the famous Orlov Trotter, *Rysak*, was bred.

The glorious white stone **Transfiguration Church**, *Preobrazheniya*, one of the few tent-shaped tower churches in the Moscow area, was built in the second half of the 16th century as part of the royal estate. The slim octagonal cone rises steeply from the cube base where twelve tiny cupolas are grouped three at each corner and sheathed with a great profusion of *kokoshniki* ogee gables. An enclosed gallery, rebuilt of brick in 1838, surrounds the church on three sides culminating in two chapels, each miniature versions of the central church. Within the narrow confines it is thrilling to look high up into the tall cone. The unusual deep-set round windows suggest foreign influence although it was almost certainly constructed by master builders from Pskov in the reign of Ivan the Terrible. The only false note is the insensitive red and white Gothic bell tower of 1830. The church has now reopened.

Amazingly, a second tower church stands at nearby **BESEDY**. *It can be approached directly from the MKAD going east from the M4/M6 junction 4 km, then turn right into Besedy. Or, from Ostrov, return through Misailovo and turn right just before the Domodedovo Airport Road to a T-junction then right to Besedy.* But this fine church, the **Nativity of Christ**, *Rozhdestva Khristova*, cannot compare with Ostrov's soaring elevation. It was built at the end of the 16th century in white limestone by the boyar Dmitry Godunov, a relative of Boris Godunov. Rising high on a sub-basement and surrounded by a 19th century gallery, it is neat and orderly with 19th century frescoes, walls and gates and all the adjuncts of a church that did not suffer closure in the Soviet period.

ON THE LOWER PAKHRA

Take the Kashira Highway M-4/M-6 from the MKAD as it branches right from the Domodedovo Airport Road signed ROSTOV NA DONU and turn left just past the 29 km post signed GORKI-LENINSKIE at the large statue of Lenin 3 km through woods and fields.

GORKI-LENINSKIE *(closed Tuesdays)* was the country house appropriated by Lenin and his wife, Krupskaya, to escape the stresses of the capital and it was here that Lenin died on January 24, 1924 of a rare congenital brain disease. Lenin founded a special farm here, later the Experimental Institute of Genetics under the Academy of Sciences, with at its head the notorious biologist, Trofim Lysenko. Gorki-Leninskie only opened to the public in 1949 as a shrine to the memory of Lenin and it still bears the hallmarks of the cult although the quasi-religious veneration of Lenin is no longer in vogue. In 1994 Lenin's lovingly preserved apartment in the Kremlin was transferred to the building by the car park. From here a fine walk along an avenue of birches leads to the house.

Before **the house** the land dips down into a steep, wooded ravine, an extremely peaceful spot that has hardly changed in the last century, for Lenin and Krupskaya left barely any trace of their stay. The furniture, the books, the paintings, and the interior decor belong not to Lenin but to the last owner before the revolution. This must surely be the only

country estate in the Moscow area where the pre-Bolshevik order has
been so perfectly preserved.

There has been an estate at Gorki since the late 18th century. In 1909 it
was purchased by **Zinaida Morozova**, the widow of Savva Morozov, the
wealthy textile merchant and Bolshevik sympathiser. It is ironic that
Lenin, the fighter against capitalism, should have died at Gorki in the
small bedroom of the daughter of Savva Morozov, old Russia's most
conspicuous capitalist. In 1910, five years after Savva's suicide, Zinaida
married for the third time (her first marriage was to Savva's nephew,
Sergei), General Anatoly Reinbot, the Moscow head of police. Reinbot,
who changed his German name to Rezvoy in 1914, fell foul of the law
and, although pardoned by Nicholas II, Zinaida divorced him. In 1917
she was evicted from Gorki but allowed to keep her estate at
Pokrovskoe-Rubtsovo (see p.319).

Zinaida employed Moscow's finest architect, **Fedor Shekhtel**, who had
designed the Morozov mansion in Moscow, to make modifications. In
1910 he masterfully embellished the classical house with new wings,
added the outside frieze, improved the portico, and built the large pond
and pavilions, grotto and bridge. Within, he created the amazingly light
winter garden with its artificial marble columns and floor-to-ceiling
glazing. All the furnishings, including the wonderful Russian furniture
in Karelian birch and mahogany, the paintings and clocks, the old
books on the left side of the bookcase and even the old telephone were
chosen by Zinaida. Her boudoir furnished with many vases and even a
porcelain dressing table suggests an extravagant taste.

In the garage an ancient **Rolls-Royce** of the imperial family fitted with
skis and caterpillar treads for use in the First World War mud was
employed by Lenin and Krupskaya to get around Gorki in the heavy
snows of winter.

*Two km south of Gorki-Leninskie within the village of Yam, (staging
post), where the M-4/M-6 commences, is the railway station, Leninskaya
(formerly Gerasimovka), completed in 1954 by Mezentsov and Shpotov in
the Stalin monumental style with a splendid central spire and a marble
interior dominated by a large statue of Lenin.*

West of Yam 4 km towards Podolsk is **DOMODEDOVO VILLAGE**
(not the airport or town), on the Pakhra. Colourful **St Nicholas**, yellow
and white with blue cupolas and a green roof, is a most unusual church

to find in a small village. It was designed in 1731-8 by the noted St Petersburg architect, Gottfried Schadel, at a time when Domodedovo belonged to the imperial palace administration. The waning influence of Moscow baroque can be seen in the form, an octagonal on a cube, but the windows reflect the fashion for the Petrine style. For such a rare building, it was fortunate that it was only briefly closed and has retained all its considerable furnishings, including the richly carved gilded iconostasis. The large *trapeza* was rebuilt 1837-41 and the tiered bell tower which fits so well into the composition was added in 1845 by Yevgraf Tyurin, the architect of Moscow's Yelokhovsky Cathedral.

From the Domodedovo Airport Road turn right signed MESHCHERINO then left across the road bridge to Lukino. The **JERUSALEM EXALTATION OF THE CROSS CONVENT**, *Krestovozdvizhensky-Ierusalimsky Monastyr*, was returned to the church in 1993 after many decades as a children's sanatorium.

Founded as the Sisters of Mercy at the Florus and Laurus Church in Yam, the convent was formed in the 1860s. Facing the central avenue is the vast red brick **Cathedral of the Ascension**, *Vozneseniya*, built 1890 to 1893 by the Moscow diocesan architect, Stepan Krygin, the grandest of his many churches, and financed by Moscow merchants. Inspired by traditional Russian design, it is divided into three bays offset with white stone detailing and topped by five large grey cupolas and gold crosses. Like the Christ the Saviour in Moscow the church is much too large for a modest convent, but placed well above the Pakhra River it has become a landmark. The pseudo-Russian bell tower has not survived although other buildings of the convent, the *trapeza* to the left of the cathedral and the house of the abbess to the right, are still in place.

On the Domodedovo Airport Road, at the airport turn left onto a poor cement road 6 km to Selvachevo then turn left (north) 4 km towards Konstantinovo. Just past Zhdanovskoe (named for a small river and not Stalin's notorious cultural henchman) turn left at the chicken farm and continue ½ km on the rutted track to the woods on the right.

On foot follow a path, right, into a field then turn left along another track and make for the woods by the river. An old graveyard and the handsome church of the elusive **ROZHDESTVENSKY POGOST** are hidden within the trees overlooking the Zhdanka river, a tributary of the Pakhra. The **Nativity of Christ**, *Rozhdestva Khristova*, was constructed in 1685-6 for the patrimony of Prince Alexander Prozorovsky who had the then prestigious position of royal carver at the courts of Tsars Fedor and Ivan. This innovative building was one of the first masonry churches to be built as an octagon on a cube, the basic form from which Moscow baroque evolved. The octagon was covered with coloured tiles – which still exist under the metal covering of the dome – in contrast to the undecorated facade. In 1902-8 the lower windows were widened, a north chapel added, a new south doorway built and frescoes repainted. The interesting bell tower which stood separately was dismantled in Soviet times. Although the church stands alone seemingly abandoned in the woods, services occasionally take place in summer for villagers from Zhdanovskoe and Pletenikha.

IN THE VALLEY OF THE ROZHAIKA

Take the old Kashira Road 37 km to Domodedovo town (not the village or the airport). In the town centre turn right at the third traffic light, go past the post office, after 4 kilometres cross the Rozhaika River and at the T-junction turn right to the Przhevalsky house, right.

KONSTANTINOVO, originally a large estate, was in 1882 when it was acquired by the prominent Moscow lawyer, **Vladimir Przhevalsky**, a small comfortable property. His brother, **Nikolai Przhevalsky**, the great Russian geographer, spent much of his time here between travels to Siberia and the Far East. After the revolution it was annexed by the local state farm and the buildings suffered accordingly. But the modest late Empire house of one-and-a-half storeys, newly painted light blue and with a grand columned hall the length of the house, has been restored for use as a small hotel and seminar centre. The portico of six Tuscan columns faces on the peaceful park side ponds, woods and a charming gazebo although, in the distance, the industrial chimneys of Domodedovo intrude. Across the river, the **Church of the Smolensk Virgin**, *Smolenskoi Ikony Bogoroditsy*, originally built in the 17th century as part of the estate, has been shorn of its dome and spire, painted a hideous red-orange colour and incorporated into the toy factory.

Take the old Kashira Road past Domodedovo town for about 4 km to Zaborye and turn right at the 46 km post signed P.L. YUNY NEFTYANIK. Go under the road bridge and after 3 km fork right to Bityagovo. On the way hidden in woods, right, is the delightful **Serafimo-Znamensky Skit** of the Sisters of Mercy founded by Grand Duchess

Elizaveta Fedorovna. Until recently the Sputnik pioneer camp, it is now reverting to its original use. Built in Art Nouveau style by Leonid Stezhensky in 1910, it is in the form of a walled square with the impressive **Church of the Sign** at the centre.

At **BITYAGOVO** the **Resurrection Church**, *Voskreseniya*, stands on the other bank of the Rozhaika across a fragile bridge – the foot bridge a little farther along seems safer. The quaint building was erected in 1670-1 by I.S.Telepnev, a courtier at Tsar Alexei's court. Repairs have been put in hand since the church was returned to worship and bells again hang in the tower. It is peculiarly composed of two equal cubes side by side, one for the main church and the other a chapel, each with their own identical apse.

On the old Kashira Road past Domodedovo town turn right at the 48 km post signed LESNOE D.O. 4.5 km. Or, on the A-107 from the Kashira Road turn right (north) signed DRUZHBA for 5 km then left at the crossroads to cross the river.

ODINTSOVO (Arkhangelskoe) was the country mansion of **Vikula Morozov**, the owner of the textile mill at Nikolskoe. A strict Old Believer who ate with a handmade wooden spoon and did not smoke or shave, he employed the then unqualified Fedor Shekhtel to design and construct this extravagant house. Shekhtel, later the outstanding Art Nouveau architect, completed the Vikula Morozov house in 1892, his first in the Moscow area. After the revolution Odintsovo became a hospital, then during the Second World War a sanatorium for exhausted pilots, and finally the trades unions' rest house now open to anyone.

The **mansion**, which faces the narrow river, is in a vigorous Renaissance style like a French chateau with lashings of Gothic details. Now painted a lurid green, probably not the original colour, every conceivable decoration is employed on the facade: shells, towers, cartouches, the date and the letter 'M' for Morozov. Permission to see around the house can be obtained from the director on a weekday, and possibly on a weekend if he is in residence. It is entered from the back courtyard up a staircase (copied uncannily a year later in the Kharitonenko house, now the British Ambassador's residence) to the ground floor where the splendid stone fireplace in the medieval hall resembles the Shekhtel fireplace in the Savva Morozov mansion. Off the hall is a Gothic dining room with a coffered ceiling and an 'M' on the fireplace. It opens onto the well-lit conservatory panelled in Karelian birch. Upstairs is a second Gothic hall with paintings in the neo-Russian style of swans and the mythological siren.

To the right of the house is the ochre-coloured **Church of Michael the Archangel**, built in 1800, when the estate belonged to the Naryshkins. In sharp contrast to the eclectic mansion the church is classical in style with rounded corners and four Tuscan porticoes. The large, heavy drum supporting the hemispherical dome is intriguingly repeated in miniature in the drum and dome. The steward's house and the early **electricity station** housed in the service wing, left, are in the same style as the mansion. The pond and pavilions lie north beyond the church while the stables and main gate are at the southern end.

From the Kashira Highway M-4/M-6 turn right (west) onto the A-107 4 km and at the top of a hill – past the right turn signed DRUZHBA (to Odintsovo) – turn left onto an unsigned road. After 1 km turn right for 1 km across a tributary of the Rozhaika to **DOLMATOVO**. The small and unpretentious **Church of the Sign**, *Ikony Bozhiei Materi 'Znamenie'*, was built in 1735 in an unequal octagon, in the manner of wooden churches. The low roof dome with an unusual belfry is completed by a single helmet-shaped cupola over which an intricate, lacey cross holds sway. The village boys refer to the church as a *skit* and the impression of a hermitage is intensified on meeting the priest in a skull and crossbones cap. He is from Moscow's Danilov Monastery which in 1990 adopted and reopened the church. Inside, an old iconostasis from another church fits the narrow space very nicely.

A COMMUNITY OF NOBLES

On the Kashira Highway 4 km south of the turning to Barybino turn sharp left signed BOLNITSA. After 1 km take the second unsigned road right, opposite a bus-stop, to **KUZMINSKOE**. The sparkling **Church of Cosmas and Damian**, *Kozmy i Damiana*, was built in 1652 for the estate of S.P. Naumov. It was beautifully restored in the 1970s, the very epitome of a mid-17th century church with its rows of *kokoshniki* gables, five cupolas, tent-shaped bell tower (19th century but in the same style) and extravagantly protruding apse. Glazed tiles within the cornice add a touch of colour to the otherwise brilliant white. It began functioning again in 1990 and before it was redecorated one could appreciate the bare forms of the vaulting, low doorways and thick walls.

From Barybino follow the railway south to cross the line and continue east through Ilinskoe with its brightly painted church 6 km to **LYAKHOVO** *at the end of the village where trees overhang the road, left.*

Lyakhovo, built in the early part of the 19th century, was yet another estate of the Vasilchikov family which before the revolution belonged to A.A. Vargin. It is in the new arrangement whereby the **Empire house** and its separate wing face the road like a town house. Of one storey with a mezzanine floor it was used as a school and is now looking desolate although people still seem to be living there. It has lost the four columns at the front but the attractive loggia of Tuscan columns survives on the courtyard side. To the right is the wing with Tuscan portico on the end facade and dilapidated roof. Stables at the back of the property are also very neglected. The wooden house of the last owner, Vargin, built in 1910, stands left, near the road.

From Barybino 30 km through Lyakhovo and Kishkino (the late red brick church is the village shop) and at Bolshoe Alexeevskoe turn left across the Severka River then immediately sharp left 1 km to **AVDOTINO**.

Since the 17th century Avdotino belonged to the family of **Nikolai Novikov**, the publisher, educator and reformer (it was named for Avdotiya, wife of an earlier Novikov). He spent his childhood and the last 22 years of his life here and is buried in the church. Novikov's influential publishing house translated French, English and German literary, economic and philosophical works and at one time was publishing one-third of all books in Russia. However, his attitudes were not admired by Catherine II and his espousal of freemasonry, the modern equivalent of a dissident movement, added fuel to the fire of her dislike. Finally, in April 1792 his estate was searched and a letter found from the leading architect, Vasily Bazhenov, about masonic books for the heir apparent. He was arrested on the spot and spent four years in the appalling Shlisselburg fortress and was only released after the death of the Empress. Thereafter he lived as a recluse at Avdotino, until his death in 1818.

On the right are the nine stone houses Novikov built for his peasants to provide them with better housing than the thatched and overcrowded wooden hovels of the time. Each building was divided into two for two families (of 8 or 9 people) each with three rooms, all with windows, separated into living quarters and storage. Today the original arrangement has long since changed but, adapted into individual units, they are still used as living quarters.

To the left behind the shop is the red brick schoolhouse Novikov
founded for his peasants. The wooden house where Novikov lived was
pulled down in 1879 but the **wing**, of which only the stone basement is
original, still stands in dilapidated condition a little distance from the
church. The carriage house beyond is an utter ruin.

In contrast to this neglect, the stone **Church of the Tikhvin Icon of the
Virgin**, stands tall and elegant, once more holding services. The main
church was built by Novikov's father 1749-53, in the baroque of Elizabeth's time, an octagon on a cube with paired pilasters on the corners
and a large dome from which the figured double drum and cupola
spring. The expressive bell tower also of stone with round windows and
paired columns was built 30 years later in 1789 reflecting the new
classical style. In the grounds to the left of the church is the grave of
Semen Gamaleya, the translator and close friend who looked after the
estate after Novikov was arrested.

Following Novikov's death Avdotino was sold to pay debts. A
poorhouse was established in the wing but the rest of the estate was
allowed to deteriorate although at the end of the 19th century the
Moscow City Duma opened a school there. In the 1970s, when the
village was amalgamated with the stock farm at Bolshoe Alexeevskoe,
the surviving buildings were placed under the protection of the state
but to little effect for the old stables were immediately demolished.

*From Avdotino return to the main road and turn left (north) away from
the Severka River. After 4 km just past the sign for RAMENSKY
RAYON, turn sharp right signed P.L. SEVERKA. Follow this road 6 km
through open country which crosses the Severka again to the ruins of*
TROITSKOE-LOBANOVO. The old estate was given in the 18th
century as dowry to Princess Praskoviya Lobanov-Rostovskaya who
married Prince Semen Volkonsky; their son, Grigory, became a friend
of neighbour Novikov in his old age. All that has survived of the
ancient property is the ruined red brick 16th century **Church of the
Trinity**, *Troitsy*. One of the few so-called Godunov churches, it is
now a sad sight, its windows and doors gaping open and covered with
graffiti from the children in the summer camp next door. The central
part of the church and two side chapels, the oldest parts, are hidden
under the later roof and oversized *trapeza*. Four round towers stand at
the corners of the territory and there are the remains of an entrance
arch.

3 km from Troitskoe-Lobanovo on the right is **Rassvet** (dawn), a childrens' summer camp. It is housed in the picturesque buildings of **MARINKA**, the former estate of the **Buturlin** family. Continue past the main gate where the road turns right alongside the camp to the service entrance where the director seems happy to show people around. The camp belongs to a Moscow knitting factory, *Krasnya Zarya* (Red Dawn) which is attracting children again after a slow period.

In the late 18th century Marinka was rebuilt by Count Petr Buturlin in Gothic style, quite possibly by the noted architect, Vasily Bazhenov, the friend of their neighbour, Novikov. Today, the house is gone and all that is left is the considerable park, ponds, the ruined **Church of the Cross**, *Kresta*, built in 1748, the old wine cellar by the service gate (used now for storing vegetables) and the remarkable stables. These Gothic fantasies of red and white round towers, some small, some large, formed the grand entrance with the avenue of limes that led to the main house. The stables have been adapted as dormitories and dining room for the Moscow children enjoying country life.

Two of Russia's greatest noble families, **Counts Orlov and Sheremetiev**, settled in this area south of Moscow. The five Orlov brothers, who assisted Catherine II to the throne, were dominant in the rolling meadows west of the Kashira Road. The more ancient Sheremetiev family, landowners since the 16th century, held the higher land to the east of the Kashira Road.

THE ORLOV LANDS

Take the old Kashira Road to Velyaminovo and turn right towards CHEPELOVO. In 5 km at Stupino turn left across a railway line through Glotaevo 6 km to **MIKHAILOVSKOE**. The wooden houses are attractively spaced in a wide circle around the church and village green with the pond a little to one side. The large white **Church of the Archangel Michael**, which remained open in the Soviet period, was built 1816-24 by the pious Countess Anna Orlova. With rusticated walls and Doric porticoes on north and south it lacks a *trapeza* linking the bell tower and the church.

3 km west of Stupino (8 km from Velyaminovo) turn left, unmarked, across a railway line 7 km to **SHCHEGLYATOVO**. In this unremarkable village, owned by Count Vladimir Orlov of Semenovskoe, is the sadly ruined rotunda **Church of St Vladimir** built in 1779-83 with a

magnificent high dome and spire. All the strikingly different segments –
apse, church, *trapeza*, bell tower – are cleverly united by high arched
ground-floor windows.

12 km west of Stupino to **DOBRYNIKHA** *on the left*. The unprepossessing
railway yards give way to a high red brick wall encircling the **Convent of
Joy and Consolation**, *Obshchina 'Otrada i Uteshenie'*. The convent was
founded in 1898 by Countess Mariya Orlova-Davydova, later the nun
Magdalina, daughter of Count Vladimir Orlov-Davydov of Otrada,
the grand estate at Semenovskoe after which the convent is named.

Within the walls are two churches, the Joy and Consolation, and the
larger **Assumption**, *Uspeniya*, consecrated in 1904. The leading Moscow
Art Nouveau architect, **Sergei Soloviev**, designed the walls, the gate bell
tower (not survived) and the five-domed Assumption church in a
reinterpretation of traditional Russian forms. The community established a school, an orphanage, a poorhouse and a hospital on the
spacious premises. In the 1930s when it was forced to close, the buildings were taken over by the psychiatric hospital based at Meshcherskoe.
Uniquely, the Church of the Assumption was put to use as a flour mill
– the mill stone was still standing outside the church on our visit. In
1991 the convent was given back and today Father Antony, a former
engineer, is overseeing the restoration and recovery.

KHATUN is some way south of the Orlov villages described above. *On
the old Kashira Road about 80 km from Moscow turn right at the GAI
post onto the A-108. After 4 km turn left onto an unsigned road which
leads in 7 km to Khatun on the Lopasnya River*. In 1785 Admiral Alexei
Orlov-Chesmensky built the attractive, somewhat squat **Church of the
Resurrection**, *Voskreseniya*, the principal ornament of today's run-down
village. A quatrefoil design with paired pilasters (the capitals left unfinished) surmounted by a cube with cut corners making an unequal
octagon, it is baroque in essence although in other respects – the use of
pediments and lucarne windows – it follows the fashion for classicism.
The interesting shape was obscured in 1820 by the *trapeza* linking the
church to the belltower. The drum and cupola removed in Soviet times
when it became a warehouse and a children's home, were quickly
replaced when it began functioning again in 1992.

*From the old Kashira Road about 80 km from Moscow turn right onto the
A-108 towards Semenovskoe and travel 7 km to* **IVANOVSKOE**, *right*.
In the straggling village turn left to **St John the Baptist**, *Ioanna*

Predtechi, a noble structure out of place with its present humble surroundings. It was built in brick by Vladimir Orlov, the youngest of the brothers and owner of nearby Otrada, in 1831, the year of his death. The massive cube with porticoes of the Doric order is topped by a heavy drum in the form of a rotunda and cupola linked to the fine triple-tiered bell tower by the low *trapeza*. The now restored church was in poor state when first seen in 1992, its windows and doors open and exposed to the weather. Only four weeks earlier it had been returned for worship and it was astonishing to find Father Valery, in a corner of the bare interior on dirt floors christening a noisy group of babies and small naked girls, their friends busily shooing away curious little boys. In the grounds on the north side is the gravestone of Andrei Rudinkin, coachman for Grand Duke Sergei who died in the same Kremlin explosion that killed the Grand Duke in 1905.

From the old Kashira Road turn right 80 km from Moscow at the GAI post onto the A-108 and travel 12 km to **SEMENOVSKOE**. *As this is still a sanatorium run by the successors of the KGB, it is wise to leave the car on the road.* The extensive stately home, **Otrada** (Joy), of the Counts Orlov, consists of palace, church, mausoleum, orangeries, greenhouses, theatre, service buildings and an extensive park straddling the Lopasnya River. Although not in mint condition, Otrada has survived better than many estates. By the long iron fence on the left is the church and, down the hill, the main gates and entrance. Opposite the entrance is a small Gothic building, the old **forge**, for long the village shop. In the 1960s an extraordinary cache of Otrada household documents from the 1780s to 1918 was discovered there. The least difficult way of entering the grounds is an inconspicuous gate left of the church used by local people, even those leading cows.

Otrada was founded at the end of the 18th century by **Count Vladimir Orlov**. Curiously, of the five heroic Orlov brothers, supporters of Catherine II, there were remarkably few descendants. Vladimir, the youngest owner of Otrada, had two daughters one of whom, Natalya, married into the ancient Davydov family and it was the son of this liaison, also Vladimir, who succeeded as owner of the estate. The old Count, who had been director of the Academy of Sciences and spent most of his life in Italy, invited his grandson to live at Otrada and in 1831 bequeathed the entire property to him. The second Vladimir, who was also long-lived, had been educated in Edinburgh where he became friends with the writer, **Sir Walter Scott**. He even acquired one of Scott's manuscripts, *The Talisman*, now in the History Museum in Moscow. In 1856

Alexander I approved the new noble house of **Orlov-Davydov** and Vladimir was made a count. There were to be only four Orlov owners of the estate from its foundation in 1774 until it was nationalised in 1918.

After the revolution a boarding school for peasants was set up at Otrada but the upper part of the main house was turned into a museum where the best paintings and sculpture and some personal belongings of the scientist, Mikhail Lomonosov, collected by Count Orlov, were displayed. But in 1925 the museum was closed and the valuable contents removed to Moscow. Eventually the Semenovskoe dairy collective farm was organised and the wonderful palace and grounds were turned over to the **security ministries**, (now the FSB, Federal Security Service), for the use of the highest in the land as a holiday venue. Vladimir Tendryakov in his amusing story, *On the Blessed Island of Communism*, described lunching at Semenovskoe with Khrushchev in 1960 along with other members of the cultural establishment.

The impressive **Church of St Nicholas**, (originally called Vladimir after the patron saint of its first owner), near the side gate on the main road was erected in only two years, 1778-80, by the Orlov serf, Babakin. It is built to a plan popular in the late 18th century involving a high central section with pediment lit by two rows of windows, one arched and one round, a square apse at one end and *trapeza* with bell tower at the other and topped by an octagonal drum and large, hemispherical dome. In 1835 Alexander Gilardi, the Moscow architect, altered the original conception by adding another tier to the bell tower and two chapels on either side of the main church. Nowadays soldiers are helping with repairs after the years of neglect and the church is functioning again.

Enter by the gate next to the church and walk across the meadow heading left, ignoring the modern building with weird antennae and the yellow brick sanatorium in the hollow. There, set against trees, is the beautiful round **mausoleum of the Orlov family** in red brick with stone portico and ornament. Sympathetic restoration completed in 1994 means that in contrast to so many dilapidated places it is gleaming and perfect. It was commissioned by Anna Orlova, Alexei's daughter, and designed 1832-5 by Domenico Gilardi but built by his cousin, Alexander Gilardi. It is the epitome of the Empire style, with its round form, plain pediment, Doric columns and rusticated walls even though the niches remained empty and the bas-reliefs representing victory were never executed. Recently, a modern bronze angel has been mounted over the pediment. The circular interior, the chapel of the Assumption, *Uspeniya*, is defined by paired Ionic columns. In the basement are the grave stands and plaques listing the Orlovs who were buried there. In 1937 when the estate was handed over to the NKVD the bodies were literally thrown out.

Permission is needed from the sanatorium director to view the fenced-in palace in poor condition guarded by soldiers. A lion (originally there were two) grins from one gate where the initials, 'O D' for Orlov-Davydov, are inscribed in the ironwork. The palace was built in 1775–9 under the careful scrutiny of the serf-architect Babakin, to the design, it is believed, of Karl Blank. It is of two storeys, heavily vaulted, with a deep basement. The facade of red brick strongly contrasting with the white cornices and rhythmically placed windows is neither stuccoed nor fronted with columns in the usual Russian manner but resembles, rather, English stately homes of the period – Vladimir and his grandson travelled widely in Britain. Semicircular curved ends on east and west face inwards as if protecting the main palace but so many additions – porches and orangeries – were later grafted on that the effect is almost lost. In front a fountain sent up a stream as tall as the palace. Across the Lopasnya River, Orlov laid out a large park in the English, natural manner. Since the 1930s this area has been built up with dachas for political leaders, first the Party *nomenklatura*, and nowadays new Russian politicians. It is therefore still inaccessible to the public.

The ground floor of the main house was mostly devoted to the extensive library, now in the Russian State Library. The finest rooms, round, oval and square, were on the second floor richly decorated with fine mouldings, laid with intricate parquet flooring, and provided with tiled stoves of which one remains. The ceilings were painted by Karl Briullov, a fashionable salon artist. The exquisite orangeries with terracotta reliefs, one on either side of the main house facing the park, were built in 1848 by Mikhail Bykovsky, the neo-Renaissance Moscow architect. Even the service quarters and pavilions that flank the palace fit into the overall design. The greenhouses to the left were so successful that peaches could be ripened in April and sent to the family in their winter quarters in Petersburg.

THE SHEREMETIEV DOMAINS

Take the Kashira Highway M-4/M-6 80 km and turn left at the GAI post onto the A-108. Travel 20 km to Fominka and turn right 2 km to

CHIRKINO. This lofty place is the cradle of the illustrious Sheremetiev family. A wide grassy lane flanked by 20 wooden houses leads to two tall tiered churches commanding a view of the broad valley of the Sukusha. The eastern church, the **Intercession**, *Pokrova*, the oldest, was built in the early 16th century but reconstructed twice – in the late 16th century and at the end of the 17th. The second, taller **Church of St Basil**, *Vasiliya*, the bell tower and mausoleum (for **Vasily Sheremetiev**) were built at the end of the 17th century. The two churches, which were closed in 1938, are both in ruins, lacking windows and doors, with huge holes in the apses and the cupolas in perilous state. In the Intercession sheep and goats take shelter from the hot summer sun.

Chirkino was granted to the **Sheremetievs** by Ivan the Terrible. A century later in 1660 Boyar Vasily Sheremetiev, commander of Tsar Alexei's army, was captured by Polish forces and maliciously handed over to their Tatar allies who demanded such a high ransome that he remained their prisoner for 20 years. On his return, he elected to live his remaining years in his peaceful village. He rebuilt the old church in the prevailing Moscow baroque style, an octagonal on a cube, and constructed the second church as the family mausoleum, also in Moscow baroque but with three diminishing octagonal towers, so that it rises higher than the first church. He did not leave Chirkino to his daughter, Anna, who had married a Golitsyn, but to his nephew, Boris, the grandee and first Russian Field Marshal, owner of Kuskovo and Ostankino and also of neighbouring Meshcherino. The Chirkino estate remained in the Sheremetiev family until the revolution.

When we arrived in mid-summer the village street was lively with people repairing their houses, airing their bedding, drying clothes, chopping nettles for soup, and keeping an eye on the children. A retired colonel and self-appointed local historian told us he was a boy when the church was closed but remembered that many valuable books had been kept in the basement of St Basil's. Curiously, it seems that in the 1890s the tomb of Vasily Sheremetiev was taken out of St Basil's, opened (the body was wrapped in birchbark), and moved to the Church of the Intercession. Although the village is only inhabited in summer, most of the residents were either born there or had some historical connection with Chirkino.

From the Kashira Highway turn left onto the A-108 27 km to **MESHCHERINO**, *left, or from the parallel Ryazan Road turn right onto the A-108 14 km to Meshcherino.* Follow the straight but bumpy road through the arch of hot-water pipes to the tall, ochre-coloured church.

The brick **Church of the Nativity of the Virgin**, *Rozhdestva Bogoroditsy*, was built at the end of the 17th century for Count Boris Sheremetiev, owner of Chirkino and close associate of Peter the Great. His son, the pious and eccentric **Count Sergei**, liked to wear tattered clothes and spend his time praying and caring for the poor. Another pious owner, Yakov Yermakov, a former serf of the Sheremetievs, purchased Meshcherino from them and founded a textile factory. In 1845 he added the large dome, altered the windows, and reconstructed the *trapeza* and bell tower. Known for his charitable works, Yermakov built a poor house in Meshcherino, the long building west of the church, with bricks from the dismantled main house. It later served as the library and House of Culture.

From Meshcherino turn right onto the A-108, cross the Severka River and at the top of the hill turn left onto an unmarked road. After 2 km at the approach to a military town(straight ahead are sinister-looking discs and strange installations) turn left. Ignore the barrier on the left and follow the increasingly poor road down an incline and along fields whence, on the right, the pyramid-shaped church at **GORODNYA** *(Zevapovo on the map) comes into view. Turn right onto the poor concrete road and in another 500 metres is the church, right.*

The beautifully proportioned **Resurrection**, *Voskreseniya*, is a superb example of the tent-shaped *shatrovy* style tower church. It was built sometime before 1578 by the Sheremetievs following the tenets laid down for wooden churches: an octagonal base from which the thick walls of the tower, also 8-sided, taper subtly to finish at the cupola and cross. The porch surrounding the octagon on three sides was given another storey in the late 17th century by Prince Yakov Odoevsky and enclosed to form a gallery with two more chapels on either side of the principal altar. On our first visit it was distressing to find such an important building in poor condition. But two years later services had restarted in the basement chapel and repairs were underway: holes in the walls filled in and new window frames installed. It is astonishing that this 16th century building, recognised as of first importance in all the architectural manuals, had been so neglected.

As above but ignore the right turn for Gorodnya and go on 1 km to **FEDOROVSKOE**, *on the banks of the Severka River.* It is a small attractive place dominated by the baroque **Church of St Nicholas**, built in 1754 by A.F. Sheremetiev of white limestone rather than the usual brick with finely carved baroque windows. An octagonal on a cube, its ground plan is a four-cusped figure in which three sides bulge out from the core most attractively. Unfortunately the large and tactless 19th century *trapeza* and bell tower in clashing red brick obscure the west end. Recently rededicated, the only furnishing within was an altar made from a simple table with a white cloth hanging behind. The village in summer was full of visitors including young girls who were leaping gaily from the wooden bridge into the Severka.

The oldest of the Sheremetiev lands is found at **Prusy**, a tiny place not far from Gorodnya and Chirkino, but approached from the Ryazan Road.

Take the Ryazan Road, M-5, 91 km to Nepetsino and turn right on an unsigned road at the bridge over the Severka River. At 8 km, after crossing the railway line and the river and negotiating the dreary pig breeding settlement, Industria, is **Shkin**. Its glory is the once splendid **Church of the Holy Spirit**, *Dukha Svyatavo*, now under repair, probably the work of Rodion Kazakov. The church was completed in 1800 in the classical style in the shape of a Latin cross with a massive rotunda over the transept and elegant north and south porticoes at the arms. Twin towers on either side of the western entrance act as belltowers. This magnificent church, so out of place in the run-down village, was constructed for General Gavril Bibikov.

Take the bumpy dirt road, right, and cross the Severka River by the dubious lower section of a precarious bridge and continue 2 km to **PRUSY** *right*. Here the ancient tent-shaped **Church of St Elijah**, *Ilii*, is surrounded by old and new dachas. It has no windows or doors but the roof is complete although there is a terrible crack and hole in the apse. An early example of a masonry octagonal tower, it rests uncomfortably on the cube with no intervening stage to soften the transition. The ogee-shaped porticoes and decorated windows are of the 17th century. Inside you can look straight up the bare walls (they were not painted originally) to the inner side of the small cupola.

St Elijah was built by the early Sheremetiev nobles who received this land from Ivan the Terrible sometime in the mid 16th century – certainly before 1578 when it is recorded that the village passed to the Bishop of Kolomna. The Sheremetievs named it Prusy after their supposed ancestral home in Prussia. In their coat of arms (two lions holding orb and sceptre) it is mentioned that 'the forebears of the Sheremetievs in Prussy were sovereign *vladiteli*'.

SOUTH TO STUPINO

Travel the Kashira Highway, M-4/M-6, 85 km from Moscow and 10 km south of Mikhnevo to **KIYASOVO**. The name probably derives from the 16th century Prince Vasily (Kiyas) Meshchersky, whose grandson owned the village. The picturesque **Church of the Kazan Virgin**, *Kazanskoi Ikony Bozhiei Materi*, stands enticingly to the left surrounded by fencing behind the shop and war memorial. For decades a grey miserable heap, since it was returned to the church it has been transformed: the cupolas have gradually reappeared, and the roof and four-tier bell tower renewed. Built in the early 1700s, it bypassed the Moscow baroque period entirely in favour of the picturesque churches of the mid 17th century with its triple bay, five cupolas, north chapel, and bell tower.

Six km south of Kiyasovo is the strangely named Sitne-Shchelkanovo, perhaps from the Tatar Khan Shchelkan. Turn left at Psarevo to Zhilevo across the main railway line and continue for 2 km across a branch railway line which loops back and forth. Take the next left turn signed KOLYCHEVO, *cross the stream then turn left and right 2 km to* **VERZILOVO**

At Verzilovo on the Kashirka River, are the remnants of a bustling 18th century estate owned 1825-9 by **Prince Fedor Shakhovskoy**, a leading Decembrist known as 'Le Tigre'. The modest early 19th century house on the south, right side of the river, used in Soviet times as a school, is now only a brick ruin. Straight ahead and across the river is the better kept **Church of the Transfiguration**, *Preobrazheniya*, built in the early 18th century. An octagonal on a cube, whitewashed with light blue cupolas, it is very pretty, especially in the cosy context of the priest's house where washing hangs on the line and domestic gear is scattered around. Two ladies busily cleaning the church as they have done for 40 years told us that in the 1930s parishioners daring to attend services were arrested and put in prison for a few days as a discouragement. The church was only briefly closed just before the war and is all in order with a tall iconostasis, two stoves on either side of the door, and masses of polished brass.

On the Kashira Highway after Sitne-Shchelkanovo take the left fork to Stupino, go under the railway line and turn left towards Malino 5 km to **STARAYA SITNYA**. This good, quiet road runs parallel to the Kashira Highway through fine countryside. At the corner shop leave the car and take the cobbled path across a bridge over the gurgling Kashirka to the unusual **Church of the Nativity of the Virgin**, *Rozhdestva Bogoroditsy*, where cherubs sport around the windows and entrances with delightful abandon.

Built in 1767 for an estate, the rich baroque reflects the taste of the reign of Empress Elizabeth. It was originally symmetrical – the square apse and the *trapeza* match one another – but the later bell tower and unfortunate south chapel flout this harmony. The curve of the baroque, however, continues upwards to the drum and cupola and in its original light colour it must have struck a joyous note in the rather sombre village. An elderly lady told us that when she and her family arrived in 1934 the church was already closed and in use as a storehouse by the newly-founded state farm. In the 1960s villagers began stealing bricks from the crumbling building for their houses. But a priest has recently appeared, services are taking place and volunteers are bent on repairing the building.

From the Kashira Road take the left fork after Sitne-Shchelkanovo to reach **STUPINO** *on the Oka River, 99 kilometres from Moscow.* For Andropov Street, the main thoroughfare, turn left away from the railway line, then right and left again. Founded in 1932, Stupino is a purely Soviet town based on machine-building and metallurgical factories. It was notorious for its Stakhanovite super-workers whose contrived production levels were impossible for ordinary workers to achieve. Nevertheless, there are some interesting Soviet apartment blocks on Andropov Street and a fine **Palace of Culture** with the obligatory statue of Lenin. The Stupino museum at No 61 contains the collection of household documents from the Orlov estate at Semenovskoe. At Srednee, in the eastern suburbs, is the **Church of the Tikhvin Icon of the Virgin**, *Tikhvinskoi Ikony Bozhiei Materi*, the sole functioning church in the Stupino area in the Soviet period.

On entering Stupino turn left across the busy railway line (there are very few crossings), then follow the parallel road towards the Oka and after 2 km cross another railway line ignoring the turn to Ozery until the **Trinity Belopesotsky Monastery** *appears across the little Kremechenki River.* Founded in 1498 it was an important defence outpost for the tsars in their struggle against the Tatars. In 1681 the monastery was linked to the powerful Kolomna archbishopric and an intensive building period was inaugurated during which the cathedral and walls and towers were rebuilt. Although Belopesotsky was a powerful and rich monastery in its time, by the early 20th century there were only 26 monks in residence supported by only 226 desyatins (about 600 acres) of land. It was not closed until the late 1920s.

Until recently the old monastery was a service and repair station for heavy lorries, which crowded the forecourt. But the walls are now gleaming with whitewash and over them towers the magnificent 17th century **Cathedral of the Trinity**, *Troitsy*. Built over a lower floor gallery, it is a tall cube topped with five onion domes and has a marvellous porch. The refectory **Church of St Sergius**, built in 1804 on 16th century foundations, and the perfectly balanced oval-shaped **St John** in Empire style of the first half of the 19th century, are located in the south-eastern corner, newly painted and functioning again. Near these churches on the east wall is the oldest building, the 16th century former Holy Gate, now blocked up, with the small and rather plain **Church of St Nicholas** and 18th century bell tower. The monastery was handed back at Easter 1993 as a convent and the nuns are now applying themselves to the daunting task of reconstruction.

BY THE OKA

Across the railway at Stupino take the road east signed OZERY parallel with the Oka River. Soon, by a minor railway line, is the striking red brick ruin of the classical **Church of the Sign**, *Ikony Bozhiei Materi 'Znamenie', built in 1816 at* **Staraya** (Old) **Kashira**. *In the early 17th century Kashira was moved to the higher bank across the river. Immediately past Staraya Kashira turn left signed GORODISHCHE and continue 7 km to a T- junction and turn right to the village of Nivki then 2 km farther to the dacha village of* **SUKOVO** *where the good road ends.* On the right is the run-down **Church of the Kazan Virgin**, *Kazanskoi Ikony Bozhiei Materi*, built in 1745, the spire of its belltower now leaning dangerously but still with its fine cross. The house has gone – the buildings flanking the church are the late 18th century stable and service building. The estate belonged in the middle of the 19th century to E.A. Yaroslavova whose attractive classical house in Moscow on Myasnitskaya was used as Stalin's headquarters in the war.

In Sukovo take the dirt road to the farm and join the bumpy track going east 2½ km to the small river at **ALESHKOVO**. On the raised bank opposite artlessly set out against a carpet of green are the red brick roofless ruins of a considerable estate – the gate, mansion, service buildings and school poke up through the nettles and tall grasses while above are the stable block and church. Only a jeep or a Niva should attempt the passage across the shallow stream and up the steep bank.

Aleshkovo was built at the beginning of the 19th century. Of its many buildings only the stable/carriage house – where the high central section with the huge semicircular window was for carriages – and the church situated higher up still have their roofs. However, the **Church of the Assumption**, *Uspeniya*, built in 1819, is unusually interesting. It is composed of three roughly oval east-west forms under a broad dome and drum. Three apses at the east end mirror three rounded forms at the west and handsome Doric porticoes flank the church on north and south. This symmetry is tactfully interrupted by the two-tiered bell tower linked to the church by an enclosed passageway. It is good to know that the church is to be reopened.

The estate passed through the female line from P.A. Novikova, under whom it was built, through the Kozhins to Novoseltsev, a local merchant, who lost it at gambling to the Shcherbakovs. The last Shcherbakov owner, who was over 2 metres tall, founded the local fire brigade. When the Bolsheviks arrived, he invited them in and gave them the keys to Aleshkovo. In return he was made captain of the fire brigade for the rest of his life which apparently suited him very well. Meanwhile, Aleshkovo became a labour colony for homeless children and then in the 1930s a state farm known for its amateur plays produced in the main house. In the 1960s when the farm moved its headquarters to Gorodishche, the buildings began seriously to deteriorate.

Continue along the river road to **Ozery***, another textile town, and turn right at the* **Trinity Church** *(1851) to cross the Oka on a fragile-looking pontoon bridge. Follow the road 4 km then turn left signed POLURYA-DENKI. Ten km on, just past Poluryadenki, turn left at the T-junction 4 km to Sosnovka.* At tiny **SOSNOVKA** (little pine) on the high bank of the Oka two churches stand side by side facing the river. The larger red brick **All Saints**, *Vsekh Svyatykh*, was built at the turn of the century in the popular pseudo-Byzantine style probably to compete with its older neighbour which in 1883 had become an Old Believer church. Although it is in poor state, a recent sign proclaims it to be a monument of architecture and there are plans for its rejuvenation.

Its neighbour, the ramshackle wooden church with pitched roof and single cupola leaning at a dangerous angle, is the **Intercession**, *Pokrova,* built in 1784 in traditional style where the three sections of *trapeza*, main church and pentagonal apse are equal in size. The logs are faced with weatherboarding outside and within are planed to make smooth walls. In the 1920s when both churches were closed the local club took over the Intercession which began to deteriorate although superficial repairs were occasionally carried out – in 1985 student volunteers patched up the roof. Now empty, its future is uncertain.

Return to Poluryadenki and continue east 5 km to **SENNITSY**. At the war memorial turn left to the red brick church, **the Ascension**, *Voznese-niya*, standing by itself in a field and now under renovation. It was built in 1709 for Prince Matvei Gagarin, a commander in the army of Peter the Great and Governor of Siberia. Gagarin's addiction to bribes incurred the wrath of the Tsar, and even the intercession of the Tsarina did not save him from execution in 1721. Also owner of Stepa-novskoe near the Ryazan Road, he has left this fine tower church 'under the bells' in the Moscow baroque style. High above the deep foundation round cusps extend from the cube on three sides like a clover-leaf, the fourth squared for the entrance. The cube supports two diminishing octagonals, each with a gallery enclosed by a balustrade the upper containing apertures for the bells, which culminate in drum and cupola.

The Gagarins ruled Sennitsy until the middle of the 19th century when it was acquired by the Princes Shakhovskoy. Of the magnificent old estate virtually no buildings apart from the church have survived and the park across the little Sennitsa river is very overgrown. Some of the estate furnishings have found their way to the museum in Zaraisk including a portrait of Princess Shakhovskaya by Leon Bakst.

LUKHOVITSY

From Zaraisk east to Lukhovitsy or via the Kolomna bypass on the Ryazan Highway M-5 across the new bridge over the Oka to Lukhovitsy, about 140 km from Moscow.

Lukhovitsy, population 30,000, straddles the Ryazan Road near the old boundary beween the Moscow and Ryazan provinces. At **SUSHKOVO**, in western Lukhovitsy on the road to Zaraisk (turn right at the cross-roads if coming from Kolomna) is a rare wooden church, the **Kazan Virgin**, *Kazanskoi Ikony Bozhiei Materi*, a heavy octagonal on a cube with a low, broad *trapeza*. Built of logs in 1754 by the owner of the village, I.V. Svechin, the church was faced in the 19th century, with weatherboarding and is painted a deep blue. Both the church and the tiered bell tower finish in long slim spires atop the domes making an elegant focus for the small wooden houses of the suburb. It remained open in the Soviet period but the iconostasis, which was contemporary with the church, was removed in the 1960s.

Continue 5km on the road to Zaraisk and turn right signed **TROITSKIE BORKI** *3 km.* The first sight is of a large new *kottedzh* in red brick with crenellated walls like a mini-Kremlin, which even has underground parking. But in summer children lark about in the long ponds just as they always did and in the distance across the water is the attractive dilapidated **Church of the Trinity**, *Troitsy*, built in 1774 and now under repair. The main cube lit by three rows of windows and the vaulted steeply pitched roof finishes at the baroque lantern and cupola.

ZARAISK

From the Ryazan Highway M-5 via the Kolomna bypass cross the Oka River and turn left at Lukhovitsy to Zaraisk, in all 165 km. It can also be approached via the Kashira Road crossing the Oka at Ozery.

Zaraisk, population 30,000, is an ancient fortified town that escaped the heavy industrialisation of the late 19th century and the Soviet period and has remained a quiet backwater. This is partly because the main Moscow-Ryazan Road in 1847 was relocated 30 km east, and the main railway line also avoids the town.

Zaraisk was founded at the confluence of the Osetr River and its tributary, the tiny Monastyrka, about the 13th century as part of the Ryazan princedom. A century later it joined forces with the powerful Moscow princes. The Kremlin walls and towers built of masonry in 1528-31 were put to the test four years later in 1535 and again in 1541 when Tatar attacks were successfully repulsed. The town was laid out on a grid pattern in the 18th century. Leave the car by the Kremlin gate for the one-way traffic system is confusing. *(If arriving from Lukhovitsy, leave the car at Sovietskaya Street left of the traffic light.)*

At the end of a row of wooden houses the **KREMLIN** is most attractively situated on a high plateau overlooking the Osetr River and rolling countryside. Of brick and stone with a tower at each of the four corners and three gates, it forms an almost perfect square instead of the usual

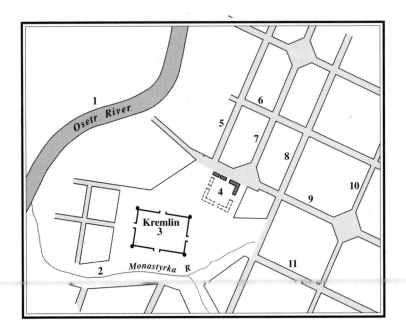

ZARAISK   1. Osetr River, 2. Monastyrka River, 3. Kremlin,
4. Market Place, 5. Pervomaiskaya, 6. Leninskaya,
7. Krasnoarmeiskaya, 8. Karl Marx, 9. Sovietskaya,
10. Dzerzhinskaya, 11. Komsomolskaya

irregular contour. This site is very ancient; just outside the main
Nikolsky Gate in 1994 archeologists dug up the tusks of a great
mammoth.

Within is a large, almost empty grassy enclave filled only with two
churches and a few school buildings. Directly in front is the heavy
recently returned **Church of St John the Baptist**, *Ioanna Predtechi*, built
in 1821, its facade reworked in the early 20th century and for many
years the local cinema. To the left is a charming new belfry, *zvonnitsa*.
But across the way in the southeast corner is the newly restored shining
white **Cathedral of St Nicholas**. Built of brick in 1681 by Tsar Fedor
Alexeevich it is a traditional church with an elaborate portal, its walls
divided into three bays finished by a rich cornice and gables (now
hidden). For five hundred years the great iron crosses have stood atop
the five cupolas.

The cathedral was closed after the revolution but began functioning again in late 1991. Some of the 1912 oil paintings survive but its once glorious baroque iconostasis has been lost and a modern one replaces it. The great treasure of Zaraisk was the wonder-working icon, St Nicholas of Korsun (Khersones in the Crimea) for which the first St Nicholas was built. The icon hung in the cathedral until after the revolution and is now in the Tretyakov Gallery. Copies are called *Nikola Zaraisky*.

Outside the walls a small graveyard left of the entrance was chosen by the Bolsheviks for burial of leading Zaraisk communists. On the wall is an odd declaration in black letters on red from the early years of Soviet rule urging the citizenry to refrain from sentimentality for the dead: *'The dead do not need songs or tears. Honour them in a different way. Walk among the dead without fear, carry forward their banner.'*

An interesting walk around the harmonious **OLD TOWN** of two-storey mostly masonry houses interrupted by tall churches can take about an hour. The trading rows, or old market place, part of which were built in the early 19th century, stand to the east of the Kremlin gate in Revolyutsyi Square. Facing them is the tall run-down brick **Church of the Trinity**, *Troitsy*, built in two periods, 1776 and 1778. It is typical of the three tall churches which are all that have survived in Zaraisk out of the 16 functioning before the revolution. Inside, the church has been divided into two floors to accommodate the town museum, which has interesting paintings from the estate at Sennitsy. *Open 10 to 5, closed Tuesdays.*

Pervomaiskaya Street, north of the Kremlin at the traffic light, has fine 19th century houses and two older mansions, No 45 built at the end of the 18th century, right, and the early 19th century mansion, No 26, left. Turn right down **Leninskaya** to see the **Church of St Elijah**, *Ilii*, on the left still being used as a workshop. It was built in 1819 and is heavily classical with porticoes and an immense rotunda. The pseudo-Russian bell tower was completed half a century later. Look back to see the brick **water tower** built 1914 in the centre of the square a block north. On the opposite corner is a fine town house with a porch which has recently been restored.

Continue on Leninskaya to the corner of the next street, **Karl Marx**, noting No 33/19, the early 19th century Loktev mansion. Turn right (south) on Karl Marx for the old school and an interesting house on the right. Turn east down **Sovietskaya Street** for the former red and white **Zemstvo** (local government) building built in 1910. The *Zemstvos*, set up by Alexander II's reforms, provided remarkably good government at local level although their powers were severely limited. Around the corner and backing onto it is the modern glass local government building built by the Communist Party which blends well in colour and height. Opposite the *Zemstvo* on the corner is a fine half-brick, half-timbered 19th century merchant's house where the descendant of an Englishman taken prisoner at the Battle of Poltava lived in the 1890s. In the centre of this main square is the ubiquitous **Lenin** surrounded by the inevitable blue firs.

Turn left from the Square on **Dzerzhinskaya Street**. At No 38 is the house, now an interesting museum, that was the childhood home of the sculptress, **Anna Golubkina** (*closed Mondays*). Golubkina, who studied with Rodin in Paris, is one of the most important Russian sculptors of the early years of this century. The museum is more interesting for the insights into her early years and her large and impoverished family than for the sculptures, mostly copies, that are displayed there. If it is closed go to the other side of the house to the Zaraisk cultural department and make enquiries.

Turn right at the Square to go south on **Dzerzhinskaya Street**. Note the solid 19th century houses, Nos 51, 54 and 65. On the opposite corner is another splendid tall church, with baroque windows in three rows and a tall elegant bell tower. This is the **Church of the Annunciation**, *Blagovesh-cheniya*, begun in 1777 and completed only at the beginning of the 19th century. It is now holding religious services again, the second active church in Zaraisk. Behind it on a small hill on Dzerzhinskaya St is an interesting black marble tablet, a memorial to the soldiers who fell in the struggle to free Zaraisk from the Poles in 1608. Return west along Komsomolskaya Street to the Kremlin.

Across the Osetr River turn left signed SEREBRYANYE PRUDY for 10 km, then turn right for MONOGAROVO, cross a stream and turn left down a track and a dam. The green wooden house is all that is left of the Dostoevsky estate of **DAROVOE** where Fedor Dostoevsky spent the summers as a child. His father, Mikhail, was so cruel to his serfs that they murdered him, an event reflected in Dostoevsky's portrayal of the father in *The Brothers Karamazov*. Nearby is a statue of the writer put up in 1993. Dostoevsky's father is buried by the ruined church in Monogarovo.

KASHIRA

Cross the Oka on the Kashira Highway 110 km from Moscow where the road divides into the M-4 and the M-6. At the end of the bridge turn right and right again to Kashira. At traffic lights turn left on Sovietskaya Street into the town centre.

Old Kashira (Staraya Kashira), a fortress on the opposite, low left bank of the Oka, was burnt to the ground by the Tatars in 1571. In the 1620s, when the Tatar threat had receded, the Polish invasion defeated and the new dynasty of the Romanovs had gained the throne, Kashira fortress was built anew on the high right bank of the Oka. It soon lost its military significance and became a provincial centre and port.

From Kashira goods could easily be conveyed to Kaluga, Ryazan and Nizhny Novgorod on the Oka and to Moscow on the 'dry' road. Even

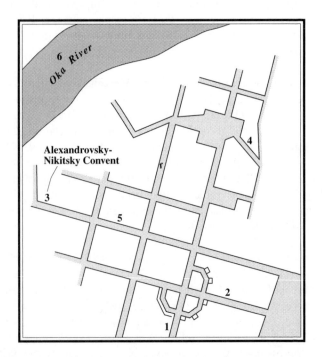

KASHIRA   1. Sovietskaya, 2. Karl Marx, 3. Alexandrovsky-Nikitsky Convent, 4. Volodarskovo, 5. Svobody, 6. Oka River

today when traffic on the river is much diminished, the port still operates. Kashira grew rich from the river trade and in the early 19th century was rebuilt in the typical grid design and embellished with remarkably similar classical churches which still provide the main focal points among the predominantly low wooden houses. All the thorough-fares seem to face the broad Oka which here circles around the high plateau on which the town is located. Everywhere there are wonderful views across to the low green meadows of the left bank.

Kashira today, population 44,000, is a small and charming town. The spacious junction of **Sovietskaya** and **Karl Marx St**, once encircled by trading rows, is watched over by the rotunda **Church of the Presentation**, *Vvedeniya*, with enormously tall bell tower built 1801–17. Occupying the northeast corner is an early Soviet cinema built in 1931 and still functioning, its salmon pink concave facade influenced by the construc-tivist style. Farther away from the river on Sovietskaya is the handsome **bank**, built 1940 in pure Soviet classical style with pediment and rusti-cated walls. A little east on Karl Marx Street the **Church of the Ascension**, *Vozneseniya*, built in 1826-42, closely resembles the Presenta-tion Church.

The remains of the **Alexandrovsky-Nikitsky Convent** lie in a pleasant residential area west of Sovietskaya Street. *From Sovietskaya turn left onto Svobody St to where the land begins to drop away.* The red brick, pseudo-Russian cathedral built 1894 by Vladislav Grudzin is now in poor condition while the other chapels and convent buildings were assimilated into the sock factory next door. In 1941 when German troops came uncomfortably close and were halted just outside the city, the convent proved convenient for Kashira's military headquarters.

Back on Sovietskaya Street walk north towards the river to a little park on the left almost opposite the old red and white **Town Duma** (local council). Within the park surrounded by flower beds stands an empty pedestal which until 1993 supported the obligatory **Lenin**. The actor, Boris Shchukin, famous for his role of Lenin in Soviet films, came from Kashira. A little farther an extensive, single-storey wooden house contains the **town museum**. *Open 10am to 5pm except Fridays and the last Thursday in the month.*

Almost opposite the museum down a small lane is the **Church of St Nicholas Ratnovo** (warrior) named after the defenders of the early fortress. It was built in 1815 by a Mme Zhdanova and even in its ruined state the skill of the builder of the powerful rotunda is evident. Interesting medallions adorn the facade, and triple Venetian windows are placed rhythmically around the drum.

At the end of Sovietskaya Street at the escarpment overlooking the Oka is the oldest part of town, the site of the **Kremlin**, only remembered now by the monumental **Cathedral of the Assumption**, *Uspeniya*, built 1829-1842 long after the Kremlin walls had gone. Its donors were Kashira's wealthy merchants of whom Lepeshkin was the most prominent. The cathedral, composed like the other churches of a huge drum on a large cube, four small domes on the four corners, two porticoes and three-tier bell tower, and with a massive *trapeza*, is functioning once more and has been newly painted light green with a new roof.

Behind the cathedral away from the river is an interesting **merchant's house** of the late 19th century in restrained Gothic where the town museum will be transferred. On the opposite side of the road a long ochre and white two-storey building (7 Volodarskovo St) with baroque detailing turns out to be the **treasury** built in the second half of the 18th century and the oldest building in Kashira; it now seems to be communal apartments. Farther on the right, at Sovietskaya 49, is the **Zubkov house** with pilasters built in the late 18th century. Down the hill is a splendid viewpoint called *blyudechko* (saucer), from which to watch the river and admire the shining Belopesotsky Convent opposite.

About 6 km **EAST OF KASHIRA** on the lower road is the very first Soviet **electric power station** (GRES). Begun in 1919 in response to Lenin's call for electrification for the whole country and adapted to use the local poor quality coal, it was finally opened in June 1922 (Lenin who had visited the year before was too ill to attend). Now greatly expanded, it supplies Kolomna, Serpukhov and parts of Moscow with electricity.

Continue east on the poor road, sometimes paved and sometimes gravel, past stagnant ponds until the road begins to climb. At the top of the hill take the bumpy dirt road left to the small but ancient village of **Baskachi** *perched romantically high above the Oka.* A thoroughly ruined but nevertheless pleasing brick church with a small bell tower majestically commands the view. The **Church of the Epiphany**, *Bogoyavleniya*, was built in 1752 by Prince Meshchersky to the tenets of 17th century architecture with the merest suggestion of the baroque.

Just beyond Baskachi also on the high bank overlooking the Oka is the small estate of **Kropotovo**. Built in the late 19th century, the attractive wooden house clad with stucco is irregular in form, sometimes one storey and sometimes two, with finely carved window surrounds. The park reaches to the edge of the steep bank of the river.

WEST OF KASHIRA. *From the M-4/M-6 Kashira Highway cross the Oka and turn right and then left away from the bridge. Or from Kashira at the traffic lights on Sovietskaya Street turn right and cross the road bridge over the M-4/M-6. In less than 1 km in* **LIDY** *turn right signed DOM OTDYKHA KASHIRA*. At the end of the drive is the two-storey classical mansion of the Litvinovs, now a rest home, with a new roof. In the unrestrained greenery of the overgrown park at the back where the ground drops sharply away to the Oka River stands an enticing sculpture of a lady in her bathing costume. On this side of the house a fine portico affords glimpses of the water meadows on the other side of the Oka.

The house was built in 1910 – in the classical style fashionable in the decade before the revolution – for Vladimir Litvinov, who named it Lidy after his mother. Vladimir's father, **Nikolai Litvinov**, was in the 1880s adjutant to the two sons of Alexander II, the future Alexander III and Grand Prince Nikolai. Litvinov, who had no fortune, met in provincial Perm on a journey with the grand princes a wealthy merchant with an only daughter, 18-year-old Lidia. Litvinov soon proposed, no doubt seeing a way out of his problems, and she must have been attracted by the move from the provinces to St Petersburg. They had two sons and Litvinov, now a general, retired early to his estate at **Korystovo** 5 km from Lidy beyond Zendikovo (where there is the ruined stately home of the Princes Baryatinsky). Unfortunately General Litvinov's fine wooden house at Korystovo, which became a home for handicapped children, was razed to the ground in 1990. It is a great pity that in Russia so many local authorities regard wooden buildings as worthless relics of the past.

From Lidy continue west 8 km to the paved right turn to **TARASKOVO** *signed KASHIRSKY SOVKHOZ*. Follow it past the execrable farm buildings down the hill and turn right to the modest, decrepit **Church of the Kazan Virgin**, *Kazanskoi Ikony Bozhiei Materi*, built in 1780. Leave the car and walk up the hill to the roofless ruin of a once fine late 19th century **mansion**. A thrilling sight even in decline, the pointed gables, round towers and wild disregard for symmetry recall mansions in Gothic horror stories.

The **Glebov** family of Moscow built the fashionable Gothic house probably sometime in the 1890s for their summer house to accommodate their eight children. In 1900 Mikhail Tolstoy, youngest son of **Lev Tolstoy**, married Alexandra, the eldest daughter of the Glebov family. Lev, not the easiest of parents, objected to what he saw as the wanton display of wealth at the wedding and refused all invitations to Taraskovo although he was quite fond of his daughter-in-law. The young couple went their own way and in 1911 with the elder Glebovs founded a society to preserve ancient monuments in Tula province and published several illustrated books on the subject.

Bogoslovskoe just across the border in Tula Oblast is famous for its schools established in the early 20th century by educational reformers to provide education at all levels for all the peasant children in the area. Little is left except the delightful **Church of John the Divine**, *Ioanna Bogoslova*, built in 1910 in Art Nouveau style by the notable Petersburg architect, Mikhail Preobrazhensky.

Beyond the turning to Taraskovo turn left signed YELKINO 8 km then turn right signed **ZLOBINO**. *Leave the car and walk along the pond south and then right.* The Moscow baroque **Church of the Archangel Michael**, standing alone among wheat fields was built in 1715 at a time when all building work other than for the new Petersburg was forbidden. But powerful interests were at work here for it was built for a courtier of Peter the Great, I.P. Ivanchin-Pisarev, and Tikhon, his relative and abbot of the influential Saviour Monastery in Yaroslavl. Lush ornamentation of white limestone crosses at the windows and doors of the beautiful building is striking against the red brick. Its height is enhanced by the two drums, one on top of the other, which support the single cupola. Rows of old-fashioned gables, *kokoshniki*, are now hidden by the later roof. What a pity this lovely church stands idle and empty and certain to deteriorate.

Road 5

RYAZAN ROAD M-5: LYUBERTSY TO KOLOMNA AND YEGOREVSK

The southeast Ryazan Road follows the Moskva River as it flows towards its confluence with the Oka at the beautiful town of Kolomna. Beyond the industrial giants of Lyubertsy and Ramenskoe is pleasant dacha country, sprinkled with estates of the nobility. To the east the Gzhel potteries and Old Believer churches lead towards the textile town of Yegorevsk and the ancient royal fisheries.

Take Volgogradsky Prospekt to the MKAD where it becomes the Ryazan Road M-5.

ON THE MOSKVA

*On the M-5 turn right at the first exit signed DZERZHINSKY/ LYUBERTSY. At traffic lights, turn right (west) then left across the railway line. After 1 km turn left again signed BELAYA DACHA and follow the road left and then right to the church on a hill at **KOTELNIKI**.*

The **Church of the Kazan Virgin**, *Kazanskoi Ikony Bozhiei Materi*, was built 1675-80 for the royal gardeners who provided food for the Tsar, his family and their many retainers in the Kremlin. With its *kokoshniki* gables, five domes and gallery (now gone) it resembled the elaborate royal church at Taininskoe. It is said that the boy tsars, Peter and Ivan, with their sister the Regent Sophia, attended the church at its consecration. In 1837 Alexander Gilardi, cousin of the better known Domenico, remodelled the interior and built the pyramidal bell tower in traditional style. In Soviet times the upper parts of the church were removed and an incongruous cement cylinder was hoisted atop the truncated bell tower for the local water supply. The neighbouring army base further abused the building but in 1992, in this wrecked hulk, services were resumed. Two years later the water tower had gone, a new roof was installed and finally, in 1997, the domes were back in place. A new iconostasis and fresh paint has transformed the interior although not to Gilardi's standard.

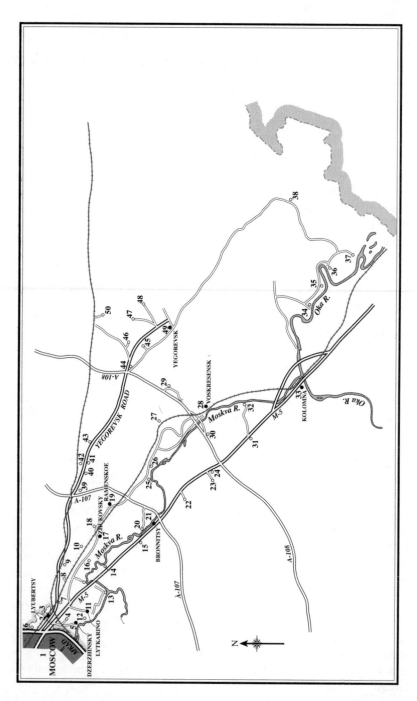

ROAD 5
LYUBERTSY TO KOLOMNA AND YEGOREVSK

1. MOSCOW
2. LYUBERTSY
3. Natashino
4. Kotelniki
5. DZERZHINSKY
6. Kosino
7. Zhilino
8. Kraskovo
9. Malakhovka
10. Udelnaya
11. LYTKARINO
12. Petrovskoe
13. V. Myachkovo
14. Mikhailovskaya Sloboda
15. Krivtsy
16. Bykovo
17. ZHUKOVSKY
18. Kratovo
19. RAMENSKOE
20. Markovo
21. BRONNITSY
22. Tatarintsevo
23. Stepanovskoe
24. Nikitskoe
25. Mikhalevo

26. Faustovo
27. Konobeevo
28. VOSKRESENSK
29. Ostashevo
30. Fedino
31. Nepetsino
32. Cherkizovo
33. KOLOMNA
34. Dedinovo
35. Lyubichi
36. Lovtsy
37. Belocmut
38. Ryazanovsky

39. Gzhel
40. Rechitsy
41. Novo Kharitonovo
42. Ignatevo
43. Karpovo
44. Ilinsky Pogost
45. Aleshino
46. Ustyanovo
47. Krasny Tkach
48. Ryzhevo
49. YEGOREVSK
50. Rudnya-Nikitskoe

Turn right from the M-5 signed DZERZHINSKY/LYUBERTSY and then right west to **Dzerzhinsky**. Closing the road is the strange brick wall like a weird medieval cityscape of the **NIKOLAEVSKY-UGRESHSKY MONASTERY**. In fact it is an idealised representation of Jerusalem built in 1866 when the monastery was extended.

In 1380 Moscow's Grand Prince, **Dmitry Donskoy**, experienced a vision of St Nicholas on his way to the famous Battle of Kulikovo and is reputed to have called out in ecstasy *'ugresha'* (this sets my heart aflame) and founded a monastery on the very spot. In the 17th century **Tsar Alexei** made so many pilgrimages here that a special palace was built for him and the patriarch. The monastery was also used as a temporary prison for **Archpriest Avvakum**, the fanatical Old Believer opposed to the reforms of Patriarch Nikon (see p.54). A century later, in 1771 a hospital for sufferers of Moscow's last plague was established here. In the mid 19th century under **Abbot Pimen** the territory was doubled and a gigantic new cathedral was erected. Closed in 1920, the monastery at the behest of **Felix Dzerzhinsky**, head of the secret police, became a camp for the many homeless children, *besprizorniki*, then living on the streets of Moscow and the town was renamed Dzerzhinsk (now Dzerzhinsky). Later the children's home was reorganised as a labour commune where the inhabitants were obliged to perform 'productive labour'.

Beginning in the 1930s rapid industrialisation transformed Dzerzhinsk but the present forbidding forest of chimney stacks and tower blocks gives way before the charm of the monastery. It has recently taken on a new lease of life. The ambulance station, the clinic for venereal and skin diseases, the metal workshops have all gone, and reconstruction and paint are returning colour to the grey, pallid buildings. The huge, terribly dilapidated **Cathedral of the Transfiguration**, not the most beautiful of buildings, has been transformed by the reconstruction of its five gigantic cupolas painted in vivid orange and lemon hues.

Enter the **monastery grounds** by the gate left of the Jerusalem-Palestine wall. The oldest building, left, is the two-storey **17th century palace** for the tsar and patriarch, and later the abbot. Connected to it is the **Assumption**, *Uspeniya*, the old chapel royal in red and white with wonderful baroque windows, the first to return to worship. On the eastern inner side of the **Holy Gate** with its baroque bell tower of 1763 is the poorhouse with chapel and then, turning the corner, a line of two-storey monks' cells with florid baroque window designs followed by more monks' cells. Cattle graze in the dry bed of the large pond.

The most impressive building, the huge **Cathedral of the Transfiguration**, *Spasa Preobrazheniya*, stands in the centre of this ensemble. It was built 1880-94 by Alexander Kaminsky to the design of Boris Freidenberg, both eminent Moscow architects, in the Russo-Byzantine style – the cube, tripartite walls and heavy cupolas, reflecting the fashion for monumental churches introduced by Moscow's Christ the Saviour. The small 16th century **Cathedral of St Nicholas** huddled under the shadow of its huge younger brother on the northwest corner until it was destroyed in 1940. For a long time the new cathedral, its long narrow windows widened and divided, served as a sports hall and workshops. Its lordly appearance is now restored.

Near the apse of the cathedral stands a small round **chapel**, erected in 1893 in the reign of Alexander III, to commemorate the spot where Dmitry Donskoy was supposed to have had the vision of St Nicholas. The chapel has been newly gilded and its medallions of heads of saints repainted. Across the only remaining pond the bright blue of the wooden hermitage, *skit*, **Church of Sts Peter and Paul**, is reflected in the water. For long it resembled an ordinary wooden house but with the domes restored, repainted and re-gilded and a newly carved iconostasis within, it too has been reborn.

From the Ryazan Road M-5 take the second exit, right, signed LYTKARINO 5 km, a Soviet town constructed after the Second World War. Turn right signed SPORTIVNAYA ULITSA and then right again to Pervomaiskaya Street. Follow this to its end then left towards the Moskva River and right at the T-junction following the river to Petrovskoe.

PETROVSKOE in the 17th and 18th centuries belonged alternately to the rival Miloslavsky and Naryshkin families as their stars rose and fell with the reigning monarch. Later it was owned by the great mining magnate, Demidov, and finally, from 1890 to 1917, Prince Baryatinsky. The **main house**, now the local clinic, of which only the ground floor survives, is in the woods overlooking the river. Its wooden upper floor with painted ceilings was destroyed by fire in the 1930s and crudely rebuilt of brick in 1959. In the main square a tellingly empty plinth once held the figure of Felix Dzerzhinsky.

The large classical **Peter and Paul Church** built in 1805 by the Demidovs stands on the main road, left. It exudes a symphony of round forms in the circular main church with porticoes on north and south, the round apse, the rounded refectory and the round arches of the bell tower. In Soviet times a sports hall occupied the narthex and a shop operated in the apse. Services restarted in 1991.

In sharp contrast to Sts Peter and Paul is the small tent-shaped **St Nicholas** on the Moskva, built between 1680 and 1691 by Boyar Ivan Miloslavsky, supporter of the Regent Sophia and enemy of young Peter the Great and his Naryshkin relatives. The old-fashioned architecture of the church – the tent-shaped tower and charming roof belfry beautifully restored in the 1970s – reflects the conservative attitudes of the Miloslavskys as opposed to the Naryshkins' more progressive views. Of course when Peter won the crown, the estate and St Nicholas reverted to the Naryshkins. St Nicholas has been reactivated as a chapel augmenting the Peter and Paul Church.

From Lytkarino (or from the M-5) past the ugly sprawl of Turaevo with its charming Old Believer church turn right signed VERKHNEE MYACHKOVO past factories and concrete panelled fencing. Here on the Moskva River is the fine **Nativity of the Virgin**, *Rozhdestva Bogoroditsy*, which never closed. Built in 1770 of the excellent limestone, the Myachkov 'marble', which is quarried here, its main decorative feature is the stylised shells like Catherine wheels in the gables.

At Chulkovo on the Ryazan Road just after crossing the Moskva, the Russian commander, Kutuzov, stood on the hill, right, to watch Napoleon's troops leave Moscow by the Kaluga Road. Beyond Chulkovo past the GAI post, left, is the **Church of Michael the Archangel** at **Mikhailovskaya Sloboda** built in 1689 but extensively rebuilt in the 1830s in the late classical style. It belongs to the *Yedinovertsy*, the sect founded in the 19th century to bridge the gap between Old Believers and the Orthodox.

Continue on the M-5 to the 51 km post and the ancient village of **KRIVTSY**. It's impossible to miss the elegant **Church of the Smolensk Virgin**, *Smolenskoi Ikony Bozhiei Materi*, with its pale blue cupola. Built in 1708 for Prince Mikhail Volkonsky, it is a fine example of Moscow baroque. Composed of an octagon poised on a cube it has a voluptuous tripartite apse, the elaborate window designs of the period and a tall three-tier bell tower. The cube is of the famous white limestone from the Myachkovo quarry while the upper parts are brick with stone dressings.

As it remained open in the Soviet period, the 18th century iconostasis has survived.

On the Ryazan Road M-5 travel 58 km from Moscow to Bronnitsy past the 1870s red and white St Elijah on the right, now a do-it-yourself shop selling prefabricated dachas. The name **BRONNITSY**, population 20,000, derives from either *bronya*, armour, or *pole brani*, field of battle, both referring to the struggle against the Tatars. Regiments of musketeers were stationed here from earliest times and there is still a military presence. In the late 17th century a royal stud-farm, one of the first in Russia, was established in Bronnitsy giving rise to associated industries in leather goods and saddlery, still a local industry. By the late 18th century Bronnitsy had the status of a town but today, bypassed by the railway 12 km away, it retains a provincial air.

The **centre** of the town opens up into a broad attractive square with two churches and an immensely tall bell tower, left, and the village green bounded by shops and trading rows, right. The **Cathedral of the Archangel Michael**, was built 1696–1705, its tall white cube lit by three rows of richly embellished Moscow baroque windows crowned with five crowded onion domes on gabled drums. The tall church is in contrast to the single-storey *trapeza*, extended in 1865 in the same style, and the equally low eastern apse. The interior with plasterwork cartouches of flowers and plants has survived astonishingly well considering it was closed in the 1930s and only reopened 60 years later. The oldest icons of the carved 19th century iconostasis are in the Rublev Museum in Moscow but requests are now being made for their return.

Outside by the apse are the graves of two outstanding Decembrists, Mikhail Fonvizin and Ivan Pushchin. Their lives were inextricably intertwined not only by their Siberian exile but by their love for the same woman. Fonvizin's wife, Natalya, owner of an estate near Bronnitsy, loyally followed her husband to Siberia in 1826 returning only in 1853 when Fonvizin was amnestied by Alexander II. But he died within the year so she returned to Siberia, found Fonvizin's friend, Ivan Pushchin, brought him back to Bronnitsy and married him. Tragically Pushchin also died only two years later. The twice-widowed Natalya erected these poignant black crosses for her two husbands.

Next to the cathedral in contrasting style is the **Jerusalem Church**, *Ierusalimskoi Ikony Bozhiei Materi*, built in the 1840s by the Moscow architect, Alexander Shestakov, in the late, rather heavy classical style with rotunda, dome and portico. The enormously tall pseudo-Russian **bell tower**, erected by the Pushchin family, makes a poor foil for the churches given its extreme height. Behind the ensemble is the Moskva River where a small **gazebo** invites one to watch the passing boats.

Follow the Ryazan Road M-5 south from Bronnitsy to Starikovo and just past the 68 km post 3 km to the right is the quatrefoil baroque **Church of the Cross**, *Kresta, at* **Tatarintsevo** *built in 1737 and never closed. Continue to the 78 km post in Nikitskoe and turn right before the stream 3 km to* **STEPANOVSKOE**. An ancient church and idiosyncratic bell tower across a long pond rise, incongruously, out of the muddle of a dairy farm. The venerable **Annunciation**, *Blagoveshcheniya*, was built before 1578 for the boyar, Nikita Zakharin-Yuriev, brother of Anastasiya, Ivan the Terrible's first and most beloved wife, and grandfather of Mikhail, the first Romanov Tsar. The church, richly decorated in brick and stone, was largely rebuilt in the 1690s by the courtier, Mikhail Likhachev, in the Moscow baroque style, an octagon on a cube although the two side chapels survive from the older building.

The huge bell tower with **St Isaac of Dalmatia**, *Isaakiya Dalmatskovo*, which stands separately was built in 1702–3 by the then owner, **Prince Matvei Gagarin**, the first Governor-General of Siberia, later executed for taking bribes. As St Isaac's nameday falls on Peter the Great's birthday, the name of the church was a clever diplomatic choice but it was only dedicated in 1732 under another owner, Count Andrei Osterman. The immensely satisfying tower consists of the two-storey cube topped by another resting on the terrace of the first, followed by the octagonal bell tower mirroring the octagon of the older church, and completed by drum and cupola. Like the Annunciation, it is in desperate need of repairs.

On the Ryazan Road M-5 to **NIKITSKOE**, *at the 78 km post. Cross the stream, go up the hill and turn right on a narrow road across a small bridge.* Closing the end of this track is the former Soviet palace of culture bearing a large head of Lenin haughtily overlooked by an elegant red brick church.

The noble estate of Nikitskoe, first developed in the 1760s by the **Apraxins**, was reconstructed in the late 18th century by **Prince Kurakin**. It sits on the brow of the hill with park and ponds at the far, western end, the church at the centre, and the main house and domestic buildings by the stream. Now fallen into serious decay, only one of the low curving galleries attaching the **Apraxin House** to the wings remains. Behind, where the portico with its six Corinthian columns stands askew, the land drops away sharply to the stream on its way to the Moskva.

The **Church of the Vladimir Virgin**, *Vladimirskoi Ikony Bozhiei Materi*, built in the early 18th century, bears characteristics of Moscow baroque – the octagon on the cube, topped by the octagonal drum with fine window designs especially of the upper tier. The *trapeza* was added in 1838 and the apse in 1886. The splendid three-tier bell tower of the 1760s with its rare spire balances the church not only in baroque features but by the use of white stone and red brick. In June 1992, when we first came upon this place, it happened to be the very moment when the service for rededication was being celebrated and a great crowd filled the building singing and chanting in the dim candle light.

FROM LYUBERTSY TO MARKOVO

Take Ryazansky Prospekt out of Moscow to the centre of Lyubertsy then turn left for the railway station, left again parallel to the line and right over the humped-back one-way bridge straddling the line. Turn left on 8 March Street – the road winds past a pond left – to the wooden cemetery church.

LYUBERTSY, population 165,000, is a gruesome industrial town on Moscow's southeast boundary. Its social problems came to a head in the mid 1980s when young men, bored with their factory jobs, donned special uniforms and invaded Moscow at night terrorising the population. The 17th century Church of the Transfiguration in the centre of Lyubertsy was demolished in the 1930s and there is little here of special interest apart from the **Napoleon museum** and the attractive **wooden church** in the cemetery.

The inhabitants of **Natashino** (renamed Ukhtomsky) in 1912 argued successfully for a new church, pointing out that the churches in Lyubertsy and Kosino were full to overflowing. They were wiser than they knew for the neighbouring churches were either destroyed or closed and only their little church remained open. The picturesque **Church of the Trinity**, *Troitsy*, completed in 1913 by Mikhail Bugrovsky, is surrounded by wooden fencing and gates, its basic form a wooden frame in which logs are set horizontally. Pointed porches and exaggerated gables lead to the tent-shaped roof supporting the blue cupola surrounded by four subsidiary ones. Inside the church the heavy gilt decorations and the paintings are in the chocolate box manner of the period. It exudes cleanliness and order and even the toilets (the squatting type) are exemplary. It being a cemetery church, open coffins are often lying within awaiting the funeral service. Outside stand the rundown old buses that serve as hearses, one of the more distressing sights in Russia.

Take Ryazansky Prospekt and turn onto the MKAD going north. Leave at the first exit signed KOSINO and turn left at the T-junction onto B. Kosinskaya to the walled enclosure, left. **KOSINO**, just outside the MKAD close to Lyubertsy and now part of Moscow, is situated on two deep ice-age lakes, the White, *Beloe*, and Black, *Chernoe*, while a little to the south is the third of the group, the Holy, *Svyatoe*. The group of churches on the lakes makes a wonderful sight, not even spoiled by Moscow's high-rise towers poking up over the water.

Kosino's history is of tsars and icons and entrepreneurs. By the 17th and 18th centuries it belonged to the **Telepnev family** among whom were many ambassadors and advisors to the tsars. In the 1680s the young Tsarevich, **Peter**, excited to find an abandoned English sailing boat at Izmailovo, had it brought to the Kosino lakes to try his hand at sailing. After he had achieved some skill he took it to Pereslavl-Zalessky where the larger lake, Pleshcheevo, accommodated him better. This small boat known as the 'grandfather of the Russian fleet' is now in a museum in Petersburg. Later, when Peter became Tsar, he presented the villagers with the icon of the **Modena Virgin**, brought to Russia from Italy. It was placed in the Telepnevs' wooden church of St Nicholas and soon credited with miracles on the Holy Lake, attracting the inevitable pilgrims.

In 1814 the Telepnevs sold Kosino to Dmitry Lukhmanov, a merchant of the first guild. Under Lukhmanov the brick **Assumption**, *Uspeniya*, the free-standing **bell tower** with **St Nicholas** and the walls and towers were constructed. The village serfs took advantage of the fact that as a merchant Lukhmanov had no legal rights over them and petitioned Nicholas I to release them from bondage. At last, in 1851, the Tsar relented and the Kosino peasants received their freedom a decade before the rest of the Russian empire. Their joy was shortlived, however, for they were granted very poor land. In the 1880s another merchant, Mikhail Gorbachev (no relation), opened Kosino's first small factory producing ribbons, transformed in Soviet times into a knitting factory. Since annexation by Moscow, tower blocks have proliferated and the walled churches and lakes have become an oasis within this urban sprawl.

The churches were closed in 1939 and reopened only 50 years later, in 1990. Take note of the sign forbidding smoking and, for women, the wearing of trousers. The tall free-standing **bell tower** built 1823-6 has on its ground floor the classical heated church of **St Nicholas** with pediments and pilasters on three sides. In 1853 the three upper tiers, two for bells, were rebuilt in the baroque manner. The **Assumption Church** opposite the bell tower was built in 1823 in the late classical style. Of brick with white stone detailing, it is a beautifully proportioned rotunda with a broad round drum and dome resting on an octagon and surrounded by an outer circular wall interrupted on three sides by Tuscan porticoes and on the fourth by the tactful apse. Within, a ring of marble columns emphasises the circular shape. The **Modena Virgin icon**, removed after the revolution, has recently been returned to the church. The wooden church next to it, originally built as St Nicholas in 1673, was rebuilt and reconsecrated in 1993 as **St Tikhon**. A small belfry, which is carefully padlocked, stands nearby.

Popular **DACHA VILLAGES** are bunched between the convenient Ryazan railway line – built by English engineers so that as in England trains pass each other on the right – and the Yegorevsk Road south of Lyubertsy. At **Kraskovo**, left, a rare classical wooden mansion with columns and pediment built in 1890 survives from the aristocratic summer estate of the Princes Obolensky, as does St Vladimir built 1831-1832. Farther along Yegorevsk Road are the dacha villages, settlements of regular streets of small wooden houses which, although all have electricity, to this day function without running water in marked contrast to the dachas and sanatoria of the ruling elite. In the 1920s one of the favourite places for the new Bolsheviks was **Malakhovka** which had a summer theatre (now demolished). In 1921 the artist, Marc Chagall, with his wife Bella ran a home there for Jewish orphan children in three confiscated dachas. At **Udelnaya** the splendid wooden **Church of the Trinity**, *Troitsy*, built in 1894 by Semen Eibushits beside the railway line, appears to travellers like a fairy tale illustration in light pink with dark trimmings and a multitude of gilded and starred onion domes, *kokoshniki* gables, porches and fat columns. **Kratovo**, formerly Prozorovskoe, was a garden city for railway workers built by the Ryazan railroad owner, Nikolai von Meck (son of Tchaikovsky's patroness) and designed by such leading architects as Alexei Shchusev, who also built the Kazan Station, the terminus of the Ryazan line.

Begun in 1912, construction was never finished although in Soviet times it continued to be an exclusive dacha settlement.

On the Ryazan Road M-5 at the second exit turn right and then left signed BYKOVO over the bridge at Chkalovo/Chasovnya, then right at the T-junction and left at the GAI post again signed BYKOVO. At **Zhilino** *where Kutuzov and the Russian army spent a night during their pursuit of the retreating Napoleon the pretty baroque* **Assumption Church,** *Uspeniya, built in 1754 stands impressively tall. For long a functioning church with a large congregation it has escaped the ravages of Soviet neglect. About 5 km past Zhilino across a railway line ignore another sign to BYKOVO, left, which is for Moscow's oldest airport serving Siberian cities. Instead turn right signed VEREYA and follow the poor road through the large village then turn right again at the second street past the war memorial. Framed at the end of the lane like some great ship is* **St Vladimir.**

One dark and forbidding January day which also happened to be Orthodox Christmas, we visited **BYKOVO** and found St Vladimir thronged with people darkly bundled up against the snowy cold, climbing up and down icy steps into the packed main church. At the conclusion of the service, the great crowd surged forth and headed to the Moskva River. Cordially invited to join we followed along to be met by a remarkable sight. On the banks of the incline young men were putting together Delta hang gliders. On the ice of the river itself a companiable group of older men sat stock still huddled around their fishing holes. Another group, mostly women, queued by the spring collecting precious holy water in whatever receptacle they had. And children shrieked with laughter as they slid past either on sleds or on their bottoms on a long, fast ice slide. Behind, St Vladimir towered protectively over the people enjoying their holiday.

St Vladimir was built in 1789, probably by Vasily Bazhenov, the talented architect in the court of Catherine II who moved to Moscow after being dismissed by the Empress for his freemasonry activities. The church was part of the grand estate of a powerful nobleman, Mikhail Izmailov, Governor of Moscow and for twenty years head of the Kremlin Expedition which oversaw important construction work in Russia. For this exacting patron Bazhenov built an oval church on two floors crowned by a veritable forest of spires and pointed forms in the Gothic manner. The church is entered by a wonderful staircase which fans out on two sides and is approached through the long *trapeza* supporting twin bell towers. (The large freestanding bell tower opposite built by Ivan Tamansky in the 1840s in the same style has long taken over this function.) The lower, Nativity, is the heated winter church. The upper, St Vladimir, with marble-lined walls, originally contained a silver organ, strange furnishing for an Orthodox church where musical instruments are not used but undoubtedly reflecting the taste of the patron. The church was given back for worship in 1990 after long use as a storehouse.

But there is more to see at Bykovo. Hidden within the overgrown park is the grand **mansion** on the bank of the Moskva. The palace can be found northwest of the church through the turnstile into the park past a perfect classical pavilion with Corinthian columns on an island in the pond. It is also a creation of Bazhenov and the only one left of the many that once embellished the park. The **palace** straight ahead and a little to the right was largely rebuilt in the 19th century and only the basement, the ramps at the front and back, and the sweeping stone terrace with its seductive caryatids remain of the original Bazhenov building.

The **Vorontsov-Dashkov** family followed the Izmailovs as owners of the estate. The present mansion was built in 1856 by the Swiss architect, Bernard de Simon, over the Bazhenov terrace. On two main floors with a tower, it is of unstuccoed red brick richly enlivened with white stone quoins and stone door and window frames. Its best feature is the splendid terrace at the back overlooking the river. The last owner before the revolution was the rich railway tycoon, **Nikolai Ilin**, a director of the Moscow-Ryazan line. There is a legend that the house was sold to him on the spur of the moment by the impetuous Countess Vorontsova-Dashkova. In the 1870s the future Alexander III, an ardent ballet enthusiast, visited the estate accompanied by dancers from the St Petersburg royal ballet. The visit had an unexpected denouement. The Countess, offended by her husband's attentions to one of the ballerinas, without further ado sold the estate to Ilin.

After the revolution Bykovo became a house of rest, the **Krasny Strakhovik** (Red Insurance Man). Now under the Ministry of Health it is a sanatorium for patients recovering from tuberculosis and other illnesses. It seems in remarkably good condition and the pre-revolutionary interiors, which were executed during Ilin's tenure, have survived well. One enters a circular hall with a white staircase, vases on the top landing, paintings on the ceiling, and original lamps hanging like coach lanterns. To the left is the panelled hall with a fine ceiling which extends the length of the house. Rooms off the hall were for billiards and the main boudoir. To the right is the library, now the patients' exercise room. The patients are housed in light and spacious wards on the top floor which might originally have been servants' quarters.

Follow the main road towards Ramenskoe through Zhukovsky, the home of the **Central Aerohydrodynamics Institute** *where the annual airshow takes place in August. Continue to Ramenskoe and turn left at a round-about over the railway line then at the first traffic light turn right signed TSENTR and follow right and left until the road runs parallel to the railway line. Impressive 19th century mill buildings stand left.*

In the 1740s **RAMENSKOE**, population 90,000, belonged to Platon Musin-Pushkin, accused of treason by Empress Anna Ivanovna who had his tongue cut out. Another owner, Count Bestuzhev-Ryumin, was the powerful Chancellor in the time of Empress Elizabeth. The property then passed by marriage to the Princes Volkonsky and then the Princes Golitsyns. The Golitsyns, later Prozorov-Golitsyns, are remembered for their reluctance to grant land to their serfs after emancipation; in 1917 in retaliation their grand wooden house was burnt to the ground. Prince Vladimir Golitsyn founded the first textile mill in 1831 which in 1866 was sold to a grim-faced illiterate factory owner from Serpukhov, Pavel Malyutin, who nevertheless was canny enough to introduce the latest English textile machinery and to employ as manager a Russian engineer, **Fedor Dmitrov**, instead of the usual foreigner. The railway line was a vital factor in the town's expansion and by 1900 nearly 7,000 workers were employed in the mills. A year later militant workers managed to reduce their working hours from 11 to 9 a day. In 1907 the main mill was purchased by the **Bardygins** of Yegorevsk. After the revolution the mills were nationalised and renamed *Krasnoe Znamya*, Red Banner.

From the main road along the railway line turn left by the yellow brick factory school. The main entrance to the largest of the textile mills with its own small museum is on the left. Beyond a large pond is the huge pseudo-Russian **Church of the Trinity**, *Troitsy*, on a hill above the factories. Built in 1852 by Malyutin it was closed in the 1930s and its domes sliced off; it reopened in 1990. Within is a sculpture by Antokolsky for the tomb of Fedor Dmitrov, the mill manager. The second church, **Sts Boris and Gleb**, built 1725-30, stands near the Trinity above the pond and park of old lime trees that date from the time of the

Volkonskys. Even with its domes missing, the white-tiered church in the form of an octagonal set on a cube with a taller bell tower is attractive. It houses the local museum (*open daily except Monday, closed 1–2 for lunch*).

From the factories in Ramenskoe turn right signed RAMENSKOE UVD (Interior Ministry) following signs to BRONNITSY STATION, past Litvino, across the River Gzhelka to **Zagornovo** *and Michael the Archangel church built 1805 and never closed. At Bronnitsy railway station (12 km from Bronnitsy), turn right on the A-107 and at 5 km turn right again signed BOYARKINO SOVKHOZ. Where the bus turns around, go straight ahead parallel with the river 5 km on a lesser road to* **MARKOVO**.

The 17th century **Church of the Kazan Virgin**, *Kazanskoi Ikony Bozhiei Materi*, with the mid 19th century bell tower resting on a high stone basement is situated on the bank of the Moskva commanding broad views of the valley which in times past was the main route to Ryazan. This ancient building, now a sad ruin, was in fine fettle only two decades ago when the local population began removing the brick for their own use, ripping up the floors, tearing out the windows, and vandalising the bell tower. Perhaps this is understandable, for this important building listed in all the architectural histories was for a long time used to house pigs.

The church was constructed 1672–80 by **Prince Yakov Odoevsky**, ambassador to Poland and head of the Kazan and Siberian *prikazy*, offices of state. It was built by the serf master builder, **Pavel Potekhin**, who built similar churches at Ostankino and Nikolskoe-Uryupino. Here at Markovo the church rises out of the enclosed gallery which abuts onto four side chapels. There are five domes, the central one the old-fashioned helmet-shape and four minor cupolas identifying the four corner chapels. Coloured ceramic tiles are used distinctively in the *shirinki* or indented squares on the exterior pilasters and the sculptural brickwork around the windows. The roof was formed by a system of unusually complex vaulting resulting in tiers of *kokoshniki* gables now hidden by the later roof. Only fragments survive of the interior originally designed by Kremlin craftsmen. One of the 17th century chapel **iconostases** is safe in the Rublev Museum Moscow, but the principal iconostasis has entirely disappeared.

A doctor whose dacha is nearby has tried on several occasions to drum up local interest to save the church but so far without success and even the materials brought to begin repairs have been pilfered. Markovo is certainly a seminal building for Russian architectural historians but nevertheless the authorities – both state and religious – have left it to rot. Try to see it while it is still standing.

THE MOSKVA AT VOSKRESENSK

The land by the looping Moskva River is marshy and flat inviting walkers although between Mikhalevo and Faustovo a large and malodorous sewage works makes passage difficult. *From Ramenskoe go south to Bronnitsy Railway Station then cross the A-107 and continue south 7 km towards Voskresensk and turn right to* **MIKHALEVO**.

The brick Empire-style **Nativity of Christ**, *Rozhdestva Khristova*, left, overlooking the Moskva River was built in 1821 in the form of a Greek cross, each arm ending in a portico with Corinthian columns. In 1992 when it reopened it was in sad condition, the fine capitals all but disappeared. But by January 1999 the spire of the bell tower had been regilded and the whole building, brilliantly white with a bright blue dome, shone like a postmodern revival. Between Mikhalevo and Faustovo a large secret enterprise that used to make rockets has taken up other products including, it is said, the manufacture of toothpaste.

Three km south of Mikhalevo on the Voskresensk road is **FAUSTOVO**. High on a knoll overlooking the green flood plain are two lonely magnificent brick churches. Both rise up from open terraces – the **Cathedral of the Trinity**, *Troitsy*, built in 1696-8, by the use of a tall cube and five soaring domes, and the **Gate Church of Sts Zosim and Savvaty**, built in the 1680s, in tapering tiers. Both have voluptuously jutting apses and both make liberal use of coloured tiles. The former **Krasnokholm Solovetsk Monastery**, *Krasnokholmskaya Solovetskaya Pustyn*, was founded in the mid 17th century by the powerful mother-monastery far to the north in the Solovki Islands (a notorious prison in Soviet times). In 1764 the monastery was dissolved and the two churches reverted to the parish. Closed in the Soviet period they had severely deteriorated when the reopening of the churches allowed repairs to be put in hand just in time.

Continue on the Voskresensk Road south of Faustovo following the railway line then turn left across the line at Shchelkino and join the Tsyurupy-Konobeevo road about 8 km in all to **KONOBEEVO**. It lies on the edge of a large expanse of marshy land where the River Nerskaya empties into the Moskva. Left of the road on the eastern edge of the village is a strange group of churches. The most remarkable, the ruined **Church of the Trinity**, *Troitsy*, built in 1702 by Prince Dolgorukov, is in the Moscow baroque style, a tower church with finely decorated windows where coloured tiles once held sway. Next to the venerable Dolgorukov church is a brash eclectic church, also the **Trinity**, built in 1911 by Fedor Rybinsky and recently re-roofed and repainted. What a pity with all this construction going on that the older church is left to rot.

South on the Ryazan Road M-5 turn left on the A-108 road signed GORKY to **VOSKRESENSK** *in 12 kilometres across the old bridge over the Moskva River.* On the right just before the bridge stands **Fedino**, a group of ugly scattered buildings, a petrol station, and the splendid pyramid-shaped church dedicated to **Serafim Sarovsky**. It was built 1909-12 by Vladimir Suslov for father and son, Dmitry and Pavel Akhlestyshev, members of the Moscow City Duma. In the Russian version of Art Nouveau it has pyramid roofs of glazed tiles and delight-fully exaggerated porches with, in the tympanum, a majolica depiction of the **Saviour Untouched by Hand**, *Spasa Nerukotvornovo*, by S.T. Shelkov. The church, covered in scaffolding, began functioning again in 1997, once again in time to save it from complete dilapidation.

The strange industrial town of Voskresensk, population 80,000, stretches haphazardly for 15 km along the Moskva River. It is an amalgam of the dyeing and textile mill villages, Gusev and Vanilovo, and is conveniently close to peat deposits, the river and the railways. Cement and brick factories were also built but it was in the late 1920s, when the first five-year plan was adopted, that the gigantic Kuibyshev chemical factory was constructed. It was followed in 1931 by the huge cement works, *Gigant*, which produced the immense quantities demanded by the grand-iose projects of the 1930s, including the Moscow-Volga canal and the Moscow metro. In 1938 it was declared a city and named Voskresensk (Resurrection) after one of the villages. Unlikely as it may seem, a few places of interest lie hidden among the smoking towers.

Once across the river turn right at the first traffic lights to where the road turns left. Leave the car at the city park. Walk through the park which is parallel to the river to a fence surrounding a large house, the former mansion of **Krivyakino**. Originally built in the late 1760s, it was rebuilt in the 19th century then considerably altered in the 1950s. On the southwest side of the house facing the river is a splendid portico of giant Corinthian columns and an elaborate baroque cornice with fine Venetian windows dwarfing the odd little porch.

The estate was purchased in the 1790s by a Kolomna merchant, Ivan Lazhechnikov, whose son, also Ivan, became a popular romantic writer in the style of Sir Walter Scott. Lazhechnikov senior liked to give magnificent dinners which featured fish from his own ponds, pears from his orchards, and other gourmet items. His largesse did not save him from the machinations of the local clergy who denounced him as a heretic and had him incarcerated in the Peter-Paul Fortress. In 1811 the estate was purchased by the Kurmanlevs but in the mid 19th century it again was in the hands of the Lazhechnikov family. After the revolution the mansion became a children's holiday home. The local museum is housed in the wing.

Return to the main A-108 road, cross it (turn left if on the A-108 from the M-5) and continue straight ahead for 1 km. The estate of **Spasskoe** lies about 3 km north of Krivyakino also on the bank of the Moskva where the pioneer camp, *Plamya* (Flame), under *Moskovsky Kombinat* has long had use of the old buildings.

The estate belonged in the first half of the 19th century to N.M. Smirnov and his wife, Alexandra Smirnova-Rosset, who kept a gossipy diary of her encounters with literary people including the writer, Nikolai Gogol. The Smirnovs sold Spasskoe to the Gagarins who, in 1872, completely rebuilt the house to the design of Robert Gedike. Before the revolution it belonged to Prince Lieven. The central part of the house was brick linked by galleries to two-storey wings built of wood to resemble brick. After the Second World War Spasskoe became a pioneer camp for war orphans and in 1961 the central section of the house burned down and was rebuilt as one tall floor flanked by the old wings. In the grounds, once famous for its English park, are rows of vases and the original rough stone 'dragon's' gate, *zmeiniye vorota*, originally the main entrance. By the river stands a modest two-storey wooden house, the Dubki (Oak) Dacha, which the Lievens built in 1909.

From Voskresensk continue east along the A-108 about 4 km and turn at the second right turn (unsigned), and cross a railway line busy with freight to Lopatinsky. Almost at once turn sharp left past a large factory and follow the road which soon turns sharp right at another factory and go past a refinery. Turn right by the bus-stop to **OSTASHEVO**, a refreshingly real village after the dreary factories, where small wooden houses bristle with magnificent carvings of horses or cocks and tall slender poles like sentinels draw water from the wells. **St Vladimir** is straight on and up the hill. Built in 1763 like a Moscow baroque tower with an octagonal surmounting the cube, the squat bell tower and *trapeza* of the late 19th century built by the mill owner effectively screen the older church. When we visited, a group of hard-working women were busy replastering the interior, and the bell tower was shining with new paint in contrast to the run-down church. Surprisingly, it was handed over in 1991 not to the Orthodox Church but to Old Believers, reflecting the present religious beliefs of the villagers. Even though it is on the edge of the Guslitsy Old Believer strongholds, the priest has to come from Moscow.

One of the women told us impassively that the blue lorry we saw leaving the village was taking away the body of her son-in-law who had died of drink that very morning. Life in rural Russia is hard.

Take the Ryazan Road M-5 to Nepetsino where across the Severka River, right, the colourful peach and blue classical **Church of the Sign**, *Ikony Bozhiei Materi 'Znamenie'*, *built in 1806 and now functioning is all that survives of the estate of the Novikov family. Just before crossing the Severka take the unsigned left turn 4 km to Myachkovo past the ruined pseudo-Russian church of 1868 with the impressively large onion-shaped dome and turn right for another 4 km to* **CHERKIZOVO**. *Turn right at the T-junction on the parallel road to the Moskva River.* In the park, left, a large pale green building of two storeys with paired Tuscan columns facing the river is the only surviving wing of the great mansion of the eminent Princes Cherkassky. One of the biggest landlords of their day with hundreds of thousands of serfs, they fought against emancipation and when in 1861 the Tsar proclaimed the new law, their great house was torn down by their own serfs. The family lived in the surviving wing until 1917.

A little farther on is the completely ruined baroque **Church of the Assumption**, *Uspeniya*, built in 1749 with a round apse once encircled by Tuscan columns. There is a fine view of the narrow Moskva River here, of barges wending their way to the Oka. Across the river is the prestigious dacha settlement of Peski where a late 19th century estate of the Sheremetievs stands among the summer homes of many well-known Russian artists. One wonders if they dare swim in the Moskva which here is very polluted.

Farther south in Cherkizovo, left, is **Starki**, where another highly inter-esting church has Cherkassky connections. The *pogost* **Church of St Nicholas** was built 1759–63 to replace a 17th century church probably by the great Vasily Bazhenov. Built for Prince Petr Cherkassky it is one of the first pseudo-Gothic churches in Russia. A highly original building with separate bell tower which from the river must have appeared fantastical, it was designed while Bazhenov was still a student in Peters-burg. Of brick with strange white stone details it rises in tiers to pinna-cles and spire with the upward thrust so typical of Bazhenov's later churches at Bykovo and Podzhigorodovo. Surprisingly, the tall drum is of wood rather than stone, which it resembles. The unusual diamond and spade designs on the facade and drum are explained ingeniously but implausibly by local people as representing playing cards and indicating that the property was therefore won at cards. The church seems never to have been closed under communism and the 18th century icons including a carved wooden virgin and child and a wooden sculpture of Christ are still in the church. Outside, the black marble tombs of the Princes Cherkassky lie undisturbed in a fenced-off section, left.

The ancient fortress town of Kolomna is situated near the confluence of the Moskva River and the Oka, 115 km southeast of Moscow on the Ryazan Road M-5 about 2 hours by car.

KOLOMNA

Kolomna, population 163,000, enjoyed a brief period of independence as a grand duchy in the 12th century until in 1306 it allied itself with the Moscow grand dukes. It was here at the strategic confluence of the Moskva River with the wide Oka that the Moscow Grand Prince, Dmitry Donskoy, mustered his troops for the successful assault on the Tatars in 1380. Although Kolomna today is a major centre of heavy industry, it is nevertheless the most seductive of all the ancient fortress towns circling around Moscow. Even the heavy presence of the army's artillery school in central Kolomna – noisy armoured cars suddenly amble down the peaceful streets – has not ruined its appearance. The museum, at 71 Grazhdanskaya Street in the 18th century **Church of Michael the Archangel** (rebuilt by the Moscow architect, Fedor Shestakov), may help those who would like further information. *Closed Mondays, and between 1 and 2 for lunch.*

At the traffic lights before crossing the Kolomenka River turn right through a pleasant suburb to **GORODISHCHE** *and the first stone*

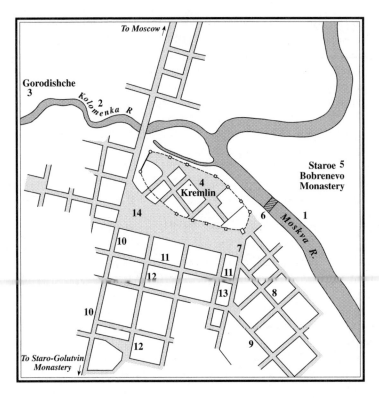

KOLOMNA 1. Moskva River, 2. Kolomenka River, 3. Gorodishche, 4. Kremlin, 5. Staroe Bobrenevo Monastery, 6. Swing bridge, 7. Pushkinskaya, 8. Posadskaya, 9. Artilleristov, 10. Oktyabrskoi Revolyutsyi, 11. Komsomolskaya, 12. Krasnogvardeiskaya, 13. Levshina, 14. Market Square

building in Kolomna. **St John the Baptist**, *Ioanna Predtechi na Gorodishche*, once again holding services, was originally built in the 1360s–70s as the seat of the Kolomna bishopric and was largely rebuilt in the 16th century. The triple-bayed facade with trefoil gables is topped by helmet-shaped domes and a charming roof belfry. The bell tower and *trapeza* were added a century later and in the late 19th century the *trapeza* was callously enlarged, thoroughly masking the older church. The apse and lower walls of limestone blocks are of the earlier, 14th century church, the upper brick walls of the 17th century. A plaster relief in the form of a snow leopard, a ducal emblem, stands over the doorway on the north wall (the original is in the Kolomna museum).

Return to the main road and cross the Kolomenka River to the impressive **KREMLIN** with its powerful red brick walls and towers. The narrow fortress in the form of an ellipse extends about 500 metres at the confluence of the Kolomenka with the Moskva. Three gates and seven of the 16 towers remain of the superb walls built 1525-31, probably by the same Italian masters who built the Moscow Kremlin.

The large round (20 sided) tower of 8 levels with gun apertures is the **Marinkina** named after Marina Mnishek, Polish wife of the first False Dmitry who overthrew the Godunov dynasty in 1605 only to be murdered in the Kremlin a year later. Nothing daunted, Marina married the second False Dmitry and local legend has it that she was imprisoned and died here after he was defeated. (In reality she died in Moscow in 1614 when her 4-year old son by False Dmitry II was murdered.) The Marinkina is at the head of the longest extant section of wall which also includes the hexagonal **Faceted Tower**, bereft of its upper section. Park the car in the market square and enter the Kremlin by Lazhechnikova Street.

On the left is **Brusensky Monastery** founded in the 16th century and recently reopened as a working convent. The oldest and most striking building is the octagonal tent-shaped tower, the **Church of the Assumption**, *Uspeniya*, built in 1552 and beautifully restored in the 1970s. Like its contemporary at Prusy, it lacks the intervening stage from cube to octagonal. Inside, the accoustics are excellent and the view unimpeded to the dome. Its triple apse juts out forcefully eastwards but the ungainly, two-storey red brick *trapeza* with poorhouse built in 1883 on the west side is a disgrace. Red brick identifies the mid 19th century abbess's house, the monks' cells and the handsome pseudo-Russian cathedral, **Exaltation of the Cross**, *Vozdvizheniya Kresta*, by Alexander Kutepov, built 1852–5. About half the monastery wall survives together with four round **pseudo-Gothic towers** by Matvei Kazakov in red brick spotted with stone suns and topped with slim spires. Kazakov, the notable Moscow architect, was sent to Kolomna in the 1770s by Catherine the Great to regularise the haphazard street plan. Thus Kolomna's straight streets follow the line of the rivers, occasionally interrupted by charming squares. Kazakov's stylish towers also enhance three other monasteries in Kolomna.

From Lazhechnikova Street turn right onto Lazareva Street with a splendid view of **Cathedral Square** and the majestic **Cathedral of the Assumption**, *Uspeniya*, where services are again being held, flanked by the bell tower and the Novo-Golutvin Monastery. Built of brick, 1672–82, and modelled on the Moscow Assumption Cathedral, the facade is divided into three vertical bays in the traditional manner, with finely carved portals, a heavy triple apse and five domes set close to one another. Inside the bare church is the wonderful, carved 18th century iconostasis and peeling frescoes (at one time it was used to store grain). On the Cathedral's left the white tent-shaped brick bell tower was built in 1692, almost contemporary with the cathedral. It is attached to the ugly pseudo-Russian **Church of the Tikhvin Icon**, *Tikhvinskoi Ikony Bozhiei Materi*, built in 1776 but rebuilt in 1861.

More churches lurk behind the cathedral near the Moskva River. In 1366 in an earlier church where the **Resurrection**, *Voskreseniya*, of 1786 now stands, Dmitry Donskoy is said to have married the Suzdal Princess Yevdokiya. Nearby is the 16th century **St Nicholas Gostiny** heavily rebuilt in the 19th century.

The walls, towers and tall belltower of the **Novo-Golutvin Monastery**, now a convent, on the south side of Cathedral Square, were built in 1778 by Matvei Kazakov. In the centre is the single-domed white **Church of the Trinity**, *Troitsy*, erected in 1680 in Moscow baroque style, while to the right of the gate is the **Church of the Intercession**, *Pokrova*, with the pinnacles and high roof introduced by Kazakov. The **Archbishop's palace**, including the old **stone chamber** adjoining the Intercession, continued in use until 1801 when the bishopric was dissolved.

East of Cathedral Square are unexpected streets of ordinary wooden houses leading to the river where in the distance the gold domes of the **Staroe Bobrenevo Monastery** beckon enticingly. Beyond some fine houses of the 19th century and the Empire **Church of the Exaltation of the Cross**, *Vozdvizheniya Kresta*, rebuilt 1832–7, is the heavily vaulted **Pyatnitskaya Gate** with crevices for the huge portcullises and a space for the town alarm bell above the icon frame.

Left of Pyatnitskaya Gate on the river quay is an alarming pedestrian swing bridge which suddenly swings back to allow boats to pass and then returns without warning. Across the river, a 20 minute walk takes one to **STAROE BOBRENEVO MONASTERY**, on its own in the flat landscape punctuated by Kazakov's familiar slim Gothic towers. It was founded as a monastery/fortress in 1381 by Dmitry Volynets, nicknamed *Bobrok* (beaver), a hero of the Battle of Kulikovo. In 1790 it was totally rebuilt for the country residence of the powerful Kolomna archbishop.

Enter the monastery not from the splendid south gate but from an inconspicuous small door left of it; pull the string and the door mysteriously opens. The ruined **Church of St Fedor**, on the right now under repair was built of brick in 1861 over the foundations of the 16th century *trapeza*. In the centre is the newly painted **Cathedral of the Nativity of the Virgin**, *Rozhdestva Bogoroditsy*, built in 1790, a tiered octagonal on a cube like the Moscow baroque churches of a century earlier but without their rich decoration. The attached tent-shaped bell tower is contemporary with the cathedral. To the left the abbot's house now houses the newly established monks.

Return from Staroe-Bobrenevo for **WALKS IN THE OLD TOWN**. Turn left to an interesting district of small wooden houses, churches, and old mansions along the high river bank. At **Pushkinskaya Street** note the **Tupitsyn House**, No 13, with a modest Corinthian portico and fine medallions built in the early 19th century. In a short distance angle off, left, onto **Posadskaya Street** to see the amazing brick church built in 1716 of **St Nicholas Posadskovo**, now functioning. Its most stunning feature, the five receding rows of gables topped by five domes on slim drums, removed in the Soviet era, were wonderfully restored in the 1970s. The tent-shaped bell tower by the entrance, however, was demolished and not rebuilt nor have the church porches been reinstated. A small wooden house by the church bears a plaque stating that **Boris Pilnyak**, the fine writer of the 1920s, lived there 1940-1. This house belonged to his father-in-law, the deacon of St Nicholas. Pilnyak's story, *The Unextinguished Moon* (1926), suggesting that the death of the Bolshevik General, Mikhail Frunze, was suspicious, incurred serious disfavour as did subsequent works and in 1937 he was arrested and sent to the camps where he perished. It seems from the plaque that he was allowed to return for a short time in 1940 to his in-laws' house which was 100 km from Moscow, the closest exiles were allowed to live to the capital. To the left on Posadsky Lane is the now shabby **Voevod (governor's) house**, built around the beginning of the 18th century in the Moscow baroque style and used as artists' studios.

A little farther on Posadskaya turn right and first left to Artilleristov Street (closed farther north by the army) to the **Church of the Epiphany**, *Bogoyavleniya*, in sparkling order which was never closed. It was built in the 1680s but rebuilt in the Empire style in the early 19th century.

On the main road, **Oktyabrskoi Revolyutsyi** at No 192 is the former 18th/19th century estate of the **Lazhechnikovs** whose son was the

romantic writer, Ivan Lazhechnikov. Kolomna's first public library
opened here in 1899. A little farther along, at No 196, is the interesting
Soviet state bank built in the early 1930s in the geometrical, constructivist style. At No 200, the former **Frolov Hotel** built in the 1860s served
as the local Soviet until the 1970s. At No 222, with baroque inspired
windows, enter the courtyard to admire the round staircase and the
carriage house of the 19th century **merchants' club**, now used by air
cadets.

Cross Oktyabrskoi and turn left onto **Komsomolskaya Street**. On the
corner with Krasnogvardeiskaya Street is the **Ascension Church**, *Vozneseniya*, built 1792–7 probably by Matvei Kazakov then working in
Kolomna. For long used to store harmful chemicals, it has now been
handed back to the church. A rotunda with a hemispherical dome,
Doric porticoes at north and south entrances and a rusticated apse, the
large heated Empire *trapeza* was added in the 1800s. Amazingly, the
original wooden iconostasis and early 19th century frescoes are intact.
The triple-tiered bell tower is also by Kazakov as is the stuccoed
priest's house next door. At the top of **Krasnogvardeiskaya** where it
joins Truda Street is a late 18th century mansion with an imposing
portico of six Corinthian columns which may also have been by
Kazakov. An exceptionally fine substantial wooden house survives
farther south at No 29 Krasnogvardeiskaya (across the square)
complete with barns and gates.

Walk along **Komsomolskaya** to explore the many early 19th century
mansions. Turn right into **Levshina Street** richly endowed with substantial houses and turn left to a little square with a steam bath on the
corner. Continue to **Artilleristov** where No 4 on the left housed the
Kolomna Zemstvo, the local government. Next to it is No 6, set back in
the square, a small **old merchant's house** of the mid 18th century.
Straight ahead is a fenced-off area with soldiers on guard, for within is
the **army's artillery school** and also one of the most interesting houses of
Kolomna. It can be glimpsed from the street and sometimes the young
soldiers will wave you through if senior officers are not around. Above
the rusticated ground floor the mansion is richly decorated with pilasters
and extravagant window designs in the florid baroque manner unusual
in Kolomna. It was built in the 1760s by the wealthy textile merchant,
I.T. Meshchaninov, who was also the mayor. His property included an
extensive garden and a small pavilion, also baroque, which is now on
the territory of the neighbouring sports stadium, *Start*. Within, are
elaborate plastered ceilings and some **tiled stoves** of which the most

colourful, a triple-tiered edifice, was removed in 1913 and installed in the old Yusupov house on Bolshoi Kharitonevsky Lane in Moscow.

The vast **MARKET SQUARE** is dominated by the soaring **bell tower** of 1846 that rises in five tiers giving the town its distinctive silhouette. The more modest **Church of St John the Divine**, *Ioanna Bogoslova*, built in 1756 and rebuilt in 1828 in Empire style, is hard to find among the market kiosks and trading rows on either side of the bell tower that serve as its walls. A delightful early 19th century **guardhouse**, with four Doric columns and pediment, is tucked into the Kremlin wall.

To the right of the market place, a spacious piazza, used in Soviet times for meetings and parades, was constructed in 1921 by the 'bourgeoisie' forced to work under Komsomol enthusiasts. In the centre is a large statue of **Lenin**, flowers at his feet, erected in 1938 by the sculptor Merkurov, a smaller version of the huge statue that was meant to surmount the gigantic Palace of Soviets in Moscow. Behind Lenin a semicircle of bright hoardings still proclaimed communist slogans in the late 1990s.

Travel south 4 km on Oktyabrskoi Revolyutsyi passing a hospital, right, in the constructivist style, a rare wooden theatre, left, of 1910, and an old engine, left, celebrating railway construction in Kolomna. Where the road crosses a railway line take the first left across a bumpy and dangerous mainline railway without barrier or signals. On the other side is the isolated **STARO-GOLUTVIN MONASTERY**, with Matvei Kazakov's elegant towers. The monastery was founded in 1374 by the great Russian saint, Sergius Radonezh, at the strategic place where the two river highways, the Oka and the Moskva, meet. The walls and Kazakov's six slim Gothic towers of 1778 are intact and the **Cathedral of the Epiphany**, *Bogoyavleniya*, built in the early 18th century, **St Sergius Radonezh**, built 1828–33, and the 18th century gate bell tower **Church of the Presentation**, *Vvedeniya*, are still standing. It has now returned to the church after use as a factory and is slowly coming back to life. In the early 1990s a lone figure, Anatoly Kuznetsov, bravely set up a furniture workshop in the monastery to raise money for the much needed repairs.

THE ROYAL FISHERIES

Four villages on the east, left bank of the Oka where it turns right at Kolomna on its way to Ryazan were chosen by the tsars to provide fish from the well-stocked river for the royal table. After the capital moved to St Petersburg, the villages still proved useful to the monarch as valuable gifts to favoured courtiers. As a result, some splendid churches that would not have looked out of place in Moscow or Petersburg were erected on the banks of the Oka. Today the almost dead fishing industry has been replaced by agriculture and these villages are in decline.

The Ryazan Road, M-5 from Moscow, continues on a bypass signed RYAZAN which crosses the Moskva. After 10 km at, Parfentievo (with the recently reopened classical church of St Nicholas), ignore the sign RYAZAN and continue eastwards about 20 km to Selnikovo then turn right 10 km to **DEDINOVO**, *the most ancient of the royal villages.* It was founded in the late 15th century by citizens of Novgorod, who by the early 17th had begun making sailing ships. In 1667 a flotilla of ships for use in the Caspian Sea was made for Tsar Alexei Mikhailovich. In 1669 the Eagle, *Orel*, was ready, the first ship of the fledgeling Russian navy. Unfortunately it soon perished from fire but the shipyard flourished, attracting visits from the sailing devotee and future tsar, Peter the Great. In 1762 Catherine II granted Dedinovo to General Mikhail Izmailov a progressive man by whose will the Dedinovo peasants were to be freed from serfdom after his death. However, the local authorities refused to implement this clause, the peasants rebelled, and most of the male population were executed.

On the attractive central square with its parade of brick and stucco houses is the large classical **Church of the Resurrection**, *Voskreseniya*, built in 1817 as a basilica and used as the club for the state farm. Walk to lower Dedinovo along the river and, where the Tsna River empties into the Oka, the stunning brick **Trinity**, *Troitsy*, comes into view. It was built in 1700 by the merchant, Nikita Shustov, according to the bell tower inscription, and recently repaired and reopened. While it resembles the assymetrical churches of the mid 17th century, the quality of its richly carved limestone flowers and plants sets it apart. Rows of *kokoshniki* gables in the form of shells climb towards the exceptionally tall drums with voluptuous onion-shaped domes and unusually fine gold crosses with crowns indicating royal origins. A relief of a lion and a unicorn on the bell tower is further evidence of royal involvement.

From Dedinovo take the main road south parallel to the Oka for about 5 km along flat, treeless fields. Look to the right for the unexpected sight of the large and elegant **Church of the Resurrection**, *Voskreseniya*, in tiny **LYUBICHI**. It was erected in the 1770s by a wealthy fisheries merchant, P.D. Larin, and displays early classical elements mixed with baroque such as the Doric cornices and decorative windows.

From Lyubichi continue 7 km south following the looping Oka to the right turn over the Shya Canal 2 km to **LOVTSY**. At this village, unlike Lyubichi, the Oka ferry is working and there is a cheerful bustle. An arresting ensemble of cupolas and porticoes turned out to be the **Church of the Resurrection**, *Voskreseniya*, built in classical style in 1835-43 with porticos and five tall domes and recently returned to the Church. The *trapeza*, like the mother church, has its own dome, spire and porticoes. The dilapidated belltower stands dejectedly apart.

Leave Lovtsy by crossing the Shya Canal and in 8 km where the road to RADOVTSY branches off left, take the right road 8 km to **BELOOMUT**. The largest of the royal fisheries lies on a dramatic loop of the Oka. The strange name, probably of Finno-Ugrian origin, derives from *omut*, a deep, quiet place or whirlpool, for here the waters of the Oka are very deep and still.

In the 1620s Tsar Mikhail Fedorovich chose Beloomut as headquarters of the royal fisheries. In 1762 Lower Beloomut was granted by Catherine II to M.S. Pokhvisnev for services rendered when she usurped the throne. Upper Beloomut was later given to M.E. Baskakov, the grandfather of Nikolai Ogarev, the liberal and friend of Alexander Herzen. When Ogarev inherited Upper Beloomut he immediately liberated his serfs fifteen years before the general emancipation.

Beyond the T-junction at the centre of **Lower Beloomut**, is the peach and white **Church of the Transfiguration**, *Spasa Preobrazheniya*, built in 1797 in classical style with baroque 'ear' windows. Now used as a club and a cinema it is shorn of its north portico, drum and bell tower. Unusual geometric shapes – ovals and diamonds – by a local artist frame the south door of the church resembling those at the Nikolo-Radovitsky monastery.

The road turns right towards the **Church of the Assumption**, *Uspeniya*. The lovely classical cemetery church built in 1840 delights by its good design in the shape of a Latin cross with attractive Ionic porticoes and pediments and elegant drum, cupola and spire repeated on the bell tower. The few parishioners, who reopened the church in 1990, have been slowly and painstakingly replacing the roof and renewing the building without any outside help.

The **Church of the Three Saints**, *Trekh Svyatitlei*, in **Upper Beloomut** stands right of the road in the cemetery. It was built in 1827 in the shape of a Greek cross and has little decoration apart from the portico. Once again it is obvious that the fashion for constructing huge *trapeza* in the late 19th century can spoil a delicate plan. On our summer visit everyone seemed to be bringing in hay for their animals – even bicycles were commandeered for this purpose and the poor horses seemed barely able to pull the overloaded wagons. In Soviet times it was illegal to produce feed for privately owned animals.

THE GZHEL VILLAGES

Take the Ryazan Road M-5 and turn left signed YEGOREVSK at Chkalovo and continue past the dacha villages 35 km over the railway bridge across the A-107.

GZHEL is the generic name for the rich clay pottery district of twenty-five villages southeast of Moscow in the marshy **Meshchera** region along the R-105, the Yegorevsk Road. The justly famous Gzhel figurines, dishes, clocks, tiles in characteristic white and cobalt blue continue to be popular following the demise of the Soviet Union. It was not until the 18th century that the first pottery works opened in Gzhel and by 1787, twenty-five villages in the chain had earthenware kilns. In 1810 the Kuznetsovs established the first porcelain factory in Novo Kharitonovo. The string of villages, each with its own pottery, now so hug the road that it is impossible to tell where one ends and the other begins.

The first of the villages is **GZHEL** on the Gzhelka River where brightly painted wooden houses stand behind neat picket fences. The big eclectic **Church of the Assumption**, *Uspeniya*, built in 1854, is functioning again after years as a branch of the pottery. Continue through Troshkovo to **RECHITSY**, the largest of the villages. In the 1930s the potteries here became the *Electroizolyator* works producing ceramic products for the growing number of power stations. Rechitsy is also remarkable for the monstrous **Church of the Ascension**, *Vozneseniya*, left, with the massive blue dome and bright yellow drum built in the 1860s and intended to impress the large number of Old Believers in the area. Beyond the church is the pottery shop.

Pass **Turygino** and its pottery and related technical college to **NOVO KHARITONOVO** where the row of cottages is suddenly interrupted by the soaring Old Believer **Church of St George**, left, in Art Nouveau style (the preferred style of Old Believers anxious to show their independence from the Orthodox). Ivan Kuznetsov, cousin of Matvei Kuznetsov of the chinaworks at Dulevo, commissioned Boris Velikovsky, the fine constructivist, to build a mansion, church and poorhouse in his family's home village. Velikovsky completed the ensemble in 1912 but the poorhouse was destroyed in 1918, the mansion was dismantled and only St George survives. It is a daring reworking of Russian 16th century tower churches – the bells are hung in the central tower like the Naryshkin churches and exaggerated arrow-like gables are employed like those of St Basil's – but the total, vigorous effect is quite independent of any of its sources. St George, which of course was closed in the long Soviet period, is again holding services for Old Believers.

Cross the stream and turn immediately left past the old factory at **Kuzlyaevo** to **IGNATEVO**. Here is another **St George** and although it cannot compare with the Old Believer St George, it is an excellent example of how attractive the pseudo-Russian style can be. In red brick with five domes on tall drums abutting a large cemetery and overlooking fields it was built in 1863 by the Moscow architect, Nikolai Finisov, who himself donated 600 roubles towards the costs. The reopened church has once again become the social centre of the community.

THE GUSLITSY REGION

Southeast of Novo Kharitonovo open fields give way to another pottery village, **Karpovo**, with yet another pseudo-Russian church in very poor condition which nevertheless has been returned to the parish. Farther on, the Yegorevsk Road passes out of the Gzhel district into the Guslitsy region. A large area of Old Believer villages is centred on the **Nerskaya and Guslitsa Rivers** in a district of low-lying fens, stunted woods, and with a soil suitable only for hops. It is only the extensive peat bogs which are useful, providing fuel for the great textile mills in the area. It was to this forbidding place that groups of Old Believers fled during their frequent bouts of persecution beginning with Patriarch Nikon in the mid 17th century. It was not until 1905 that restrictions on Old Believer worship were lifted and by 1917 each of the fifty or so Old Believer villages in the Guslitsa area had its own church, however modest.

Continue from the Yegorevsk Road across the A-108 and turn towards ILINSKY POGOST on the old road to Yegorevsk which runs parallel to and west of the new road. At Pominovo turn left to **ILINSKY**

POGOST, the most important village in the Guslitsa area, where there is an exceptionally large church. This part of the Guslitsa was crown land which the tsars granted to court favourites: Peter the Great presented it to his friend Alexander Menshikov and after Menshikov's fall it was given to the powerful Lopukhins.

The **Church of the Resurrection**, *Voskreseniya*, built 1822-40, in the centre of the attractive village green, seems too large and grand even for the considerable village. Its size was meant to intimidate the large Old Believer population who were obliged to contribute to its construction. If it was also an attempt to woo Old Believers away from their church, it was clearly unsuccessful for travellers in the 19th century reported only 40 regular parishioners when 2,000 could be comfortably accommodated. It is in Empire style of brick with white stone detailing, porticoes, a hemispherical dome on a huge drum and two smaller drums and domes on the eastern corners. The overly-long *trapeza* supported by six interior columns, and the overly-tall bell tower in brick and stone bands, not completed until the 1850s, destroy any sense of unity. In 1920 the church was closed, the priest was shot and the important *pogost* (cemetery) destroyed. Today with a new roof, the church is functioning once more.

On the old road 10 km from the A-108 turn left 2 km to **ALESHINO** *(signed)*. Across a field, the **Church of the Kazan Virgin**, *Kazanskoi Ikony Bozhiei Materi*, is a pink and white vision with a blue dome. Built 1886-89 by the Yegorevsk textile merchant, Nikifor Bardygin, it is saturated with 17th century Russian motifs. Although originally an Orthodox church, it has been reopened as an Old Believer church and renamed St George. We found the ebullient priest, Father Sergei, with a beautiful white beard and flowing locks, in the yard chopping his own wood. He told us he is from a poor family of eleven children and that in the difficult Soviet period he was a priest in the Ukraine and near Moscow. His main worry nowadays is how to stop the frequent robberies of the church.

Join the new Yegorevsk Road, the R-105, from the A-108 and soon, after crossing a small bridge, turn left to USTYANOVO (signed). In a few km turn right 2 km to **USTYANOVO** *through sandy pine woods.* In the village turn left for the charming Old Believer **Church of St Nicholas**. It recalls the medieval Transfiguration Church in Novgorod with its triple-bayed indented facade and the trefoil arch of the main bay echoed by the sharply pointed roof gable. Old Believers preferred architectural

styles that predate the schism in 1653 whereas the Orthodox revival
looked to the 17th century. St Nicholas was built 1910-11 by a Moscow
architect closely associated with Old Believers, Nikolai Martyanov, for
Feodosiya Morozova, one of the Morozov clan from Bogorodsk. It has
recently been returned to the villagers who have carried out vital
repairs.

YEGOREVSK AND BEYOND

*From the new Yegorevsk Road, the R-105, 9 km short of Yegorevsk, turn
left towards KRASNY TKACH then turn right at Kurbatikha 2 km on a
rough dirt road* to **RYZHEVO**. Turn left at the main street to the attractive pink and blue wooden cemetery **Church of the Presentation of the
Virgin**, *Vvedeniya vo Khram Presvyatoi Bogoroditsy*. With its bright
colours, extravagant towers and ogee-shaped gables, it resembles a
Bilibin fairy tale illustration. It has an unusual history. Designed by
Nikolai Shokhin in the Russian national style for the 1872 Polytechnical
Exhibition in Moscow, it was purchased by Konnon Golofteev, and
transferred to his estate at Lyublino (now in Moscow) as the summer
church of Sts Peter and Paul. In 1927, after the advent of Soviet power,
permission was somehow obtained for the church to be moved from
Lyublino to this remote village where, rededicated as the Presentation of
the Virgin, it never closed. The move almost certainly saved it from
destruction.

On the Yegorevsk Road R-105 about 110 km from Moscow. **YEGOREVSK**,
an attractive industrial centre, population 70,000, was part of Ryazan
province until, after the revolution, it was swallowed by the greatly
enlarged Moscow Oblast. A small village known as Yegor-Vysoky after
the church of St George, its position at the junction between Moscow
and Kolomna and Kasimov on the Oka, made it a busy trading centre
and the intermediary point in the important grain trade from Kolomna
to the industrial towns of Orekhovo-Zuevo and Pavlovsky Posad. In
1778 Yegorevsk was replanned on a grid pattern which has remained
largely unchanged.

During the 19th century Yegorevsk's cottage industries were replaced
by the great textile mills of the machine age. The energetic **Khludov
brothers**, who moved to Moscow and established a notable clan,
opened the first spinning mill in Yegorevsk in 1845 soon adding a
cotton mill and dyeing works. Their factory on the Guslyanka River
grew ever larger, as the sons and then the grandsons ran the business,

using English managers and opening an office in Liverpool. Alexei Khludov amassed an outstanding collection of Old Believer manuscripts and books now in the Russian State Library. Alexei's son, Ivan, took over the business but died tragically young of an illness contracted while visiting Samarkand. (One of Alexei's daughters, the famous blue stocking, Varvara, married Abram Morozov, scion of the textile dynasty at Tver.) The Khludov factories were eventually bought out by their rival, **Nikifor Bardygin** who, for 30 years as *golova* or mayor, dominated Yegorevsk. Today the great textile factory still functions but not on the scale of the pre-revolutionary mills when the huge Asian market was there for the taking via the newly built Siberian railway.

Enter the town past a cemetery on the right to the former **Holy Trinity-Mary Convent**, *Svyato-Troitsky Mariinsky Monastyr*, left. Built in 1901 by the Moscow architect, Ivan Baryutin, for Nikifor Bardygin it has a rather sombre history. Bardygin's first wife died of cholera aged 35 in the same year as the death of their eldest son and a disastrous fire which all but destroyed the factory. The convent was intended to provide a place for his second wife, Mariya, in case of his death – she was thirty years younger – but as she died first Bardygin built it in her memory. After the revolution the convent became the prestigious **Civil Aviation Institute** for training pilots. Here Valery Chkalov, the Soviet pilot who made the pioneering flight from Moscow to the USA over the North Pole in 1937, received his training. Most of the pseudo-Russian convent buildings survive although the bell tower was blown up and new buildings have been added in the usual higgledy-piggledy fashion. It is not difficult to enter the grounds where cheerful students in dark blue uniforms lark about.

Yegorevsk's one-way streets are lined with pretty, wooden houses, interspersed with fine merchants' mansions but the major churches have nearly all gone. **Oktyabrskaya Street** parallel to and west of the principal street, Sovietskaya, has an imposing poorhouse at No 48 built by the Khludovs in 1862, now a TB clinic. Farther on is one of the **Bardygin mansions**, No 62, built in 1820 and 1910, and the **town prison** (next to it are the brick foundations of the 18th century wooden church, the Kazan Virgin, which burned down in the 1980s and is awaiting reconstruction).

On the main street, **Sovietskaya**, in a former merchant's house, No 58, is the interesting local museum. *Open 11-6, but closed Mondays.* The central square halfway down Sovietskaya Street is flanked by delightful pink and brown pseudo-Gothic shops built in 1873. The ubiquitous Lenin stands here on the site of the **White Cathedral**, blown up in 1935. Just behind, at No 87-89, is the Bardygin mansion built in 1868 of two storeys, the ground floor devoted to shops and the upper the living quarters. After the revolution with its grand reception rooms it served as the local city council and is now the mayor's office.

Perhaps the best of the Yegorevsk buildings is the Technical College complex, originally the **Mechanical-Electrical School**, on Profsoyuznaya 30–32 (turn right at the corner of the Trinity-Mary Convent and continue across the river to the School). It was built 1907–9 by Bardygin to Baryutin's design in Art Nouveau style with a lively use of ironwork and consists of the three-storey teaching block and laboratories, teachers' houses and stables and student hostel. Within, the staircases and halls have retained the original decor.

A little to the east of Sovietskaya on **Stepan Khalturin Street** is the tall **Church of Alexander Nevsky**, heavily ornamented in the pseudo-Russian manner. It was begun in 1879 by Bardygin as a memorial church to the unsuccessful attempt on the life of Alexander II. Ironically, Alexander II was to die only two years later at the hands of another assassin and the church was only completed in the reign of his grandson, Nicholas II, by the noted Moscow architect, Alexander Kaminsky.

Travel southeast of Yegorevsk about 45 km on the R-105 through Yurtsovo and Stary Spass crossing the Tsna River to the railway settlement of Ryazanovsky, then turn left to a second **RYAZANOVSKY** *in an area of peat bogs and lakes.* Turn right on bumpy Sovietskaya Street to the village centre, where the little wooden houses sit at right angles screening the small **Holy Lake**.

At the end of the street on the left are the red brick walls and ruins of the once powerful **Nikolo-Radovitsky Monastery** founded in the 16th century. The huge pseudo-Russian Cathedral of the Nativity of the Virgin built in 1868 is now roofless and ruined although the amazing six-sectioned apse can still be appreciated. The monastery was closed after the revolution and in the 1930s the new walls and the second, Nicholas, Cathedral were destroyed leaving the empty southeast corner. The most dynamic surviving building is the classical bell tower and gate church of **Sts Peter and Paul**, built 1750s to 1780s, which still has its spire and gold cross and engaging geometrical designs similar to those of the Transfiguration Church in Beloomut. In spite of the dilapidation, the old red brick of the ruins harmonises sweetly with the green grass and the rolling countryside. Boys cycle in and out and climb the dangerous towers, cows contentedly crop the grass, and local people arrive burdened with pots and buckets to tap the holy water from the still-functioning monastery well.

From Yegorevsk take the R-105 north towards the A-108 but turn right (unsigned) opposite the left turn to Ilinsky Pogost. In 12 km past Abramovka and Stepanovka turn right at the T-junction by the railway line and in 2 km turn right again signed NIKITSKOE and MALKOVO. Here at **RUDNYA-NIKITSKOE** are two stunning wooden churches in a *pogost*, cemetery, on the Volnaya River. The churches both date from the 18th century and it must be a miracle they are still standing considering the risks of fire, vandalism, and Soviet hostility. The tall summer **Church of the Nativity of the Virgin**, *Rozhdestva Bogoroditsy*, an octagon on a cube, was built in 1782 with a tent shaped bell tower. In the 19th century the wide *trapeza* with entrance steps was added which embraces and hides the old church on north and south. The interior is a rare delight. The ceiling, as in northern wooden churches the *nebo* or heaven, is lined with canvas on which biblical scenes are painted. The iconostasis too is original although many of the old icons have been stolen. The smaller winter **Church of the Nativity of Christ**, *Rozhdestva Khristova*, stands modestly in a corner of the cemetery. First built in the early 18th century and rebuilt a century later it is of logs covered with weatherboarding under steep saddlebacked roofs and single cupola, the whole painted a dark blue. The beams within are covered with traditional ornamental designs and the small iconostasis of 1806 also includes some fine icons.

NIZHNY NOVGOROD HIGHWAY M-7: ZHELEZNODOROZHNY TO NOGINSK AND FRYANOVO

The land east of Moscow has long been an industrial area. The first manufactures – leather and silk – appeared in the 1700s under Peter the Great. In the late 19th and early 20th centuries, textile mills grew rapidly especially in Noginsk and Orekhovo-Zuevo. As electricity came into use new towns were evocatively called Elektrougli, Elektrostal and Elektrogorsk. Nevertheless, *dachniki* enjoy the deep countryside away from industrial centres among dilapidated former stately homes.

AROUND ZHELEZNODOROZHNY

An unnumbered road south of and parallel to the Nizhny Novgorod Highway follows the Vladimir railway linking small industrial towns before it merges with the A-107.

From Rogozhskaya Zastava Square take Shosse Entuziastov passing Izmailovsky Park and turn right onto the MKAD, then take the next exit left to Reutovo signed NIKOLSKO-ARKHANGELSKOE 3 km onto Nosovikhinskoe Shosse.

Where the high rises and cotton mills of Reutovo end, the wooden houses of **NIKOLSKO-ARKHANGELSKOE** begin. Moscow's depressing modern crematorium, right, is more than compensated for, left, by the attractive **Church of Michael the Archangel** where in fine weather people sit on welcoming benches and children run to and fro. The best time to visit is during the June festival of the Trinity, when deliciously scented grasses are strewn over the floor.

The church was built between 1748 and 1771 for Prince A.V. Dolgorukov of nearby Saltykovka. The Dolgorukovs' traditional views are reflected in the church's 17th century features – the tower of airy octagonal tiers over the tall cube and the deep basement containing the winter church. But elements of Petersburg baroque visible in the cornices, the window architraves and the semicircular arches were creeping in. The covered staircases and gallery linking the small bell tower to the church were originally open. Within the main, upper church is a gilded 19th century iconostasis with some fine icons but more spectacular is the ornamental plasterwork in a complicated baroque design of flowers and plants which follows the vaulting of the tower then separates to form cartouches.

From Nikolsko-Arkhangelskoe continue on the heavily trafficked narrow road parallel with the railway line. Or from the Nizhny Novgorod Highway M-7 turn right to Saltykovka then left (east) to **ZHELEZNO-DOROZHNY (Railroad City)**.

Any town uninvitingly called Railroad City implies a settlement built up around a busy railway junction – and Zheleznodorozhny (Zheldor for short) is no exception. Yet it also has fascinating villages on its periphery – Kuchino, Fenino, Savvino, and Poltevo. Moreover the busy railway station before 1939 was known as **Obiralovka** where Tolstoy placed the suicide of his despairing heroine in *Anna Karenina*.

Nowadays Zheldor, with a population of 100,000, is a modern town of tower blocks and a uniquely large statue of Lenin. An exception is the quiet district of **Zhilgorodok**, (right, before the railway station coming from Moscow) entered by an unusual pair of pink gates. Blocks of handsome wooden two-storey apartment houses with interesting stylised arrows and curves line the road interspersed with trees and open spaces while at the centre is a piazza bordered by four curved single-storey shops. Zhilgorodok was constructed by German prisoners of war as housing for the ceramics factory using the red clay of the Pekhorka River. The Germans, who were not repatriated until the 1950s, built several such wooden suburbs in other towns but most of these suburbs did not survive the reconstruction mania of the 1960s.

Enter Zheleznodorozhny and just past Kuchino station where tower blocks begin turn left under the railway line. The road soon turns sharp right then crosses the Pekhorka River to the meteorological institute, right, in the grounds of the former Ryabushinsky estate at **KUCHINO**.

The large estate was purchased from the Ryumins by Pavel Ryabush-insky not long before his death in 1899. His 8 sons and 5 daughters built dachas at the extremities of the property not caring for the gloomy Ryumin mansion. In 1904 **Dmitry Ryabushinsky**, the seventh son then 22 years old, founded the **Institute of Aerodynamics** at Kuchino assisted

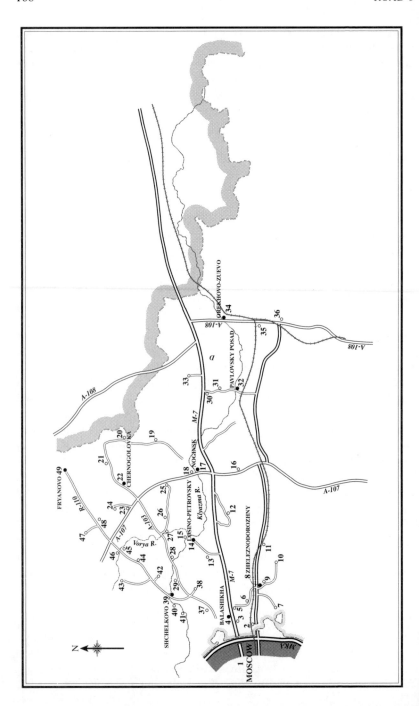

ROAD 6
ZHELEZNODOROZHNY TO NOGINSK AND FRYANOVO

1. MOSCOW
2. Nikolsko-Arkhangelsky
3. Gorenki
4. BALASHIKHA
5. Pekhra-Yakovlevskoe
6. Kuchino
7. Fenino
8. ZHELEZNODOROZHNY
9. Savvino
10. Poltevo
11. Elektrougli
12. Ivashevo
13. Monino
14. LOSINO-PETROVSKY
15. Glinki
16. Elektrostal
17. NOGINSK
18. Glukhovo
19. Mamontovo
20. Novosergievo
21. Stromyn
22. CHERNOGOLOVKA
23. Makarovo
24. Ivanovskoe
25. Yamkino
26. Voskresenskoe
27. Avdotino
28. Raiki
29. Aniskino
30. Kuznetsy
31. Zaozere
32. PAVLOVSKY POSAD
33. Elektrogorsk
34. OREKHOVO-ZUEVO
35. Kabanovo
36. LIKINO-DULEVO
37. Pekhra-Pokrovskoe
38. Almazovo
39. SHCHELKOVO
40. Khomutovo
41. Obraztsovo
42. Grebnevo
43. Bogoslovo
44. Trubino
45. Zdekhovo
46. Kablukovo
47. Petrovskoe
48. Dushonovo
49. FRYANOVO

by Nikolai Zhukovsky, the great scientist. Thus only a year after the Wright brothers' flight, aerodynamics was being seriously studied in Russia funded by the immensely rich Ryabushinskys. In 1914 the Institute's first decade was celebrated by 200 guests who watched delightedly as a pilot from Khodynka airport in Moscow landed in front of them. Dmitry's brothers distinguished themselves in other fields – Nikolai famously bankrupted himself sponsoring avant-garde artists – but Dmitry was the only pure scientist. He emigrated after the revolution to Paris where he became Professor of Hydrodynamics at the Sorbonne.

A small museum to the Ryabushinskys is located in the hydro-meteorological institute. Near the Pekhorka River, only the stone steps of the old house survive along with the remains of a sad fountain. To the right is the pseudo-Russian **stone chapel**, that was altered in Soviet times for use as an observatory.

On the main road pass Kuchino railway station cross the Pekhorka River to a traffic light and turn right. After 2 km past tower blocks turn right again at a T-junction to **FENINO** *and its stunning church.*

Count Petr Rumyantsev, dubbed *Zadunaisky* (beyond the Danube) for his exploits in the Russo-Turkish war, was given the large estate by the Pekhorka in 1760 and renamed it **Troitskoe-Kainardji** after the Turkish peace agreement. Various points in the roughly triangular property were named for Turkish fortresses and the victory was celebrated annually in the most extravagant fashion. Troitskoe was even graced by a visit of Catherine II. It is no accident that Tolstoy chose the station of Obiralovka for Anna Karenina's suicide for he based the sumptuous estate of Anna's lover, Count Vronsky, on that of the Rumyantsevs.

As none of the Count's three sons married (the eldest, Nikolai, founded the Rumyantsev museum in Moscow) Troitskoe was divided in the 1830s between his two married daughters after whom the villages, Fenino and Zenino, were named. The mansion, thus abandoned, is now gone without trace. The large statue of Catherine II by Demut-Malinovsky was removed in 1934 to the Moscow Architecture Museum. So only the church, which never closed, the mausoleum and a chapel survive.

The splendid **Church of the Trinity**, *Troitsy*, built in 1778 was designed by Karl Blank in brick and stucco with elaborate stone dressings combining elements of the early classical style and the baroque. The impressive triumphal entrance designed by Rumyantsev himself is framed by twin triple-tiered bell towers with tall spires. Within, where the old iconostasis and fittings are barely visible in the dim light, an old lady with a lovely face can sometimes be found polishing the brass.

The **cemetery** behind the apse contains graves of Apraxins and Golitsyns who married into the family. A great marble mausoleum with four Tuscan porticoes built in 1838 holds the tomb of the Count's younger son, Sergei. By the graveyard is a second chapel, the red brick **Assumption**, *Uspeniya*, built in 1867 in pseudo-Russian style by V.S. Mukhanova, great-granddaughter of the Count, over the grave of her husband.

In Zheldor turn right at the railway station, go past the Lenin statue following the road 2 km to **SAVVINO** *and turn sharp left at traffic lights for a few hundred metres.* The **Church of the Transfiguration**, *Spasa Preobrazheniya*, was built 1870-85 then later enlarged. The unique iconostases – the main screen and those of the two side chapels – are in shiny gold, pink and blue **ceramic**, a bold material that clashes with the warm serenity of the icons. They are the gift of Vikula Morozov whose mill was on the main road and were made 1906-9 at the Kuznetsov works.

From Savvino cross the Chernaya River, turn left at the barely legible sign, and travel 5 km to **POLTEVO**. In the park of the old Apraxin estate, left, is a pioneer camp, being redeveloped for use as holiday homes. On the right the tall, elegant ship-like **Church of St Nicholas** with a bell tower like a funnel at its centre was built in 1706 by Count Fedor Apraxin, an admiral although he had never been to sea. As the Count had no children it was acquired in 1729 by **Andrei Osterman** of Westphalia who had served Peter in important diplomatic negotiations but who, after service with Empress Anna, was exiled when Elizabeth came to power.

The high austere church, lit by two rows of finely carved windows, is not a cube but an unequal octagon, almost an oval. The eastern and western ends are identical, one serving as the apse and the other as the *pritvor* or entrance. The single chamber with a few late frescoes is well lit and spacious without the encumbrance of columns or interior walls. But St Nicholas, a rare example of Petrine architecture, is suffering from dangerously large cracks in the walls and the cost of repairs is too large for the small parish of summer *dachniki*.

NOBLE ESTATES ON THE VLADIMIR ROAD

For the **Nizhny Novgorod Highway M-7** *from Rogozhskaya Zastava join Shosse Entuziastov. Pass the Guzhon/Serp i Molot factory with its interesting Palace of Culture, left, and the huge expanse of Izmailovsky Park, left, to cross the MKAD where the Shosse becomes the M-7.*

Before the revolution the road was known as the *Vladimirka* along which thousands of prisoners, many of them in chains, made their way on foot to exile in Siberia. Levitan's canvas of 1892, *Vladimirka*, depicts the lonely track going on into the empty distance enlivened only by a church and the vast lowering sky. At the first post station called **GORENKI**, from *gore* meaning grief, families of the prisoners could get a last glimpse of their loved ones whom they might never see again.

Today, the lonely track has become the sprawling industrial city of **Balashikha**, population 137,000. *On the M-7 after the third traffic light beyond the sign BALASHIKHA by the Sanatori bus-stop are the ochre walls and gates of* **Gorenki**, right. Most of the principal buildings of the palatial **Razumovsky** estate survive in reduced form – the main house and wings, the orangerie, some service buildings, the gates and guard houses, and part of the park, long pond, grotto and even some Karelian birch furniture. Since the 1920s it has been the *Krasnaya Roza* (Red Rose) sanatorium for treating tuberculosis but visitors can explore the grounds.

Gorenki belonged from 1714 to 1747 to the influential **Prince Alexei Dolgorukov**. The conservative Dolgorukovs who opposed the reforms of Peter the Great became the dominant faction during the reign of the boy-king, Peter II, 1727-30. Alexei Dolgorukov's second daughter, Catherine, was betrothed to the young king but on January 30, 1730, which should have been their wedding day, Peter II died of smallpox. On the accession of Anna, the Dolgorukovs including the royal fiancee were sent into exile. Catherine returned a decade later and married Alexander Bruce, owner of Glinki farther along this road, but died in the same year, aged only 33.

In 1747 Empress Elizabeth granted the estate to **Count Alexei Razumovsky**, the former shepherd boy who became her lover and probable husband. On his death, Gorenki passed to his nephew, another **Count Alexei**, whose father, Kirill, was the last Hetman of the Ukraine. In 1795 at the end of Catherine's reign, Count Alexei retired to Gorenki and devoted himself to botany in the gardens of the estate. In 1810 under Alexander I, he was recalled to court to serve as Minister for Education and was responsible for opening many parish schools and for establishing the remarkable lycee in Tsarskoe Selo which so influenced Pushkin and his generation. In 1816 he retired a second time, in protest against Alexander I's harassment of Jesuits.

It is probable that the English architect, **Adam Menelaws**, resident in Russia from 1784 and responsible for several Razumovsky properties, built Gorenki. The main house was constructed 1780 to 1790s in the classical manner but its severe facade is untypical of Menelaws' later buildings (e.g. the Razumovsky palace in Moscow). Of three storeys, the central section with a portico and pediment of six Ionic columns is flanked by attractive bays. Two-storey wings on either side of the bays reach into the garden to embrace a spacious courtyard.

The single-storeyed **orangerie**, right when facing the house, is also by Menelaws, now much altered since it was adapted as housing. Here in forty hot-houses Razumovsky indulged his passion for the delicate plants he collected from around the world. His **gardens** by the ponds made from damming the little Gorenki River, a tributary of the Pekhorka, were filled with strange trees and plants and lovingly cared for by the German botanist, Dr Teodor Fischer, later the first director of the new Petersburg botanical garden. The English gardener, John Claudius Loudon, who visited Russia in 1814 described Gorenki in his *Encyclopaedia of Gardening* published in 1827:

> remarkable for its botanical richness and its huge quantity of grass ....The house, which was built by an English architect, is highly elegant and the adjacent pavilions, grottoes and lawn decorated [with flowers] form a magnificent and gay spectacle which is not surpassed in Russia.

Of these remarkable gardens only abundant wild flowers flourish today in the hugely overgrown park. When Razumovsky died in 1822 two buyers divided the estate: **Prince Nikolai Yusupov**, who removed many of the rare plants to Arkhangelskoe (other plants were taken to Moscow University's botanical gardens on Prospekt Mira), and **Volkov**, a merchant, who used the mansion to manufacture textiles. In 1910 Gorenki was purchased by **V.P. Sevryugov**, who commissioned the architect, Sergei Chernyshev, to return the old house and grounds to its former elegance. The work was only completed in 1916 leaving

Sevryugov little more than a year in which to enjoy his achievement before the revolution swept away all private property.

Sergei Chernyshev, then in his early thirties, followed Menelaws' classical style in the impressive curving **colonnades** ending in pavilions which enclose the terrace and the **loggia** of 14 columns and richly decorating the interiors. The former gold room (right of the entrance up some steps) with its wonderful oak doors, fine parquet flooring and delicate columns with gilded capitals must be the most magnificent dining room in any Russian sanatorium.

On the M-7 travel 3 km beyond Gorenki to a traffic light where the Pekhorka River and a church are on the right. Turn right signed ZHELEZNODOROZHNY, and immediately right again to the agricultural college milling with students that occupies the former estate of **PEKHRA-YAKOVLEVSKOE**.

The Princes Golitsyn owned Pekhra-Yakovlevskoe from 1591 for nearly 250 years. After 1828 it passed rapidly from hand to hand until in the 1870s it was acquired by General Khristofor Roop, dealer in wood and wine, who owned it until the revolution. The church, the theatre, the wings and orangerie are still standing.

The most impressive building is the classical **Church of the Transfiguration**, *Spasa Preobrazheniya* built 1777-82 for **Prince Alexander Golitsyn**, vice-chancellor of Catherine II. The triumphal arched entrance with twin bell towers similar to Karl Blank's church at Troitskoe-Kainardzhi leads into an airy inner and outer rotunda in soft rosy colours lit by two tiers of windows. The massive drum and dome with a tall spire rest on the inner rotunda where fluted Corinthian pilasters support a grand entablature. Services resumed in 1992.

The original mansion, probably by Karl Blank, was damaged by a hurricane in 1917 and then in 1924 by fire. It was subsequently rebuilt in a pared down classical style with an extra storey resulting in the present unsympathetic building. However, the late 18th century two-storey **wings** with porticoes of Tuscan columns attached to the main house by beautiful open colonnades survived the fire. To the left is the **theatre**, built in 1810 (windows and interior later altered), thought with the **orangerie**, right (hidden by a Soviet building), to be by Adam Menelaws, the architect of neighbouring Gorenki.

Great, broad steps lead into the **park**, once planted in the regular French manner. Statuary including some amusing lions survive although the fountain of the three graces has long disappeared.

Take the Nizhny Novgorod Highway M-7 past Balashikha and Staraya Kupavna 26 km. At Obukha, left, Peter the Great pardoned escaped serfs and convicts who agreed to work at his new mill. Turn right signed ELEKTROUGLI then, after 4 km, left in the direction of Noginsk to **Ivashevo**, *where only the church and a few service buildings survive of the modest 18th century* **Troitskoe-Ratmanovo** *estate. The* **Trinity**, *was built in 1815 of brick and stucco in the classical style, its beauty still evident in the Doric rotunda surrounding the apse. Return to the Nizhny Novgorod M-7 Highway to traffic lights at the GAI post and turn left signed MONINO 4 km (where there is an interesting* **museum of military aircraft**) and under the railway line to Losino-Petrovsky.

The run-down rambling town of **LOSINO-PETROVSKY**, population 22,000, at the confluence of the Vorya and the Klyazma was founded by Peter the Great for processing moose/elk hides (hence the name, *los*, moose or elk) to make knapsacks, gloves, and even ammunition for the tsar's army. Losino-Petrovsky has three interesting Empire churches, all built about 1820 and all functioning, and one great estate.

On the left past modern tower blocks on the territory of the former moose/elk factory is the tall bell tower and church of the **Consolation of All Sorrows**, *Vsekh Skorbyashchikh Radosti*, built in 1819 to celebrate the victory over Napoleon. This fine church with a massive drum and dome, Doric columns and pediments still has the original iconostasis and iron floors. The second church, also **Consolation of All Sorrows**, was built in 1819 on the Valuev estate in the former village of **Timonino**, now within Losino-Petrovsky. *Turn right towards the river before reaching the centre.* It is centrally planned, under a broad dome with Tuscan porticoes, semicircular windows on three sides and a round apse on the fourth. The third church, of the **Aristov Pogost**, is at Prechistoe. *On entering Losino-Petrovsky under the railway line follow the main road left past wooden houses, an old mill and fields. At a second mill turn left onto a narrow road to the cemetery/pogost within 1 km.* The handsome **Church of the Trinity**, *Troitsy*, now surrounded by modern brick *kottedzhi*, remained open throughout the Soviet period. It was built in 1822 with a heavy rotunda and massive drum pierced by windows, a rusticated facade divided by pilasters, and Doric porches on north and south. The large *trapeza* and three-tier bell tower are nearly the same date. On the north facade is an unusual painting, a cartoon of a man petitioning the Virgin with words coming out of his mouth in a balloon.

In the centre of Losino-Petrovsky turn right near the first Church of All Sorrows and cross the bridge over the Klyazma River. Follow the signs left to Monino sanatorium.

GLINKI (now the Monino sanatorium), at the confluence of the Klyazma and Vorya, was built in the reign of Peter the Great by James Bruce of Scottish origin. Not only is the house still standing but also the stables, the orangerie, the so-called Bruce laboratory, storeroom, and the guard house. Although still a sanatorium, strangers are welcome, especially to the small museum.

William of the Bruces of Airth came to Russia as a mercenary soldier in 1649 and his two sons born in Russia were able to make fine careers in the fluid times of Peter the Great. The eldest, **James Daniel** (Yakob Vilemovich), was well-educated with a scientific bent and a talent for military engineering. He accompanied young Tsar Peter to England on his Great Embassy in 1698, where he met Sir Isaac Newton and visited Greenwich Observatory and on his return set up the first Russian observatory. He also served Peter in diplomatic negotiations, as engineer of fortifications, and as general of the artillery (he is mentioned in Pushkin's poem, *Poltava*), was head of the mint and an ingenious inventor. Indeed, his gifts were so numerous that superstitious Russians thought him a dangerous sorcerer. Peter, however, appreciated his talents and in 1721 made him a count. Bruce purchased **Glinki** in 1727 from Prince Alexei Dolgorukov of Gorenki, whose daughter was to marry Bruce's nephew and heir.

The two-storey **mansion** with grimacing masks facing south to the square and watchmen's lodge may have been designed by Bruce himself. The main feature, the central loggia, rises through both storeys – the ground floor is distinguished by rusticated arches and the upper by the balcony of paired Corinthian columns. The roof belvedere and the exact north-south axis suggest that the house may also have been Bruce's observatory. Indeed the well-lit central hall on the second floor surrounded by smaller rooms could have been used for telescopes.

On the west side, left of the house are the 'Bruce storage rooms' (now the museum) built at the same time as the house. The single-storey 'Bruce laboratory', with shell niches framed by paired pilasters, stands a little to the northeast. Beyond the square pond at the end of the park is the unrecognisable ruined church of 1756 vandalised in the 1930s when it was adapted as a dormitory.

James Bruce died in 1735 aged 66 and his scientific instruments, his collection of maps and his extensive library were taken to Peter the Great's *Kunstkamera* in Petersburg where they were consulted by later scientists, including Lomonosov. Bruce was buried with his wife in the cemetery of the Lutheran church in Moscow on what is now Radio Street. In 1929, when the church was destroyed, the graves of Bruce and his wife, Margarita, were discovered with Bruce's fine kaftan of gold thread still intact.

Glinki then passed to his nephew, **Alexander Bruce**, who also inherited his uncle's title. Alexander married two Dolgorukovs, the first died and the second was the unfortunate Catherine who had just missed becoming Tsaritsa to Peter II (see Gorenki). At the end of the 18th century Glinki was inherited by James Bruce's great grand niece, another Catherine. She married a Musin-Pushkin who thereupon added Bruce to his already cumbersome name. In 1815 Catherine sold the estate to the Kaluga landowner, Ivan Usachev, who promptly opened a paper works then a textile mill. In 1899 the house was struck by lightning setting fire to cotton bales within and destroying all the interiors.

After the revolution, Glinki was used to house homeless children then, in 1931, it became a rest home of the Commissariat for Food Industries. During the war a military hospital was established and in 1948 the sanatorium opened. Visitors are welcome to the delightful museum where the caretakers fiercely maintain that James Bruce is the direct descendant of the Scottish kings via Robert the Bruce.

NOGINSK

Noginsk lies left of the Nizhny Novgorod Highway M-7, 40 km from the MKAD. To the right is ELEKTROSTAL, population 150,000, founded in 1916 by the powerful Siberian magnate and banker, Nikolai Vtorov. But the factory only came into operation in late 1917, after the revolution, the first furnace in Russia to be powered by electricity and to make high quality steel. Vtorov, living in his Moscow mansion (now the American Ambassdor's residence) died suddenly in May 1918 – his was the last public funeral the new government allowed to a bourgeois businessman. Turn left into Noginsk at the hammer and sickle onto 3rd International

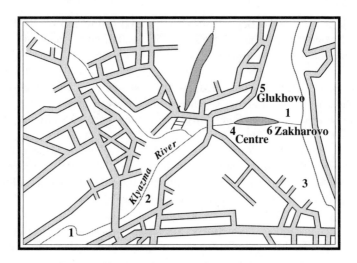

NOGINSK   1. Klyazma River, 2. 3rd International, 3. Uspenskoe,
4. Centre, 5. Glukhovo, 6. Zakharovo

Street past a ruined chapel and the Istominskoe mill and left again onto
wide Komsomolskaya Street, then left again to 9 January Street and left
once more onto Rabochaya Street.

Noginsk, population 120,000, was the staging post, Stary Rogozhsky
Yam, between Moscow and Nizhny Novgorod. By the 18th century silk
began to be produced and in 1781 the town was renamed **Bogorodsk**
and granted a coat of arms. Modern expansion began in 1842 when
Zakhar Morozov, a member of the Morozov dynasty of Orekhovo
Zuevo, founded the cotton mill in Glukhovo, on the left bank of the
Klyazma. As the Zakhar Morozovs were Old Believers of the
Rogozhskoe Accord, Bogorodsk became an important religious centre.
Zakhar's son, Arseny, took over the mill and was in turn succeeded by
Nikolai, his nephew, who after study in England introduced many
improvements. Zakhar Morozov and his son, Arseny, were great philan-
thropists, particularly in the educational and medical fields, attracting
some of the best architects for these new buildings in Art Nouveau, the
preferred style of the Old Believer merchants. After the revolution the
mills were nationalised and in 1930 the town was renamed Noginsk for
Viktor Nogin, a leading Bolshevik, who had no connection with the
town. Noginsk today has the best Art Nouveau buildings of any provincial town around Moscow.

In **CENTRAL NOGINSK** a glimpse into the town's history can be obtained at the local **museum** at Bugrova Square off Rabochaya Street. Among the exhibits are items from Arseny Morozov's house including a strange statue of Columbus. Among the few churches is the ungainly **Cathedral of the Epiphany**, *Bogoyavleniya*, on Rabochaya Street built in 1873 and now functioning again. Down the street to the east is the more attractive **Tikhvin Church** of 1853 with a pseudo-Russian facade which was a cinema in the Soviet period.

On nearby **Sovietskaya Street** (parallel to Rabochaya one block south) and **Trudovaya** is the *univermag*, the main shop, built in the 1900s as the Sidnev restaurant with pointed gables and an Art Nouveau entrance. Farther along Sovietskaya St at No 57 is the admirable **Girls' Grammar School**. It was built in Art Nouveau style in 1908 by Alexander Kuznetsov, principal architect of the Morozov factory at Glukhovo. The differently treated windows and attractively curved roof line, combine with the corner towers and use of bays to make it one of Kuznetsov's best buildings.

Complementing the Girls' Grammar is the science-oriented **boys' school**, now a pedagogical institute, on 3rd International Street. Built in 1910 it was well equipped including a still-functioning observatory and reflects the advances made in education before the revolution. Like the girls' school, it was the gift of Sergei Morozov, grandson of Zakhar.

The old Morozov mill at **GLUKHOVO** is on the other side of the Klyazma River, across the bridge to the left. The **Bogorodskaya-Glukhovskaya Manufaktura**, where all aspects of cloth manufacture were performed from spinning cotton to dyeing, was one of the largest enterprises in Russia before the revolution employing over 11,000 workers. The mill now called *Glukhovteks*, still functions although lethargically, since it has become difficult to obtain cotton cheaply. It is amazing how the old buildings with their Art Nouveau touches, erected 1903-8 by Alexander Kuznetsov, look more solid than the rapidly decaying blocks of the Soviet period. Kuznetsov devised the centralised ventilation and the roof skylights in the form of pyramids, now commonplace but then a highly original innovation.

The whole neighbourhood well served with parks has the atmosphere of a garden city. On the main road, 8 March Street, almost opposite the factory are some **workers' dormitories** still displaying their original lettering *Dom No.1* although they have long since been communal flats.

They were built to the latest standards on the corridor system with communal kitchens and storage in the central areas of each floor and laundries in the semi-basement. They are probably by the local architect, Alexander Markov, who built in 1908 the attractive **boys' trade school** nearby. Still a school, it has retained the coloured tiles, brick and stone cladding dotted with Art Nouveau designs, and in the central hall the frieze of classical figures and fine iron staircase. Not far away in the park is the **maternity hospital**, (now the Neurological Institute) also a gift of the Morozovs and another building by Markov. Art Nouveau tiles and metalwork decorate the exterior while within the splendid white staircase and other fittings have survived.

A delightful street in this area is the tree-lined *Ulitsa Tikhaya*, Quiet Street. It has the fine **wooden houses** with peaked gables and touches of Art Nouveau of the lesser managers, engineers, and skilled weavers. One of the houses now divided into communal flats still has the old stove in the hall. It is hard to believe that these fine buildings, still owned by the factory, may be earmarked for demolition.

In the city park by the pond two houses were built for the **Morozov family**. That of Arseny Morozov, designed by Alexander Kuznetsov, has been thoroughly altered but the second, for Arseny's son, also in wood and stucco, is better preserved. Now a club for children not only the interesting fireplaces have survived but even the original door handles. In the attic a panelled room served as the secret Old Believer's chapel for the Morozovs until the ban was lifted in 1905.

Another interesting corner of Noginsk is the tiny suburb of **ZAKHAROVO**. Take 3rd International Street left across the railway line and turn immediately right. Here the Old Believers under the redoubtable Arseny Morozov built a community centre in the years just before the First World War. The **Church of St Zakhary**, named for Arseny's father's patron saint, was an outstanding example of Russian Art Nouveau built in 1911 by the architect, **Ilya Bondarenko**, whose Old Believer church in Moscow's Tokmakov Lane was much admired by the Morozovs. But Bondarenko today would not recognise the church, now a bakery. The cube with its ogee-shapes still stands but the strong drum and powerful onion-shaped dome are gone. The *zvonnitsa* bell tower on the southwest has had its top aperture destroyed and the two lower ones are filled in. Although the ground floor west window retains its original architrave, the low entrance beside the bell tower is blocked up and built over. And the portable altar donated by Arseny Morozov is lost.

The neighbouring building where the famous Zakharovo choir trained, has survived better.

But the oldest buildings are at the former estate of **USPENSKOE**. Take 3rd International Street east, across the railway line and at traffic lights turn left and follow the road, turning left again across a stream and then right on Kalayev Street. The **Church of the Assumption**, *Uspeniya*, and the two-storey **mansion** of the mid 18th century were used until recently for weaving cloth. The octagonal church with the tall drum is functioning again but the much altered mansion is in poor condition.

NORTH OF NOGINSK

An interesting way to return to Moscow is by following the Sherna River northeast from Glukhovo through villages most of which are embellished by pleasant Empire churches of the 1820s. Within 7 km is **Mamontovo** and the appealing 1820 Church of St Elijah; then 5 km farther is **Novosergievo** where the greatly ruined Empire church is under repair. Within another 7 km at Chernovo turn left to **Stromyn**, and the impressive Assumption Church of 1827. Ten km west are the dreary high-rises of **Chernogolovka**, the biophysics scientific town founded in the 1960s. Turn right at the roundabout and then right to join the A-107 and in 2 km take the right fork to **Makarovo** and the early 20th century **St Nicholas**. At **Ivanovskoe** 2 km farther on the Pruzhenka River the old wooden church burnt down in the early 1980s but the winter church of St John the Baptist built in the late 19th century is functioning again. Twelve km south on the A-107 towards Noginsk is **Yamkino** and another Empire church of the 1820s, the Nativity of Christ. Here the companion wooden church of the 1720s was barbarously dragged apart by tractors in 1963, a victim of Khrushchev's anti-religious campaign.

From Yamkino travel west 8 km to **VOSKRESENSKOE** where a complete ensemble survives of a wooden summer church, a masonry winter church, a priest's house and, an exotic new guesthouse with steambath. The wooden church is the most remarkable. The log-built **Ascension**, *Vozneseniya*, was constructed in 1705 just as Petersburg was being founded, and is relatively unchanged except for the addition of weatherboarding and the loss of the outer gallery, *gulbishche*. The tall cube, with the sloping roof and single dome, has a pentagonal extruding apse and low *trapeza*. Within are exquisite ceiling paintings on canvas *(nebo*, heaven) modelled on those of northern Russia. The iconostasis and rare carved figures of St Nicholas and St Paraskeva also survive.

The neighbouring masonry **Church of the Intercession**, *Pokrova*, was built to a standard design over a period of thirty years, 1833-63, at a time when the classical style was beginning its long decline. Painted yellow and white, with an impressive dome astride the main cube, the tiered bell tower, which is used as the village fire alarm, guards the entrance. During repairs the remarkable old heating system was uncovered and is now reactivated. It lies in the basement, a narrow cavern 8 metres long into which logs are placed every three days. Even in the coldest weather the logs burn evenly, hot air flows through vents, and the church is kept beautifully warm.

The wooden Church of the Ascension was closed soon after the revolution but the Intercession continued holding services until 1937 when local officials formally asked if anyone wished to keep the church open. Naturally, in the atmosphere of 1937, no one dared speak out but the church warden courageously hid the key in the wall of his house and no-one could open the huge padlock. Thus the interior was not vandalised but the bells were wrenched from their hangings and smashed to the ground. In 1944 the church reopened.

Voskresenskoe was a poor parish until in the early 1990s a miracle happened in the form of Alexei, a wealthy entrepreneur from Noginsk, who took upon himself the organisation and finance of the restoration work.

Four km west of Voskresenskoe at **AVDOTINO** on the Vorya River is the **St Nicholas-Berlyukov Monastery**, *Nikolaevskaya-Berlyukovskaya Pustyn*. It was founded in the early 17th century then abandoned until the 1770s when the Moscow Metropolitan, Platon, decided to restore the romantic ruins. By the 1830s the cathedral was renewed and at the end of the century other buildings including the magnificent bell tower were built. In the 1930s the monastery was closed and turned into a psychiatric and tuberculosis hospital for which its secluded position was well suited. Nowadays there are plans to return it to the church, but new accommodation will have to be found for the hospital.

The walls, gate and belltower survive as does the dilapidated **Cathedral of Christ the Saviour**, *Khrista Spasitelya*, completed in 1842, which stands opposite the entrance. The design for this church, rejected in the competition for St Isaac's Cathedral in Petersburg finally found acceptance here. To the right is the refectory Trinity Church, *Troitsy*, and the abbot's All Saints, *Vsekh Svyatykh* both in the pseudo-Russian style.

More striking is the **gate/belltower** which soars upward for 104 metres. The noted Moscow architect, **Alexander Kaminsky**, suffered a setback in 1888 when one of his buildings under construction in central Moscow collapsed crushing several passers-by and he was reprimanded and fined. However, he continued working and the magnificent bell tower is witness to his skill; constructed 1895-1900, it has not yet collapsed despite decades of neglect.

Continue north 3 km to join the A-103 left. After 6 km are the large gates, left, of **RAIKI**, *the Foreign Ministry holiday home.* The property was purchased in the 1890s by the rich Siberian gold merchant, Ivan Nekrasov, for his country dacha. The delightful two-storey stucco house with steeply pitched roofs built by **Lev Kekushev**, the notable Art Nouveau architect, for the Nekrasovs in 1909 still stands but the romantic wooden house used for guests at the end of the central avenue suffered badly from fire in 1996. **Leonid Pasternak**, the artist and teacher, and his family – including young Boris – spent their summer holiday here in 1907 and 1909. In 1915 Sergei Chetverikov, the Gorodishche (Sverdlovsky) mill owner purchased Raiki for use as a hospital for soldiers injured in the war.

Travel east through Yunost to **ANISKINO** *and the shining white* **Church of the Nativity**, *Rozhdestva Bogoroditsy, right, built in 1759 in a subdued baroque style.* Closed in 1938 and used as a workshop for the mill, it was handed back in 1990 the walls barely standing. The last private owners of the mill, the Chetverikov brothers, were great patrons of Aniskino and today after 70 years of neglect the mill has again been in the forefront of rescuing the church. From here Moscow is reached in about 20 km.

PAVLOVSKY POSAD

En route to Pavlovsky Posad, travel on the Nizhny Novgorod Highway M-7 past Noginsk 7 km to **Bogoslovo** *at the confluence of the Sherna River and the Klyazma.* The cemetery **Church of the Assumption**, *Uspeniya*, right, was built in 1826 in Empire style and has been functioning since 1992. Stone detailing beautifully enhances the red brick and the strong rotunda resting on the cube repeats the curve of the round jutting apse. Across the Sherna River is **Bolshoe Bunkovo**, once a post station for prisoners returning from Siberia including the radicals Alexander Radishchev and Alexander Herzen.

Thirteen km beyond Noginsk is **KUZNETSY** *which as its name, smiths, implies, served horses and carriages before the advent of the motor car.* The bizarre **wooden house**, No 42 on the left, is fitted with inexplicable spires and metal balls, solar panels and odd folkloric designs. Turn right at the traffic lights by the GAI towards Pavlovsky Posad. The large white building, right, is all that remains of the once picturesque Old Believer **Church of St Ann** constructed in 1910 by the architect Ilya Bondarenko for the same patron, Arseny Morozov, as his St Zakhary in Noginsk. Bondarenko favoured the exaggerated Novgorod style employing piquant touches in the the varying heights and shapes of the large onion-shaped dome, sloping roofs, porches and bell tower. Altered for use as a club, all that is left is the main cube with its triple-bayed indented facade and the entrance which has been made level with the rest of the building. How spectacular it would be if restored to the original design.

Two km beyond Kuznetsy going towards Pavlovsky Posad just before a small lake take the paved road left (ignore the no entry sign) to **Zaozere**. The handsome classical **Nativity of Christ**, *Rozhdestva Khristova*, built in 1809 and never closed, is surrounded by an old overgrown graveyard overlooking the pretty lake.

Continue from Zaozere 4 km to **PAVLOVSKY POSAD** *through Bolshie Dvory, where the old mill produces linen.* Pavlovsky Posad, population 70,000, is a well preserved late 19th century industrial town. Situated on the Klyazma River and its tributaries, the Vokhna and Khotsa, its streets are pleasantly lined with wooden houses embellished with carvings and bargeboards, the odd church and tower, handsome merchants' houses and many old textile mills.

In 1844 four silk-weaving villages joined together to form Pavlovsky Posad. With the opening of the railway line in 1862 woollen and cotton as well as silk could be quickly carried to the great markets of Nizhny Novgorod and Moscow. In 1812 Semen Labzin began making the distinctive kerchiefs and shawls in the large flower design on black, cream and wine-coloured backgrounds known as *pavlovsky*. Until recently no respectable Russian woman was properly dressed without such a shawl.

Across the Klyazma left on Gorky Street is the recently reopened red brick **Intercession-St Basil Convent**, *Pokrovsky-Vasilievsky Monastyr*, founded in 1885 by sisters of mercy, by the town cemetery. Cross over

the Klyazma to the green **Cathedral Square** and the magnificent triple-
tiered **belltower**, all that is left of the Cathedral of St Dimitry dismantled
1954-7 in Khrushchev's time. It houses the interesting town museum
(open 10 to 5, closed Mondays).

Pavlovsky Posad's several districts are each focused on a particular
factory. One of the most attractive is **FILIMONOVO**, 2 km west,
reached from the bell tower by turning right before the bridge over the
Vokhna onto 1st May Street. Delightful wooden houses lead to the
large red brick mill founded by Andrei Sokolikov, a refugee from
Moscow escaping the French in 1812. He so liked Filimonovo he settled
down and began silk weaving. Under his descendants the workshop
grew into a sizeable enterprise which in 1909 employed over 300 people.

Return to Cathedral Square, cross the Vokhna, and pass through
market square with the usual statue of Lenin to **MELENKI** where the
large red brick **Labzin/Gryaznov factory** is on the right and the 1895
Russian-French Manufaktura stands on the left. The Labzin/Gryaznov
mill sold silk scarves and shawls in Persia and the East as well as Russia
and was a generous benefactor of the town.

Another interesting suburb, **GORODOK**, is in the eastern part of
Pavlovsky Posad. From the market square turn left (coming from the
north) onto Kirov Street, a main avenue with fine houses, past the
railway station to a traffic light. Turn left here and then left again at
the railway crossing signed GORKOVSKOE SHOSSE (or Nizhny
Novgorod). Note the old Kudin factory on the left by the Klyazma then
turn right onto a sandy lane and then immediately left. The road leads
to a tree-lined square and, right, the large church and cemetery of
Gorodok. The red brick pseudo-Byzantine **Annunciation**, *Blagoveshcheniya*, with its peaked arched facades and huge blue dome stands behind
a fence with a delightful free-standing wooden bell tower in the corner.
It was built in 1908 by the Kudin brothers, Alexei and Ivan, who,
although peasants, had risen as master weavers through the silk mill
hierarchy and established their own large wool and silk mill. Although
they generously built the churches, hospitals and schools of the community, they lived modestly on nearby Shkolnaya Street at Nos 14 and 16.

For the oldest building in Pavlovsky Posad at **SAUROVO** turn left past
the railway station and continue straight ahead past another large
factory and a new red brick Old Believer church in front of tower
blocks. Turn left here through Korneevo to the Klyazma and follow the

embankment east 2 km to Saurovo. The **Church of the Nativity of the Virgin,** *Rozhdestva Bogoroditsy,* built in 1830 overlooking the river is in Empire style with a strong rotunda and pediments on north and south balanced by the tall, three-tiered bell tower and low refectory. Closed for only two weeks in the 1930s it has retained the early 20th century iconostasis.

OREKHOVO-ZUEVO

On the Nizhny Novgorod Highway M-7, 5 km past Kuznetsy, ELEKTRO-GORSK stands on the left, population 18,000. It was founded in 1912 when a power plant producing electricity using peat was developed by R. Ye Klasson, the first in the world. 13 km farther at Malaya Dubna (18 km from Kuznetsy) turn right on the A-108 10 km to Orekhovo-Zuevo.

With a population of over 135,000 Orekhovo-Zuevo, yet another large mill town on the Klyazma, is named for the two villages which face each other across the river. Closest to the M-7 is **Zuevo** on the left bank while **Orekhovo** (with Nikolskoe) stands on the right bank. The history of the villages is closely linked with that of two giant merchant families, the Morozovs and the Zimins. After the emancipation of the serfs in 1861 and the founding of the railroad in 1863, the textile industry boomed taking advantage of cheap labour, cheap power from abundant peat supplies, and improved access via the rail network to the large markets in the east.

The Orekhovo-Zuevo mills, like those of Noginsk/Bogorodsk and Pavlovsky Posad, had their beginnings with enterprising silk weavers working from their cottages. The founder of the **Zimin Family**, which controlled the mill in Zuevo and in Drezna, was Semen Zimin, born in 1760, a silk weaver who drew his three sons into the business. The Zimins were Old Believers of the priestless sect. One of their most interesting descendants was Sergei Zimin who founded the famous **Zimin private opera** in Moscow where Chaliapin sang and many Russian operas were first performed.

ZUEVO was thoroughly rebuilt in the 1960s and 70s with the usual ugly tower blocks. To the right of the main road on Volodarskovo Street is the tall heavy Orthodox **Cathedral of the Nativity of the Virgin,** *Rozhdestva Bogoroditsy,* in pseudo-Russian style which reopened several years ago. Beyond, at No 15, 2ya Sovkhoznaya Street, is a new Old Believer church and community building in ugly cement brick.

Turn left, before the bridge, to Nos 41 and 43 Volodarskovo Street, the Old Believer **prayer house** built in 1884 by the Zimin family helped by the Vikula Morozovs who were members of the same congregation. In 1906 after the ban on Old Believer churches was lifted, the prayer house was officially registered and also dedicated to the **Nativity of the Virgin**. The Moscow architect, Ilya Bondarenko, in 1912 added the fine bell tower on the west, and the north and south halls. Closed in Soviet times and turned into a truck depot, it reopened in the 1990s. It lies opposite one of the Zimin houses in pink stucco where the beauteous **Zinaida Zimin** once lived. Her three marriages, one of which was to Savva Morozov, head of the Nikolskaya Manufaktura in Orekhovo, either ended in divorce or, as in the case of Savva, suicide (see Gorki-Leninskie).

Cross the Klyazma to the Morozovs' **OREKHOVO**. The founder of the **Morozov clan**, Savva Morozov, a serf and strict Old Believer, began making his fortune as purveyor of silk ribbons in Moscow after the 1812 fire. Count Ryumin, his owner, allowed Savva to purchase the freedom of his wife and four sons in 1820 with the proceeds gained from the Moscow sales. The Count was not being particularly generous: Savva had to find 17,000 roubles to ransom his sons. But, alas, in 1823 another son, Timofei, was born who was not part of the agreement and it took Savva another ten years to obtain his freedom.

In 1823 Savva moved the mill, now also producing woollen and linen cloth, to the Orekhovo side incorporating the next village of **Nikolskoe**. By 1837 he had 11 buildings and 200 workers, and had made the daring conversion to cotton production, importing bales from America and later Egypt and Central Asia. He moved permanently to Moscow in the 1840s and died in 1860 aged 90, only a few months before Alexander II granted freedom to all the serfs. He left his four sons (the fifth, Ivan, died young) with four different textile empires: Yelisei, with his son, Vikuly, acquired the mills in Orekhovo; Timofei, the youngest, and with the most business acumen, got the main factory in Nikolskoe; Abram the works in Tver; and Zakhar the mill in Bogorodsk/Noginsk.

In some ways the Orekhovo-Zuevo peasants merely exchanged serfdom for an even harsher rule in the mills for the factory owners controlled employment, housing, provisions, all social amenities and even the church. Unlike serfs, however, the mill workers received wages and were free to seek work elsewhere. Timofei Morozov, one of the more ruthless owners, called in the Cossacks in the bitter cold of January, 1885, to brutally put down the strike of his 8,000 workers protesting against unreasonable fines and wage reductions. However, the resulting court case, one of the first in Russia to use Alexander II's new jury system, went against Morozov and not only were the strikers declared not guilty but a large fine was imposed on him. Timofei never recovered from this humiliation.

Timofei's son, named **Savva** after his grandfather, had an entirely different approach. As so often happened in the third and fourth generations of these merchant dynasties, he was passionately interested in cultural pursuits. He loved the theatre giving considerable financial and other assistance to Stanislavsky and the **Moscow Art Theatre**. Through his friend, the writer **Maxim Gorky**, he even subsidised Lenin's mouthpiece, the journal *Iskra*. Naturally, he tried to ameliorate the harsh conditions of the mill workers in the huge factory complex he had inherited. The contradictions in his life – factory owner of one of the largest enterprises in Russia yet sympathetic to the revolutionary movement, and under the thumb of his authoritarian mother, Mariya Fedorovna, who criticised any concessions he made to mill workers – led to his death at his own hands while on holiday in Nice in 1905. That he managed to improve the living conditions of the mill workers in Orekhovo/Nikolskoe can still be seen today in the fine buildings he constructed for them.

Turn left at the T-junction for Leninsky Prospekt which has a few richly decorated 19th century local government offices, left, and the modern former offices of the communist party on the right. Farther on, old factory buildings flank the road. On the right, set against the modern factory building with the clock, are the two-storey offices of the old Morozov mill. The **factory shop** stands behind, in the small square, where the mill workers had little choice but to pay the prices demanded. It is now an interesting museum devoted to the social and economic history of the Morozov mills (*closed Mondays*). An obelisk erected in the 1920s stands in front with a figure carrying a flag commemorating the 1885 strike.

Savva's first cousin, **Vikula**, controlled the second Morozov factory in Orekhovo. He not only imported English machinery but had the foresight to employ managers from the mills of northern England, a policy which was to play a decisive role in the introduction of the game of **soccer** to Russia. Turn right at the first traffic light on Leninsky Prospekt and cross the bridge over the railway. The Vikula Morozov mill works are to the right while on the left can be seen the large wooden house of Vikula Morozov's **English manager**, Harry Charnock from Lancashire. Situated at 18 Terentieva Street near the river the fine two-storey wooden house, now a tuberculosis clinic, is best approached on foot.

The energetic **local historian** in Orekhovo-Zuevo, **Vladimir Lizunov**, a retired colonel in the Soviet army, has linked the origins of Russian football with the Morozov mill through Harry Charnock. In 1894 he organised the first **RUSSIAN FOOTBALL CLUB**, the players drawn from the mill workers, called the **Morozovtsy**. Charnock thought that by establishing the Sunday matches he could solve the drink problem that wreaked havoc on attendance at the mills on Monday mornings. Although it is doubtful if the second objective was achieved, the Morozovtsy quickly became so popular that even ladies attended the games. Objections from the Old Believer clergy were at first a problem – they insisted that the players wore long trousers. Charnock was so irritated by this that in the middle of a game he cut the legs off with a pair of scissors and from that time on, they stayed short. When the Russian league was formed in the early 1900s, the Morozovtsy were by far the strongest team winning the title four years in succession, easily beating the new St Petersburg and Moscow clubs.

Across the railway bridge turn right, then right again past the steam baths built by the Morozovs for their employees. Turn right again at the railway line to see the football ground of the Orekhovo-Zuevo club (no longer the best in Russia). The first football pitch is now subsumed in the grounds of the local park but this pitch, built in 1914 from turf brought over from England, is so even and well drained that it is still in use.

Retrace the route west along the railway line past the steam baths and turn left at the next road, Bugrova Street. Here is the **centre** of the Morozov mill workers' settlement. Immediately on the right are two attractive **kazarmy** (barracks) built to house mill workers and their families. In Soviet times the buildings were used for communal apartments, although nowadays the ground floors are given over to commercial shops. Built in 1908 – the date is over the entrance – they are on four floors in red brick with lavish white stone trim that breaks through the roof line in the manner of Art Nouveau. Across from the barracks is the **smithy** with its fine decorated water tower, also similarly vivid in red and white, like a 17th century monastery fortress.

Next to the smithy and past the police station, is the impressive **WINTER THEATRE**, the first workers' theatre in Russia constructed long before the revolution. Its stark form clad now in painted stucco (underneath is the original red brick) prefigures the development of constructivist architecture of the 1920s. Commissioned by Savva Morozov, it was begun in 1904 by Alexander Galetsky and not completed until 1912 owing to Morozov's tragic death in 1905. Such a sophisticated, avant-garde building with its stepped vertical fenestration and differing roof levels would seem to reflect the hand of a master like Fedor Shekhtel for whom Galetsky worked as assistant. However, here Shekhtel apparently did no more than advise on the machinery required for the stage. The plays staged by the amateur mill workers were such a success that **Stanislavsky** came to advise on new productions. He must have been a great nuisance, dispensing advice in his customary imperious manner and at the same time secretly persuading young promising actors to desert to Moscow. The theatre still uses **amateur actors**, many of them from the mills, but the town council has difficulties in maintaining the subsidy to keep the theatre going.

Further along this remarkable street is the handsome **hospital** on the left, also given by the Morozovs in typical red brick with white trim, and also by Alexander Galetsky. Across the street stands the charming hospital chapel in red brick and white stone with its slim octagonal tower and porch with peaked roof.

LIKINO-DULEVO

In Orekhovo take Leninsky Prospekt west and follow it south across the railway line, the A-108, signed LIKINO-DULEVO to Kabanovo.

In **KABANOVO** where the road curves sharply left take the dirt lane, right, to the delicate green and white wooden **Church of St Nikita**. It was built in 1862 in nearby Dubrovka but moved here in 1890 and rededicated in the Orthodox campaign against the many Old Believers in the area. It remained open in Soviet times and was therefore not mutilated although in 1957 the bell tower burned down. Around the octagonal drum are paintings of saints and within are icons saved from the church in Drezna before it was pulled down.

Continue to **Likino-Dulevo**, population 34,000, which extends in a long narrow ribbon for five kilometres along the main road and railway line. In 1870 the Likinskaya Manufaktura was founded here by A.F.

Smirnov replaced nowadays by the LIAZ bus works. On the right is the modern building of the old **porcelain works** founded by **Terenty Kuznetsov** of Gzhel in 1832. In 1843 the Kuznetsovs opened a similar works in Riga and then bought out all their rivals' businesses including the fine Gardner porcelain at Verbilky. By the end of the century they owned two-thirds of all pottery and chinaware production in Russia.

The Kuznetsov works after the revolution were renamed in honour of the *Pravda* newspaper and are now the **DULEVO PORCELAIN FACTORY**. In the 1920s exciting avant-garde designs for porcelain by Malevich and other leading artists were produced here, now avidly collected. In the early 1930s the first US Ambassador to the Soviet Union, William Bullit, ordered a new dinner service for **President Franklin Roosevelt** from Dulevo for 1200 people based on a Ukrainian folk design. The huge order, examples of which can be seen in the factory museum, was prepared in four months and shipped to America and the proceeds used to build a metallurgical factory. The factory continues to stagger on somewhat out of touch with modern requirements.

Continue down the long main road. To the left, is the **workers' club** of the china works. A dull building at first glance it repays careful observation for, built 1927-8, this is one of the famous factory clubs in constructivist style by **Konstantin Melnikov**. A deep courtyard is flanked by two wide wings which narrow back to the main entrance. Melnikov here shows his romantic and quirky side for the club, if looked down on from above, is an ingenious design in the form of a human body. The wings on either side of the courtyard are the legs, the front door is at the crotch, arms swing out from the central core on either side, and at the farthest end the auditorium makes a heavy neck and the stage, the head. It is in sad need of repairs.

The large Orthodox church next door, **St John the Divine**, *Ioanna Bogoslova*, was built at the beginning of the 20th century by the Kuznetsovs and has recently been returned to the congregation. It is a splendid example of pseudo-Russian design, the basic cube with gables is flanked by chapels, the extruding apse at the eastern end balancing the western entrance. The inferior domes emphasise the large central one rather like the 17th century Church of the Trinity at Ostankino.

THE SILK ROAD TO FRYANOVO

The minor R-110, Shchelkovskoe Road, runs north of the Nizhny
Novgorod Highway to Fryanovo, near the border with Vladimir Oblast.
At first built-up and industrial, once past Shchelkovo the road becomes
rural linking age-old villages. Its intriguing name sounds like *shelk*, silk,
and silk weaving was long the main occupation of the two towns at
either end of the road, Shchelkovo and Fryanovo.

*From Kalanchevskaya Square go east on Stromynka and Bolshaya
Cherkizovskaya past Shchelkovskaya Metro and cross the MKAD to
the A-103. 7 km from Moscow pass a GAI post to* **PEKHRA-
POKROVSKOE**. Set back on the left just before the bridge over the
Pekhorka River is the fine Empire **Church of the Intercession**, *Pokrova*,
built 1825–9 by the notable Moscow architect, Osip Bove. It is in the
form of a rotunda encircled by paired columns interrupted by the 1902
trapeza. When it reopened in the 1990s the cross and golden cone were
restored but only grisaille paintings on the underside of the dome
survive of the original decor.

*Continue on the A-103 to Medvezhe Lake, then right on an unsigned
paved road. Past the lake 3 km where the road divides, ignore the paved
road left and take the hard dirt road right 2 km through woods and across
a bridge over a dry canal to the ruined estate of* **ALMAZOVO**.

The grand estate built in the 1760s by Nikita Demidov, scion of the
wealthy mine-owning family and patron of the arts, is now a forlorn
ruin housing a few orphans. The huge heavily overgrown park was
originally laid out in a series of canals and large ponds dotted with
islands and pavilions linked to each other by bridges. The Demidov
mansion which stood on a man-made hill called Sion situated between
the ponds and canals (left facing the orphanage) was destroyed in the
early 19th century when a new house and church were built. In 1915 the
second house burned down.

The **Church of the Kazan Virgin**, *Kazanskoi Ikony Bozhiei Materi*, in
red brick with white stone detailing was built 1814-19, possibly by
V. Tkachev, although Domenico Gilardi, working at that time at
Almazovo, might have been involved. It is a cube with a central
rotunda and drum resting on four internal pylons. The square apse
juts out at one end, the three-tier bell tower with spire balances it at
the other, and no *trapeza* spoils the strict symmetry. Father Andrei

of nearby Nikolskoe-Trubetskoe intends to establish a brotherhood here.

To the left of the church is the orphanage, a two-storey house with a rusticated entrance of Doric columns contemporary with the church, perhaps originally the **guest house**. There is talk of restoring the large **pond** and **canals** and plans for new cottages. For the orphaned children, the wild although lonely surroundings are a wonderful playground.

Continue on the A-103 to the crossroads where the airplane monument denotes the Gagarin cosmonaut training centre at Zvezdny Gorodok (Star City) on the A-103 right. Take the left turn to Shchelkovo.

SHCHELKOVO on the Klyazma River, population 110,000, arose out of the silk-weaving hamlets of the late 18th century and has swallowed up many small villages including Khomutovo and Obraztsovo on the Klyazma River.

In the centre of Shchelkovo, right, shortly before the bridge, a sign on the wall of a mill announces the **Cathedral of the Holy Trinity**, *Troitsy*, within. Go through the mill entrance and inside among dilapidated buildings is the huge, red brick, late 19th century **Trinity Church** in pseudo-Russian style and a ruined poorhouse. It is difficult to see how, marooned within the factory walls, the church can serve a parish.

Before the bridge over the Klyazma turn left on 1st Sovietsky Lane to the square where a fat statue of Lenin still stands. Turn left at the traffic lights and then right at the roundabout to Tsentralnaya Street. At 3 km turn right signed ZAGORYANSKY and right again at the dead end formed by the former Zagoryansky textile mill. In a few metres where the road bends right, turn left between two houses on a dirt road down a steep bank to an unstable bridge. Leave the car and walk across the bridge and up the bank to the **Nativity of the Virgin**, *Rozhdestva Bogoroditsy*, at **Obraztsovo**.

From the church the view is of the winding Klyazma, a large reservoir, and to the north the factory chimneys of Korolev. The church was never closed and everything about it is in apple pie order. Built in 1736 by Count P.I. Musin-Pushkin, the then owner of Obraztsovo, there are hints of baroque in the tiered octagonal on the cube and the tall bell tower. Contemporary with the church is the finely carved iconostasis and some interesting icons. In the churchyard a huge black cross stands over the grave of Zagoryansky, the mill owner.

From Shchelkovo cross the Klyazma and immediately turn left. At 2 km, past a large hospital, turn left onto the poorly paved but attractive Sverdlov Street to the church. The large white and ochre **Intercession**, *Pokrova*, at **Khomutovo** on the left bank of the Klyazma, like its rival across the river remained open in the Soviet period. Its long construction, 1800 to 1856, reflects changes in architectural tastes: the severely classical church of 1800 is in the form of a cylinder topped by a dome with a delightfully round apse and curving Tuscan colonnade; in 1836 the Empire-style *trapeza* was added with windows set in arched niches; finally in 1856 the *trapeza* was lengthened and the eclectic three-tier bell tower was grafted on, the least attractive of the three parts.

From Shchelkovo continue east 7 km on the R-110 to Fryazino, where the Institute of Rocketry is situated. Cross the narrow Lyubosivka River and turn first right (no sign) for 2 km. **GREBNEVO** consists of two exceptionally lovely churches, the gutted main house, entrance gates, stables, a carriage house, and extensive park.

Originally a property of the Princes Trubetskoy, it was given in 1781 to **General Gavril Bibikov** by Catherine II in gratitude for putting down the Pugachev rebellion. He rebuilt most of the buildings in the severely classical style and put the poor Pugachev rebels to work digging the lakes. Although **Prince Sergei Golitsyn**, who purchased Grebnevo in 1811, largely reconstructed it in Empire style, he also stripped it for his preferred estate at Kuzminki even taking large quantities of top soil. The Golitsyns departed in 1845 and a bewildering number of mill owners and merchants followed, culminating in 1914 with F.A. Grinevsky, the last owner before the revolution. After 1917 it became a sanatorium and now houses a school.

The first sighting is of the **two churches**. The nearest is the cylindrical, ochre-coloured winter **Church of St Nicholas** built in 1817-23 by Ignaty Oldelli and N.I. Deryugin inspired by the Moscow baroque 'churches under the bells'. The base is octagonal with four Doric porticoes on alternating sides, from the centre of which rises the tall cylindrical bell tower containing a clock. Within, the circular kernel of the church matches the cylindrical tower bounded by artificial marble columns and there is a wonderful silver chandelier and late 19th century curved iconostasis. It is full of sculpture, some by Gavril Zamaraev who was working at this time on the Moscow Senate and Kuskovo. It is thought that the noted Petersburg architect of the Admiralty, Andrei Voronikhin, may have been responsible for the design, and that Domenico Gilardi may have assisted with the interior.

The even lovelier, older second church, surrounded by trees, the **Grebnevo Virgin**, *Grebnevskoi Ikony Bozhiei Materi*, is named for an icon brought to Moscow by Dmitry Donskoy after defeating the Tatars in 1381. It was built in 1786-91 by Ivan Vetrov, a student of Matvei Kazakov, as the summer, unheated church. Whereas St Nicholas is octagonal, the Grebnevo church is quatrefoil in plan. Its four arms finish in elegant porticoes with pediments under a domed rotunda over which a shining gilded angel holds the cross. The rich effect is enhanced by the red background and contrasting white stone detailing of the columns, porticoes, and window frames. The richly sculpted interior by Stepan Gryaznov is enhanced by artificial marble columns and a white iconostasis with carvings in gold. Names of the builders and architects are listed on a bronze plaque within.

East of the church complex is the main courtyard of the estate with the great **entrance gate** of Doric columns and massive entablature, like a Roman triumphal arch, built 1818-19 for Prince Alexander Golitsyn in memory of his travels with Alexander I. Designed by Deryugin it closes off the long courtyard leading to the main house behind which the ground slopes down to the lake. The palatial **house** of three storeys was built for Bibikov 1780-90 in the severely classical style, its sombre facade highlighted by the six-columned portico and pediment and linked by galleries to the two Empire wings built in 1820. Sadly the two upper floors were badly damaged by a fire in 1992 and little of the interior remains. The carriage house and barns with Gothic overtones east of the courtyard survive from the late 18th century and the stable was built in 1821 by Deryugin.

Behind the main house and the churches the little Lyubosivka River was transformed in the late 18th century into a large lake. Islands in the centre once were laid out in broad avenues in a star pattern but have now reverted to wilderness.

On the R-110 turn left at the eastern end of Fryazino onto a poorly paved road by the bus-stop. Within 6 km, keeping right past Saburovo, is **BOGOSLOVO** *where shabby farm buildings suddenly give way to an elegant late 18th century church.*

The **Church of the Kazan Virgin**, *Kazanskoi Ikony Bozhiei Materi*, was built for the estate of Mme P.F. Astafyeva in 1795-1801, most likely by an architect of the Kazakov school. In contrasting red brick and white stone the rotunda church, its bulging apse exactly matching the equally protruding entrance, is ringed by six pairs of Tuscan columns with alternating pediments. A covered gallery links the entrance to the belltower, the only breach in the otherwise perfect symmetry. Avenues of limes from the old estate still stand in the overgrown woods behind and a large pond stretches into the distance beyond the church. The old building, almost in ruins in the early 1990s, has been revived and a young priest, his small son acting as a vigorous bell ringer, conducts services for a smattering of parishioners.

Continue east from Fryazino on the R-110 through **Nazimikha**, one long ribbon of houses which turns into **Trubino**. The ruined **St Vladimir** in pseudo-Gothic style built in 1849 stands to the right in a cemetery.

Less than 2 km after Trubino turn right at the crossroads onto a paved road. Soon the delightful white **Church of St Nicholas** with a large dome and tall gold cross rises above the horizon at **Zdekhovo**. Continue to **Kablukovo** where the Vorya River meets the tiny Lashutka and the slim **Saviour**, *Spasa*, built in 1775, and saved from collapse by a return to worship, stands right.

Fourteen km farther on at Ogudnevo turn left onto an unmarked paved road 3 km to **PETROVSKOE**. The disorderly mess of farm buildings and ugly blocks of flats gives way on the right behind a wall to the **Church of the Saviour**, *Spasa*, built in 1828 for S.A. Melgunova. The church, which remained open in Soviet times and has kept its original iconostasis, resembles the work of the Empire architect, Afanasy Grigoriev, in its use of round and arched forms. The cube with its rusticated *trapeza* and round apse is pierced by tripartite windows set in arched niches topped by a rotunda. The upper tier of the bell tower serves as a resonator for the bell peal. From the high point of the church there are good views of the valley of the Pruzhonka although the foreground is spoiled by industrial jumble.

On the R-110 road turn right just past Ogudnevo onto a paved, unmarked road to **DUSHONOVO** *in 1 km.* Here the listed wooden Church of All Saints of 1670 was destroyed by fire in 1986, some say to hide the fact that funds for its restoration had been stolen. It stood to the left of the awkward **Church of the Tikhvin Virgin**, *Tikhvinskoi Ikony Bozhiei Materi*, built in 1839.

At the end of the R-110 some 55 km from the MKAD is the delightful town of **FRYANOVO**, *population 7,000*.

Fryanovo sits on a small plateau high above the winding, narrow Shirenka River an unusually pretty town of small wooden houses, a tall arresting church and an elongated wooden mansion. Cross the bridge and climb the gentle slope on Leninskaya Street past the park and rambling **wooden house** of the Lazarevs. To the left stands **St John the Baptist**, *Ioanna Predtechi*, no ordinary village church. Beyond on the right is the large public square, with the war memorial, where fairs and markets were held, and in Soviet times public meetings. Today one of the buildings used for the **old silk manufactory** on the square has gone but the second still stands. The Soviet factory producing woollen cloth (wool replaced silk before the revolution) is just beyond the hill.

Like many other towns, Fryanovo's existence depended on the manufacture of silk. In 18th century Russia, silk, the main material of the upper classes, could only be imported and was therefore prohibitively expensive. To reduce costs native silk mills were encouraged and in 1735 the Armenian, Ignaty Sherimanov, established the first one in Fryanovo. Another Armenian, **Lazar Lazarev**, who came to Russia to escape persecution in Persia, and whose family founded the Lazarev Institute in Moscow, bought the village and mill from Sherimanov in 1758 and bequeathed it to Ivan, his eldest son. Ivan's business so prospered that he was able to present the Empress Catherine with a large diamond, now in the royal sceptre, and was granted the title of Active Counsellor.

At the end of the 18th century Ivan expanded the mill and laid out the town in a grid pattern. At the same time he commissioned the fine wooden house as a summer residence on the brow of the hill overlooking the Shirenka. To the left and west of the house he built the splendid church, St John the Baptist, his patron saint. When the male Lazarevs died out in the 1820s, the village and mill changed hands many times – the last owner before the revolution was Vasily Zalogin.

Nowhere else in the countryside around Moscow has a wooden mansion of this early date and its related church survived so well nor has the layout of a town and its early manufacturing buildings remained so unchanged. Stretching for 110 metres, the **house**, now in need of restoration, compares very favourably in size with other grand country houses of the nobility. It is of wood on a stone foundation reflecting the Russian view that wooden houses were more hygienic and easier to heat. And materials were easily obtained. Local oak from nearby forests was used for the support beams, for the frames of doors and windows and stairs, and local pine was employed for the walls and floors. Roofing was of iron sheets from the Lazarev ironworks placed on wooden rafters. At the centre is the main entrance with columns and pediment including the second, mezzanine floor, with smaller family rooms. Linking the main block to the end wings were single-storey galleries containing oval-shaped orangeries equipped with large stoves for growing flowers and exotic fruit trees. They were remodelled at the end of the last century as quarters for mill workers when the extensive glazing was replaced by the present wooden walls. However, the five-roomed end wings for guests remain largely as they were. It has been suggested that the architect of the house may have been **Ivan Podyachev**, a serf of the Lazarevs who designed the Lazarev Institute in Moscow and afterwards was granted his freedom. Appropriately the director of the evening school for young workers that now occupies the main house is a Podyachev.

If the churches at Bogoslovo and Petrovskoe were excellent examples of their kind, then the **Church of St John the Baptist** at Fryanovo built 30 years earlier is the crowning touch. St John was built in 1797, about the same time as the foundation stone was laid for the Lazarev house, in the form of a Latin cross like some of the churches in Petersburg. The large dome rests on a wide drum over the transept and the long nave ends in the elegant three-tiered bell tower. The short arms of the transept are completed by porticoes of pediments and columns on which the capitals, surprisingly, were left unfinished as were the pilasters of the long body of the church. (Perhaps there was a dispute over payment as Ivan Lazarev died in 1801 before the church was completed.) The bell tower with its vases and paired pilasters at the corners and round topmost tier with a rose-window at the centre, originally intended for a clock, reflect the fashion for baroque detailing. As the church's large interior can accommodate over 1,000 people it acted as the central church for the surrounding villages, especially during important festivals. Fryanovo's second church of wood was dismantled in the 1980s.

The church was closed in Soviet times and used for various purposes including the repair of tractors. In 1991 it reopened and year by year is re-acquiring its former grandeur although the gilded carved iconostasis bestowed on it by the Lazarevs is gone for ever. It acts today as a sort of village club; elderly ladies sit on benches waiting their turn to talk to the busy priest in his colourful robes.

Fryanovo is fortunate to have a fine historian in **Vladimir Moroshkin**, a retired military officer who lives in a wing of the Lazarevs' house. When he first founded the local history society in 1988, the authorities were extremely wary but now give him every assistance. He is especially worried about the future of the wooden Lazarev house.

Road 7   YAROSLAVL HIGHWAY M-8: MYTISHCHI TO SERGIEV POSAD

The fast north-easterly Yaroslavl Highway M-8 is reached via Prospekt Mira and Yaroslavskoe Shosse crossing under the MKAD. This was the ancient pilgrim's road taken by tsars and common people alike to the Trinity-Sergius Monastery at Sergiev Posad. It is now prime dacha country, easily accessed by the *elektrichka* railway, enlivened by fascinating associations with Stanislavsky and Chaliapin, Lenin's mistress, the great artistic centre at Abramtsevo and the superb Trinity-Sergius Monastery itself.

INDUSTRIAL TOWNS ON MOSCOW'S BORDER

MYTISHCHI, population 150,000, which extends seamlessly from Moscow's tower blocks along the Yaroslavl Highway, was in the early days of Russia an important portage point where goods (*myt* means customs dues) were carried between the Yauza River to the broader Klyazma. In the late 18th century Mytishchi's springs provided Moscow with clean water; today Moscow's water needs are met by the huge Klyazma, Ucha and Pirogov reservoirs built in the 1930s west of Mytishchi.

The brick **Church of St Vladimir**, 1 km north of the MKAD, left, was built in 1713, an octagon on a cube in the Moscow baroque style. The *trapeza*, widened in the 19th century, hides much of the older church apart from some of the original windows. It has been returned to worship in time to save it from becoming completely derelict although the bell tower was levelled. Attached to Savva Mamontov's railway (now metro) carriages factory of 1896 is a workers' club built in 1929 in the interesting constructivist style. Mytishchi is also home to the foundry where huge statues of Soviet-approved historical figures were made – Yury Dolgoruky, Lenin, Stalin.

Modern Mytishchi has swallowed up the dacha village of **Perlovka** (the railway station survives) built by Vasily Perlov, the tea merchant, on his extensive property. The wooden church there by Petr Zykov in the romantic Russian style is now being lovingly rebuilt by volunteers.

15. **Gorodnya.** The Resurrection is a superb example of the tent-shape that dominated church architecture until the mid 17th century. Patriarch Nikon banned this indigenously Russian form in preference for the Byzantine model with one, three or five cupolas.

16. **Lukhovitsy.** As was common practice, the wooden Church of the Kazan Virgin was faced with weatherboarding in the 19th century to protect the logs from rotting.

17. OPPOSITE. **Bykovo.** The highly original Vladimir Church on Izmailov's estate is probably by Bazhenov, the great Moscow architect spurned by Catherine II for his masonic beliefs.

18. LEFT. **Nikolaevsky-Ugreshsky Monastery.** The 19th century wall and gate of the expanded monastery was meant to convey an impression of the holy city of Jerusalem.

19. BELOW. **Kolomna.** The Kremlin's truncated wall contains the 20-sided Marinkina tower named after the ambitious wife of the Russian pretender who led the successful Polish invasion against Tsar Boris Godunov in 1604.

20. RIGHT. **Staro-Golutvin Monastery.** Surrounded by slim, elegant towers the monastery stands on the point of land where the Moskva River flows into the great Oka on its way to the Volga.

21. BELOW. **Glinki.** The owner of the estate, James Bruce, born in Russia of Scots parentage, was Peter the Great's leading scientist. Bruce was regarded by the public as a dangerous sorcerer but the Tsar greatly admired him and made good use of his immense knowledge.

22. ABOVE. **Grebnevo.** General Bibikov, granted the estate for quelling the Pugachev rebellion in 1774-5, erected this classical summer church with its richly sculptured interior.

23. BELOW. **Orekhovo-Zuevo.** The workers' theatre, built in the early 1900s for Savva Morozov's mill workers, was so successful that Stanislavsky tried to poach the actors for his Moscow Art Theatre.

24. ABOVE. **Ivashevo.**
The Trinity Church, an
excellent example of the
Russian classical style, is in
such poor condition that
revived services have to be
held in the less damaged
bell tower.

25. RIGHT. **Abramtsevo.**
The community of
outstanding artists at Savva
Mamontov's estate
designed the stylised
Saviour Untouched by
Hand in 1881, a seminal
building for the modern
movement.

26. **Klyazma.** It was rare for dacha communities like this one of the early 1900s to be graced with masonry churches, let alone one as splendid as the Saviour Untouched by Hand.

For **TAININSKOE** *join the MKAD going west and after 2 km take the first right turn onto an unmarked road, Trudovaya St. Turn left onto Krestyanskaya Street and then left again onto Vera Voloshina Street and where the houses end across a bleak field near the improbable new statue of Nicholas II (recently blown up then rebuilt), is a truly splendid building.*

The **Church of the Annunciation**, *Blagoveshcheniya*, makes an unlikely oasis in the barren landscape bordered by the rushing motorway and Moscow's high-rise towers. It was completed in 1677 for the palace of the pious Tsar Fedor Alexeevich, the second station after Alexeevskoe in Moscow in the chain serving the **royal pilgrimage** to the Trinity-Sergius Monastery. The cuboid church is richly sculptural with firmly etched cornices, columns, and window surrounds and three tiers of receding *kokoshniki* gables leading to tall drums holding aloft five domes. Its rare and beautiful ogee-shaped porch is composed of twin staircases with pointed towers leading to parallel galleries which meet in the main church, allowing ritual processions to divide and then merge. Within, the choir stall rests on massive pillars and the vaulting of the bare interior is immensely impressive.

On the M-8 cross the Yauza River and turn right onto Pionerskaya in **KOROLEV** (KorolYOv). Korolev, population 160,000, lies to the right of the Yaroslavl Road beyond Losiny Ostrov park. Industry only came to the then dacha settlement of Podlipki (Under the Limes) in 1918 when the Petrograd armaments factory, under threat by the German Army, moved here. The first five-year plan brought more factories and in 1938 it became the town of **Kaliningrad** named for Mikhail Kalinin, the first president of the Soviet Union. In 1996 it was renamed Korolev thus eliminating the confusion that has reigned since 1946 when Koenigsburg was also named Kaliningrad. Caught up in the ugly modern sprawl are two old villages which have a special relationship with Korolev: Kostino in the south and Bolshevo in the north.

Sergei Korolev, the oustanding rocket engineer, was arrested in 1938 and forced to work in the NKVD's special science laboratories so poignantly described in Solzhenitsyn's *Third Circle*. Released in 1946, he was sent to a new space institute in the highly secret town of Kaliningrad where the rockets that lifted Gagarin and other cosmonauts into space were developed.

From Mytishchi continue on the Yaroslavl Highway and turn right before the railway bridge signed KOROLEV onto Pionerskaya Street then right

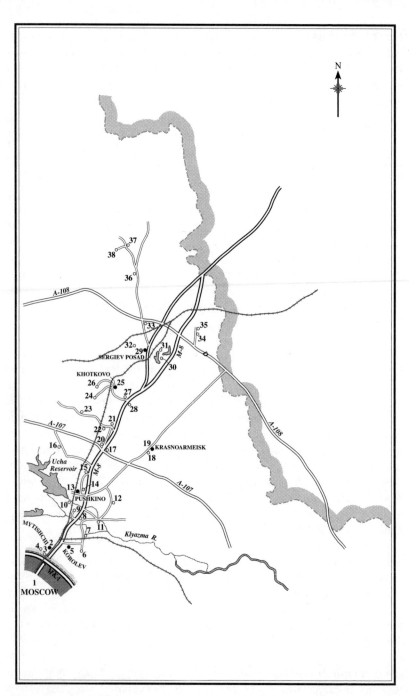

ROAD 7
MYTISHCHI TO SERGIEV POSAD

1. MOSCOW
2. MYTISHCHI
3. Perlovka
4. Taininskoe
5. KOROLEV
6. Kostino
7. Bolshevo
8. Lyubimovka
9. Klyazma
10. Mamontovka
11. Ivanteevka
12. Komyagino
13. PUSHKINO
14. Novaya Derevnya
15. Bratovshchina
16. Yeldigino
17. Mogiltsy
18. Tsarevo
19. KRASNOARMEISK

20. Talitsy
21. Rakhmanovo
22. Sofrino
23. Muranovo
24. Abramtsevo
25. KHOTKOVO
26. Akhtyrka
27. Radonezh
28. Vozdvizhenskoe
29. SERGIEV POSAD
30. Vifany
31. Gethsemane
32. Blagoveshchenie
33. Deulino
34. Putyatino
35. Gagino
36. Iudino
37. Shemetovo
38. Akim-Anna

again at Matrosova and right again to narrow Lenin Street at the sign to the local (**krayevedchesky**) *museum.*

Kostino was the summer home of the textile magnate, Alexander Kraft. In the distance is the pond and remnants of the wood and gardens and on the right the heavily rebuilt house of two storeys. To the left a wooden house with a charming peaked porch, once the house of Kraft's manager, was home to Lenin in 1922 for a few weeks. It was inevitably turned into a Lenin museum but has now broadened out into the town museum. Here the furniture of Kraft's manager charmingly recreates the atmosphere of a middle-class home of a century ago. *Open 11-5 except Mondays.*

Felix Dzerzhinsky, the first head of the Cheka, made the arrangements in great secrecy for **Lenin**, with his wife Nadezhda Krupskaya, to spend January to March 1922 at Kostino recuperating after his first stroke. According to the museum director the winter of 1922 was particularly harsh and feed for horses was in short supply so the Cheka in Central Asia presented two camels to Lenin for use at Kostino. Camels can go longer without food than horses and can withstand severe cold so they were useful if a little bizarre in the remote winter fastness of the estate.

In 1924 after Lenin's death, the Kraft estate became home to the first **labour commune** composed of boys and girls housed in the long main house opposite the manager's house. Set up by Dzerzhinsky, it was intended to provide a purposeful life for the thousands of homeless children, the *besprizorniki*, who were living by their wits on Moscow's unhealthy streets. The first director was Matvei Pogrebensky who set out the principles of the commune and chose the children, all under 18. They were to engage in trades such as shoemaking and textiles, to be educated and stimulated, and above all were to be fully trusted and not heavily guarded. Proudly it was reported that no-one tried to run away in the first winter. This open regime and advanced educational theory of which Kostino was the flagship was copied in other children's communes and seems in the early stages to have been successful. But in the 1930s these libertarian ideas were gradually discarded and the children (now older) were exploited as labour for Kostino's burgeoning industries. Finally, in the terrible year of the purges, 1937, the commune was closed down.

In Korolev turn left (north) on Matrosova, cross the tracks to the church on the left. Or, from the Yaroslavl Highway at the end of the long railway bridge turn right signed BOLSHEVO. **Bolshevo** is unexpectedly rural and attractive in the early autumn when the many rowan trees are red with fruit and it is not surprising that Shostakovich had a dacha here in the 1940s and 1950s. In 1776 Bolshevo was given to the Moscow Charitable Society as a 'sanctuary for the poor'. The Society built an orphanage and a large poorhouse for women near the church, often visited in the 1860s by Sergei Alexeev, Stanislavsky's father, on his way to his estate at Lyubimovka.

It is obvious that the **Church of Cosmas and Damian** was not closed in the Soviet period for it is in such good condition. Built in 1786 of brick and stucco the cube base is topped by a large rotunda and the north facade is distinguished by a portico of the Tuscan order. The bell tower, with a long slim tier for the bells and tall spire, is contemporary with the church as is the rare white and gold iconostasis within. Lower down the hill is a blue-grey building flying the Russian flag with a tell-tale bulge at the eastern end. It is the former **Church of the Annunciation**, *Blagoveshcheniya*, now the office of the village council.

DACHA COUNTRY

On the Yaroslavl Highway, M-8, after crossing the Klyazma River turn right under the bridge 2 km to the centre of **KLYAZMA**. In the early 1900s farming land was laid out in a regular grid of streets, lined with big houses and gardens, some in picturesque national styles, and named for Russian writers and artists. In 1903 a local society set up a park, tennis courts, a football field, bicycle paths, a dance platform, postal facilities and even provided electricity.

At the railway station turn right onto Turgenievskaya Street to the T-junction closed by the small wooden **Church of the Grebneva Icon of the Virgin**, *Grebnevskoi Ikony Bozhiei Materi*, designed by Petr Vinogradov in 1902 and recently revived. Turn right onto Lermontovskaya Street to one of the finest Art Nouveau churches in Russia: the **Saviour Untouched by Hand**, *Spasa Nerukotvornovo*. Commissioned by I.A. Alexandrenko and based on 16th century tent-shaped churches, it was built 1913–16 to the design of Sergei Vashkov, chief artist for the Olovyanishnikov firm of church furnishings. Vashkov was one of many Art Nouveau artists who turned to architecture and the splendid tiered gables and coloured tiles – especially the stylised white angels and head of Christ – betray his training. When the church was given back in the early 1990s the crumbling tiles were beautifully cleaned and repaired. Inside, not even the iconostasis survives of the original decor.

On the left of the church is the old **Klyazma Parish School** designed by Vashkov at the behest of the Alexandrenkos and named for their daughters, Anya and Pelageya. The large stylised neo-Russian **dacha** of the Alexandrenkos, also by Vashkov, is at No 8, Pushkin Street, parallel to and north of Turgenievskaya. Although it always seems to be closed, one can have a glimpse over the fence.

From the Yaroslavl Road turn as for Pushkino then left at the T-junction onto the old Sergiev Posad Road and almost immediately turn right signed MAMONTOVKA STANTSIA, 3 km. The next station up the line, **MAMONTOVKA** (named after the owner, Savva Mamontov) was also a fashionable dacha village. Leave the car, cross the line and turn left to No 1 Lentochka, a large wooden turreted house, left, behind a high fence. The familiar blue firs immediately betray the fact that it was a rest house for communist pary officials. The L-shaped house forming two sides of an inner courtyard with long balconies and verandahs was built in 1875 by Alexander Kaminsky for Miss A.N. Mamontova, a cousin of Savva Mamontov who married Mikhail Gorbov, the financier. A rare treat is the central room two storeys high which still has a splendid chandelier, the original fireplace and walls decorated in the pseudo-Russian manner. In the 1930s Mamontovka was still a popular dacha village but by the 1960s factories had moved in and it began to lose its rural identity. Most of the inhabitants now commute by train to jobs in Moscow or Mytishchi.

On the Yaroslavl Highway M-8 cross the Klyazma River and turn right (don't dip under the bridge for Klyazma), and go straight ahead signed LESNYYE POLYANY. The remains of **LYUBIMOVKA** *(Beloved) are just beyond the bend behind the fence, right.*

The wealthy Alexeev family's eldest son, Konstantin, better known as the theatre director Stanislavsky, liked to spend summers at the family home at Lyubimovka. Indeed, the famous **Moscow Art Theatre** was born here on June 22, 1897 after all-night discussions between Stanislavsky and his friend, the director and teacher Nemirovich-Danchenko. Actors and actresses, including the newly graduated **Olga Knipper**, later to be Chekhov's wife, rehearsed the first season of the new theatre at Lyubimovka.

In the summer of 1902 **Anton Chekhov** and Olga Knipper, who had been married just over a year, spent a holiday at Lyubimovka. Stanislavsky and his wife were travelling at the time but the place was full of his relatives and other guests including his half-French mother, Maman. Chekhov enjoyed the woods and the fishing, and, especially, the company. He based at least three characters of the *Cherry Orchard* on people he met there: the student Trofimov, the clerk Yepikhodov and the governess, Charlotta Ivanovna. She was modelled on an English governess, Lily Glassby (her father was sculptor to Queen Victoria), who came with the Smirnovs, relatives of the Alexeevs. Small and lively, Lily would leap onto Chekhov's shoulders when she met him out walking and doff his hat to passers-by just as Charlotta does in the play.

The once comfortable **wooden house** ranged in front of the river in the early 1990s was a sorry sight with rotting porches and roofs askew and was finally pulled down in 1995. The wooden church, too, the **Intercession**, *Pokrova*, with its brick bell tower is extremely dilapidated. In this now rotting building, Stanislavsky married the actress, Mariya Lilina, in great style in the summer of 1889. Guests were ferried to and from Moscow in special trains and the reception was suitably lavish.

The former theatre is the unlikely two-storey wooden house left of the drive which has long since been divided into offices. It is now occupied by the **Union of Theatre Workers**, *Soyuz Teatralnykh Deyatelei*, the successors of the Soviet theatre union, who want to restore the buildings and rebuild the house as the Stanislavsky memorial centre. The striking brightly painted oval structure like a ship standing by itself in the centre of the property, now used as a theatre studio, is the **pavilion** of the Alexeev manufactory designed by the Moscow architect, Dmitry Chichagov, for the industrial exhibition of 1882 at Khodynka Field in Moscow.

The old **stables** and **carriage house** flank the driveway. Farther to the left is the bright **green wooden house**, also of two storeys, of Vladimir Stanislavsky's brother. The **White Dacha** which belonged to the Sapozhnikovs, mill owners and relatives of the Alexeevs, burned down recently.

About 18 km from the MKAD turn right from the Yaroslavl Highway signed **PUSHKINO** *over the road west.* The old town on the Ucha River, population 75,000, is named for Pushkin's reputed ancestor, the Boyar Pushka. On the pilgrims' route to Trinity-Sergius Monastery, it later belonged to Patriarch Adrian who built the striking **Church of St Nicholas** in 1692-4. A cube with five domes and tiers of gables (hidden by the later roof) the style reflects the conservative views of Adrian, the last Patriarch before the office lapsed under Peter the Great. The north and south chapels and the convincing three-tiered bell tower were built in 1871.

After the railway opened, wool and cotton mills, including those of the Armand family (see below), began to proliferate at Pushkino. It also became a popular venue for summer visitors and by 1900 there were over 1,000 dachas in the town. **Vladimir Mayakovsky**, the poet of the revolution, lived on the fashionable Aulova Gora (No 6) but the dacha was demolished in 1993 and only a dull statue of the poet identifies the site.

When the Ucha Reservoir was built many fine dachas were moved to **Novaya Derevnya** on the old Yaroslavl Road (parallel to the M-8) 2 km north of Pushkino Station. The charming wooden **Church of the Purification**, *Sreteniya*, right of the road is also a newcomer. It was originally built in 1895 by Nikolai Nikitin for *dachniki* by the railway station in Pushkino but was moved here in 1922 to remove it from the sight of passengers. Here the famous Orthodox priest, **Father Alexander Men**, preached for twenty years. But his Jewish mother had converted to Orthdoxy and this Jewish background made him a target for anti-semitic extremists. One Sunday, in September, 1990, he rose early in his home in Semkhoz near Sergiev Posad and set out to take the *electrichka* down the line to Novaya Derevnya. On the lane he was ambushed, bashed over the head with an axe, and left for dead and although he managed to crawl to his house he died before help could be summoned. This atrocious crime has never been solved and many suspect the connivance of the authorities. His burial place left of the church has become a shrine for his enormous following. Father Vladimir, Father Men's assistant, has continued his pioneering work in children's hospitals and schools and keeps Father Men's study in the house, left, as a memorial. The new brick chapel is used for the Sunday School and baptisms.

Continue on the old Yaroslavl Road towards Sergiev Posad to the **Church of the Annunciation**, *Blagoveshcheniya*, on the right up a hill. **BRATOVSHCHINA**, with its wooden palace (demolished in the early 1800s) was the **third station** in the royal pilgrimage (after Taininskoe) of the five to the Trinity-Sergius Monastery. The portly Empress Elizabeth would walk a certain distance, then have her carriage take her to one of the palaces or back to Moscow for the night. The next day she would arrive by carriage at the place where she had left off and continue on foot. The present church, functioning and newly painted, was built in 1808 long after the Russian monarchs had ceased making pilgrimages. Built of stone, it is quietly classical, an octagonal on a cube with pediments, engaged columns and a nicely proportioned bell tower.

In the 18th century the estate and village was owned by **Prince Mikhail Golitsyn** whose fortunes had a strange habit of veering from the sublime to the ridiculous. His grandfather, Vasily, a powerful figure during the regency of Sophia, was exiled at her fall with his family to Siberia. In 1714 after the death of Vasily, the Golitsyns were allowed to return to European Russia and Mikhail was sent to study in France and Italy where he married an Italian. This happy state was cruelly ended when the Empress Anna Ivanovna in 1730 ordered him to return to Russia, declared his marriage to a catholic foreigner null and void, and reduced him to the position of court jester. Anna, who loved outrageous practical jokes, ordered Mikhail one cold January to marry a spectacularly ugly Kalmyk woman. An ice palace was built for their wedding night on the frozen Neva and both were obliged to remain there in the excruciating cold until morning. Prince Mikhail soon retired to Bratovshchina.

From the Yaroslavl Highway M-8 turn right, under the road, to PRAVDA and TISHKOVO. At the T-junction turn right and then left signed ZAVETY ILICHA across railway tracks (straight on is Bratovshchina). After 1 km at the edge of the settlement turn right, unsigned, for Yeldigino in 6 km.

YELDIGINO was acquired in 1662 by the powerful **Princes Kurakin**. Prince Boris Kurakin was a well educated man, a diplomat of Peter the Great's time and close to the Tsar. Kurakin's son, Alexander, commissioned the elegant Trinity church and his son, in turn, Boris-Leonty, a Senator, added the grand mansion and the park. Today, the big house has gone, little is left of the park, and the village is in the shadow of an ugly farm.

The Church of the Trinity, *Troitsy*, was built in 1735 at the height of the fashion for baroque in Russia but its shape, a square ground plan with angled corners, shows an unusual discipline and firm handling. The large central octagonal drum springs from the central cube and the

210 ROAD 7

decor is restrained with paired pilasters and modest window designs.
The bell tower was added in 1842.

Near the church, on the southeast side, is a modest two-storey wooden
house where **Inessa Armand**, Lenin's intimate friend, lived with her
husband, Alexander Armand, the Pushkino textile mill owner. Perhaps
the stately home of the Kurakins was too dilapidated or perhaps with
their three children they preferred a more rustic ambiance. The lovely,
independent Inessa deserted Alexander in 1904, joined the communist
party, and set off to tour western Europe in the pursuit of human happi-
ness through socialism. Alexander faithfully sent her money, looked
after the children, and seems to have accepted the situation stoically.
She became a close friend perhaps mistress of Lenin and returned with
him on the famous sealed train through Germany to Russia in 1917. A
spokesman for women's affairs in the new Bolshevik government, she
never returned to her family and fell victim to the 1920 cholera
epidemic. The unfortunate Alexander joined the local state farm,
working until his death in 1943 at Aleshino, 5 km northwest of Yeldigino where his descendants still live.

FOUR UNUSUAL CHURCHES

*From the Yaroslavl Highway M-8 turn right into Ivanteevka. Because of
the one-way system, at traffic lights on the main square turn right onto
Sovietskaya St, then left at more traffic lights, and, at the third set left
again onto Tolmachev Street. (At the farthest end of Tolmachev Street,
past the old mills on the river bank, turn left to return to the Yaroslavl
Road.)*

Russia's first paper mill in the 16th century for Ivan the Terrible's new
printing presses was set up at **IVANTEEVKA**, population 50,000, on
the Ucha River. Textiles have been made here since the 19th century
and are still being produced.

Past the House of Culture, right, is the startling red and white **Church of
St John the Baptist**, *Ioanna Predtechi*, built 1803–8 by Alexei Bakarev, a
student of Matvei Kazakov. In the late 18th century the classical and
pseudo-Gothic styles were both fashionable but the use of Gothic in
Russian architecture, as here where it is so overstated, has always been
eccentric. Yet the forms are surprisingly simple. The ground plan is a
Greek cross of equal arms with the two-storey bell tower at the western
entrance all in sober red brick which by itself would not have been out

of the ordinary. The masterly stroke is the white stone detailing sprinkled liberally everywhere – on the quoins, arches, windows, and walls. The total effect is of a highly decorated festive cake.

To reach the interesting wooden **Church of St George** in Novoselki turn right at the end of Tolmachev Street, cross the river, go past the turn to Komyagino and up a small hill. St George, which never closed, was built in the pseudo-Russian manner of the late 19th century. Its bright colours – the blisteringly blue dome, green roof, yellow columns and white door frames – rival St John.

Follow the route as for St George in Ivanteevka but turn left to **KOMYAGINO** *3 km on the paved but bumpy road. Or from the Yaroslavl Highway turn right signed KRASNOARMEISK for 5 km and turn right through Levkovo 3 km to Komyagino.* On a small hill the picturesque, white **Church of St Sergius** stands in a garden sown carefully with flowers and cabbages and with fine views over the countryside. It was built in 1678 for the conservative courtier, the *dumny dvoryanin*, Nikita Akinfov, who lost favour in Peter the Great's reign opposing his reforms. Assymetrical with receding tiers of gables, five fat domes clustered tightly together, tent-shaped bell tower and bulging apse, it is typical of the mid 17th century Russian style. The proportions are particularly extravagant: the roof gables together with the drums and domes are approximately the same height as the cube of the church, and the apse protrudes to the same degree as the cube is wide. Notice how the window frames are all differently executed and how the building has two doorways, the larger for the main church, the smaller for the second altar to St Makary. Soviet restorers had already returned the church to its original look before it reopened for which the new parishioners must be grateful.

From the Yaroslavl Highway turn right opposite Pushkino signed KRASNOARMEISK and travel 16 km to **TSAREVO** (TsarYOvo). *From Komyagino continue north to Levkovo and turn right to Tsarevo, about 10 km.*

The unusual **Church of St Nicholas** is left of the main road on the edge of the textile town of **Krasnoarmeisk**. Built 1812-15 with its pointed windows and doors and pinnacles and spires it is pseudo-Gothic like St John in Ivanteevka but here the similarity ends for this is an altogether finer building. The main church is a rotunda with a circular apse and massive round dome. On the western side two oval rooms act as the *trapeza* and there is a small belfry over the western entrance. White stone detailing stands out sharply against the red brick walls and more colour is provided by the light blue dome and spire. It was built for the influential **Durasov** family probably by the fine architect Ivan Yegotov.

The elegant church provides a splendid backdrop for the visual arts. A painting of the last supper marks the western entrance and a marvellous frieze of bas-reliefs encircles the apse, probably by the Moscow sculptor, **Gavril Zamaraev**. Paired pilasters enhance the sculptural effect. As the church was not closed, the original fine iconostasis of four tiers has survived.

On the Yaroslavl Highway M-8, 30 km from the MKAD turn right signed NOGINSK. After 1 km turn left to MAYAK DOM TVORCHESTVA, the holiday home of Gostelradio, the state radio station. Walk right and then left, past the shop, *Dom Byta*, to the freshly painted lemon and white **Church of St John the Divine**, *Ioanna Bogoslova*, surrounded by a fence with gates and pointed towers enclosing a spacious churchyard, a caprice among the ugly five-storey blocks. Built in 1767 and twice rebuilt in the 19th century, the baroque apse and bell tower are all that remain of the original church. The bell tower stands not at the western end but in the middle, linking the unheated eastern and the heated western church. The effect is remarkably harmonious.

St John was built in 1767 for the **BOGOSLOVSKOE-MOGILTSKY** estate which in the late 18th century was purchased by **Prince Gavril Gagarin**, a childhood friend of Paul I and Minister of Commerce under Alexander I. In 1850, it was bought by the Aigin forestry entrepreneurs who lived in neighbouring Talitsy and by 1912 it was owned by the mill-owning Armands, the Russianised French family. By 1920 the house had disappeared and only the extensive park and the church were left.

ON THE THRESHOLD OF SERGIEV POSAD

From the Yaroslavl Highway M-8 turn right marked SOFRINO over the highway and right at the intersection onto the old Yaroslavl Road. Note the large house at **Talitsy**, left, with the garden full of anodyne sculptures of Russian saints, the work of **Vyacheslav Klykov**, owner of the house. It was built at the end of the 19th century for Vasily Aigin, the forestry and brick entrepreneur, who chose to live in Talitsy, his ancestral village, rather than the opulent estate in Mogiltsy. A little ahead by the Talitsy River, is the dilapidated Aigin chapel, until recently used as housing.

Ignore the turn in Talitsy signed SOFRINO (to the dacha settlement only) and continue 4 km to **Rakhmanovo** *where the attractive Ascension church, built in 1802, was never closed. Turn left signed MURANOVO 7 km and left again in 2 km at the bus-stop.* The **Church of the Smolensk Virgin**, *Smolenskoi Ikony Bozhiei Materi*, stands on the other side of the pond.

In the late 17th century **SOFRINO** belonged to **Fedor Saltykov** whose daughter, Praskovya, married Tsar Ivan, the feeble-witted brother of co-Tsar Peter at the time their sister, Sophia, was acting as Regent. Praskovya bore three daughters before Ivan's death of whom one, **Anna**, was to become Empress in 1730. By this time Sofrino belonged to **Mikhail Golovin**, Chancellor in the reigns of Anna and Ivan VI. When Elizabeth seized the throne, Golovin along with other statesmen, was exiled to Siberia. His faithful wife, Yekaterina, who followed him, setting a precedent for the Decembrists' wives in the next century, inherited the village. Sofrino seemed to attract strong female owners for in the 19th century it passed to the idiosyncratic **Varvara Yaguzhinskaya** who granted freedom to her serfs in 1843 angering other landowners. Her marble tomb still rests in the church.

The church built in 1691 alongside the old boyar *palata* (which was only demolished in 1866) is a fine example of the Moscow baroque style. It rises high above the pond in five receding red and white tiers, the top four octagonal, the white stone cockscombs making a lovely contrast with the red brick of the tall tower. Spoiling the effect is the 19th century bell tower – unnecessary in these 'under the bells' churches – and the *trapeza*. Even more disturbing is the 1912 pseudo-Russian south chapel which upsets the harmony of the building at ground-floor level. But from afar the graceful tower is unforgettable.

For several years the church was used to store furniture from the nearby estate at Muranovo while it was under restoration. Finally the Muranovo museum took back its belongings and in 1995 services resumed at Sofrino. The regime seems unusually strict: a sign implores ladies not to bare their heads in the presence of men.

From Sofrino continue west 5 km to Muranovo.

The modest estate of **MURANOVO** on the Talitsa River is associated
with the lives of two important poets, Yevgeny Baratynsky and Fedor
Tyutchev, and the slavophile writer, Ivan Aksakov. Muranovo consists
of a two-storey wooden and brick house, a small box-like wooden
church, now functioning, and service buildings and guest houses on the
slope overlooking the pond and park. The successive families who lived
here from the early 19th century were connected to each other by
marriage through the female line thus ensuring a direct descent from the
first owners, the Engelgardts, to the last, the Tyutchevs. Closed for
many years for repairs, it finally reopened in 1997. *(Closed Mondays
and Tuesdays.)*

In 1816 the property was purchased as a summer residence by **Lev
Engelgardt**, a major-general in Catherine's army with literary interests
who turned Muranovo into a haven for writers and poets. A frequent
visitor was **Denis Davydov**, the hero of the 1812 war who introduced the
Engelgardts to one of Russia's finest poets, **Yevgeny Baratynsky**.
Baratynsky married the eldest daughter, Anastasia, and thus became
master of the estate. He died in 1844 of a sudden illness during a trip to
Italy but has left an indelible mark on Muranovo for he personally
redesigned the house and grounds.

Baratynsky's comfortable but idiosyncratic **house** is composed of three
parts: the two-storey central section of vertical logs (usually logs are
placed horizontally) clothed in brick, plastered and bearing a shallow
dome; a low western wing finished in wood; and the southwest brick
tower. The grand central hall dominates the ground floor off which
other rooms recede. The original paintings, china and mahogany furniture combine to give an unusually complete picture of the lifestyle of a
modest Russian gentleman of the 19th century.

In 1859 the Engelgardts' youngest daughter, Sophia, wife of **Nikolai
Putyata**, also a writer, inherited the estate. In 1869 the Putyatas'
daughter, Olga, married **Ivan Tyutchev**, son of the poet **Fedor Tyutchev**.
A contemporary of Pushkin, Fedor Tyutchev served in the diplomatic
service for 22 years, only returning to Russia in 1844 at the age of 41.
Although a leading nationalist and panslavist, popular in the Moscow
and St Petersburg salons, it was not until 1850 that he obtained literary
recognition. Tyutchev visited his son's family often and at his death in
1873 the furnishings from his rooms in St Petersburg were brought to
Muranovo for safe keeping. The room in which the great satirist,
Nikolai Gogol, stayed was also kept as a memorial.

The third writer connected with Muranovo was **Ivan Aksakov**, the political journalist and slavophile who lived at nearby Abramtsevo – his father, Sergei, was the author of *A Family Chronicle*. Ivan married Anna, the sister of Ivan Tyutchev, and when Aksakov was exiled from Moscow in 1878 for attacking the Congress of Berlin, his brother-in-law tried in vain to get permission for him to live at Muranovo. Nevertheless, when Aksakov died the contents of his study were also transferred to Muranovo which was rapidly becoming a museum of 19th century writers.

After the revolution **Nikolai Tyutchev** (grandson of Fedor) became the first curator of the museum – he and his father Ivan are buried by the odd little church. Relatives of the Tyutchevs, the Pigarevs, still live in the grounds in the attractive wooden house near the car park. Thus at least one family of landed gentry have been able to cling to a fragment of their ancestral home throughout the Soviet period.

From the Yaroslavl Highway M-8 turn right signed LESHKOVO and RADONEZH for1 km to **VOZDVIZHENSKOE**. The singularly lovely **Church of the Exaltation of the Cross**, *Vozdvizheniya Kresta*, was built in the late Empire style in 1845. The cube with Doric porticoes on all four sides supports the powerful helmet-shaped dome and tall drum hung with bells without a jutting apse or bell tower to spoil the symmetry. Although a sign claims the church to be by Afanasy Grigoriev it is more likely the work of the fine classicist, Fedor Shestakov.

At Vozdvizhenskoe, where the monarchs rested at the **fourth royal travel palace** on the way to the monastery, the struggle between Peter the Great and his half-sister Sophia was played out. The **Regent Sophia** had come to power on the back of the Streltsy uprising in May 1682 when many of Peter's Naryshkin relatives were slain. To control the still rebellious Streltsy, Sophia appointed as their head Prince Ivan Khovansky. Only four months later during her pilgrimage she stopped at Vozdvizhenskoe, ordered Khovansky and his son, Andrei, to join her, and that very day had them executed on the square by the Moscow road. Seven years later, the situation was reversed. In 1689 Sophia set out for the Trinity-Sergius Monastery in a desperate attempt to win over the audacious Tsar Peter, then gathering support in the monastery. When Peter sent orders not to advance further she took refuge in the Vozdvizhenskoe palace and waited for him to arrive. But he refused to see her and she finally returned, humiliated, to Moscow. There her closest minister was executed and she herself was forced to enter the Novodevichy Convent and take the veil. Peter had won the battle for the throne. (Moussourgsky's opera, *Khovanshchina*, interprets these historical events very freely.)

From the Yaroslavl Highway M-8 turn right signed LESHKOVO and RADONEZH and, past the Church of the Exaltation of the Cross, go under the motorway west 2 km to **RADONEZH**. In the 14th century this was a bustling place where the Boyar Kirill settled with his wife and sons including Sergius, who was to become the monk canonised as Sergius Radonezh in memory of his home town. Radonezh was destroyed in 1610 by the Poles and thereafter remained a village, even changing its name to Gorodok (little town). Nowadays, it is dominated by the impressive classical church at the top of the high bank overlooking the pretty Pazha River.

The **Church of the Transfiguration**, *Spasa Preobrazheniya*, was built in 1840 possibly by the Moscow architect, Afanasy Grigoriev. It is of brick stuccoed over but unlike the Vozdvizhenskoe church it is traditional in plan with cube and heavy rotunda, round apse, Doric porticoes on north and south, and on the west the rusticated *trapeza* and three-tier bell tower. The iconostasis is in good order as are the wall paintings, repainted in 1968 when the church was a museum. In preparation for the return to worship, the later layer was scraped off to reveal the earlier frescoes. Radonezh is an important place of pilgrimage and the costs of restoration are being met from central church coffers not, as is usual, from parishioners.

Travel 5 km west to **KHOTKOVO** *to the southern gates of the convent perched on a hill above the Pazha River*. Now a small town of over 20,000, Khotkovo's traditional crafts include carving, lace-making and painting of lacquer trays.

The ancient **Convent of the Intercession**, *Pokrova*, was founded in 1308, although no buildings survive earlier than the 18th century. Sergius Radonezh and his brother took their monks' vows here over five hundred years ago – at that time the monastery served both sexes. Their parents, Kirill and Mariya, also entered the monastery in old age and are buried there. In 1504 the monastery became a convent, the recipient of rich gifts from boyars and tsars but a century later it was destroyed by the Poles and only rebuilt in the 18th and 19th centuries. It was Peter the Great who suggested that a Dutch craftsman teach the nuns of Khotkovo the art of lace-making. The convent soon became famous for its lace which together with wooden toys turned Khotkovo into a crafts centre and gave the nuns a steady income.

After the revolution a children's home which opened in the convent was named for the Soviet leader, Kamenev, but changed to Krupskaya when he fell from power. By 1930 the children's home was closed, the tall bell tower demolished, and the buildings given over to the local agricultural college. Fifty years later, in 1989, the cathedral and other buildings were returned to the church and gradually the convent has been re-established.

Within the southern Water Gate, built in 1833 and guarded by a benign lion, are the former poorhouses built into the wall. Farther on the left is a small wooden newly constructed belfry followed by the handsome pink and cream **Cathedral of the Intercession**, *Pokrova*, with five domes constructed 1812-16 on the site of the 17th century wooden cathedral. In spite of its pastel colours, it is rather lugubrious, with a massive rotunda dome over the cube and Corinthian porticoes on north and south. Unusually, it has no entrance from the west as the ground drops away precipitately on that side to the river below. Attached to it are the nuns' quarters who scurry in and out in their black robes. In the *trapeza* where the walls are still bare and a temporary iconostasis has been erected, are the tombs of Sergius Radonezh's parents.

Across the forecourt is the astonishing brick pseudo-Byzantine church of **St Nicholas** with its immense burnt orange dome built 1900-4 by Alexander Latkov to commemorate the 600th anniversary of the founding of the convent. Like so many late 19th century churches, size (it held 2,000 people) seems to have taken precedence over other considerations. During the Soviet period it was closed and used as a garage to repair the large tractors of the agricultural college.

Farther on, opposite St Nicholas, is the small blue guest house where the Metropolitan stayed on his visits. On the left just beyond St Nicholas is the house of the abbess with Soviet-style columns. At the end are the impressive mid 18th century Holy Gates where the Khotkovo museum was housed in the former **Church of the Nativity of St John the Baptist**, *Rozhdestva Ioanna Predtechi*, up the stairs, left. St John, a popular venue for weddings, had an entrance from the street ensuring that the nuns could be safely screened from the newly-weds.

From the Khotkovo convent cross under the railway line and turn right and then left reaching **AKHTYRKA** *in 4 km.* The pretty village on the banks of the winding Vorya is where the artist brothers, Viktor and Apollinary Vasnetsov, associated with the Mamontov Circle, rented a dacha for they could easily walk along the Vorya River to Abramtsevo. Akhtyrka was also known for the splendid wooden palace of the Princes Trubetskoy but today only the red and white church at the edge of the village survives. The Akhtyrka estate was in the Trubetskoy family from 1734 to 1879 when Prince Nikolai Petrovich, a great musical patron, was obliged to sell it to pay his brother's debts. The last owner, Matveev, in a fit of despair after the revolution, deliberately fired and destroyed the remarkable palace.

The church (and the palace) were built in the 1820s by a student of Domenico Gilardi, **Alexander Kutepov**. The handsome red brick and white stone Empire church is composed of a central cube topped by a rotunda, and monumental Doric porticoes north and south. The eastern apse perfectly matches the rounded *trapeza* on the west; the three-tier bell tower and spire are linked to the church by a gallery. The interior has not survived but the church has been repaired, a new floor laid and choir rebuilt since it was restored to the parish in 1992.

From Khotkovo convent go left under the railway to a roundabout and continue straight on for 2 km crossing the Vorya River to Abramtsevo, right, opposite the car park.

ABRAMTSEVO, the home of the Aksakov family of writers, was also the summer residence of Savva Mamontov whose encouragement of the arts at the estate initiated the great flowering of Russian culture that erupted at the turn of the century. And what is more, like Muranovo but unlike nearly all its sister estates, Abramtsevo has not deteriorated with time.

The modest estate was purchased in 1843 by **Sergei Aksakov**, one of the foremost prose writers of his generation. It was at Abramtsevo that Aksakov wrote much of his best work including *A Family Chronicle* published in 1856, three years before his death. His two sons, Konstantin and Ivan, were also writers; Ivan married the poet Tyutchev's daughter at nearby Muranovo. Gogol, Turgeniev, and of course, the Tyutchevs, were frequent visitors to Abramtsevo which is often mentioned in the poetry and literature of the time. It was here that Gogol in 1849 read the first chapter of the second volume of *Dead*

Souls. Those who heard it were especially privileged for later, in a fit of despair, he destroyed the entire manuscript.

In 1870 Abramtsevo was purchased by the young and newly married **Savva Mamontov**, the owner of the Yaroslavl-Arkhangelsk railway line and a passionate patron of the arts. He and his wife, Elizaveta, donated a hospital for victims of the 1871 cholera epidemic and a year later opened the first school in the district. But their real contribution was to provide a creative environment for Russia's most talented artists, sculptors and singers. What occurred at Abramtsevo was a catalyst for the modern movement that had such a brilliant beginning in Russia.

Savva Mamontov, the railway tycoon, was also an amateur sculptor, singer, director and dramatist. During trips to Italy and France with his wife and sickly son he befriended the sculptor **Mark Antokolsky**, the artists **Vasily Polenov** and **Ilya Repin**, and the widow of the composer, Alexander Serov, with her small son, **Valentin Serov**, who was to become a noted portraitist. In the summer of 1874 when the expansive Mamontovs invited this group to join them at Abramtsevo the Mamontov Circle came into existence. Repin settled nearby, giving the boy, Valentin Serov, drawing lessons. Polenov made studies of archeology and Russian artistic history at a time when the early icons were not even cleaned or properly studied.

In 1890 Mamontov invited **Mikhail Vrubel**, then a poor artist eking out a living in Kiev, to join the group. He thus rescued the most important Russian artist of the age who was to have enormous influence on the avant-garde of the next generation. The circle at Abramtsevo included many other noted artists: **Apollinary and Viktor Vasnetsov**; **Konstantin Korovin**; **Vasily Surikov**; **Mikhail Nesterov**; and **Mariya Yakunchikova**. The artistic commune worked together painting, writing and producing plays and staging operas helped by **Chaliapin** and **Stanislavsky** who were frequent visitors. In 1890 Polenov's sister, Yelena, opened the **ceramic workshop** and Vrubel experimented and composed some outstanding work using new lustre glazes. Abramtsevo ceramics can still be seen on the Metropole Hotel and the Yaroslavl Station in Moscow.

But misfortune suddenly struck the Mamontovs. In September 1899 Savva was accused of fraud over the construction of the railway. He languished in prison many months until finally, in June 1900, he was cleared in a famous court case. But by this time he was a broken man and the magic Mamontov Circle had disintegrated.

Abramtsevo does not have a great mansion, only a low rambling single-storey wooden **house** with a small mezzanine floor, shutters, simple pediment and open balconies probably built in the 1820s and 30s. It was enlarged in the early 1870s by the Mamontovs who added several rooms and was reconstructed in 1947 when the old house was rebuilt to the original design. Although the house is largely a museum to Sergei Aksakov, the paintings of the talented Mamontov Circle hang on the walls and Vrubel's masterly tiled stove dominates the hall. The old photographs are particularly poignant.

Other buildings on the estate relate to the Mamontovs. To the right of the house is the **sculptors' studio** of logs built for Savva Mamontov in 1873 by the gifted Moscow architect, **Viktor Gartman** who sent his assistant to oversee the construction then died suddenly and never saw the finished building. It makes use of traditional carved peasant decoration like lace patterns, in the spirit of Gartman's other buildings. In the 1960s the glazed stoves of Mamontov's Moscow house were transferred to the studio, which now exhibits ceramics produced at Abramtsevo. To the left is the fanciful **bath house** or *teremok*, built in 1877 by the architect, **Ivan Ropet**, known for his love of old Russian motifs. It was used as a bath house for some years and then altered as a guest house for the Mamontovs' many visitors. Not far away and behind the church is the delightful **'hut on chicken's legs'**, a fairy tale pavilion designed in 1883 by Viktor Vasnetsov as a playhouse for the children with a thatched roof and carved owl and bat.

The jewel in the crown, however, is the **Saviour Untouched by Hand**, *Spasa Nerukotvornovo* (the mandilion or image of Christ imprinted on Veronica's veil – in Russian literally 'untouched by hand'). In 1880 when the Vorya River flooded preventing everyone from attending the Easter service, Elizaveta Mamontova spearheaded the building of a church at Abramtsevo. Everyone embarked on the project in 1881 with enthusiasm but the overall design belonged to Viktor Vasnetsov. Direct inspiration was the Church of the Saviour Nereditsa in Novogorod, but elements of Moscow, Pskov and Vladimir-Suzdal architecture crept in and in the end it was the brilliant adaptation of features of the early churches, exaggerating some, reducing others, that makes this the **first Art Nouveau church** in the neo-Russian manner. The dome looks Pskovian, the bells hang above the western entrance like an old *zvonnitsa* and a frieze rings the cornice as in Moscow architecture.

The inner walls of the church were unpainted to focus on the intricately carved **iconostasis**. Like the *tyablo* of northern churches, the festivals are ranged on shelves left of the royal gates while on the right are early Russian saints. To Polenov is ascribed the Annunciation, Repin the Saviour, Vasnetsov the Virgin of the royal gates. Yelena Polenova added St Fedor and his sons Konstantin and David. Viktor Vasnetsov not only designed the **mosaic floor** in the form of a single spreading flower, but personally helped to lay it. The vestments were designed by Polenov (whose marriage to Mariya Yakunchikova was the first service) and in 1890 Vrubel added the brilliant **tiled stove**. In 1892 Vasnetsov added the north chapel for a sadder occasion, the burial of Mamontov's son, Andrei, an artist who had also contributed to the interior decoration of the main church. Mamontov himself was buried in this chapel in 1918; the graves of his daughter, Vera and his wife, Elizaveta, are just outside.

Abramtsevo was nationalised in 1919, the museum was established shortly after and Mamontov's youngest daughter, Alexandra, became the first director. In 1993 the Saviour church reopened its doors to religious services.

SERGIEV POSAD

Take the Yaroslavl Highway M-8, 45 km from the MKAD and take the left fork signed SERGIEV POSAD 7 km into the town.

The pilgrims' ultimate goal, the Trinity-Sergius Monastery, is not only the most important religious institution in Russia but one steeped in Russian culture and history. After the revolution Sergiev Posad became Sergiev and then, in 1930, **Zagorsk**, in honour of the Moscow communist, Vladimir Zagorsky, blown up by anarchists in 1919. Fortunately Soviet industrial development was confined to new suburbs and even the Palace of Culture built in 1954, the largest in the Moscow region, could not upstage the monastery which retains its dominant position among the quiet streets of wooden houses and winding Konchura River.

HISTORY of the monastery. The walled **Trinity Monastery of St Sergius**, *Svyato-Troitskaya Sergieva Lavra*, was founded in 1345 when two young monks, Stefan and Sergius (Sergiy), sons of Kirill of Radonezh, established a lonely hermitage in the wild land 10 km north of their home. Stefan soon left the hard life but the pious Sergius continued alone. He was gradually joined by others and slowly walls, chapels and monks' cells were built and the hermitage became the

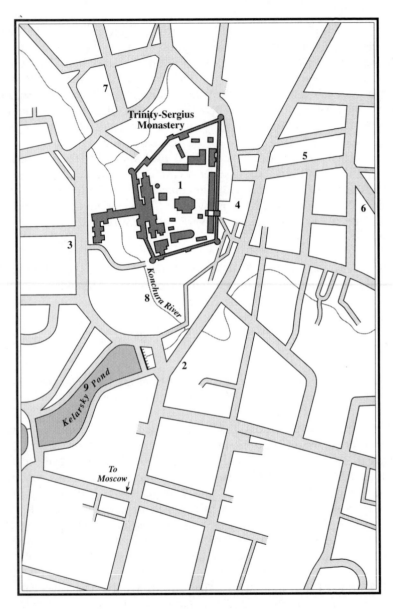

SERGIEV POSAD 1. Trinity-Sergius Monastery, 2. Prospekt
Krasnoi Armii, 3. Proletarskaya,
4. Monastery Square, 5. Karl Marx,
6. Komsomolskaya, 7. Akademik Favorsky,
8. Konchura River, 9. Kelarsky Pond

Trinity Monastery. Sergius's fame spread so far he became spiritual advisor to Dmitry Donskoy, the Grand Prince of Moscow who encouraged the spread of new monasteries, especially in the southeast where they could double as defence bastions against the dreaded Tatars. Sergius founded 22 monasteries in all, many in the far north, before his death in 1392. As Russia's greatest saint the Trinity Monastery was embellished with his name.

When in 1380 Dmitry gathered his forces for a desperate assault against the Tatars he visited the Trinity Monastery to receive Sergius's blessing and to take with him two warrior monks, Alexander Peresvet and Rodion Oslyava. Against great odds the Russians successfully routed the Tatars at the **Battle of Kulikovo**. Nevertheless, in 1408, the Tatars mounted a particularly devastating raid, putting many towns to the torch and completely destroying the wooden monastery. Sergius had died in 1392 but his body in the small chapel miraculously survived the fire.

In 1422 the Moscow Grand Prince, Vasily I and his uncle, Prince Yury of Zvenigorod, endowed the construction in stone of the serenely beautiful **Cathedral of the Trinity**, the earliest extant building. In the troubled times of the 16th and 17th centuries, heavy masonry walls were built and the monastery took on the aspect of a fortress. Nevertheless, scholars like the Greek monk **Maxim** came to consult the great library. (In his old age Maxim met **Ivan the Terrible** in the monastery and advised him to help the families of those he had murdered or he would lose his son. The prophesy seemed to be fulfilled in 1581 when the unrepentant Tsar, in a fit of rage, murdered his eldest son.) In 1608 the **Polish army** under False Dmitry succeeded in capturing Moscow but they could not take the strongly fortified Trinity-Sergius Monastery even after 16 months siege. And when the Russian patriots, the aristocrat **Prince Pozharsky** and the merchant **Kuzma Minin**, gathered an army to defend Muscovy, their first act, like Dmitry Donskoy before them, was to come to the monastery for a blessing. In 1618 the Poles again attacked but this time the new Romanov dynasty was on the throne, Muscovy was united, and a peace treaty was signed at nearby Deulino.

In 1682 when the **Streltsy**, the palace guards, rioted in the Kremlin, the future Peter the Great, then 9 years old with his half-brother, Ivan, and their sister Sophia fled to the Trinity-Sergius Monastery for protection. Seven years later, in 1689, the young 17-year-old **Peter**, now opposed to the Regent Sophia, again sought refuge in the monastery whence he was able to march on Moscow and take the throne unopposed.

Although the capital moved to St Petersburg in 1712 the monastery remained an important focus of national aspirations and during the 18th century was frequently the object of **annual pilgrimages** by the powerful empresses. In 1742 the **seminary** opened and two years later the monastery received the highest title, that of *Lavra* or Laura (in Greek it means a row of cells). By this time it was very wealthy owning 214,000 desyatins of land and over 100,000 serfs, more than four times that of the next richest monastery. However, by the decree of 1764 the Lavra, like other monasteries, lost much of its land and serfs.

At about this time Catherine the Great conceived the idea of cladding all the buildings in marble to bring them in line with 18th century ideas of classical beauty. Fortunately, like her project to redesign the Moscow Kremlin, it was never realised. But during her reign the great commanding **bell tower** was completed, several tiers higher than originally planned. In 1814 the famous **Moscow Academy**, Russia's first institute of higher education, was transferred to the Lavra and in the late 19th century the hotel and the huge poorhouse/hospital by the west wall by Alexander Latkov were constructed.

In November 1918 **the Bolsheviks** closed the monastery and invited hostile left-wing students from Moscow to take over the buildings. As in many monasteries where there were holy relics, the coffin of St Sergius was opened for a Soviet commission hoping to expose the remains as a hoax. However, they concluded that they were those of a 15th century person and for a while, to the delight of pilgrims, the coffin was left open. In 1919 the Moscow students were sent packing and 43 monks were allowed to remain as guardians. But this was only a respite for in 1920 the monastery was finally closed. The **great library** was transferred to the Rumyantsev Museum (later the Lenin now the Russian State Library) and stored in closed churches in Moscow. By 1921 trials and executions of religious leaders had begun all over Russia.

What saved the Lavra from ruin was the decision in 1920 to turn it into a **Soviet museum** of the churches and their treasures. In comparison with other Russian monasteries, the Lavra's fate was comparatively mild. Indeed, the same government that hounded its priests also carried out important and sensitive restoration work returning buildings, distorted by 19th century additions, to their original form. And the Lavra has acted in a small way as a safe haven for paintings and iconostases from some of the many demolished churches in Moscow.

With the relaxation in 1943 of Stalin's policy towards the Orthodox Church the position eased. In 1946 the great Easter service was again held in the Lavra and **monastic life**, albeit on a small scale, resumed. The monastic side has now been fully reinstated (there are 15 applicants for every place in the seminary) and the church authorities, in a reversal of roles, have begun agitating for the removal of the museum. But the museum with its outstanding collection of religious artifacts is still holding on.

THE MONASTERY TODAY. The **motor route** into Sergiev Posad along Prospekt Krasnoi Armii passes the old walled prison and a succession of elegant baroque churches of the 1770s. On the left can be glimpsed the **Church of the Assumption**, *Uspeniya*, at Bolotnaya Ulitsa 39 built in 1769 in the wealthy suburb of Klementcvo. On the right, is the late 18th century church, the **Ascension**, *Vozneseniya*, of the icon-painters' district with an absurdly small cupola, never properly completed. Another, the delightful red and white **St Elijah**, *Ilii Proroka*, built in 1773 which served the armoury district, stands opposite the southwest corner of the monastery on Proletarskaya Street, left.

At Prospekt Krasnoi Armii 136, left, before the green slope of the monastery is an interesting **museum of old Russian toys** attached to the Institute of the Development of the Personality, founded in Moscow in 1918 but moved to Sergiev Posad in 1931. *Open 10-5 except Mondays and Tuesdays.* The main car park is on the right – parking in the monastery square is not allowed.

On the left just outside the monastery wall, two beautiful 16th century churches of the former Pyatnitsky Monastery huddle close together, the **Presentation**, *Vvedeniya*, the former cathedral, and the sister winter church, **Pyatnitskaya**, next to it heavily rebuilt in the 17th century. Facing both across the road is the charming early 18th century **Pyatnitsky chapel** built over a holy well in the colourful Moscow baroque style, roofed with aspen shingles.

Beyond these churches the monastery square opens up. At the north end near the 1926 statue of Lenin by Sergei Merkurov, is the former **monastery hotel** built in 1823. On the east side are the old trading rows built in 1902, now used as souvenir shops, and in the southeast corner, the baroque **Krasnogorsky Chapel** built in 1770 on the spot where St Sergius's wooden coffin was laid to rest when saved from the 1408 fire.

The **monastery** presents a wonderful picture of massive white walls, gold domes and colourful towers, in which the simple forms of early Moscow architecture combine successfully with the highly decorative features of full-blown baroque. It forms an irregular square surrounded by strong walls built 1540-50 punctuated by 13 gates and towers – octagonal on the corners and square in the middle. The decorative upper parts were added in the 17th century. The evocative names starting from the south-east corner going north are; Pyatnitskaya, Krasnaya (the main gate), Assumption Gate, Drying, Duck (from which in 1689 Peter the Great liked to shoot ducks in the Bely Pond), Ringing, Stable Gate, Carpenter, Cellarer, Beer (with ice house), Water, Water Gate, and Bow (as in bow and arrow). Enter by the main **Krasnaya Gate** which has a second gate containing the colourful **Church of St John the Baptist**, *Ioanna Predtechi*, built in 1692-7 by the Stroganov family, the wealthy northern merchants.

Tickets for the museum and permission to photograph can be obtained from a kiosk on the right. There is no charge for admission to the monastery itself. Primitive toilets are situated a little to the right of the main entrance (or through the Assumption/Uspensky gate right of the Krasnaya Gate).

Straight ahead, left, is the long building of the **refectory** with its open porch containing the **Church of St Sergius** rising two floors above the rest of the building. The refectory was built of brick with lush stone detailing 1686-92 in the reign of the young co-tsars, Peter and Ivan. The exuberant rusticated stone facade combines with vine leaves and grapes in relief on moulded columns, heavily adorned niches, decorated windows and doors, and scallop shells at roof level. The long dining hall, still used for important assemblies, is not interrupted by columns. The magnificent late 17th century iconostasis was rescued from the Church of St Nicholas of the Large Cross, *Bolshovo Kresta*, in Moscow when it was demolished in 1933.

Tucked into the wall of the refectory is the oblong **Church of St Mikhei** in baroque style built in 1774 over the grave of the saint, a pupil of St Sergius. To the right of St Mikhei is the graceful white **Church of the Descent of the Holy Spirit to the Apostles**, *Soshestviya Svyatovo Dukha na Apostolov*. Built in 1476 by Pskov master builders it is the second oldest church in the monastery, one of the first to use coloured tiles. The cube, with protruding triple apse and two rows of pointed ogee-shaped gables, bears a tiled frieze which repeats the leaf motif of the limestone frieze on the Trinity Cathedral next door. Bells originally hung in the tall drum were rung not by chiming in the Russian manner but by ringing from the ground with ropes as in western churches. The strange dome, a splayed onion with a gold band around the middle and stars on a blue background, was only added in the 1780s. The frescoes within were painted in 1906.

Beyond the Church of the Holy Spirit lies the oldest and most wonderful building in the monastery, the **Trinity Cathedral**, *Troitsy*. After a terrible famine Vasily I of Moscow and Prince Yury of Zveni-gorod buried their differences to jointly sponsor in 1422 the new stone cathedral. Its equally ancient iconostasis was painted by two of the greatest artists of the 15th century, Andrei Rublev and Daniil Cherny. Except for the period 1918 to 1946 when the monastery was closed, the cathedral has remained open 24 hours a day and the service never ceases to be intoned over the body of St Sergius in its silver casket before the altar. Pilgrims crowd the narrow church chanting and holding candles in the murky light

The walls of the cathedral are divided into three sections, cut horizon-tally by a fine **triple frieze** and finished in **peaked gables**, the *zakomary*. Above is the tall drum punctuated by narrow windows and the **helmet-shaped cupola**. The north entrance is a splendid receding ogee-shaped **portico**; the similar west and south porticoes are hidden on the west by the 16th century entrance *papert* and on the south by the 1623 chapel to the Archimandrite Nikon and the *palatka* over the grave of one of the early archimandrites.

Within, lit only by candles and the drum apertures, there is sufficient light to display the splendid iconostasis and its wonderful icons, many painted by Rublev and Cherny in 1427. The screen of icons was then just developing in Russia and this is one of the first to extend across the entire east end of the church. To the right is an early copy of the icon of the **Trinity by Rublev** which is now in the Tretyakov gallery. The lovely *deesis* row, above, with the figures of Mary and John the Baptist and the apostles on either side of Christ is believed to be by Rublev and Cherny as is the smaller row of the festivals of the church below. The wall frescoes painted in 1635, which seem pale by comparison, were rediscovered and cleaned in 1949.

Behind the Trinity Cathedral on the south wall are two-storey richly decorated **Metropolitan (later Patriarch) Chambers** built in the 17th century. The letters '*PL*' in the cartouche refers to Platon Levshin, the Moscow Metropolitan and Archimandrite.

At right angles to the Trinity is the large **Assumption Cathedral**, *Uspeniya*, built 1559-85 by Ivan the Terrible to celebrate his victory at Kazan. Although modelled on the Assumption Cathedral in the Kremlin, it is larger and heavier, the domes crowding together, and unlike the Moscow cathedral, the apse accounting for one-third of the church. Inside it is unusually spacious and filled with wonderful frescoes of 1684 executed by the Yaroslavl artists, under Dmitry Plekhanov. **Tsar Boris Godunov** and his family are buried in the stone sepulchres west of the entrance, the only early Tsar not to be buried in the Archangel Cathedral in the Kremlin. He died in 1605 as Polish forces marched on Moscow and was removed from the Kremlin by False Dmitry and finally reinterred here.

A miniature brightly coloured late 17th century tower in the central square by the Assumption Cathedral contains the chapel over the **holy well** whose pure water is especially valued by pilgrims. The heavily ornamented tower of diminishing octagonals is even more florid than the richly embellished refectory.

Behind the **obelisk** of 1792 inscribed with the history of the monastery, is the immensely tall and stunning **bell tower**. It was begun in 1741 by Ivan Shumakher, court architect to Anna Ivanovna, then taken over by Ivan Michurin, the Moscow architect, and finally entrusted to a third architect, **Prince Ukhtomsky**, the great exponent of the baroque. It was he who persuaded Empress Elizabeth to approve two more tiers in addition to Shumakher's three. Over the solid platform the tower rises 88 metres through a series of ever diminishing levels, the dominant feature by far in the surrounding low-lying countryside. The giant flat pilasters of the massive base change into paired columns in the second and third tiers and single columns in the two upper tiers. Decoration is dramatic. White stone and plasterwork cartouches, cornices and vases – Ukhtomsky wanted statues but the church, as always dubious about statuary, objected – against a turquoise background are set off by the gold cupola flanked by alabaster crowns representing the monarchy. Completed at last in 1770 it was higher even than Ivan Veliky in the Moscow Kremlin. This is the only known example of Ukhtomsky's work to survive in the Moscow area.

West and north of the bell tower stands the small, round **Church of the Smolensk Virgin**, *Smolenskoi Ikony Bozhiei Materi*, built 1746-8 possibly also by Ukhtomsky. This stunning example of Elizabethan baroque with its rich plasterwork and white stone decor, is more like a pavilion in a tsar's country estate than a church. The open undulating staircase which beautifully follows the curve of the round pediments above, was dismantled in the early 19th century but expertly replaced in 1956 and 1977 by skilled Soviet restorers. The richly carved **iconostasis** is not original but comes from the destroyed Moscow church, St Paraskeva, and reinstalled here in 1956.

Several secular buildings line the **western wall**. Behind the Trinity Cathedral is the 18th century *riznitsa* or sacristy, now the excellent **museum** of monastery treasures of the 14th-17th century. It adjoins the **treasury**, *Kaznacheisky Korpus*, the administrative centre of the monastery, built in the 17th and 18th centuries and containing another exhibition of treasures. At the northeast corner is yet another beautiful building. Rising out of the second storey of the **infirmary** built 1635-7 is the ribbed tower church of **Sts Zosima and Savvaty**, the two saints who in the 15th century founded the great Solovetsk monastery in the inhospitable White Sea. The green tiles on the tower depict cannon and other military subjects of the Time of Troubles.

The tsars' palace, the *chertogi*, a two-storey brick building of the late 17th century stands against the north wall. It is not normally accessible as it is the **theological academy and seminary** but it also has a fine museum. Another example of the rich Moscow baroque style, the painted facade is rusticated and embellished with tiles and white stone. Within, although largely rebuilt in the 19th century, there are two magnificent tiled stoves of the 17th century.

BEYOND THE MONASTERY WALLS. Three km east of the monastery is the **Gethsemane Hermitage**, *Gefsemansky Skit. On Prospekt Krasnoi Armii turn right at traffic lights onto Karl Marx Street which leads into Komsomolskaya/Vifanskaya. In 1 km turn left into Karbushinsky Pereulok then right into Novo-Ogorodnaya St past new red brick 'kottedzhi', the Korbushny pond, and the Zagorsk Sewing Factory (which includes the cemetery church, Kinovaya Bogolyubskaya.)*

The Hermitage, or *skit*, was founded in 1843 by Filaret, the Archimandrite, and named after the garden of Gethsemane in Jerusalem. If the idea of a hermitage is modesty and self-reliance, then the *skit* is something of a shock for it is large and magnificent, embellished with churches, walls and tall belltower, like a monastery itself. Built over the Chernigovsky caves, it is dedicated to the 17th century icon, the Chernigov Virgin, credited with miraculous cures. The tall pyramid-shaped gate **bell tower** in three giant tiers was designed in 1895-1900 by Alexander Latkov, the gift of the Moscow merchant, P.G. Tsurikov. The huge red brick pseudo-Russian **Church of the Icon of the Chernigov Virgin**, *Chernigovskoi Ikony Bozhiei Materi*, was constructed in 1886-90 by Nikolai Sultanov, the specialist in Russian medieval architecture. Closed after the revolution the hermitage was used as a prison, then a hostel for the blind, and its poorhouse north of the church as a home for invalids. It was handed back in 1990.

Accompanied by a priest, one can climb down to the cave or narrow underground church, from the south doorway. Here is the gravestone of a famous *starosta*, elder, the monk Barnabas, known for his uncannily accurate predictions. He is reputed to have told Nicholas II that the Romanov family would end tragically, and to have foretold the persecution of the Orthodox Church and its eventual rebirth. After the hermitage was closed 1921-2 the faithful removed Barnabas's remains to the Trinity-Sergius Monastery for safe-keeping. In the past women were only allowed to enter the hermitage once a year on 17 August but these days they outnumber the men.

From the Gethsemane/Chernigovsky hermitage travel north 2 km, turn right through the unpleasant farm, Smena, then thread through shabby garages for 1 km and turn left to the **Paraklit-Tarbeeva Monastery** (*pustyn*).

The Paraklit Hermitage was founded in 1858 for monks of the Gethsemane hermitage who wished to take a vow of silence. At that time, dense woods gave it complete isolation but today the land is increasingly under threat by dachas. The shabby white church of **St Paraklit**, built in 1861 by P. Ya. Mironov, bears a plaque stating that Partriarch Pimen took his vows here in 1927 just before it was closed. The tall brick gate bell tower that stands alone was built in 1898 by Alexander Latkov.

Vifany (Bethany), another reference to the holy city of Jerusalem also lies east of the monastery. *From Komsomolskaya (formerly Vifanskaya) Street, cross the railway tracks and in 2 km bear left following Ptitsegradskaya Street, past a military base to Vifany, in the narrow strip of land between two small lakes.*

In 1783 Metropolitan Platon built a magnificent residence, later a seminary, on the lake as a retirement home with an unusual church named Vifany (Bethany). Today, the suburb is undistinguished except for a chicken research institute, the attractive ponds and some of the seminary buildings. The **Church of the Transfiguration of the Saviour** and the **Palace of Platon**, as far as can be made out, stood on the unkempt square behind the bus-stop surrounded by walls and gates. A statue of Lenin was erected there but it too has been dismantled. The iconostasis of the strange church was placed on top of a mound representing Golgotha and covered in moss, bushes and flowers and even stuffed animals.

The **seminary** with a large library donated by the Metropolitan, was built 1797-1800 on the high bank of the lake across the road from Platon's walled retreat. With round corner towers behind a large courtyard, it was built in the shape of a Russian 'P' (upside-down Latin 'U') for the name of its patron, Platon. Still standing but depressingly squalid, it is now an unkempt hospital for venereal diseases. To the right of the old seminary is the **new building** constructed 1826 to 1830 by Mikhail Bove (brother of the famous Moscow architect) in the Empire style, badly damaged by fire. To the left of the old seminary is another in the red brick pseudo-Russian style much favoured by the church.

For **Blagoveshchenie** (Annunciation) *take Proletarskaya Street behind the monastery, and turn left onto Akademik Favorsky. At the end of the town in 1 km, turn right following the road past the new red brick 'kottedzhi', then left for 2 km to the town cemetery. Where the buses turn around, turn left to the monastery farm.* Here is a new delightful **wooden church** dedicated to Sergius Radonezh erected in 1990. It resembles a Bilibin illustration with its exaggerated ogee-shaped gables, *bochki*, and lacey decoration. The old late 17th century wooden Ascension Church which stood at the edge of the forest was dismantled in 1977 with the intention of rebuilding it. But the restorers moved elsewhere, the logs were seized by local people, and the church is no more.

AROUND SERGIEV POSAD

The Sergiev Posad countryside remains little touched by modern development. In the words of Vladimir Got'e (Gautier), the historian and librarian of the Rumyantsev museum who visited Sergiev Posad often in the early years after the revolution:

'... how beautiful the environs of the Posad are; such an expanse, such a wealth of forests, such space for human activity, such considerable vestiges of the primeval forest in which Sergius once took refuge.'

From the Yaroslavl Highway M-8 turn right onto the A-108 signed GORKY and after 3 km turn left to **PUTYATINO**, *left of the road, and* **GAGINO** *which have links with the great bass singer,* **Fedor Chaliapin**. His friend, Tatiana Lyubatovich, a singer at the Mamontov private opera, had a house at Putyatino to which the young Chaliapin was often invited. In the summer of 1898 Chaliapin married his first wife, the Italian ballerina, Iola Tornagi (by whom he had four children) at **Gagino**, 2 km north, and celebrated the wedding at Putyatino. Chaliapin noted in his memoirs that a group of friends led by Savva Mamontov and the composer Sergei Rakhmaninov arrived at 6 a.m. the next morning bombarding the newly-weds with a horrible cacophony of banging buckets and whistles and demanded they all get up and go mushroom picking. Only the pond remains of Lyubatovich's dacha in Putyatino and Gagino's two churches – the baroque Saviour and the summer Kazan Virgin – are both in lamentable state.

From Prospekt Krasnoi Armii in Sergiev Posad north of the monastery turn left at traffic lights signed DMITROV onto Novouglichskoe Shosse 4 km to **DEULINO**.

For a brief moment in 1618 Deulino was at the centre of Russian events. Polish invaders having failed to capture Moscow or the monastery had finally signed a peace agreement in this little village. The wooden church commemorating the treaty has been replaced by the **Church of the Saviour**, *Spasa*, built 1849-53. With four arms like a Greek cross it supports a highly stylised octagonal pyramidal tower abruptly foreshortened to accommodate the strangely squashed cupola. In 1876-82 the Moscow architect Lev Lvov added the two-tier bell tower also in pseudo-Russian style. Beyond the church, which reopened in 1991, pretty wooden houses circle the pond.

Continue north past the A-108 to **IUDINO** *14 km from Sergiev Posad.*

In 1992 although the cupolas of the **Church of the Nativity of Christ**, *Rozhdestva Khristova*, were skeletal, a confident sign declared that the church, closed 1936, had reopened and that it was the most beautiful church in the Moscow region and donations would be appreciated.

Since then the cupolas have been recovered, the church renewed and its charm is undisputed. It was built by Prince Luka Nesvitsky, of the Preobrazhensky Guards, in the early years of Catherine's reign, 1763-71, as an octagonal on a cube in the old-fashioned Moscow baroque manner with the rich window frames, cartouches and corner quoins in white stone set against the peach-coloured background.

3 km north of Iudino take the left fork, unmarked, towards Konstantinovo. 4 km on the right is **SHEMETOVO** with the attractive white **Church of the Kazan Virgin**, *Kazanskoi Ikony Bozhiei Materi*, in a neat churchyard and cemetery so unlike the many ruined churches on this route. It was built by the powerful boyar, Ivan Miloslavsky, about 1676 and rebuilt by his son in 1706 adding elements of Moscow baroque. But it is only the core of the church and the apse with its two-storey elaborate window frames and gables that speak of the 17th century for it is masked by the large *trapeza* and bell tower of 1868. The odd-looking cupola was added in 1913 and the wall paintings and iconostasis are of the late 19th century.

For **AKIM-ANNA**, *travel 3 km past Shemetovo, crossing a stream and dachas, left, and under electricity pylons take the indicated left turn onto an unpromising, bumpy dirt road of several lanes. Take the middle dirt road for less than 1 km to another crossroads where again choose the middle lane. In less than 1 km turn left onto a track which becomes impassable just as the hamlet becomes visible.*

The satisfaction at finally arriving at Akim-Anna, named for the *pogost* cemetery of Sts Joachim and Anna, is enhanced by its location. A row of small cottages looks across the pond to the principal attraction, a ruined classical church of 1833, surrounded by fields. The remote village stands on a high plateau where farming land is curtailed by thick woods on every side. The **Church of the Presentation**, *Vvedeniya*, built in 1833 is immensely beautiful even in its ruined state. It is unusually tall with three sets of open windows through which the light pours. The five naked cupolas are barely standing, the one on the bell tower hangs at a rakish angle and a forest of trees grows out of the roof. Boys fish lazily in the pond on a hot summer day and across the water by the dozen or so wooden houses a woman busily gathers hay for her animals.

Road 8   THE DMITROV ROAD A-104: ALONG THE MOSKVA-VOLGA CANAL

The secondary Dmitrov Road A-104 is much quieter than the busy Yaroslavl and Leningrad Highways. It passes splendid estates, craft centres and picturesque churches and is parallel for much of the way to the wide Moscow-Volga Canal, constructed with such anguish.

Take Butyrskaya Street and Dmitrovskoe Shosse and pass under the MKAD to join the Dmitrov Road A-104.

DOLGOPRUDNY

On the Dmitrov Road 2 km north of the MKAD turn left signed **DOLGO-PRUDNY** *(named after the long ponds at Vinogradovo, a little farther).* Founded in the 1930s as **Dirizhablestroi** to produce Soviet airships, it has the usual factories but the association with flight continues in the Central Aerological Laboratory and the Physical Engineering Institute. As a prestigious new Soviet town pleasant residential streets of terraced housing were built in the 1930s although, as the population grew to 70,000, new districts were added with the familiar high-rise blocks.

In the north part of Dolgoprudny across the railway line on Parkovaya Street at **Kotovo** (also approached from the Dmitrov Road at Gribki) is the miraculously restored **Saviour Untouched by Hand**, *Spasa Nerukot-vornovo*. Built in 1684 for Prince Ivan Repnin it was later owned by the **Yusupovs** – the tomb for Princess N.B. Yusupova is by the north chapel. Typical of the mid 17th century with its pedimented window surrounds and gables, it was horribly mutilated in the 1930s when the dome and tent-shaped bell tower were sliced off and it was turned into a soap factory, then a printing press. In spite of Yeltsin's decree about reopening churches, local people had to campaign hard before the authorities agreed that the printing press should find other premises. Their crippled church was skilfully renewed 1995-9 by V.V. Ovchinni-kova and even the bell tower is whole again.

For **Gnilushi-Likhachevo** *(Starbeevo on the map) in western Dolgoprudny cross the railway line 2 km to a T-junction, turn left onto Likhachevskoe Shosse and, opposite a garage, turn right down a rural lane.* The original

THE DMITROV ROAD A-104

wooden church of St George erected in 1573 was built anew in 1774 at
the request of Prince Dolgorukov, and since then has been repaired
many times. Today, it is once again renewed using some of the old logs
and many pungent new ones. It follows the traditional cell plan of
wooden churches: the main cube with a square altar and single cupola
topped by an elaborate 17th century cross is reached through the
trapeza and entranceway. Outside, a miniature wooden belfry holds one
bell. Next door is the clergy house and chapel built in 1989.

*On the Dmitrov Road 3 km north of the MKAD past modern tower blocks
at Severny, right (population 5000, serving the water pumping station),
just before the traffic lights look left beyond the long 1.5 km pond, to a
superb mansion, one of two in a wooded glade, and, right, to the ochre and
white church on a hill.*

VINOGRADOVO (Grapevine) has borne its exotic name since the
time of Gavril Pushkin, a leader of the Streltsy (Musketeers) under
Boris Godunov and distant ancestor of the poet. He was followed by
the Dolgorukovs, the Princes Vyazemsky, and Alexander Glebov,
Catherine II's Procurator-General dismissed for bribery in 1764.
Glebov's daughter married into the Benkendorfs who owned Vinogradovo from 1790 to the 1870s. It was then purchased by Mikhail
Buchumov who rented out dachas and in 1905 witnessed the fire in the
main house. In 1911 it was sold to Emma Banza, who, with her
husband, Konrad, rebuilt Vinogradovo only to lose it a few years later
after the revolution.

Turn left across the causeway of birches dividing the pond from the
estate. The **mansion** built in 1911 is possibly by Ivan Zholtovsky whose
Rupert house at Lipki is not far away. The grand house, wooden under
the stucco in the prevailing neo-Empire style, is of two storeys, with a
portico on the pond side and a round porch of four Corinthian columns
facing the park. Wings at either end are linked by galleries. A few steps
to the west is a **neo-baroque wooden house** also built by Emma Banza in
1912 meant for her son, German. It too is of two storeys with
Corinthian pilasters and a centrally placed tower and is connected to the
western kitchen wing. White tiled stoves, light fittings and even a desk
survive from this time. Soon after its construction it was being used as a
hospital for soldiers of the First World War. After the revolution these
two houses became sanatoria and were planted with the blue firs
favoured by high Soviet officials. An experimental institute of agricultural chemicals, still in situ, took over the park. The heavily rebuilt

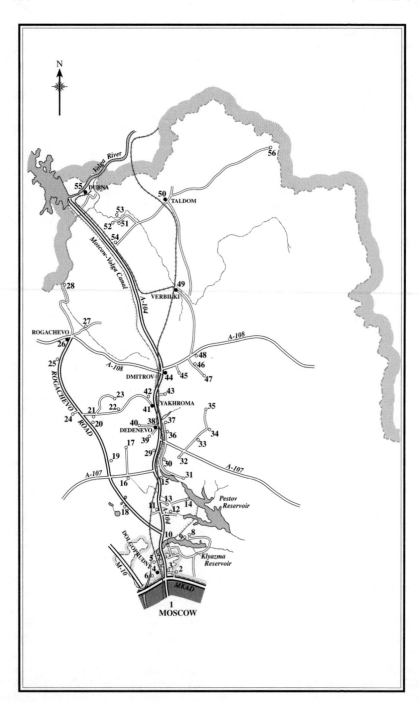

ROAD 8
A-104
ALONG THE MOSKVA-VOLGA CANAL

1. MOSCOW
2. Lipki
3. Mark
4. DOLGOPRUDNY
5. Kotovo
6. Gnilushi
7. Vinogradovo
8. Zhostovo
9. Ostashkovo
10. Troitskoe
11. Troitse-Seltse
12. Fedoskino
13. Marfino
14. Nikolo-Prozorovskoe
15. Trudovaya
16. Bely Rast
17. Gorki
18. Ozeretskoe
19. Udino
20. Khrabrovo
21. Podyachevo
22. Olgovo
23. Novo-Kartsevo
24. Matveikovo
25. Ivanovskoe
26. ROGACHEVO
27. Nikolo-Peshnoshsky
    Monastery
28. Medvedeva Pustyn
29. Iksha
30. Ignatovo
31. Rozhdestveno-Suvorovo
32. Selevkino
33. Surmino
34. Assaurovo
35. Vankovo
36. Batyushkovo
37. Svistukha
38. DEDENEVO
39. Shukolovo
40. Paramonovo
41. YAKHROMA
42. Andreevskoe
43. Peremilovo
44. DMITROV
45. Vnukovo
46. Budennovets
47. Voronovo
48. Zhestylevo
49. VERBILKI
50. TALDOM
51. Starikovo
52. Veretevo
53. Zyatkovo
54. Tempy
55. DUBNA
56. Spas-Ugol

stables are right of the lane with, amazingly, the small brick cinema
where the Banzas showed films to the hired hands.

On the other side of the main road via a path is the **Church of the
Vladimir Virgin**, *Vladimirskoi Ikony Bozhiei Materi*. Built 1772-7 for
Alexander Glebov in the unusual form of a triangle, it is a brilliant
example of Russian classical architecture with hints of baroque. As
usual there is controversy over whether it is by Kazakov or Bazhenov,
the leading Moscow architects of the time. The three facades with
Tuscan porticoes and pediments are identical, their rounded corners
filled by elaborate window architraves. A cylindrical tier supported by
the triangular base is surrounded by six sets of paired Ionic columns
with entablatures. Exceptionally, the church was not closed and the
rich, surprisingly light interior survives as does the fine iconostasis with
18th and 19th century icons. Two side chapels are cleverly included in
the corners flanking the altar; the left neo-Russian iconostasis was saved
in 1936 from the church at Kievo-Spasskaya. The graves of Glebov and
the Benkendorfs are in the cemetery.

*From Moscow take the Altufyevskoe Shosse (parallel to Dmitrovskoe),
cross the MKAD towards Veshki ignoring, like everyone else, the no entry
sign.* In a surprisingly wild and wooded area just north of the MKAD
near Veshki at **LIPKI** or Lipovka-Alexeevsk – although you won't find
it on a contemporary map – is a mysterious mansion. Take the first left
turn after crossing over the MKAD, past the children's hospital at
Lipki I, and around a bend where the arched bridge of the Lipki estate
can be seen, right, to the firmly closed gates of the house.

The property belonged to Alexander Alexeev whose son, Nikolai, was
the popular mayor of Moscow until he was assassinated in 1894, and
whose nephew was Stanislavsky. Alexeev's daughter, Elizaveta, married
in 1888 **Eduard Rupert**, who took over Lipki and began breeding turkeys,
then rare in Russia. In 1908 the young architect, **Ivan Zholtovsky**, just
returned from his travels in Italy built for them a Palladian-style
mansion. Zholtovsky was to become one of the favourite architects of
the Soviet regime and a leading proponent of Stalin classicism.

In the late 1930s, perhaps because it was conveniently close to Moscow,
it was decided to turn the two-storey mansion into a dacha for **Stalin**'s
use. Ironically, the same architect, Zholtovsky, was invited to adapt, or
rather bastardise, his own work. With security in mind for the paranoid
Stalin, the Ionic portico, curving colonnades and even the pediment

were removed. At that time too the villages and farms in the immediate area were emptied and armed secret police were installed. But Stalin seldom came here, preferring the dachas at Kuntsevo and Zhukovka. **Svetlana Stalin**, in *Twenty Letters to a Friend*, decribes how the rooms in all the dachas were identical, the furniture was the same, and even the same flowers and bushes were planted in the gardens. If a motorcade did set off in the direction of Lipki, 'pandemonium would break loose there, and everyone, from the cook to the guard at the gate, from the waitresses to the commandant, would be seized by panic.' Later other Soviet leaders, including Eduard Shevardnadze, Gorbachev's foreign minister, stayed at Lipki.

After peering through the gate, you can continue west towards the **Dmitrov Road** through the avenue of beautiful trees planted by the Ruperts – first larches, then limes, then birches and finally Siberian silver fir – until you reach a barrier closed by a huge padlock. When we thus arrived the GAI, who were sitting happily in a little hut drinking tea, refused to open the barrier. Eventually, after we had stewed for a bit, they produced the key and, highly amused, let us through.

Through the barrier is **MARK**, formerly **Arkhangelskoe-Tyurikovo**, named for the last owner, Sergei Mark, a merchant from Odessa who built a dairy farm and houses here for his large family. *A more normal route would be to take the Dmitrov Road 2 km from the MKAD and turn right at the first paved road ignoring the no entry sign.*

All that survives of the Mark estate is the pond, the decaying park and the 18th century **Church of the Assumption**, *Uspeniya*, built in 1758 in baroque style with a congenial 19th century bell tower. Closed in 1930 it was used as a storehouse, while in the 1980s the bell tower, bizarrely, became a training ground for mountain climbers practising rope climbing. The little church, in spite of terrible dilapidation, reopened for services in 1992.

BY THE RESERVOIRS

From the Dmitrov Road at Vinogradovo turn right at traffic lights for 5 km to a T-junction. Turn right again and in 2 km at Belyaninovo turn left 2 km to BOLTINO. Go past the **reopened Church of the Trinity**, built in 1861, following the road left at Pirogovo over a level crossing and across the dam. Turn first left 2 km through woods across a crossroads to Zhostovo where the black and green lacquered trays decorated with hand-painted flowers have been crafted since the middle of the 19th century and where there is a small museum and shop. *Turn left to* **OSTASHKOVO** *by the reservoir*. In the 1930s the Klyazma and Ucha valleys were flooded to make a network of reservoirs linked by canals and rivers. Moscow's water and electricity supply was thus ensured and the new lakes became favourite places for summer dachas. But many villages, including the textile mill at Ostashkovo, were inundated.

Tiny Ostashkovo is fortunate to have such a splendid church, the **Nativity of Christ**, *Rozhdestva Khristova*, built in 1699 by the elderly Prince Mikhail Cherkassky for his hunting lodge. The year before, Tsar Peter, newly returned from his European tour, exempted Prince Cherkassky from the indignity of losing his beard because of his great age. The **Cherkasskys** are descended from the Turk, Mameluk Inal, Sultan of Egypt, whose great great granddaughter, the wild and temperamental Mariya, adopted Christianity when living in the Caucasus and became Ivan the Terrible's second wife, the only one, as legend has it, who dared stand up to him. Mariya's many brothers, the Cherkassky (from the Russian for Circassian), entered Russian service. Ostashkovo was later owned by the Sheremetiev counts.

The church remained open in Soviet times and is in good condition. The apse, the main cube with cupola (there were probably five initially) and the two side chapels are original although the windows have been modified. The small bell tower was added in 1815, the entranceway in the early 20th century but the lovely cross is original to the church. Inside, are early 20th century oil paintings and a mid 19th century iconostasis. The Cherkasskys also built the late 17th century church at **Troitskoe** across the reservoir long used for restoring metal sculptures from old estates and now being restored.

On the Dmitrov Road cross the Klyazma reservoir. Left is KHLEBNI-KOVO where there is a monument on Leningradskaya Street to Nikolai Gastello, the wartime pilot who four days into the war in Belorussia deliberately crashed his stricken plane onto a convoy of German tanks and petrol carriers blowing them all up including himself. Six km beyond the Klyazma bridge turn right signed FEDOSKINO 3 km. **FEDOSKINO**, on the Ucha River just before it widens into the reservoir, is well known for the production of lacquered papier-mâché boxes. Past the church and across the Ucha the workshop with a small museum is on the right and facing it is the dilapidated wooden house of the Lukutins, owners of the enterprise for over a century.

In 1795 Petr Korobov, a Moscow merchant, brought to Russia the art of making lacqeur papier-mâché boxes from Germany. His daughter's husband, Petr Lukutin, continued the business introducing Russian folklore motifs. When Nikolai Lukutin, grandson of Petr, died in 1902 his widow closed the workshop but in 1910 the master artists regrouped, formed an artel, and began making the boxes once more. After 1917 the themes of the boxes expanded to include Lenin portraits, workers in noble poses, and scenes of Moscow.

The wooden church of **St Nicholas** was built in 1877 for Petr Lukutin, another grandson, probably by the Moscow architect, Alexander Pomerantsev. (Some think it is by Iosif Kaminsky, whose gravestone lies behind the church, and whose brother was the better known architect, Alexander Kaminsky.) Closed in the 1930s it was used for the 1980 Olympics as an exhibition hall displaying the lacquer boxes and in 1992 handed back to the church. It is simply designed, a long body with two small pyramid structures rising from the roof, one for the cupola and the other the bell tower.

Five km beyond the turn to Rogachevo (18 km from the MKAD) the Dmitrov Road divides, the main road continuing right. For **Troitse-Seltse** *take the minor left fork to the impressive* **Church of the Trinity**, *Troitsy, built in 1849 in a heavy version of the Empire style. For Marfino follow the main right fork past a brickworks at Sukharevo and turn right by a new brick house with stepped gables for 2 km to the gates.*

MARFINO, the country estate of the Panin family watered by the Ucha River, comprises two churches, the shell of the main house devastated by fire in 1992, the wings, the elegant 'kennels', a magnificent bridge, the park with pavilions and sculptures, the ponds, dilapidated stables and a carriage house. It is a fine place to escape to on a summer afternoon.

In the late 17th century **Boris Golitsyn**, Peter the Great's friend and tutor, acquired the estate, renamed it Marfino in honour of his wife, and built the interesting summer church. In 1728 the estate was purchased by the powerful **Counts Saltykov** who remained for nearly a century adding the winter church, the mansion, the two lodges or 'kennels', the summer theatre (Karamzin wrote a play especially for Marfino), and landscaped the park and ponds. Although Count Petr Saltykov, Field Marshal under Catherine II and Military Governor of Moscow, was dismissed in 1771 for abandoning his post during the plague riots, his son, Ivan, was not prevented from becoming Field Marshal and Governor of Moscow in turn. French soldiers in 1812 burned and pillaged the estate and Ivan's only son, Petr, died in 1813 from war wounds. Marfino, now in a sorry state, passed to his sister, **Countess Anna Orlova** but the huge cost of rebuilding the estate combined with her brother's debts forced her to sell to her father-in-law, **Count Vladimir Orlov**, owner of Otrada. Marfino was then inherited by the Count's daughter, Sofya, wife of **Count Nikita Panin**, a diplomat and Vice-Chancellor under Paul I and a conspirator in the murder of the Tsar although he did not actually participate in the deed. Ironically, Nikita Panin's son, Viktor, became an arch conservative who served three decades as the harsh Minister of Justice under Nicholas I and Alexander II. **Countess Sofya Panina**, mother of Viktor, commissioned the Moscow architect **Mikhail Bykovsky** 1837-9 to enhance Marfino in the romantic Gothic style which harmonises surprisingly well with the existing classical and baroque buildings. The last lady of the house, also Countess Sofya Panina, was a fervent supporter of the liberal Kadet Party and even served a few months as **Minister of Education** in the Provisional Government of 1917. The Bolsheviks, on taking power, arrested her but she was soon released after a farcical trial and emigrated to America.

Since the revolution Marfino has been used variously as houses of rest or sanatoria. In 1988 modern three-storey **sanatorium buildings** were grouped around the old avenue where the two **'kennels'**, point the way to the main house. These elegant structures with their fine porticoes were not used to keep noisy hunting dogs but as homes for the dogs' keepers. The modern boxes look absurd next to them.

The **two churches** by the pond are holding services again. The attractive **Nativity of the Virgin**, *Rozhdestva Bogoroditsy*, left, was built 1701-7 for Boris Golitsyn by Vladimir Belozerov. Of plastered brick with white stone detailing (the shockingly bright mustard colour will hopefully fade) and Corinthian pilasters, it is a quatrefoil with a central cylinder supporting drum and low dome. The use of four large pylons to support the cylinder apparently so enraged Golitsyn that he had the unfortunate Belozerov, aged 59, so cruelly beaten by birch rods that he died. Perhaps the tale is true, for Belozerov's gravestone lies in the grass behind the church.

Sts Peter and Paul, right, overlooking the pond painted a softer, more attractive ochre, is the smaller, heated winter church. Built in the 1770s by the Saltykovs, it is in the round, interrupted by the altar and entrance. Eight elegant columns within are arranged in a circle surpporting the octagonal central drum where the bells hang. Bykovsky added renaissance motifs to the facade.

On the left is the dilapidated **mansion**, painted a soft pink. It was originally built in the 1760s in baroque style but is clothed in Bykovsky's castle-like facade. At the centre two towers protect the entrance flanked by two storeys of arched windows and surmounted by many pinnacles. The two separate wings were faithfully rebuilt in the 1940s. In the **wooded park** are statuary and pavilions from the Saltykov era and at the farthest end of the estate are the crumbling triangular stables with a magnificent Gothic entrance and the carriage house.

Bykovsky's wonderful red brick and stone **Gothic bridge** between the two ponds, resembling a monastery cloister, offers a glorious vista from the south bank. The bridge acts as a foil to the mansion which descends to the water by a series of wide terraces.

Continue beyond the Marfino gates 2 km towards the Pestov Reservoir to a grassy lane, right, just before modern brick four-storey blocks. Leave the car and walk down the lane to the old estate of the Prozorovskys and Trubetskoys, right. If lovely Marfino seems crowded with visitors, **NIKOLO-PROZOROVSKOE** appears deserted with a delicious sense of abandon.

Through the ugly Soviet archway of heating pipes the principal buildings – the house, the two separate wings, and the church – seem lost among the straggling woods and overgrown pond. The classical **Church of St Nicholas** on the right newly painted and bearing a gold cross is holding services again on major feast days but it is hard to imagine there are many worshippers. Some authorities ascribe it to a late work by Matvei Kazakov or at least by his school. It was built in 1792 in the form of a Greek cross embellished with Tuscan porticoes and pediments on north and south and on east and west pilasters of the same order. The dome is pierced with lucarne windows, and a tall drum and small cupola rise above it. The bell tower has been demolished.

West of the church is the 19th century gutted **mansion** and two separate wings. Baroque flourishes decorate the windows, and rounded pediments and balconies hang dangerously over the bays. Farther along

to the right is the 18th century **grotto**. The atmosphere of decay is
enhanced by old scaffolding from abandoned restoration work.

The Prozorovsky Princes owned the property from 1623 to 1812. An
elderly gentleman told us that the great **General Suvorov** whose summer
estate was not far away in Rozhdestveno-Suvorovo came here to woo
Princess Varvara Prozorovskaya. It was Prince Alexander Prozorovsky,
the General/Field Marshal and commander in the first Turkish war,
who built the church and other buildings, many of them with Turkish
prisoners of war. In the middle of the 19th century the estate passed to
the **Princes Trubetskoy** who rebuilt the main house and wings in the
neo-baroque style. The aristocratic era came to an end at the close of
the century when the property was acquired by the Rabeneks, mill
owners in Reutovo.

Since the revolution Nikolo-Prozorovskoe has been a grand sanatorium
for various organisations. In the *perestroika* years it was the holiday
home for Energomash, based in Khimki, who built the ugly modern
blocks but who now have no money to repair the quietly rotting
buildings.

ALONG THE CANAL

TRUDOVAYA-SEVERNAYA, *is to the right and left of the Dmitrov
Road just beyond the narrow railway bridge, about 30 km from the
MKAD*. The name from *trud*, meaning labour, refers to the huge
colonies of political prisoners forced to construct the Moscow-Volga
Canal, 1932-7. Many thousands died, for the digging was done by
hand without machines in terrible conditions. At Trudovaya they were
lodged in crude barracks and taken every day to the construction sites.
Nowadays the land by the canal where the prisoners' barracks once
stood has become desirable property for new dachas.

The nature of Trudovaya if not the name changed dramatically when
Stalin toured this new Soviet achievement in 1945 just after the war
ended. At this particular spot struck by the beauty of the woods he
stopped and declared that his **generals** and **marshals**, who had fought
so valiantly in the war, must be given dachas here. By the end of
the 1940s the woods had been cleared for large masonry houses with
extensive grounds for the marshals, while lesser two-storey wooden
houses on smaller plots were allocated to the generals. The settlement
with a fine marina was placed under a military commandant with

carefully controlled access. Today the dachas used by the sons and grandsons of the marshals and generals are no longer so strictly controlled.

The first dirt road to the right after the 45 km post leads to the street of wooden generals' dachas. Turn left and cross the railway line to see the marshals' houses, large mansions, with in some cases over two acres of land. On the right at the end behind high gates is the elaborate house given to Marshal Sokolovsky. Nearby, right, is the yellow house that belonged to Sergei, Khrushchev's son, now a US citizen. During the August 1991 putsch there were many mysterious comings and goings around these houses.

On the Dmitrov Road a lively trade in building materials for dacha owners goes on at **Iksha** *at the 50 km post and the second lock of the canal. Three km north is the bridge over the canal signed YAROSLAVL, the continuation of the A-107. Cross the canal bridge and turn south past Ignatovo with its fine views and the recently reopened* **Church of the Tikhvin Virgin** *built in 1835, past red brick kottedzhi 14 km to* **ROZHDESTVENO-SUVOROVO**.

Turn left and cross the pond to the stunning **Church of the Nativity of the Virgin**, *Rozhdestva Bogoroditsy*, set in an old graveyard which returned to worship in 1990. It was built for Prince Baryatinsky's estate in 1714 and richly decorated in the manner of the asymmetrical churches of the mid 17th century, although the window frames have the intricate sculptural shapes of the Moscow baroque style. The triple apse protrudes voluptuously, the bays end in *zakomary* gables, and five cupolas, the central one in gold leaf, decorate the roof. The only false note are the wrought iron lamps.

In 1773 **General Vasily Suvorov** purchased Rozhdestveno from Prince Baryatinsky for his retirement (the mansion was burnt to the ground during the French invasion). General Suvorov's son, Alexander, was the legendary generalissimo who in 1799 saved the Russian army by marching it across the Alps. General Suvorov senior enjoyed Rozhdestveno for only a few years – he died in 1778 and is buried in the crypt. Svyatoslav Fedorov, the wealthy eye surgeon and promoter of laser surgery who had a dacha nearby, is the modern patron who revived the church. He died in an air crash in June 2000 and is buried next to General Suvorov.

Seven km on the A-107 from the Iksha bridge turn left (north) at Selev-
kino. Note the attractive baroque church, the **Nativity of the Virgin**,
right, built in the 1770s by Princess Baryatinskaya of Rozhdestveno-
Suvorovo. Pass **Surmino**, right, with the ruined **Church of the Ascension**
built 1834 to 1837 in the late classical style with a massive rotunda. In
3 km at rural **Assaurovo** is another ruined church built in the 1810s, the
Consolation of All Sorrows, with porticoes of the Tuscan order. In 2 km
is **Shadrino** and across the Yakhroma **Vankovo** where the artist and
architect of the Tretyakov Gallery, **Viktor Vasnetsov**, purchased a small
estate after the Abramtsevo colony broke up. His log house, missing the
mezzanine floor and verandah, was moved to the pioneers' camp at
Shadrino in 1952.

From the Iksha bridge take the first left, a wide dirt road, signed
BATYUSHKOVO 2.7 km. Restored in the 1960s the picturesque **Church**
of St Nicholas at **BATYUSHKOVO** with its receding tiers of ogee-
shaped *kokoshniki* gables, tight cluster of five cupolas, and tent-shaped
bell tower is truly breathtaking after so many ruined churches. It was
built in 1666, the year many Russians believed the world would end, on
the estate of A.I. Nesterov, a nobleman at Tsar Alexei's court. Apart
from the glorious church only the pond and grove of old limes remain
from Nesterov's time.

Continue on the dirt road north of Batyushkovo 5 km (7 from the road
bridge). Turn left where the road turns right, towards P.L. TURIST.
SVISTUKHA consists of two rows of wooden houses separated by a
wide swathe of grass like villages before the advent of the motor car. It
was the summer home of the artist, **Sergei Ivanov** (not Alexander
Ivanov, the artist of religious subjects, or another Sergei Ivanov, a
sculptor). This Ivanov, a member of the Young Wanderers, painted
pictures with a social message like the famous *On the Road; Death of a*
Refugee (1889, Tretyakov Gallery). As the Bolsheviks admired the
subjects of his work, Ivanov's family were able to hold on to their
considerable property after the revolution.

Ivanov's dacha is a few metres farther and right through some woods by
the large spring-fed pond which Ivanov dug himself and from which the
villagers still draw their water. Opposite is the Ivanov property, a large
fenced area of dachas and gardens. It is a special world, in June dark
with trees, redolent with wild berries and buzzing madly with mosqui-
toes. Ivanov's descendants (he died in 1910) spend their summers here
with their families in their different houses. His daughter had six

children including the elderly Daniil, who lives in Ivanov's modest house containing the library and attractive Art Nouveau furniture made by the artist. Ivanov also built wooden studios with the main window of each facing different directions so the artist could have light at all times of day. These are now dachas for the extended family which includes great great grandchildren, not one of whom is an artist. Ivanov's grave is near the stream.

On the Dmitrov Road 46 km from the MKAD turn left at the traffic lights in Dedenevo towards the railway station. Where the road turns sharp right, take the dirt road ahead then turn left to TURIST, the former convent now a sanatorium for veterans.

DEDENEVO, (DedenYOvo), population 6,000, is named according to legend after the Tatar Khan, Deden, who was killed at this spot in 1293 by citizens of Dmitrov. The **Saviour Convent of the Vlakhern Virgin**, *Spaso-Vlakhernskoi Ikony Bozhiei Materi* took nearly a century to complete. In 1798 Vasily Golovin commissioned the church, **Saviour Untouched by Hand**, *Spasa Nerukotvornovo*. The work went slowly, his son, Pavel, took over, and only in 1811 was the exterior finished. Interior work, held up by the French invasion and other problems, was not complete until 1850. At this time the aged Anna Golovina, Pavel's widow, established an *obshchezhitie* for women, a low-ranking religious community, which opened in 1854 enabling the huge church, so long in the making, to be dedicated. In 1884 architect Nikolai Nikitin (the younger) added the huge bell tower connected to the church by the *trapeza*. By 1917 there were 300 members of the community.

After the revolution the convent was closed but for 20 years left to its own devices and some of the nuns quietly remained, living a secret life of prayer and worship. In the anti-religious campaign of the dreadful purge year of 1937 the authorities tried to blow up the huge church but were unable to destroy the strongly built walls which yet stand The children's psychiatric hospital which took over the other buildings was evacuated at the beginning of the war and the convent was used to train dogs to throw themselves under enemy tanks with explosives attached to their collars. At this time the last eight nuns were still somehow eking out an existence but in the cold winter of 1942 when there was no fuel they were found frozen to death in their beds. After the war the buildings became a sanatorium for invalid veterans who sit around on benches under the trees. Services have now recommenced in a chapel in the vast church.

In Dedenevo cross the tracks at the railway station and turn left. Where the road continues right, through gates to a hospital, go straight ahead on the dirt road which winds up the hill to **Shukolovo**. The pretty **Church of the Assumption**, *Uspeniya*, by the pond, now functioning again, was built in 1701. Five km farther on is **Paramonovo** where the ground falls away steeply to the valleys of the Yakhroma and Volgusha. There is even a **downhill skiing** establishment with tow ropes and the usual appurtenances, but a better one has been built at Yakhroma. The large war memorial commemorates Soviet soldiers killed here in autumn 1941.

THE ROGACHEVO ROAD

For the quiet Rogachevo Road, R-113, that runs parallel to the Dmitrov Road, turn left at Trudovaya onto the circular A-107 that joins the Rogachevo Road in 11 km. For **BELY RAST** *6 km on the A-107 before joining the Rogachevo Road turn left at the sign of a cow. (The right turning just beyond leads to Sokolniki and the Gorki estate, now a Naval children's camp, of Elizaveta Yankova, who kept a fascinating diary of Moscow life in the early 1800s published as* Rasskazi Babushki, Tales of a Grandmother.*)* Beyond the jumble of collective farm buildings an impressively tall red brick church is surrounded by wooden houses. Near the church an unusual war memorial depicting an anchor and sailors' caps commemorates the sailors from Leningrad and the Soviet Far East rushed here in December 1941 to wrench the village from determined German troops firing on the Russians from the convenient bell tower.

The **Church of Michael the Archangel** which never closed, was built in 1878 by Sergei Sokolov in traditional Russian style. Five light blue cupolas and another over the bell tower give it piquancy although the white detailing is only painted on. The interesting marble iconostasis comes, so it is said, from the Christ the Saviour Cathedral in Moscow just before it was blown up in 1931, and had to be trimmed to fit. Perhaps it will be returned now that the Cathedral is rebuilt.

On the A-107 turn left on the Rogachevo Road 8 km to Ozeretskoe.

OZERETSKOE – *ozero* means lake – is at the centre of three round ice-age lakes: Krugloe and Dolgoe to the west (the dachas built in 1991 on the south side of Krugloe are still occupied by former Soviet officials who moved in just before the August coup) and the deep

Nerskoe Lake to the northeast, the source of the small Volgusha (Little Volga) River.

The Church of St Nicholas in Ozeretskoe was built in 1704-8 by the master stonemason, Maxim Parfeniev, for Patriarch Adrian. In the Moscow baroque style it is an octagonal on a cube with a bulging triple apse and small tent-shaped bell tower topped by a single cupola and fine cross in metal tracery. Note the elaborate old-fashioned portal and windows with triangular pediments. Closed in the 1930s and used to store grain, St Nicholas's deteriorating condition worried the 1980 Olympic Games organisers when they realised that foreign athletes would see the church travelling to the sports centre at Krugloe Lake. Accordingly it was quickly painted red with white details, but the bell tower, roof and cupola were painted a startling, bright blue. In 1990 it reopened and is now less garish. Another benefit brought by the Olympics was the sudden appearance of road signs where none had been before.

On the Rogachevo Road 3 km north of the A-107 is **Dmitrovka** with another poignant war memorial on the maritime theme. At **Udino** with fine views over the Volgusha is the ruined **Church of the Intercession**, *Pokrova*, built in 1789 in classical style, a square church with porticoes and spire. About 2 km past Udino take a narrow paved road, right, 2 km signed P.L. DRUZHBA to Gulnevo and the ruined 18th century **Nativity of the Virgin**, *Rozhdestva Bogoroditsy*, for long a paint factory. Army officers' dachas built here by the Volgusha in the 1940s were supplied with water and gas, then rare in the countryside. Continue on the Rogachevo Road 11 km to **Khrabrovo** and yet another ruined church, the **Intercession**, *Pokrova*, built in classical style in 1800 by the Princes Obolensky. The modest house behind the church was brutally pulled down in the 1990s to make way for dachas for the newly rich.

Continue north on the Rogachevo Road 2 km past Khrabrovo (16 km from the A-107) and turn right signed YAKHROMA (ignore the first poor parallel road). After 1.5 km the road left signed OVCHINO leads in 6 km to Novo-Kartsevo where there is the beautiful but ruined **Intercession Church**, *Pokrova, built 1717 by Petr Tolstoy, the statesman who tricked the Tsarevich Alexei into returning to Russia and death at the hands of Peter the Great, his unforgiving father. On the Yakhroma Road continue 2 km then turn right into* **PODYACHEVO**. *The estate was purchased in 1802 by* **Petr Obolyaninov**, *Paul I's harsh prosecutor, and renamed Nikolskoe-Obolyanovo. After Obolyaninov's death in 1842 the property*

was acquired by the sociable **Count Adam Olsufyev**, a close friend of
Lev Tolstoy, who often enjoyed the Count's hospitality and indeed
would escape to the Olsufyevs during bitter rows with his wife. In 1887
Olsufyev invited leading scientists including Dmitry Mendeleev to
observe an eclipse of the sun from his estate but Mendeleev left early for
Klin to watch the phenomenon from his balloon. The Olsufyevs
founded the village school and hospital.

The village was also the home of the 19th century peasant writer and
farmer **Semen Podyachev** after whom, in the 1930s, it was renamed; his
descendants still live here. Podyachev's stories such as *Mytarstva*
(Ordeals), published in 1902, give a sorry picture of drunkenness and
cruelty in the countryside at the turn of the century.

Although in poor condition, the **Olsufyev house** has survived, as has the
ruined church and the beautiful wooded park and ponds. The single-
storey house with a mezzanine floor was built of wood stuccoed over in
the early 19th century. For a long time it served as a house of rest and
only some tiled stoves survive of the interior furnishings. The two brick
single-storey wings are connected to the main house by curving galleries,
originally glazed (only the left survives), that enclose the courtyard with
its great oak. Apparently after Olsufyev's little son drowned in the pond
that stood in the middle of the courtyard it was filled in and the oak
planted in remembrance. Podyachev had rooms in one of the wings
after the revolution. The house has been purchased privately and is to
be reopened again as a house of rest.

The red brick **Church of St Nicholas** to the right overlooking the valley
was built in the second half of the 18th century. An octagonal on a cube
with *trapeza* and two-storey bell tower, it is now in a lamentable state.
There are lovely walks in the old park.

Continue towards Yakhroma for 6 km to two red obelisks indicating
OLGOVO, *left.* Olgovo, the second estate on this minor road, was
acquired by Field Marshal Stepan Apraxin through marriage with the
Soimonovs in the 1740s and remained in his family until 1915. **Field
Marshal Apraxin** was in charge of the Russian army under Empress
Elizabeth in the war against Frederick of Prussia. When Elizabeth fell ill
Apraxin prevaricated expecting she would be succeeded by the pro-
Prussian Peter III who would certainly stop the war (which he later
did). Unfortunately for Apraxin the Empress recovered, relieved him of
his position, and charged him with treason but the Field Marshal died

before he could come to trial. His son, also Stepan and a General, took over the estate and it was at his invitation that the noted architect, **Francesco Camporesi**, rebuilt the house. In 1915 the last Apraxin, Alexander, died and Olgovo was inherited by **General Alexei Ignatiev**, then military attache at the Russian Embassy in Paris. Ignatiev's father had been shot by Tsarist secret police in 1906 and his son now took his revenge. In November 1917 he turned the Russian Embassy in Paris over to the new communist state and purchased munitions for them with the considerable funds entrusted to him for the Tsar's armies. However, he was never able to enjoy his fine estate at Olgovo.

Olgovo was famous for its social and political gatherings, its theatre and concerts. The Bolsheviks early recognised its cultural and historical importance and at first turned Olgovo, with all its furnishings, into a museum of itself. But as the 1920s went on the expense of looking after such a grand place became difficult to sustain and greedy local institutions began to cast covetous eyes. In 1929 the furniture and paintings were moved and Olgovo became a sanatorium and then a house of rest for various organisations. Although the interiors inevitably declined, all the buildings survived and it was considered the most complete early classical estate near Moscow. Sadly, a disastrous fire in the 1980s changed all that. The great house now lies decomposing into a skeleton, its walls roofless and shattered. Plans have been made to rebuild it and articles appear in the press urging action before it is too late. Perhaps the Ministry of the Chemical Industries, under whose aegis it lies, will take action.

Nevertheless, apart from the great house, the rest of the estate is more or less complete. The avenue leads from the two obelisks past the elegant **cattle and grain barns** on the right and **round manege, horse stables and offices** on the left to the main house complex where another, identical pair of obelisks once stood. The large **courtyard** is made up of four separate buildings which curve back from the ruined main house, right, to make a fine square. The formal **entrance gate** with one surviving tower is at the western end in the direction of the church. The large **ruined mansion** which overlooks the park and large pond was rebuilt by Francesco Camporesi in 1786 adding wooden chambers to either side, and an Ionic portico facing the park. The north and south **curved buildings** in the courtyard, also by Camporesi, were intended as living quarters for the peasants: the north for the unmarried and the south for the married ones.

The Gothic gate leads from the courtyard to the now functioning
Church of the Presentation, *Vvedeniya*. It was built in 1751 in baroque
style for the Soimonovs by a Yaroslavl stone mason, K.L. Druzhinin. In
1828 it was substantially widened and a new Empire facade and the
three-tiered bell tower added. Near the church is the parochial school
opened in 1894.

On the Rogachevo Road again 2 km past the turning for Yakhroma are
two pioneer camps BAZA MIR (peace base) and P.L. ZARYA (dawn).
The first has an amusing gate resembling a castle, and the second bears
the saccharine title *Schastlivoe Detstvo* (Happy Childhood). **Matveikovo**,
right, is one long lane ending in meadows and woods with the dilapidated baroque **Church of the Sign**, *Ikony Bozhiei Materi 'Znamenie'*,
built in 1785 by Prince M.I. Obolensky. Continue on the Rogachevo
Road to **Ivanovskoe**, left, with another, striking but ruined church, the
rotunda **Consolation of All Sorrows**, *Vsekh Skorbyashchikh Radosti*,
built 1823-36 in the Empire style by the Moscow architect, Fedor
Shestakov.

At the end of the Rogachevo Road, about 70 km from the MKAD, is
ROGACHEVO. Population 3,000, it is the centre of a farming area
with few manufacturing enterprises, remarkable for its enormous
church. Before the advent of the railways, Rogachevo was an important
link in the water route joining the Yakhroma River (shrunk since the
building of the Moscow-Volga canal) with the Volga and therefore
connecting Moscow, Petersburg and Nizhny Novgorod. In the 19th
century its enterprising merchants organised two large trade fairs
annually, attracting some 10,000 people (their houses of solid brick still
face the trading rows on the main square). The villagers with their
mercantile leanings objected to the Bolshevik takeover and in 1918 had
to be put down by a company of red guards, 13 of whom died in the
process. The number of villagers killed is not recorded.

The astonishing church can be seen from miles away in the flat
landscape. It is simply enormous, not quite the magnitude of Moscow's
Christ the Saviour but for this small town, totally out of scale. **St**
Nicholas, financed by the town's merchants, took over twenty years
1863–86 to build. The sparkling white summer church faces the square
with five domes of a deep, hard blue and with what seems to be a porch
but is really a chapel abutting onto the eastern end. The *trapeza* behind
with three dark grey domes and a soaring bell tower doubles as the
winter church. Although borrowing from traditional Russian architec-

ture in the tripartite division of the facades and pointed gables, it employs large arched windows making the interior light and spacious. St Nicholas has been returned to its congregation and is under intensive repairs after a long closure. It would seem an enormous undertaking for the villagers to restore this monstrous building but they have embarked on it with great enthusiasm.

From the main square in Rogachevo go east across the A-108 bypass through water meadows and, where the road becomes gravel, an avenue of willow trees 8 km to Lugovoi and the **NIKOLO-PESHNOSHSKY MONASTERY**. Where the Peshnoshsky stream flows into the Yakhroma the monastery walls and towers rise up invitingly like a mirage in the flat landscape. It is in a way a mirage for the ancient monastery is a mental home for 400 male patients.

It was founded as a hermitage in 1361 by the monk Methodius. The strange name *Peshnoshsky* is said to derive from Methodius laboriously carrying wood on foot (*nosya, pesh*) across the river to build the chapel. The hermitage soon became a regular monastic establishment attracting pilgrims including grand princes and tsars. In 1553, a year after the victory at Kazan and shortly after a serious illness, the young Tsar Ivan IV with his first wife and baby son visited Nikolo-Peshnoshsky. Here he was advised by the Arkhimandrite, Vassian, to govern hard and be suspicious of boyars. Ivan, soon to become the Terrible, certainly took this advice to heart and rewarded the monastery with many gifts.

Nikolo-Peshnoshsky closed in 1924 and eventually became the asylum. The great manuscript library is now in the Russian State Library and the most precious of the icons including the 15th century John the Baptist by a follower of Rublev are in museums. Nearly all the buildings seem to have survived. Permission needs to be obtained from the head doctor to view the buildings.

As we arrived we saw the strange sight of patients cleaning a shiny aluminium statue of **Lenin** that stands outside the main gate. Other patients, probably drugged, sat dejected and apathetic around the grounds in the warm weather. One wonders about their fate when, as must happen, this historic monastery is handed back to the church.

Astride the main **Spasskaya (Saviour) Gate** is a wonderful octagonal 17th century tower with look-outs in the topmost reaches. The 17th to 19th century building immediately on the left contains **monks' cells**. On the right is the hospital with the late classical church, **Dimitry Rostovsky**, built 1811-29, its long construction a result of the Napoleonic war. Farther right is the octagonal tent-shaped tower of the western wall followed by the old 16th century **refectory** with its **Church of the Purification**, *Sreteniya*, reconstructed in 1812 in classical style.

The **Cathedral of St Nicholas** at the very centre of the monastery is thought to date from the late 15th century. A tall monumental church, it follows the restrained early Moscow style of a cube with a tripartite facade, a frieze, *zakomary* gables, a protruding triple apse, single tall drum with slit windows, and a helmet-shaped cupola. This noble building is impaired by the late 19th century low chocolate brown and yellow structure, now the dining room of the mental home, clinging like a limpet to three sides of the older building.

Opposite the cathedral, on the west wall, are the former 17th and 18th century monastery offices. Next to them are the **Holy Gates**, *Svyatye Vorota*, where river boats would disgorge their passengers. The gates are surmounted by the **Church of the Transfiguration**, *Preobrazheniya*, built in 1689 in the plain monastery style with a single cupola, frieze and *kokoshniki* gables. Left of the gates are the former **abbot's quarters**, built in the 17th century and heavily altered in the 19th.

On the left past the cathedral is the pseudo-Russian ruined 19th century **Church of Sergei Radonezh** built over Methodius's grave. It is attached to the octagonal **bell tower** of brick with stone facing. The first two tiers occupied by the **Church of the Epiphany**, *Bogoyavleniya* with an arcaded open gallery are nearly contemporary with the cathedral. The upper tiers with apertures for the bells and a staircase embedded in the walls were added in 1793. Against the south wall are additional monks' cells.

Another monastery lies north of Rogachevo, almost at the border with Tver Oblast. *From Rogachevo cross the A-108 past Pozdnyakovo and Alexandrovka which has unusually fine houses in Scandinavian style for the model collective farm. Five km from Alexandrovka the excellent paved road once it crosses the Sestra River deteriorates into a dirt road. Continue through Ust-Pristan, 4 km to* **MEDVEDEVA PUSTYN**, *15 km from Rogachevo.*

The *pustyn* or hermitage was founded in this remote place by the Sestra River by a monk from the Nikolo-Peshnoshsky Monastery. The ancient cathedral, the **Nativity of the Virgin**, *Rozhdestva Bogoroditsy*, was built in 1547 with a small bell tower of the same date. Even in ruins it is impressive, a simple cube with tripartite facade divided by pilaster strips and gables surmounted by the tall, heavy drum and powerful cupola. It must have been the gift of an important boyar or a grand prince for stone churches of this date are extremely rare. In 1764 the *pustyn* was dissolved and attached to a women's poorhouse which functioned until 1814. In 1809, the wooden **Saviour**, *Spasa*, church was brought here from neighbouring Dulova as the winter church but it burned down in 1991 during revels by the village youth. The Nativity Church was closed in 1935 and has languished ever since. Occasional attempts at repairs are made but the walls are so heavily cracked that restoration would be a difficult task.

A woman tending graves explained why the river is called the Sestra (sister). Catherine II was visiting an estate where the two rivers, the Sestra and Yakhroma, meet when one of her ladies fell into the water. In the excitement Catherine shouted 'Sestra khroma' (our sister is lamed), so they named the one river Sestra and the other, Yakhroma. Popular etymology at its most ingenious and far-fetched!

AT THE HEADQUARTERS OF THE CANAL

Approaching Dmitrov from the south on the A-104 near Yakhroma there is a sudden flash of gold, right, at the third lock of the canal where two sailing ships in bright copper modelled on Christopher Columbus's galleons stand. Turn left signed YAKHROMA to the central square.

In the 1820s a textile mill was founded at **YAKHROMA**, 45 km from the MKAD, which rapidly expanded under Ivan Lyamin (Moscow Mayor 1871-3) when it employed 2,000 workers and was renamed Pokrovskaya Manufaktura. In 1900 the mill was the first in the Dmitrov area to use electricity. But the construction of the Moscow-Volga canal in the 1930s divided the town in two, inundating the eastern districts and cutting off the railway. On November 28, 1941 the Germans captured Yakhroma and the canal but by December 8 Soviet shock troops had forced them back. A striking war memorial at Peremilovo celebrates this event.

The town sits above the Yakhroma River with straight attractive streets of small wooden houses leading to the old mill buildings on the north side of the main square. Follow Bolnichnaya Street up the hill to the impressive **Church of the Trinity**, *Troitsy*, built by Ivan Lyamin for his mill workers, which can accommodate 10,000 people. Of red brick and white stone, in a free interpretation of the classical style it was completed in 1895 to the design of the local architect, Sergei Rodionov. The free-standing bell tower of four square tiers rich in columns and pilasters was built in 1908 by the Moscow architect, Sergei Zalessky.

In Yakhroma follow the main bus route to the Olgovo road and after 2 km turn right signed **ANDREEVSKOE** where the main road curves left to Astretsovo. This splendid church standing in an unprepossessing farm yard under repair has now returned to worship. The **Church of the Intercession**, *Pokrova*, was built in 1803 to a plan by Francesco Camporesi by Countess Elizaveta Orlova whose small estate abutted the church – only the old limes survive. The church is composed of a great rusticated cylinder lit by large arched windows with smaller ones above, the low *trapeza* with porticoes and pediments and the elegant three-tier bell tower with spire, a little taller than the cylinder. All these cunningly combined geometrical shapes are enhanced by delicate details picked out in white stone. In the 1930s the authorities considered keeping it open but in the end chose the Ascension Church at Peremilovo.

PEREMILOVO is poised between Yakhroma and Dmitrov. *Follow the A-104 across the canal and ignore the first right turning to the railway station. The large war memorial of a young soldier holding a gun aloft can be seen high above. Turn right at the next road signed MONUMENT, cross the railway line and go up the hill and left to the church.* The yellow and white **Church of the Ascension**, *Vozneseniya*, in refreshing good order, was built in 1792 by General Stepan Apraxin of Olgovo. Square in shape, resembling a large house more than a church, with Gothic, ogee-shaped windows mixing with the strange pseudo-Russian crown around the drum, it is sometimes ascribed to Camporesi. Oil wall paintings within were repainted in 1988 in honour of the millennium of Christianity. An alarm system has been installed to counter the increasing threat of burglary.

In the 1930s the local Soviet had to decide which of two local churches, the Peremilovo Ascension church or the Intercession in Andreevskoe, should be left open. Parishioners in Peremilovo took matters into their own hands by grabbing the keys to the church and disappearing into the woods ensuring that it was the Andreevskoe church that was closed.

Father Anatoly, his wife, Lyubov, their four children and her brother,

live in the small wooden house behind the church with the huge
vegetable garden. Both he and his dedicated wife distribute aid packages
for Caritas, the Catholic care agency, to the children's home in
Yakhroma and elsewhere.

*On the Dmitrov Road, A-104, 65 km to Dmitrov from central Moscow.
The town can be entered either from Peremilovo and the right bank of the
canal or via Yakhroma, right into Zareche, over the canal and right again.*

DMITROV

Dmitrov, population 65,000, was founded in 1154 by the same prince,
Yury Dolgoruky, who founded Moscow, and is younger than the
capital by only seven years. Yury named Dmitrov for his son, Vsevolod-
Dmitry, later known as Vsevolod *Bolshoe Gnezdo*, Big Nest, because he
had 12 children. Prince Yury chose a fine spot for Dmitrov at the hub
of water and road routes to the Volga River. By the mid 15th century
the town was producing flax, salt, fish, grain, leather, and ceramic tiles.
Razed to the ground by the Poles in 1610, it revived to become in the
18th century the gateway to the Volga with a population of 10,000. Its
wealthy merchants have left a legacy of elegant houses and churches.

The main railway line to Petersburg bypassed Dmitrov although a
minor line opened in 1900. In spite of a large iron foundry – Russia's
first tank was made there in 1915 – Dmitrov remained a backwater,
its population in 1926 only 6,000, on a par with neighbouring
Yakhroma and less than in the 18th century. It was the building of
the Moscow-Volga Canal in the 1930s, centred on Dmitrov, which
literally divided the town in two, that caused sudden and rapid growth.
Luckily the Kremlin and old quarter of attractive wooden houses
managed to escape both the inundation and subsequent intensive
redevelopment.

From Peremilovo follow the main road, Tsentralnaya, past the
handsome early 1900s railway station, left. At traffic lights by the tank
war memorial the spacious main square opens out, left, containing a
large statue of Lenin with the slogan 'precisely in work and only
through work is man great – *imenno v trude i tolko v trude velik
chelovek*'. To the right are the ancient earthen ramparts of the
KREMLIN. *(Park on Zagorskaya Street, right, closed at the top by the
imposing classical Soviet Palace of Culture.)* Near the Kremlin's south
entrance, stands an early Soviet memorial to the Red Guards killed at

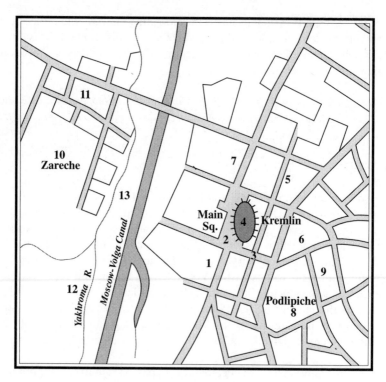

DMITROV 1. Tsentralnaya, 2. Main square, 3. Zagorskaya,
4. Kremlin, 5. Kropotkinskaya, 6. Bolshevistskaya,
7. Professionalnaya, 8. Podlipiche, 9. Inzhenernaya,
10. Zareche, 11. Staro-Rogachevo, 12. Yakhroma River,
13. Moscow-Volga Canal

Rogachevo in 1918. The oval-shaped Kremlin on rising ground is curiously lifeless; apart from the cathedral, one other church, administrative buildings, and the former boys' gymnasium, it is mostly a park used by citizens as a short cut.

By the south entrance a fine square of modest classical buildings of the early 19th century include, right, the administration office, *prisutstvennye mesta*, with a central bay and pediment, the rusticated two-storey prison opposite, and service buildings. The serenity of this architecture is broken by the compelling, pseudo-Russian prison church, **St Elizabeth**, right, beyond the office. Raised high on a sub-basement, with a tent-shaped central tower, *kokoshniki* gables, elaborate 17th century window frames, traditional belfry and fine sculptural effects, it was completed in 1896 by Sergei Rodionov, the Dmitrov architect, and financed by E.A. Lyamina, wife of the Yakhroma mill owner. It has not yet reopened.

The huge **Cathedral of the Assumption**, *Uspeniya*, with dark grey cupolas, the most striking structure in the Kremlin, was built between 1509 and 1533 by the Dmitrov Prince, Yury Ivanovich (ruled 1504-33). Built on a high sub-basement of white limestone, it has five cupolas and tripartite walls divided by a strong cornice from the gables in which small round windows are cut like the just completed Archangel Cathedral in the Moscow Kremlin. In the 17th century it was surrounded on three sides by a gallery, rebuilt 1822-48 by Fedor Shestakov and Dmitry Borisov in the inappropriate Gothic form. The bell tower of three tiers was added in 1796 by M. Agafonov, the upper part by A. Yelkinsky in 1820. The apse is faceted, not round, a feature of 12th century Vladimir-Suzdal architecture.

High on the north and south central gables are rare glazed reliefs of the crucifixion possibly of the late 15th century, although some think they were gifts of Prince Vladimir Staritsky, Dmitrov's last princely ruler from 1566 to1569. Within, on the south wall, is another no less astonishing round ceramic panel of St George and the Dragon (the symbol of Muscovy) probably made between 1460 and 1560.

The cathedral closed in 1918 but reopened as the Dmitrov museum thus saving the fine 17th century iconostasis although some of the oldest icons were removed. (There is an excellent view of the iconostasis from the second-floor gallery.) Services have resumed in the cathedral but the museum continues to occupy the galleries, both institutions striving to make the best of the awkward situation. Among the museum's few treasures are a wooden sculpture of St George and items from the Olgovo and Podyachevo estates.

The former *gymnasiya*, grammar school (now a craft centre), stands opposite the cathedral, built in 1915 in the neo-classical style by the versatile Sergei Rodionov whose pseudo-Russian St Elizabeth of twenty years earlier is only a few yards away.

The east gap in the ramparts opens onto **Kropotkinskaya**, the lowest of the network of pleasing streets of wooden houses with gardens in the old **CENTRE** placed regularly up the small hill overlooking the

Kremlin. These streets have electricity (television aerials stand on every house) but water, which is surely more essential, is available only from stand pipes. Kropotkinskaya is largely pedestrian with, at the corner with Zagorskaya Street, some fine wooden houses. No 83, the single-storey **Novoselov house**, was built in 1842 with Doric pilasters dividing the windows and a frieze under the simple pediment. The **Klyatov house** next door, No 85, was built in 1822 of logs covered with plank siding with a mezzanine floor and balcony. Across Zagorskaya Street, Kropot-kinskaya continues past high-rise modern buildings to a wooden house with touches of Art Nouveau, formerly owned by the Olsufyevs of Podyachevo, now the Kropotkin museum. **Prince Petr Kropotkin**, the anarchist, geographer and Bolshevik sympathiser returned to Russia in 1918 after forty years of exile in Britain and lived here with his wife, a native of Dmitrov, until his death in 1921. As he had known the Olsufyevs well, they would surely have approved.

Just beyond, overwhelmed by high-rise modern buildings, is another attractive wooden house in Art Nouveau style of the early 20th century. It is of two storeys with an overhanging second floor, its windows sharply picked out against the darker wood. It belonged to **Countess Olga Milyutina**, who was patroness of the girls' grammar school. She generously gave one-half to an orphanage while she lived in the other.

Up the hill on **Bolshevistskaya** is the splendid walled **Monastery of Sts Boris and Gleb**, the first Russian martyrs, founded by 1472. The mainly wooden buildings were soon rebuilt after the Polish invasions and by the late 17th century the walls and gate and most of the buildings were of masonry. In 1929-30 the monastery was closed and in the 1930s the Gulag (concentration camp) used it as barracks for those forced to construct the Moscow-Volga canal. After these long years of misery and neglect, it was repaired and reopened for worship at Easter 1993.

Enter through the Holy Gates under **St Nicholas** built 1685-7. The brick **Cathedral of Sts Boris and Gleb** occupying the central space opposite the entrance was built sometime before 1537 as the summer church in the early Moscow style of four tiers and three bays, single powerful drum, and dark cupola supporting the gold cross. The plain, square bell tower, its cupola recently renewed, was placed at the south-western end to avoid cluttering up the principal entrance. The tripartite walls are divided by pilasters and the heavily extruding apse is also in three sections. Tucked in the south corner of the cathedral is a tiny, highly decorated chapel of 1656 by the wife of the courtier, Alexei Chaplin,

and dedicated in his honour to St Alexei, a contrast to the plain,
monumental form of the cathedral. Inside, oil paintings of the 1900s
have been cleaned of whitewash. The ancient stone cross that hung on
the wall is now in the Dmitrov museum. North of the monastery at No
17 Pushkinskaya Street is the newly reopened **Trinity-Tikhvin Church**
built 1794-1801 by its wealthy parishioners, a variation of Rastrelli
baroque.

*Professionalnaya Street continues from Tsentralnaya north of the Kremlin
and main square. (Notice the little octagonal chapel of 1868 next to the
Kremlin ramparts.) Where most traffic turns left at traffic lights signed
ROGACHEVO, go straight ahead to the startlingly red brick* **Church of
the Purification**, *Sretenskaya, left.* Built in 1814 it mixes the early
classical style in the flat pediments on the facade with 17th century
traditional forms in the five cupolas and faceted, heavily extruding apse.
In 1883 Sergei Rodionov built the bell tower in pseudo-Russian style
which adds another exaggerated note to the strange building. Recently
the church has been given to the Invalid Society, which carries out excellent work with the handicapped of Dmitrov.

The estate and village of **PODLIPICHE**, to the east of old Dmitrov,
was absorbed into Dmitrov in the 1930s. *On Bolshevistskaya Street past
the Monastery turn right onto Inzhenernaya Street then, after a small hill,
right again onto Podyachevo and right on an unmarked rural lane to
Podlipiche.* Podlipiche belonged to the **Khitrovs** until the end of the 18th
century and from 1860 to 1917 to the **Lyamins** of the Pokrovskaya
Manufaktura mill in Yakhroma. The baroque **Church of the Kazan
Virgin**, *Kazanskoi Ikony Bozhiei Materi* built in 1735 is one of only two
in Dmitrov that were not closed and its shiny blue and white facade is a
surprise after so many dilapidated buildings. The carved iconostasis
which dates from 1867 includes some icons of the 16th and the 17th
centuries; the oil wall paintings were done in 1907.

Beyond the church is the former **estate house**. Built by the Khitrovs, the
impressive eclectic tower at the centre of the facade was added in the late
19th century. The house has been for some time a **home for handicapped
children** for which the south wing was added in the 1960s. (It seems
strange that the Soviet authorities allowed a church to function right
next to a children's home.) Although perenially short of cash and under-
staffed, the care of the children is first class and the home maintains a
close relationship with the priest. The director was very proud that one
of her boys had succeeded in entering Moscow University.

The old **ZARECHE** (beyond the river) district is located across the canal and the River Yakhroma. *Take Professionalnaya Street past the Kremlin and turn left at the traffic lights signed ROGACHEVO. Cross the railway line, then the canal and the river and turn left signed AVTODOR and first right onto Staro-Rogachevo Street. If coming from Yakhroma, the Zareche area will be immediately on the right.* The wooden houses on **Staro-Rogachevo Street**, the old highway to Rogachevo, are overshadowed by the tall, slim bell tower of the **Church of the Presentation**, *Vvedeniya*. The church was built in 1766 by merchants, including Alexei Tolchenov and his son, in a grand baroque style. The tall cube with a five-sided apse lit by two tiers of windows supports an octagon surmounted by a high dome pierced with lucarne windows and topped by a double cupola. The upper part and spire of the four-tiered bell tower were added in 1832. Inside is a magnificent carved six-tier iconostasis contemporary with the church. Worship has recommenced and a new church house has been built by the village pond where women wash their clothes.

The peach and white mansion of two storeys in Petersburg classicism at No 28 Staro-Rogachevo Street was built in 1785 by Alexei Tolchenov's son, the town mayor. Ten years later it belonged to Ivan Tugarinov, another wealthy mill owner whose son, Pavel, also became mayor. In the 19th century, the house declined, and the garden and park pavilions disappeared but in the early 1970s the original facade was lovingly restored. A children's home after the revolution, it is now an army driving school where young soldiers intently study theory before taking the wheel. The former Tugarinov poorhouse is also on Staro-Rogachevo Street at No 26 on the corner.

It is worth exploring the area between the canal and the railway for the fine wooden houses at **Nos 16 and 24 Rogachevo Street**, the dilapidated baroque **St Elijah** on Staro-Yakhromskaya Street, the brick **Titov house** at 2 Shkolny Lane (one of the oldest in Dmitrov) and on Fabrichnaya Street the ruins of the former **textile mill** of Ivan Tugarinov (from the 1840s to 1917 it belonged to the Nemkov brothers).

NORTH OF DMITROV

In Dmitrov take the main road, Professionalnaya Ulitsa signed DUBNA from the main square past the invalids' Kazan Church. Cross the railway line and take the second right turn onto the A-108 signed SERGIEV POSAD. About 2 km from Dmitrov turn right signed VNUKOVO.

VNUKOVO makes an attractive wooded triangle at the top of a hill with the **Church of the Trinity**, *Troitsy*, and the school at the centre, and the houses on all three sides facing inwards. In the late 19th century, when the textile industry in Yakhroma was expanding, Ivan Chuksin established a formal workshop at Vnukovo making trimmings for fashionable dresses and braid for the uniforms endemic in Tsarist Russia. As the village economy expanded, it was decided to rebuild the existing wooden church in brick in a greatly enlarged version. A brickworks was founded providing the materials not only for the church but for the parish school and a number of spacious houses, numbers 3, 5, 6, and 7, belonging to the leading citizens – the Chuksins, Lesnikovs and Sachkovs.

The now dilapidated church built 1877 to 1893 by Ivan Petrov is indeed large for such a small community. In the ponderously expressed pseudo-Russian style, the large three-bayed cube with gables, powerful drums and cupolas lacks the balancing effect of an apse. Services have restarted but the building requires hugely expensive repairs.

On the A-108, 6 km northeast of Dmitrov, turn right at the sign with a picture of a pig proclaiming **BUDENNOVETS** (*named after Semen Budenny, the Bolshevik civil war hero) founded in 1931 in the first wave of state farms.* As **Danilovskoe** it was the country estate of a number of aristocratic families including the Golitsyn princes who constructed the buildings in the mid 18th century. Later it was acquired by the Polivanovs whose nephew, Mikhail Bestuzhev-Ryumin, the leading Decembrist, visited often as a child.

Along the farm road is a cluster of poorly kept buildings. Among them on the right is the empty, two-storey **main house**, now stripped of plaster its brickwork exposed. Not even a plaque graces its walls and its original baroque features have mostly disappeared. Of the original four wings the left survives although the gallery linking it to the main house has been heavily rebuilt, the right has been replaced by a modern three-storey building, the northwest curved wing still stands but the southwest has been demolished.

The **Church of St Nicholas** by the pond east of the house was built 1768-71 under the Golitsyns, quatrefoil in shape with an octagonal tower which supported a tall, wooden drum and dome, now lost. The truncated lower tier of the bell tower, now the entrance, is still attached to the western arm of the quatrefoil. The inspiration is Moscow baroque but the curving window architraves relate to the western, Rastrelli baroque of Elizabeth's reign. The shell-like niches at the corners were originally filled with statues of the apostles. The loss of the tall drum, baroque cupola and cross has significantly reduced the height of the church but they will probably be restored in time. Worship was reintroduced in 1994.

From Budennovets continue east across the little Yakot River and about 4 km along a good dirt road turn left signed VORONOVO. **VORONOVO** (*voron* means raven) perfectly situated among green fields and woods consists of one street of wooden cottages with gardens, a green common and, as counterbalance, the dilapidated heavy looking classical **Church of the Nativity of the Virgin**, *Rozhdestva Bogoroditsy*. Commissioned in 1824 by two local craftsmen, Iosif Abramov and Semen Ivanov, and built to a standard design using local brick, it is a cube with a round apse, Tuscan portico on north and south, heavy dome and three-tiered bell tower. The 19th century iconostasis frame survives.

An elderly lady carrying a huge sack of grass for her rabbits invited us to sit with her on her garden bench for a while. Anna Nikolaevna, known as Nura, is about 70 with a smiling face and air of calm acceptance of her difficult life. Her husband, the local forester, died over a decade ago and her two children live far away, in Moscow. The plot given to her husband because of his position as forester is divided between the three of them although Anna Nikolaevna does most of the work as her children only visit occasionally. She has 20 rabbits, three goats, cats and hens and a dog in addition to her plot of land. Only old people live in the village now, very dependent on each other and the indispensable postmistress who visits every day and once saved Anna's life when she was ill. She said the church had been closed ever since she moved to the village on her marriage in 1947 to a handsome veteran. She added that the owners of new wooden dachas springing up on the other side of the village were robbing the church of its good floor tiles and other materials. We left her cheerfully collecting her three goats from the pasture.

On the A-108 Road 10 km from Dmitrov across the Yakot Reservoir to **ZHESTYLEVO**, *right (the left turn to Taldom is opposite).* The handsome red brick church, the **Intercession**, *Pokrova*, was built in 1899-1904 by Sergei Rodionov, the talented architect of so many fine churches in the Dmitrov area. In pseudo-Russian style, its charming window frames break through the cornice like medieval windows and

27. RIGHT. **Sergiev Posad.**
In the 15th century cathedral of Russia's pre-eminent monastery, the Trinity-Sergius Lavra, lie the remains of Sergius, the country's most revered saint.

28. LEFT. **Sergiev Posad.**
Like most monasteries, the Trinity-Sergius Lavra provided medical care when there were no public hospitals. This 17th century infirmary is crowned by the splendid tent-shaped Church of StS Zosima and Savvaty.

29. ABOVE. **Gnilushi.**
Like all wooden churches,
the logs of 18th century St
George are constantly being
renewed. (Gnilushi means
rotten wood!)

30. LEFT. **Vinogradovo.**
The Vladimir Virgin
Church, in the unusual
form of a triangle with
three identical facades, was
built by a leading Moscow
architect for a courtier of
Empress Catherine.

31. OPPOSITE. **Yakhroma.**
The abandoned bell tower
of the grandiose Trinity
Church was built in 1908
for workers of the huge
Lyamin cotton mill.

32. ABOVE. **Peremilovo.** The late 18th century Ascension Church carries an intriguing mixture of Gothic and Russian historic styles.

33. BELOW. **Taldom.** Russian wooden houses are traditionally decorated with carved window surrounds – classical or Art Nouveau or lace-like – which vary according to locality.

34. ABOVE. **Serednikovo.** The poet Lermontov spent his boyhood summers at his grandmother's comfortable estate. It is now the Lermontov Centre administered by his descendants where forgotten crafts are being revived.

35. BELOW. **Klin.** During the last years of his life Tchaikovsky lived at this quiet provincial retreat where he composed some of his best works including the *Nutcracker* and *Sixth Symphony*.

36. ABOVE. **Klin.**
A book shop in the old
trading rows still bears the
date – 1886 – and the name
of the original proprietor,
Ivanov, in spidery lettering.

37. LEFT. **Podzhigorodovo.**
The extraordinary
silhouette of St Michael the
Archangel, with its elegant
spires and long body, gives
the impression of a tall
ship.

38. ABOVE. **Archangelskoe.**
St Michael the Archangel
with its tiers of *kokoshniki*
gables provides a striking
contrast with the classical
ambiance of the great
Yusupov stately home.

39. RIGHT. **Ubory.** The
symmetry and soaring
tower of the red brick
Saviour Church is typical of
Moscow baroque, the new
style embraced by Peter the
Great's family.

40. ABOVE. **Volynshchina.** This small but exquisite estate was once strewn with Turkish mementoes gathered by General Dolgorukov, the victorious commander at Perekop in the Crimea where he triumphed over a huge Turko-Tatar force in 1771.

41. LEFT. **Joseph-Volokolamsk Monastery.** The splendid gate church of StS Peter and Paul was meant to astonish pilgrims and introduce them to the wonders of the monastery, one of the richest in Russia.

two rows of gable *kokoshniki* end in five cupolas. Closed in 1935 and used as a warehouse it deteriorated badly, its five cupolas and spire hanging at rakish angles, the ruin exacerbated by house owners stripping it of building material. But in the mid 1990s services resumed and the building is at last under repair.

Near the church are some interesting **wooden log houses**. The oldest, built in 1850 for the Storonkina family, and almost sunk into the earth, has window frames supported by figured consoles. The Gvozdev home, about 20 metres away, was built in the 1880s of notched fitted logs overlapping at the ends and a steep overhanging roof.

Turn left from the A-108 at Zhestylevo onto the R-114. After 12 km turn left again signed VERBILKI for 2 km. In 1766 an English entrepreneur, Francis Gardner, founded a **china works** at **VERBILKI**. Gardner, who came to Russia in the 1740s with the lumber business, chose this thickly wooded area for the fuel necessary to the manufacture of fine china. Access to markets was also good via the Dubna connecting the china works both to Moscow via the Sestra and the now disused Catherine Canal, and to St Petersburg and Nizhny Novgorod via the Volga.

In the 18th century there was a race among the European states to set up porcelain manufacture and avoid expensive imports from China. Gardner's china works, in operation by 1754, was the second in Russia after the Imperial Porcelain Works and the first to be privately owned. Gardner's reputation grew when in 1778-85 he made a service for the imperial court decorated with the orders of St George, St Andrew, St Alexander and St Vladimir. The factory was also known for its fine figurines of peasants and tradesmen. In 1892 it was bought by **Matvei Kuznetsov**, owner of several china works in the Moscow region, who retained the Gardner trademark.

After the revolution the factory was nationalised and for a while still used the old moulds and techniques. In 1989 the employees, taking advantage of *perestroika*, formed themselves into a **joint stock company** but inexperienced in marketing and distribution, and unused to any kind of competition, they are struggling. The young manager complained that no-one acts as middleman, a role adopted in the past by the state. The factory, he said, needs to be paid in advance to fulfill orders; the whole town of about 8,000 depends on the china works which only sporadically provides employment. It is hard to see what the future will be for

Verbilki unless it can adopt more aggressive marketing techniques. An interesting **museum** includes plates with portraits of Stalin in the main building and there is a shop selling china by the stream.

From the A-108 turn left at Zhestylevo on the R-112 and continue for 33 km to Taldom entering via the main square.

TALDOM, population 15,000, on the minor Savelov railway line, lies in pretty wooded countryside 110 km from Moscow. By the end of the 19th century when the **Bychkov footware firm** was founded, it had become a major centre for shoe and boot production; Lenin cited the rise of the shoe trade in Taldom as an example of capitalist exploitation. The wars with Turkey in the 1870s and consequent need for army boots were good for Taldom although not so good for the soldiers as no distinction was made between right and left boots. In the First World War orders for army boots again came flooding in. After the revolution, in 1919 its name changed to Leninsk but in 1929 the old name was returned because too many towns aspired to Lenin's name. Today leather goods and footware (left and right shoes) are still produced.

Three parallel streets of well kept attractive wooden houses with intricate lace-like carving and deeply recessed gable windows, like old-fashioned ladies' bonnets, run from the railway line to the main square. On the square, beyond the two-storey trading rows and the statue of Lenin, stands an attractive blue and white building with the Russian flag flying built in 1910 for the *prisutstvennye mesta*, **local government offices**. Once communist party headquarters, today it is the Mayor's office. On Saltykov-Shchedrin Street to the left are a few sorry-looking shops and the almost ruined fire station. On the right is the local library in red brick and next to that the green-tiled former mansion of the merchant Volkov, built in 1895, now the local museum (*closed Mondays*). The unlikely building left on Saltykov-Shchedrin Street is actually the church of **Michael the Archangel**, truncated and rebuilt chaotically when it was turned into a shoe factory. Recently, it has been tidied up and services have restarted.

West of Taldom are three fascinating hamlets grouped together on the Dubna River. *In Taldom turn left at the junction before the main square signed DUBNA to the railway station, then turn right and then left across the tracks, or follow Saltykov-Shchedrin Street west to cross the railway and travel 8 km, cross the Dubna then turn sharp right onto a hard unpaved road 7 km for Starikovo.*

STARIKOVO is on the left bank of the Dubna and Zyatkovo on the right. The very ruined church with a huge squashed cupola built in 1912-15, the 'new' St George as opposed to the 'old' one at Veretyevo, seems beyond repair. Across the Dubna at **ZYATKOVO**, is an altogether different story. The **Church of the Kazan Virgin**, *Kazanskoi Ikony Bozhiei Materi*, was built in 1852 in classical style with a tall bell tower, long refectory and five charming cupolas in the form of vases. As it remained open until the 1960s, services were able to recommence more easily than elsewhere.

Masha is a summer visitor whose grandfather, Father Petr Alekseev, was the priest at the time of the revolution. She relates how when three commissars arrived demanding the piano, Father Petr's son, Vanya, enquired if they could play and when the answer was negative, suggested he would teach them. At first all three arrived for the lesson, then two, then it dwindled to one, and so in the end they kept the piano. Father Petr remained with his large family until 1929 when they had to flee threats of arrest. The village was then composed of 42 houses of peasants and artisans; the **priest's wooden log house**, built in 1818, still stands behind the church by an avenue of old limes.

Less than 2 km beyond Starikovo right of the bumpy road is the attractive hamlet of **VERETYEVO**. A dozen pretty wooden houses with a well and gardens of red poppies form a row along a grassy lane. In a cemetery in the woods beyond, is a rare and beautiful wooden church, the tall 'old' **St George** built in 1778. It is thrilling to find a wooden church still standing after more than two centuries and this one, in reasonable condition, does not disappoint. Resting lightly on a foundation of large stones, it is composed of an impressive octagon on a particularly tall cube made of fitted planed wood elegantly put together hiding the notched logs underneath. The apse is a five-sided affair with a pointed roof attached to the east end of the cube. The two tiers rise high above the trees to its apex at the single onion dome and cross. A gallery once surrounded the church on north and west (the entrance door is three metres above the ground). St George seems to blend in seamlessly with its surroundings.

The family estate of Mikhail Saltykov-Shchedrin, the famous satirical writer, was located at **SPAS-UGOL** *in the remote country east of Taldom near the border with Yaroslavl Oblast. From the main square in Taldom turn right, then right again for 1/2 km, then left at the next junction going north. In 8 km turn right signed SPAS-UGOL at Kvashonki (straight*

ahead is Makarovo with an interesting convent). At Kvashonki the
classical church of the Transfiguration has been handed to the patri-
archate. Continue east to **Spas-Ugol***, about 30 km from Taldom.* At the
T-junction turn left to the pretty village, lined by houses with lace-like
carvings around the windows and interesting corner designs. Where the
land falls away at the end of the village is the tall, ochre-coloured
church, all that remains of the Saltykov estate.

Mikhail Saltykov spent his childhood on the family estate at Spas-Ugol
where his father was the local squire. He studied at the same excellent
school as Pushkin, joined the civil service in 1844 and began writing
satirical stories using the pseudonym, Shchedrin. Exiled under Nicholas
I, he came back to favour with Alexander II, only to fall out again
under Alexander III. In his last years he wrote *Old Years in Poshekhonie*
about a family of gentry in the provinces which was clearly autobiogra-
phical, describing life in Spas-Ugol which he called Malinovtsa.
Saltykov-Shchedrin's books have become classics and the state library in
St Petersburg is named after him.

The early classical **Church of the Transfiguration**, *Preobrazheniya*, was
built in 1795 by the Saltykovs in brick; the bell tower and *trapeza* added
in the early 19th century are in the more decorative Empire style. Badly
in need of a coat of paint, it is not holding services but is a museum of
the writer (*closed Mondays*). The cemetery has an enclosure for the
Saltykov family.

On August 7, 1887 the villagers, already amazed by the eclipse of the
sun, were astonished to see a large balloon land, carrying the scientist,
Dmitry Mendeleev, who had been viewing the eclipse from Klin and
came down 100 km away at Spas-Ugol.

From Dmitrov travel north via Orudevo hugging the east side of the canal
all the way to **DUBNA***, 128 km from Moscow.* The quiet, fast road with
the railway line on the right and the broad canal on the left is noticeably
empty apart from **Tempy**, one of the centres of canal construction. Its
odd name means tempos, the accelerated rate at which the canal was to
be built using forced labour. Finally, 14 km from Tempy, is **DUBNA**,
population 67,000, founded in 1956 as a **research centre for the nuclear**
sciences with the largest synchro-cyclotron in the world. The Soviet
slogan 'the atom is not a soldier, the atom is a worker' (*atom-ne soldat,*
atom – rabochy) giving the impression nuclear energy is for peaceful
purposes only, is still in evidence. Here is the only place in the Moscow

Oblast touched by the mighty Volga River. The town is surrounded by water – by the Moskva, by the Dubna and by the Volga itself.

At the GAI post turn right, cross the railway line, and continue 5 km then turn right, pass the cemetery, and then left across the main railway line (by the station) and then right and left onto the road to Ratmino. Continue past the shop Universam and turn left again through woods near the High Energy Institute for 3 km and at last the beautiful church at the confluence of the Dubna and the Volga appears. In the 18th century the estate belonged to the Vyazemskys who commissioned the church, **Praise to the Virgin**, *Pokhvaly Bogoroditse*, built in 1827 in Empire style and greatly extended by Yuly Dideriks in 1907-10 in the same style. Prince Alexander Vyazemsky built the **estate house** of brick in 1861 and although it survived into the 1970s, it was demolished to make way for a dispensary for the nuclear research institute. The church too had fallen into almost complete ruin when in 1989 it was painstakingly restored and returned to worship. Otherwise, all that survives of the former estate is the extensive park, a few graves of the Vyazemskys, and the dramatic position overlooking the Volga and the Dubna.

Road 9 LENINGRAD (PETERSBURG) HIGHWAY M-10: KHIMKI TO KLIN

Among old churches and fine estates of the Leningrad (Petersburg) Highway are intriguing associations with cultural and scientific figures – Blok, Lermontov, Mendeleev, Tchaikovsky and the historian Vasily Tatishchev.

Leave Moscow by Leningradsky Prospekt passing the Petrovsky Travel Palace and cross over the Moscow-Volga Canal and the MKAD.

TO ZELENOGRAD

KHIMKI, population 135,000, is bisected by the Moscow-Volga Canal and the busy highway to Petersburg; it is also divided between Moscow and the Moscow Oblast. Khimki's sudden growth in the 1930s was generated by the construction of the Khimki reservoir and the Moscow-Volga Canal.

After crossing the canal take the first right turning to the MKAD signed BOLNITSA. Ignore the left fork to the MKAD and continue straight ahead on Pravoberezhnaya Street to No 6a, Hospital No 1. It is surprising to find in this dormitory suburb of Moscow tucked away in a corner between the canal and the MKAD a large early 20th century mansion built by a leading Moscow architect, Fedor Shekhtel. In 1918 it was confiscated as a sanatorium for communist party leaders and is now part of the main Khimki hospital.

Shekhtel built the **mansion** of **Stepan Patrikeev**, a jurist and member of the Moscow Duma, in 1907. His first private house after five years designing office blocks, it illustrates the change in his style from flamboyant early Art Nouveau to a more ascetic interpretation. Clad with the usual light coloured glazed brick, it is distinguished by round corner towers like English vernacular houses of the time. A tall Venetian window distinguishes the front bay. Coloured tiles form a roof frieze that spills over into the corner towers and appear elsewhere. Shekhtel seems to have been toning down his more extravagant solutions in preparation for his next stylistic leap into the revived classicism of the 1910s.

For Kurkino continue east past the hospital and turn left under the MKAD on Kirova Street. At the T-junction turn right and first left onto Proletarskaya Street then left again at the lights onto Mayakovskaya Street which goes under the Leningrad Highway to Yubileiny Prospekt. (Or from Moscow cross over the MKAD then a road bridge and turn right to go under the bridge joining Yubileiny Prospekt.) Turn left at the junction with Nagornoe Shosse (Rodionovskaya St) and just over1 km left again at a four-way junction onto Zakharinskaya Street past a military base where a small new church looks strange among the red brick barracks. Continue veering left and then right to **KURKINO** *and the church.*

The white, blue-domed **Church of the Vladimir Virgin**, *Vladimirskoi Ikony Bozhiei Materi*, was built in brick about 1678 (although the plaque says 1672) for Prince Ivan Vorotynsky. It stands above the wooded valley of the winding Skhodnya River, a surprisingly rural place considering its proximity to Moscow.

The Vladimir Church was closed at the end of the 1930s but reopened in 1946, its comparatively unstressful history reflected in the well kept building. It seems to be in constant demand for baptisms, weddings and funerals and even for blessings of expensive Mercedes and other cars of doubtful origin. The two-storey apse facing the road has typical 17th century window designs but the original gallery and porch are hidden by the late 18th century broad *trapeza*. Likewise, the old *kokoshniki* gables have been replaced by an ordinary roof. The bell tower was built in the 1840s.

It is impossible to miss the large, rather pompous stone tomb with the mosaic panel of **Dr Grigory Zakharin** which hugs the south wall of the church. Built in 1899 it is by Fedor Shekhtel, the architect of the Patrikeev house. Dr Zakharin was a fashionable doctor in the late 19th century who developed new methods of diagnosing illnesses, particularly of women. He was often accused of being a difficult character – he certainly charged his wealthy patients huge fees. However, he diverted a large part of his considerable income into medical charities, a practice continued by his widow. Not far away south of the Kurkinskoe Shosse – *from the church at Kurkino turn right and left to join the Shosse, then immediately right* – is the charity (now TB) **hospital** built 1911-14 by Yekaterina Zakharina and named after their son, Sergei, who died young. The facade was designed by the well known art historian, **Igor Grabar**, in a free classical style and the later Soviet additions harmonise well with its strong lines.

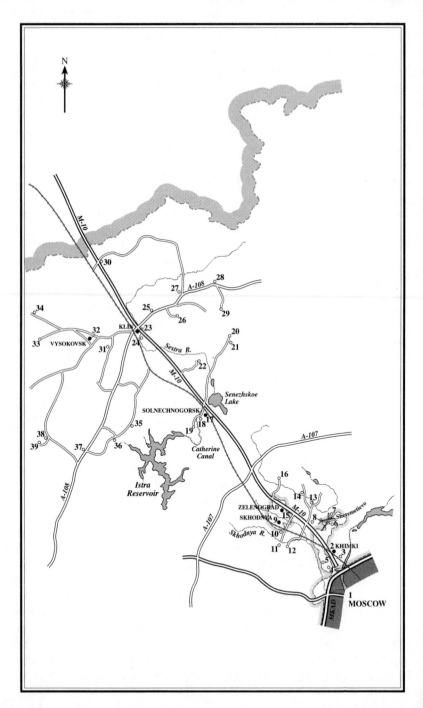

ROAD 9
KHIMKI TO KLIN

1. MOSCOW
2. KHIMKI
3. Patrikeev Dacha
4. Kurkino
5. Novogorsk
6. Sheremetievo Airport
7. Chashnikovo
8. Chernaya Gryaz
9. SKHODNYA
10. Firsanovka
11. Serednikovo
12. Podolino
13. Poyarkovo
14. Tsesarka
15. ZELENOGRAD
16. Lyalovo
17. SOLNECHNOGORSK
18. Spasskoe
19. Obukhovo
20. Tarakanovo
21. Shakhmatovo
22. Boldino
23. KLIN
24. Demyanovo
25. Novoshchapovo
26. Klenkovo
27. Voronino
28. Dorshevo
29. Boblovo
30. Spas-Zaulok
31. Selinskoe
32. VYSOKOVSK
33. Zhestoki
34. Vozdvizhenskoe
35. Nikolskoe
36. Podzhigorodovo
37. Vysokoe
38. Vertkovo
39. Teploe

Beyond Kurkino north at a sharp bend on the winding Nagornoe Shosse was the dacha of **Lavrenty Beria**, the monstrous accomplice of Stalin. Following Beria's death it became a house of rest, *Dom Otdykha Nagornoe*, although still under KGB control. Ordinary Russians, even those who had served decades in concentration camps, could simply purchase a holiday there, which former *zeki* (prisoners) found deeply ironic.

On the Leningrad Highway M-10 on the outskirts of Khimki among fields a surreal footbridge straddles the road: Khrushchev ordered its construction in the early 1960s after his escort ran over a child. The two Sheremetievo Airports 15-20 km from the MKAD are right of the busy road.

A remarkable **war memorial** stands left, about 8 km from the MKAD near the turn to Sheremetievo 2. Built in 1966 in the shape of a tank trap of interlinked railway tracks, it is at the place, only 30 km from the Kremlin, to which German scouts penetrated in the winter of 1941-2. Wedding couples like to pose here for photographs.

On the Leningrad Highway turn right for Sheremetievo 1 Airport (2 km beyond Sheremetievo 2). Where the road divides turn left at the bright blue prefabricated building and cross railway tracks for a few hundred metres to **CHASHNIKOVO** (there is a second Chashnikovo farther north).

It is as if one stepped through a magic gate. The busy modern airports melt into a village of wooden houses and tethered goats on the narrow Alba River overlooked by the venerable **Church of the Trinity**, *Troitsy*. Crowned by six startlingly blue bulbous cupolas and with a tent-shaped bell tower it is crudely juxtaposed with a second, extremely tall red brick bell tower/gate built in 1895 by Alexander Latkov. The church is first mentioned in 1585 when it is listed as belonging to Nikita Zakharin-Yuriev, the ancestor of the Romanov tsars, but its long history began in the early 16th century. It was probably constructed by one of the Italians rebuilding the Kremlin for the usual voluptuous apse is absent – the Assumption Cathedral in the Kremlin by Fioravanti has only the barest suggestion of one. Another unusual detail is the faint frieze of terracotta tiles on the eastern end.

In 1688 Chashnikovo was granted to Lev Naryshkin, uncle of Peter the Great who headed the Foreign Office in Peter's government. Under Naryshkin, the church was considerably enlarged by the addition of the entrance and tent-shaped bell tower and two side chapels, also without apses. It was at this time that the seven ballooning cupolas were built on their tall stalk-like drums like weird flowers, together with the shell gables popularised by the Archangel Cathedral in the Kremlin. Chashnikovo remained in the Naryshkin family until the 19th century when it was purchased by Alexander Karepin, a Collegiate Assesor. About 1895 when the massive bell tower was built, the walls were painted with frescoes and icons by Nikolai Safonov. It was until recently the only working church for many kilometres.

To get an idea of how the church first looked one must imagine the central cube without the side chapels, the triple-bayed walls topped by ogee-shaped gables, tall drums and helmet-shaped cupolas, a small *zvonnitsa* bell tower on the roof, and the terracotta frieze around three sides.

On the Leningrad Highway between the two airports is tiny **Cherkizovo** where the large **Church of the Saviour**, *Spasa*, right, had become the village cinema but was totally metamorphosed in 1992 when services restarted. **CHERNAYA GRYAZ** *(black mud)*, about 4 km from Cherkizovo, was the closest **post station** and inn to Moscow before the advent of the railways on the long journey to and from St Petersburg. In the ochre two-storey 18th century post house, right, 100 horses at a time could be stabled. It is now a clinic. Post stations were provided every 60 km or so by the state where travellers could spend the night and obtain fresh horses for the next leg of the journey. The last chapter of Radishchev's critique of contemporary Russia, for which he was imprisoned, *A Journey from Petersburg to Moscow*, 1790, is entitled *Chernaya Gryaz*.

ON THE KLYAZMA RIVER. *On the Leningrad Highway turn right signed PIKINO (after the left turning to Skhodnya). At 3 km where the road divides take the left fork. In less than a kilometre turn right to* **Poyarkovo**. In the early 1990s the ancient gabled church by the pond, the **Nativity of the Virgin**, *Rozhdestva Bogoroditsy*, had windows open to the elements, a rusty cupola and a heavily cracked bell tower in danger of toppling over. It has now been completely restored, mostly through the efforts of local people.

The church was built in 1665 (see the plaque over the north door) for **Artamon Matveev**, the first minister of Tsar Alexei. Matveev, married to a Scot, Mary Hamilton, was fascinated by western ways and deeply shocked Muscovites by hanging paintings and clocks in his house, staging theatricals, and allowing his wife to dress in European clothes.

His ward, Natalya Naryshkina, became the second wife of the Tsar and mother of Peter the Great. Matveev was to die a horrible death in 1682 when the Streltsy, the regular infantry, rioted in the Kremlin and hacked him to pieces. He leaves a fine memorial in the church at Poyarkovo.

It is a simple cube with a deeply projecting apse and three tiers of gables pointing the way to the drum and cupola. The original small belfry was replaced in the 1670s by the tall tent-shaped bell tower of two tiers decorated with coloured tiles. But the ground-floor arch proved unequal to the task of supporting both storeys and in the 19th century was reinforced with buttresses. During 1970s restoration the buttresses were removed to recapture the original form but cracks soon developed and the tower began leaning. This has now been corrected.

For **Tsesarka**, *from the Leningrad Highway turn right signed PIKINO, continue straight on (ignore the right turn to Poyarkovo) across the narrow Klyazma River on a bumpy road past the cemetery, right, to an army base for a tank regiment, left.* Within the walls stands the forlorn figure of the **Church of the Sign**, *Ikony Bozhiei Materi 'Znamenie'*, all that has survived of the Iovlevo-Znamenskoe estate. The young soldiers on duty sometimes allow views of the sad building, sometimes partially hidden by a tank, through the dirty window of the reception area.

The Empire church originally built in 1733 was rebuilt in 1830 by the Martynovs. The bell tower is now only a mound of bricks on the ground, and the *trapeza*, too, is nearly gone. Father Oleg of Poyarkovo has a job on his hands to resurrect this building.

The Martynovs' most famous son was Nikolai, an officer in the Caucasus who encountered the poet, **Mikhail Lermontov**, while taking the waters at Pyatigorsk. Martynov became the butt of Lermontov's scathing jokes and challenged him to a duel that at first no-one took seriously. But as they met, preparing to fire into the air, Lermontov insulted Martynov yet again and in anger Martynov shot and killed the 27-year-old poet who had prefigured his own death in his poem *The Dream* and his prose masterpiece *Hero of Our Time*. Through the intervention of Nicholas I, Martynov's punishment was mild: four years in the monastery of the caves at Kiev. At his death in 1875 he was buried next to this little church on the family estate. Ironically, Serednikovo, the country house where Lermontov spent his boyhood summers, lies only a few kilometres away across the Leningrad Highway.

At the traffic light and GAI post at Zelenograd, beyond the huge war memorial, turn right signed LYALOVO. Continue, turning right and then left to **Mendeleevo**, the small town built for the physics and radio technology institute and named for Dmitry Mendeleev, whose country home, Boblovo, is not far away. At Mendeleevo, turn left to cross the Klyazma River to Lyalovo.

Lyalovo named for one of the Starodub princes, became the property of E.I. Kozitskaya. In 1800 she built the impressive classical **Nativity of the Virgin**, *Rozhdestva Bogoroditsy*, in the form of a rotunda; the *trapeza* and bell tower were added in the second half of the 19th century. After the revolution the church was closed and used as a club for the local collective farm, the Morozovka. In 1958 the first rural art gallery in the Moscow district opened in the church with paintings by leading Soviet artists like Sergei Gerasimov, Nikolai Tomsky, and Isaac Brodsky. The church is once again holding services.

Next to the church behind a wall a large mansion was built before the revolution for **Nikolai Morozov**, the Anglophile owner of the Bogorodsk (now Noginsk) textile mills. But the present huge building behind the carefully guarded gate is more like a luxurious hotel, with iron lamp stands and Corinthian pilasters and a magnificent hall of marble columns. Expensive cars are parked in the forecourt. This is not the mock Tudor/Gothic mansion of Nikolai Morozov, but a luxurious **house of rest** for the high and mighty. It seems that in the 1930s the Morozov dacha had been turned into one of the many Stalin dachas dotted about the countryside. But in the early 1950s it burnt down and the present mansion was constructed for the Soviet Council of Ministers. Since then it has come under Gazprom and is a guest house for high-ranking official visitors.

On the Leningrad Highway 4 km north of Zelenograd is **Chashnikovo** (Sobakin) *at the 43 km post. Turn right to the Moscow University Soil Ecological Centre.* Across the pond are the modern buildings of the university but only the stables are left of the once extensive estate of the **Sobakins**. They attained the rank of boyar in the 15th century when their relative, Martha Sobakina, was unlucky enough to be chosen as Ivan the Terrible's bride – within two weeks she was dead. Beyond the little square is the classical red brick stable like a palace, its long facade interspersed with bays of arched windows and a portico of four white Doric columns. Colonnades, one of which is now missing, link the side wings to the central bay. If this was the stable one wonders what the main house was like. In one of the wings a shop operates, in another is a garage, and curtains at windows suggest people are living there.

BY THE SKHODNYA. *From the Leningrad Highway take the difficult left turning signed SKHODNYA past the turn to Sheremetievo 1.* The town squeezed between two rivers, the Skhodnya which flows into the Moskva and its tributary, the Goretova, is built up all the way to Firsanovka, the next railway station.

For **Podolino** *turn left at the railway and then right over the line, and straight on to the bridge over the tiny Goretova. Turn right past the shop (produktovy magazin) and then left. As the houses recede a delightful new wooden church rears up silhouetted against the woods and the green meadow.*

Father Georgy gives a most hearty welcome to visitors to the **Church of the Smolensk Virgin**, *Smolenskoi Ikony Bozhiei Materi*, and likes to relate its history. A new Russian entrepreneur, Vladimir Griev, in the early 1990s purchased 136 hectares of land from the local state farm and hired the villagers to work it at good salaries. He soon began making a healthy profit, an unusual situation for Russian agriculture which is usually in the doldrums. In 1992 he decided to build a church on this lovely spot on his farm. Griev's plan was realised by an architect-restorer he met in Moscow who shared his enthusiasm for Podolino. The architect turned out to be Father Georgy himself who after constructing the church took holy orders and returned to serve at the very church he built.

The model for the church is northern wooden architecture. It is in the familiar three sections: the large *trapeza*/entranceway, the main church, and the extruding apse. Logs especially imported from the Novgorod area are notched and fitted together, the method described as *v oblo*. Dried moss and hemp are inserted between them for insulation. A single cupola on a narrow drum and a delightful tent-shaped belfry with seven bells emerge from the steeply pitched roofs and a long covered porch surrounds the church on three sides. Within, the wooden walls give off the smell of the forest and bright new icons hang in the iconostasis.

For **Serednikovo** *continue from Podolino 2 km. (Or turn left from the Leningrad Highway at traffic lights signed FIRSANOVKA. At the division in the road past the Lada garage, take the left fork and then left*

again and then turn right to the Firsanovka railway station. Cross the
bumpy tracks and continue 3 km across the narrow Goretova River to the
gates of Serednikovo, right, signed MTSYRI SANATORY.)

The classical buildings of the estate at Serednikovo are intact, the main
courtyard retains its sense of intimacy, the park sweeps down to the
river, the church is open for worship. Yet there is a Chekhovian feeling
of decay and melancholy, a romantic clinging to the past, that is
certainly not evident in neighbouring Podolino.

Serednikovo and the surrounding villages belonged from 1775 to 1806
to the **Vsevolozhsky** family who, from 1784 to 1796, oversaw the
construction of the present house and related buildings and laid out the
park. Serednikovo changed owners many times before the rich and
influential **Stolypins**, Lermontov's relatives, purchased it in 1825. Then,
from 1869 to 1917, it belonged to the **Firsanovs**. Ivan Firsanov was the
owner of Moscow's most luxurious steam baths, the Sandunovsky, and
of 23 apartment houses. He and his daughter Vera built a richly
festooned and well appointed apartment house for Moscow's poor
where low rents were charged. Under their ownership, Serednikovo
became a salon for the Moscow intelligentsia – Chaliapin was a frequent
guest at the parties of the discriminating Vera. Its most notable resident,
however, half a century earlier, was the Russian romantic poet, Mikhail
Lermontov.

Under the guardianship of his grandmother, Elizaveta Arsenieva, born
Stolypina, who took over his upbringing after the early death of his
mother, the young **Lermontov** spent three summers, 1829-31, at Serednikovo. Because of Lermontov's fame as the second poet of Russia after
Pushkin, this fleeting period in the estate's history is heavily emphasised
although Serednikovo is not mentioned in any of his writings. The man
who killed Lermontov, Nikolai Martynov, is buried only a few km away
at Tsesarka.

Serednikovo is entered through the main gates. An avenue of old limes
leads past five single-storey rusticated arched buildings, the stables.
Those on the left were for cattle while those on the right, where one is
now missing, were for horses – the round manege is to the far right. An
inner courtyard is approached through a second gate. Within this
carefully balanced square the two-storey mansion with its porch,
pediment, belvedere and weather vane surmounted by a cock, is framed
by four smaller houses or wings, two on each side, linked to each other

and the main house by colonnades. These smaller houses were used as bedrooms; Lermontov's was in the left nearest the mansion.

Vera Firsanova greatly loved the Lermontov connection and for the fountain in front of the house she commissioned **a statue of the poet** by the well known classical sculptress, Anna Golubkina (removed for safe keeping). The romantic Firsanovs also erected an obelisk to Lermontov's memory in 1914, the hundredth anniversary of his birth, which can be seen through the colonnade at the left side of the house.

Of brick construction the **house** is in desperate need of repairs. A balcony on columns divides the ground and first floors and the small pediment and belvedere above give the house just the right sense of height. Within, although somewhat altered, the main oval room of the first floor with walls of shining artificial marble looking onto the garden is in reasonable condition. The impressive ceiling painting on the theme of Lermontov's most famous poem, *The Demon*, was done in the 1890s by the artist V.K. Shtemberg at the behest of the Firsanovs.

The estate has survived surprisingly well since the Firsanovs left in 1917. At first it was used as a sanatorium for the *nomenklatura*, where Lenin once came for a few days, and renamed *Mtsyri* after Lermontov's famous poem. It subsequently became a hospital for prisoners suffering from tuberculosis for which the ugly buildings on the edge of the property were built.

The present director of Serednikovo is Irina Tyzhnova, an energetic physicist from nearby Zelenograd. She is a member of the **National Lermontov Centre** which in January 1992 was given Serednikovo on a lease for fifty years with the task of capitalising on its connection with the poet. All the Lermontov descendants in Russia and many from abroad (the Lermontovs are descended from the Scottish Learmonts) are members of the association and lend their support. Irina says their intention is to open a Lermontov centre in the main house, rather like a museum, and use the smaller houses as guest houses. They hope to resurrect the crafts practised here in the 19th century, furniture making among others. They also have an idea for bottling mineral water imported from the south. But the main task, restoration of the house, is a daunting prospect. Irina complained that film companies like to use it but they rip up the floors and harm the decor and do not make good before they leave.

There is a pleasant walk of about 1 km from the house to the **Church of the Metropolitan Alexei**. Left of the cattle yard is a path leading across the old **Chertov bridge** (in poor condition) to a hamlet where the furniture and woodwork for Serednikovo used to be made. The church stands almost alone. Built in 1693, its facade was later altered to conform with classical precepts and it little resembles a 17th century church except for the heavy vaulting. Two chapels and a refectory were added in the early 19th century and in 1865 the bell tower was constructed. The interesting interior oil paintings are probably the work of Shtemberg while he was engaged on *The Demon* painting in the main house. Perhaps because of its isolation, the church was never closed.

From the Leningrad Highway M-10 Zelenograd (green city) lies 20 km northwest of the MKAD on the left.

Zelenograd on the Skhodnya, population 170,000, was specially built in the 1960s as a satellite town of Moscow for the electronics industries with high-rise buildings and broad, impersonal avenues. The principal architects were Igor Pokrovsky and Igor Rozhin. But whereas in the crowded city an argument can be made for tower blocks, in rural surroundings they look not only out of place but, forty years on, shabby and run down. It is sad that the idea of bringing the city to the countryside remained a Soviet principle for so long.

Unusually for a Soviet new town, Zelenograd has two churches. From the highway the bright red **Church of St Nicholas** can be seen, the survivor of an old estate. *Turn left at the first paved road into Zelenograd, then take the first left to the church.* Astonishingly the strange heavy building with primitive Gothic windows is almost new for the old church of 1827 was so ruined when it was handed to parishioners in 1988 it had to be reconstructed. The bell tower stands separately.

On the Leningrad Highway at the main entry into Zelenograd by traffic lights stands a large and impressive **war memorial**, right. It is a tall rendered tower shaped like a bayonet beside a sculptured relief set into the hill designed partially by Pokrovsky. There is another memorial by the railway station and farther along the highway yet another in the form of a tank. Turn left at the traffic lights onto Panfilovsky Prospekt and just beyond the Olga supermarket turn right where a delightful, new, wooden church, **St Filaret**, built on traditional lines, nestles somewhat uncomfortably against the white tower blocks of the 11th District. This, Zelenograd's second church, was only completed in January, 1994.

IN AND AROUND SOLNECHNOGORSK

On the Leningrad Highway M-10 some 45 km from the MKAD and straddling the St Petersburg Road is Solnechnogorsk.

Solnechnogorsk, population 60,000, is associated with the building of the grandiose Christ the Saviour Cathedral. To carry the heavy stone needed for the cathedral it was decided to build a canal to link Moscow with the Volga thereby cutting the journey by 1,000 km. Construction commenced on the Catherine Canal in 1825 when the Sestra River was dammed to form Lake Senezh but work dragged on for 20 years and even then the canal was unable to handle the large boats needed for carrying the stone. A further blow occurred in 1851 when the new Moscow-Petersburg railway opened making the canal redundant. All that remains now is Lake Senezh and small sections of the canal including one right of the Leningrad Road at Solnechnogorsk. The lake, some seven square kilometres of water well stocked with fish, has come into its own as ideal holiday country. The Union of Artists have their dachas at **Senezh** on the southeastern side of the lake. Turn right at the GAI post and continue to **Chepchikha** and the once fine wooden house of a relative of the imagist poet, Apollon Maikov, who frequently stayed there. Maikov was much admired by his contemporaries, including Gogol and Dostoevsky, although he is half forgotten now.

On entering Solnechnogorsk look left to see the delightful pseudo-Russian brick **Church of St Nicholas** bristling with cupolas built in 1875. It is surrounded by a large and interesting cemetery of which the tomb of Alexander Glazunov, a successful publisher in the 1870s, is the most elaborate. St Nicholas is painted a soft caramel colour offset by an array of white arches, gables, pilasters, pendules and all manner of traditional Russian ornament. The church has been functioning for much of the Soviet period and is in good order.

The fine **Church of the Saviour**, *Spasa*, is at **SPASSKOE**, the western suburb of Solnechnogorsk. *Turn left at the traffic lights signed PYATNITSKOE SHOSSE, go under a railway bridge and turn left at the sign Ts.M.I.S. past the palace of culture.* Turn right onto a dirt road to the church standing by itself looking over the Catherine Canal to the slightly later church at Obukhovo.

The Saviour Church was built in 1759 by the wealthy landowner, **Prince P.I. Lopukhin** possibly by Vasily Yakovlev. It is a fascinating amalgam of old-fashioned Moscow baroque, half a century out of date, and western baroque. The influence of the former is clear in the two octagonal towers, one the main church and the other for bells with the clusters of columns at the corners, and the unique open north and south gallery flanking the square apse. The spacious summer church with its mid 18th century iconostasis and excellent accoustics is on the first floor, bounded by the gallery, while the winter heated church is in the vaulted ground floor. The old church, which remained open, is in need of repairs but must give one-third of the takings from the tiny congregation to the diocese to help other churches which have recently reopened.

For the century prior to 1917 it belonged to the **Princes Lvov** who had purchased it from the Lopukhins. Lev Tolstoy was friendly with the jurist, Georgy Lvov, and visited him at Spasskoe in 1859 where he was impressed by Lvov's zeal in trying to close the cruel schools for sons of soldiers. In the 1960s the Lvov wooden mansion was demolished to make way for the present palace of culture.

In Solnechnogorsk turn first right after traffic lights signed TARAKA-NOVO 18 km. Past the run-down farm buildings and wooden houses of **TARAKANOVO** stands a very ruined brick tower by a pond wrapped in ancient scaffolding. It is impossible to see how the **Church of Michael the Archangel** could ever be restored although attempts have been made and then abandoned. It was in this church that the handsome and gifted **Alexander Blok**, the leading symbolist poet of the early 1900s, married Lyubov, the daughter of Dmitry Mendeleev, the brilliant scientist. Lyubov (meaning love) deeply inspired Blok's early poetry especially his *Verses About the Beautiful Lady.* The marriage, however, soon ended in divorce.

Blok's summer estate at Shakhmatovo (not the Shakhmatovo near Boldino north of Lake Senezh) is only a few kilometres from Taraka-novo but is not on the map. From Tarakanovo turn right signed SHAKHMATOVO and GUDINO. In 2 km after passing through Osinka turn right onto a dirt road. Almost immediately on the right is a small hill with a white marble stone and a plaque stating Blok lived here 1881–1916.

Blok's grandfather, Andrei Beketov, an eminent biologist, rector of St Petersburg University and a good friend of Mendeleev, had his wooden summer house here where now all is reverting to nature. Blok's mother separated from his father not long after his birth and she took him every summer to his grandfather at Shakhmatovo. Blok used to boast that looking due north from his house he was able to see the Mendeleev estate at Boblovo. After the revolution although he embraced Bolshevism for a short time, Blok could no longer come to his beloved Shakhmatovo for, like other estate owners, he was evicted. Nowadays lovers of Blok's poetry gather here every year on 9 August for Blok readings. Still a lovely, empty place surrounded by woods with long views over the Lutosnya valley, the wooden house is now being rebuilt.

From the Leningrad Highway at Davydkovo 12 km north of Solnechnogorsk turn right at the GAI post signed ZUBOVA 9 km. In 5 km after crossing the Catherine canal turn right, cross a stream and take the next right turn on the cement block road and cross the canal again to Shakhmatovo (not the Blok estate) where the road improves. At a concrete fence at a T-junction where the road turns right leave the car. Through the left gap in the fence is the path to the former estate of **BOLDINO**.

Boldino (not to be confused with Pushkin's Boldino near Nizhny Novgorod) was the home of the scholar and statesman of Peter the Great's reign, **Vasily Tatishchev**. He took part in Peter's military campaigns, pushed through mining reforms, founded Yekaterinburg and was the first Russian archeologist. It was he who formulated the theses presented to the Empress Anna under which she was to relinquish some powers. He spent some time in the Peter-Paul Fortress during the reign of the infant Ivan VI but was released when Elizabeth took the throne. He also laid the grounds for modern historiography with his five volume *History of Russia from the Earliest Times* which he wrote at Boldino after he retired in 1745. He is buried in the cemetery of the inaccessible Rozhdestvensky Pogost near Shakhmatovo.

Boldino, a children's camp after the revolution, survives only in fragments. A pleasant caretaker with his friendly dog, Mika, whose large wooden house is the only habitable building, is happy to show visitors around. The ruins of the large mansion still stand up to ground-floor level flanked on the left by a smaller building of red brick which still has its roof. On the left also are the ruined stables. To the right are woods which lead to the river and a series of ponds where a marble stone in honour of Tatishchev is the only evidence of public interest. However, there is a rumour that Americans intend to restore the buildings.

TO MENDELEEV'S HOME

*In Klin take the A-108 road from Papivin Street east towards Rogachevo
and Dmitrov.* After 5 km at **Novoshchapovo** the large ruined **Trinity
Church**, *Troitsy*, on the right built in 1835 with Corinthian porticoes and
Gothic niches had been used as a glass factory until services restarted.
8 km farther on at **Opalevo** turn right onto an unsigned paved road. In
June 1993 an unusual sight here attracted much interest. A man and a
woman leading a horse and small plough were digging up a field in the
age-old way. This was then an almost forgotten sight: private ownership
of horses was forbidden in the Soviet Union and the collective and state
farms had long abandoned horse-drawn ploughs for large tractors. It
seems that in the new Russia the old ways are returning.

In 4 km is Zolino where a left turn across a stream to **KLENKOVO**
brings one to the lovely but dilapidated **Church of the Kazan Virgin**,
Kazanskoi Ikony Bozhiei Materi. It was built in 1814 at the height of the
passion for the Empire style by M.I. Vysotskaya and P. Vishnevetskaya,
the local landowners (Vysotskaya owned Nikolskoe, at Zolino where
the main wooden house was only recently demolished). The church is all
soft curves – the round second tier of the bell tower, the rotunda of the
central part, and the thrusting round apse. The roof of the *trapeza* is
completely gone but the roof of the church itself is intact. Some oil and
grisaille paintings survive within. The old graveyard has gone but the
grounds have been tidied up, old bricks are stacked neatly, and there is
an air of hopeful anticipation.

*Four kilometres from Opalevo (12 from Klin) on the A-108 Road at the
Sestra River is* **VORONINO**. On the left is the large white classical
Church of the Smolensk Virgin, *Smolenskoi Ikony Bozhiei Materi*, in
unusually good order for it never closed. Built about 1820 by Princess
E.O.Volkonskaya it has giant Tuscan porticoes, pediments, hemispherical dome and square apse. The tympanum over the south portico
bears a mosaic of the Virgin. Within, the wall paintings have recently
been renewed and the gilded carved iconostasis is of the 1880s.

From Voronino a pleasant **circular drive** to Klin encompasses attractive
villages in the pretty Sestra and Lutosnya valleys. Cross the Lutosnya
and turn left following the road curving north and west 35 km to Spas-
Zaulok and thence to Klin.

On the A-108, 8 km beyond Voronino is **Dorshevo**. The large 18th century mansion that was in the Zasetsky family from the 16th century to 1917 still stands, left, flanked by four service buildings, but has been completely altered. The park and ponds lie behind the old house and to the east are the sad remains of the Transfiguration Church, now only a pile of bricks.

For the Mendeleev estate at **BOBLOVO**, *turn right a little beyond Dorshevo, 10 km from Voronino, signed MENDELEEV MUSEUM. The road, which turns sharp left, becomes for 4 km an avenue of limes, elms and poplars, many planted by Mendeleev himself. Just after the bus-stop turn right for ½ km and then left to Boblovo (avoiding the military base).* At the farthest end of the secluded summer colony is the museum devoted to the great chemist, Dmitry Mendeleev.

Mendeleev, a successful businessman as well as the inventor of the periodic table, purchased an estate here with his friend, N.P. Ilin, in 1865 and each built a house in the extensive grounds. Mendeleev's summer home had a ground floor of stone and upper of wood faced with brick. He also built a laboratory and planted many unusual trees and plants in the large park. In 1892 the Ilin property was purchased by the Smirnovs and it is their house in which the museum is now situated for the Mendeleev house burned down in 1919. The museum launched in 1987 is rarely open.

KLIN

Klin is 67 km from the MKAD on the Leningrad Highway M-10, situated on the wide loop of the **Sestra River**. By 1482 the town had come under the rule of the Moscow princes and after St Petersburg was founded it became an important staging post to the new capital. Klin's coat of arms displays its affiliations: the Moscow emblem of St George and the Dragon above, and below a mounted rider with a horn illustrating its postal role. Textile mills and a glass factory introduced at the end of the 19th century are still functioning together with others associated with metalwork and the building trade.

Klin, population 95,000, was occupied by the German army November to December 1941 and suffered heavy damage when Soviet troops retook the town. Nevertheless, most of the old central streets including a remarkable 16th century church are intact. **Petr Tchaikovsky**, the composer, frequently stayed in the area before renting, towards the end

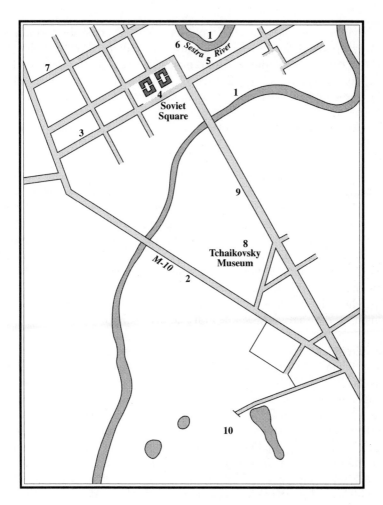

KLIN   1. Sestra River, 2. M-10, 3. Gagarina, 4. Soviet Square,
5. Papivina, 6. Kremlin, 7. Gaidara, 8. Tchaikovsky Museum,
9. Tchaikovskovo, 10. Demyanovo

of his life, a wooden house on the Leningrad Road. The children's
writer, **Arkady Gaidar**, also lived in the town.

The Leningrad Road crosses the Sestra River and continues as a boulevard. On the right is the attractive Art Nouveau church, **St Tikhon
Zadonsky**, built in 1909 and returned to worship in 1991. Just where the
boulevard commences, on the left at Gagarina Street, is the local

museum which has fascinating photographs of old Klin including a picture of Mendeleev taking off in his huge balloon. At the next street on the left is the impressive **war memorial**. Behind the memorial on Liteinaya Street, is the cheerful red brick and white stone **Church of the Consolation of All Sorrows**, *Vsekh Skorbyashchikh Radosti*. It was built between 1847 and 1860 in the form of a Latin cross to a standard design in a mixture of Russian and classical styles. As it remained open in the Soviet period, the wall paintings and iconostasis are intact.

Turn right into Gagarina Street which leads to Soviet Square and eastwards where it becomes Papivina Street and the A-108 road to Dmitrov. On the left where Gagarina Street widens into **Soviet Square** are attractive red brick market buildings, the **trading rows**, built 1886–1888 to a design by Sergei Rodionov. The single-storey buildings in pseudo-Russian style form squares around two extensive courtyards linked by an archway. One of the gates still declares the date – 1886 – and the name of the book shop, the Ivanova Lavka. The dilapidated little shops have taken on a new lease of life in the revived Russia and some of those that had been demolished are being rebuilt.

Beyond is the echoing space where parades were held in communist days. Facing the parade ground is the monumental **Palace of Culture**, built in the early 1950s out of the **Cathedral of the Trinity**, *Troitsy*. The basilica form of the cathedral was a convenient size for the palace which apart from the semicircular Doric porch has the same dimensions. Go to the insalubrious lane behind the palace to the site of the old **Kremlin**, where three strange buildings huddle together by the winding Sestra. The ramparts have long since been demolished and the right-angled streets and main square, built when the town was replanned in 1785, have displaced the Kremlin's central position. Of the decaying buildings, one is the unrecognisable **Church of the Resurrection**, *Voskreseniya*, built in 1712 in red brick in the Moscow baroque style. The removal of the octagonal upper tier and the cupola in Soviet times and the alteration of the windows leave it looking like a two-storey house. The octagonal **bell tower**, built 1769, stands opposite like a pillar stiffly clad in concrete, its smooth surface broken by small windows and bell apertures and topped by a new gold dome. The third building is the old Cathedral Hotel.

Ranged along the south side of Soviet Square is a **chemist** in Art Nouveau style built in 1914 for the Orlov Brothers. At the corner with Tchaikovsky Street is the old **posting station**, still a post office, built by the fine classical architect, Nikolai Lvov. It is composed of a central two-storey building with pediment flanked by smaller houses and stables behind.

Across the old Moscow road on **PAPIVINA STREET** (note the old sign to Moscow and St Petersburg) is a group of two-storey modest classical buildings built in the 1830s. The first, painted pink, Nos 2-4, housed the **town administration**. Next door, No 4, is a small pseudo-Russian **chapel and poorhouse** designed by Sergei Rodionov in 1890, followed by the **hospital** at No 10 financed by the Moscow merchant, Semen Lepeshkin. On the corner opposite at No 18 is the two-storey red brick boys' **grammer school** built 1904-12. The local police occupied the upper floor which must have been good for school discipline.

The oldest building in Klin, the whitewashed **Church of the Assumption**, *Uspeniya*, is at No 16a on Papivina Street now restored to the parish. Built in the middle of the 16th century as the cathedral of the Assumption Monastery it became a parish church in 1764. In the 19th century, it was heavily rebuilt in the prevailing Empire style but in 1960 the old church was lovingly restored by Soviet architects to its original aspect. It is a cube with a high triple apse supported by four internal columns on an inscribed Greek cross plan. The single tall drum supports the old-fashioned wooden helmet-shaped cupola. The facade is divided into the usual three sections but finishes in triangular gables, a wholly original resolution to the bays not encountered elsewhere. Within are traces of the original altar rail.

The home of the famous children's writer, **Arkady Gaidar**, now a museum, is located at **No 17 Gaidara Street** to the right of the Leningrad Highway beyond Gagarina Street. In the 1930s Gaidar rented rooms in the small house and was so taken with the daughter of his landlady that she became his second wife. Before the war, when Klin was a small town Gaidar, like Tchaikovsky before him, found it an ideal place for serious work and it was here that he wrote the popular *Timur and His Gang*. However, he was killed fighting in the early days of the German attack on the Soviet Union. After the Germans were thrown back from Klin, his widow returned to find their house looted and the door hanging open. Arkady Gaidar is the grandfather of Yegor Gaidar, the reformer and prime minister in Yeltsin's early days. *Open Wednesdays to Sundays, 10 to 5 p.m.*

TCHAIKOVSKY'S last home has also become a museum to his memory. It faces two streets, the old road to Moscow, and the Leningrad Highway that forks left on the approach to Klin. The well signed entrance is from the latter road where there is a small parking lot, concert and exhibition halls, and the house set deep in the park. *Open Friday to Tuesday 10 to 6 except the last Monday of every month.*

For the last ten years of his life, **Petr Tchaikovsky**, Russia's outstanding composer and deeply sensitive musician who suffered greatly from his unexpressed homosexuality, preferred the peace and quiet of life in and around Klin. In May 1892 he took the comfortable wooden house and garden belonging to a Mr Sakharov, the last house on the Moscow road. Klin was very convenient for the composer for he could easily travel by rail to either of the two capital cities, Moscow and St Petersburg. Here working at his usual frenetic pace, he completed the *Nutcracker Suite* and composed the *Sixth Symphony* and many other works. In the course of 1893 he travelled abroad giving concerts and, in Britain, accepting an honorary degree from Cambridge University. In October of that year he left Klin for Moscow and thence to St Petersburg where on the night of October 24-5 he suddenly died, aged 53, of cholera after drinking unboiled water. Some think it may have been suicide.

Tchaikovsky's faithful servant, Alexei Sofronov, to whom the composer had left the bulk of his property, purchased the house and grounds early in 1894 when visitors were already knocking at the door. In 1897 Tchaikovsky's brother, Modest, and his favourite nephew, Vladimir Davydov, to whom Tchaikovsky had dedicated the *Sixth Symphony* and who had inherited the rights to his published music, managed to find the money to purchase the house from Sofronov and open it as a museum to the composer. In 1916 Modest died and by his will the house was transferred to the **Russian Musical Society** who continued to keep it as a museum. In 1921 it was nationalised by the Soviet government. Twenty years later the Germans marched in using the ground floor to garage their motorcycles and the upper floor, including Tchaikovsky's rooms, as barracks. But by May 1945 the damage had been made good, Tchaikovsky's personal effects were returned from safekeeping, and the museum was reopened for Victory Day, May 9.

Although Tchaikovsky stayed here such a short time, it is one of the most romantic places near Moscow. His servant (and lover), Alexei Sofronov, lived with his family on the lower floor while Tchaikovsky occupied the upper rooms which are furnished as they were in the composer's lifetime. The winners of the International Tchaikovsky

Competition, held every four years, are invited to play on the master's grand piano, and every year on May 7 and November 6, the anniversaries of his birth and death, Russian pianists give concerts here.

Tchaikovsky often visited his friends, the Taneevs, at their estate at **Demyanovo**, across the Leningrad Highway. *Take the left fork on the Leningrad Highway and, before the Tchaikovsky Museum, take the first unmarked road, left, Proezd Taneeva, by the tall blocks of flats and wall of concrete slabs and cross the stream to the main house.*

It is immediately apparent that this once grand estate is now nothing but a rotting hulk. The **house** was built in the 1770s, by the Naumov family who also built the equally ruined church. It then passed through various owners until in the early 19th century it was settled on D.B. Mertvy as dowry settlement. The Mertvys entertained their friend, Vladimir Pushkin, in 1811 on his way to St Petersburg with his young nephew, the future poet Alexander, to enter him at the Tsarksoe Selo lycee. In 1883 Demyanovo was acquired by the philosopher and liberal barrister, Vladimir Taneev, whose brother, the composer, Sergei Taneev, was a close friend of Tchaikovsky. The Taneevs attracted many members of the intellectual and artistic elite including Kliment Timiryazev, the biologist expelled from the University in 1911 for espousing Darwin, Alexander Skryabin, the composer, and Andrei Bely, the symbolist writer who wrote about Demyanovo. Taneev lived in the two-storey **guest house**, left, near the long weavers' block with the impressive buttresses.

The **Church of the Assumption**, *Uspeniya*, is located in the overgrown cemetery – from the house turn right and then left. The church is equally ruined but it is just possible to discern its restrained baroque details. The remaining buildings of the estate are used as a long-stay tuberculosis hospital. But the terribly overgrown grounds, the dilapidation and the neglect, scarcely provide an encouraging ambiance for patients seeking to regain their health.

SOUTH AND WEST OF KLIN

Going north on the Leningrad Highway in Klin make a U-turn at the end of the boulevard, return to the traffic lights and turn right at the war memorial and Church of All Sorrows onto Liteinaya Street (A-108). Go past the old glass factory, over the railway bridge, keeping left in the suburb of Pershutino where a delightful chapel of 1905 has recently been rescued. At the GAI post turn right signed VYSOKOVSK. In 3 km a main road joins from the right and less than 1 km farther, turn left for **SELINSKOE.**

In the centre of the village stands the green and white **Church of the Transfiguration**, *Preobrazheniya*, bearing a blue cupola. It was completed in 1831 in the late classical style and was never added to or rebuilt. The north and south entrances are enlivened by Tuscan porticoes with pediments and the round apse juts out provocatively imitating the curves of the rotunda with its small cupola. It was closed only for a short time during the war and has kept its fine iconostasis of the 1880s. The **war memorial** almost hidden in the undergrowth bears a painfully long list of names of those who gave their lives in the war, almost fifty from Selinskoe alone.

Return to the A-108 at the GAI post signed NOVOPETROVSKOE. The quiet road passes through dense woods dotted with signs to rest homes and pioneer camps. Turn left for Nikolskoe at the 21 km post signed NIKOLAEVKA, ignore the next right turn to Nikolaevka, and follow the paved road for 7 km to Nikolskoe.

NIKOLSKOE nestles on the bank of the small Chernaya River surrounded by green fields which roll away to distant woods. A broad lane with a wide grassed area separates two rows of fine wooden houses closed at the northern end by the church. In the summer children whizz around on bicycles, meeting periodically at the bus-stop which seems to serve as the local club.

Originally known as Sverchkovo, it is famous as the birthplace of two serf/master builders of the late 17th century. **Yakov Bukhvostov**, a serf born in the mid 17th century to the influential Boyar, Mikhail Tatishchev. Little is known of Bukhvostov's early life but he was granted his freedom by Tatishchev when he was recognised in the 1690s as an outstanding builder of Moscow baroque; his masterpiece is the great tower church at Ubory, west of Moscow. **Trofim Ignatiev**, who rebuilt the Joseph-Volokolamsk Monastery in the late 17th century, was also born here.

Elegant **St Nicholas**, its windows bare of glass, trees firmly rooted in its upper parts, and bereft of the bell tower, was built in 1738 in the western baroque style with fine brickwork, and white stone pilasters, windows and doorways. It is rectangular with a round apse, a tall round upper storey, and drum, dome, and onion-shaped cupola. When we visited, it was very clean inside where a makeshift altar of twigs had been erected at the eastern end. A group of ladies from the Klin excursion bureau told us services had restarted and there are plans for repairs although a sponsor has yet to be found.

As for Nikolskoe on the A-108 from Klin but instead of following the road as it curves left towards Shekino, turn sharp right at some shabby farm buildings and three-storey blocks of flats onto a dirt road (muddy if wet). After a few metres cross the bridge over the Nudol River up the hill to **PODZHIGORODOVO**.

The **Church of Michael the Archangel** built 1778-83 for the Yuriev family, ancestors of the Romanov tsars, stands alone on the left, a slim Gothic fantasy like the silhouette of a ship. All the elements of the Orthodox system of bell tower, *trapeza*, church and apse are expressed in a most individual way suggesting it might be by Vasily Bazhenov or his pupil. The round bell tower rises like a lighthouse from the cube base to the platform balcony where the bells hang and culminates in a slim conical spire. The square *trapeza* on the west perfectly matches the apse on the east in size and shape. The Gothic pointed windows of the lower church are repeated in the main church above which is also lit by round windows. Arrow-like chevrons over the central windows remind one of Moscow's St Basil. The broad roof is punctuated with lucarne windows and topped by a lantern and small conical spire and cross. Originally dramatic in red brick with white stone detailing, in 1906 it was stuccoed and painted white losing something of its vigour. Interior oil paintings of the early 20th century survive but the interesting original iconostasis has lost its icons. Fortunately services have restarted and repairs instituted for this unique building.

On the A-108 travel south 28 km from Klin. Just before crossing the Nudol River take a right turn on a good unmarked road and then immediately left and park by a gate. This is the former estate of **VYSOKOE**. Now a house of rest, the first impression is of a jumble of unrelated run-down buildings. But on the left on the high river bank stands a once fine wooden house with columns and pediments in the Russian classical style. It is approached by an avenue of limes and flanked by two smaller wooden houses or wings.

It is in appalling condition. At the front the columns have been sawn in half, it has been painted garish colours – happily now much faded – and its insides are literally falling apart. But from the back the four columns, porch and pediment face the slope to the river and marvellous views beyond, a perfect setting for the Rostov family in *War and Peace*. The Tuscan columns are in such a state of decay that one can see how they were made: circular discs were placed at intervals around a thin log, the space between filled in and an outer layer of curved thin strips of wood placed to cover the whole, giving the impression of solid wood. Vysokoe was built in the early 1800s by the Volkov family who owned it until the revolution. The connection with Tolstoy's *War and Peace* is not just imaginary: Volkov's sister, Mariya, describes in her memoirs how her young brother, Nikolai, returned suddenly to Vysokoe from Paris, an episode which Tolstoy used for Nikolai Rostov. Sadly there seems to be no interest in repairing this unique building which so clearly evokes the life of the gentry of the early 19th century.

A little farther on, turn right at Nudol to Vertkovo and from there 5 km to the former grand estate of the Soimonovs, **Teploe**, where only the lonely **Church of the Sign**, *Znamenie*, built in 1797 in the Palladian style (possibly by Nikolai Lvov) survives.

Leave Klin on Liteinaya Street over the railway bridge to the GAI post and turn right signed VYSOKOVSK for 10 km. At Vysokovsk turn left and then, where the main road leads to Teryaevo, turn sharp right. Pass **Shipulina***, right and the Church of the Resurrection, Voskreseniya, built in 1800-2, and continue to join the bypass. Turn left in 5 km towards Vygol through woods and lonely fields to* **ZHESTOKI** *(cruel) a strange name for the lovely village.* To the left, sitting unselfconsciously in a field, is an enchanting **octagonal wooden chapel** repaired in the early 1990s with a single cupola and, as was usual in chapels, no apse. It is *v lapu*, of notched logs, covered with planed boards, an attractive cornice and arcaded frieze. The gently sloping ceiling within was painted with saints as a *nebo* or heaven. It was apparently built in 1873 to provide a place of worship for the isolated village, often cut off by floods and snow. In Soviet times it was used to house horses. Compare it with the new chapel at Vozdvizhenskoe, 15 km west, built of ugly concrete bricks to replace the five churches pulled down there after the revolution.

Road 10   VOLOKOLAMSK HIGHWAY M-9:
ARKHANGELSKOE TO
VOLOKOLAMSK

The Volokolamsk Highway stretches 120 km from Moscow encompassing the two ancient monastery towns of Istra and Volokolamsk, and many delightful places on rivers and reservoirs including, on the Moskva River, former summer homes of the nobility and secluded dachas of the Soviet elite.

The unpolluted Moskva River west of the city was a popular place for summer retreats. The aristocratic Ilinsky Road, A-106, on the left, north bank is replete with opulent houses of princes and grand dukes while facing them, on the Uspensky Road, A-105, on the right, south bank are the luxurious dachas of the Soviet leaders.

THE ARISTOCRACY ON THE LEFT BANK:
ILINSKY ROAD A-106

Take the Leningradsky Prospekt/Volokolamskoe Shosse and pass under the Moscow-Volga Canal and then the MKAD veering left to join the Ilinsky Road, A-106. Continue past Krasnogorsk and under the M-9 to the well signposted Arkhangelskoe. The car park is just past the estate, right. (Closed Mondays and Tuesdays.)

The **ARKHANGELSKOE** estate is associated with some of the greatest families of Russia. In the 1660s it belonged to **Prince Yakov Odoevsky** who constructed the church, Michael the Archangel, which gives the estate its name. From 1681 to 1703 in the hands of the boyar, Prince Mikhail Cherkassky, it then passed to **Prince Dmitry Golitsyn**, the erudite friend of Peter the Great and a great bibliophile. On the death of Peter II, Prince Golitsyn with others tried to limit the powers of the new empress, Anna, but she tore up the agreement and Golitsyn was sent to the notorious Shlisselburg fortress where he died. His great library of 6,000 books confiscated by Anna's ministers was partially returned when Empress Elizabeth restored the estate to Golitsyn's son, Alexei. Golitsyn's grandson, **Nikolai**, the senator and ambassador, built the present house in the 1780s and laid out the park. In 1810 his widow

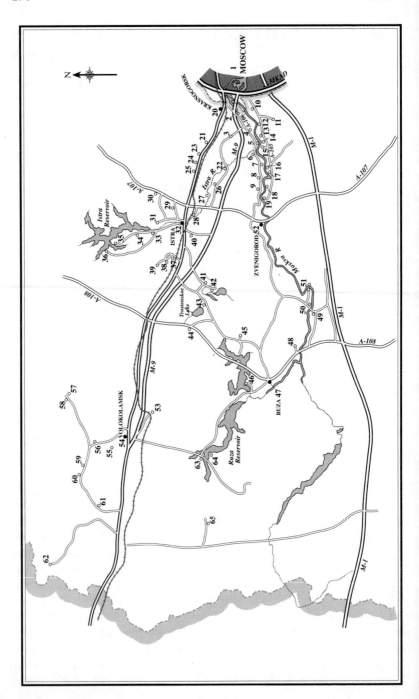

ROAD 10
ARKHANGELSKOE TO VOLOKOLAMSK

1. MOSCOW
2. Arkhangelskoe
3. Nikolskoe-Uryupino
4. Ilinskoe
5. Petrovo-Dalnee
6. Dmitrovskoe
7. Ubory
8. Nikolina-Gora
9. Aksinino
10. Razdory
11. Barvikha
12. Zhukovka
13. Usovo
14. Kalchuga
15. Znamenskoe
16. Uspenskoe
17. Gorki 10
18. Islavskoe
19. Dunino
20. KRASNOGORSK
21. Nakhabino
22. Pavlovskaya Sloboda
23. Dedovsk
24. Sadki
25. Lenino
26. Anosino
27. Luzhki
28. Troitskoe
29. Darna
30. Kholmy
31. Polevshino
32. ISTRA
33. Buzharovo
34. Lamishino
35. Rozhdestveno
36. Ivanovskoe-Kozlovskoe
37. Brykovo
38. Glebovo
39. Filatovo
40. Pokrovskoe-Rubtsovo
41. Nikolsky Pogost
42. Yurkino
43. Onufrievo
44. Nikolskoe-Gagarino
45. Annino
46. Volynshchina
47. RUZA
48. Maleevka
49. Tuchkovo
50. Poreche
51. Vasilievskoe
52. ZVENIGOROD
53. Dubosekovo
54. VOLOKOLAMSK
55. Ivanovskoe (Bezobrazovo)
56. Kashino
57. Spirovo
58. Joseph-Volokolamsk Monastery
59. Yaropolets
60. Fedorovskoe
61. Belaya Kolp
62. Markovo
63. Ostashevo
64. Brazhnikovo
65. Peski

sold the property to another equally remarkable grandee, **Prince Nikolai Yusupov**. The peripatetic library was then removed to the Golitsyns' estate at nearby Nikolskoe-Uryupino but, like homing pigeons, some of the books since the revolution have found their way back to the considerable Arkhangelskoe library.

Prince Nikolai Yusupov was highly educated, head of the imperial theatres and a connoisseur of the visual arts. Commissioned in 1791 by Empress Catherine to purchase paintings abroad, he took the opportunity to add to his own collection (virtually no Russian art) which he moved to Arkhangelskoe. But as Yusupov settled in, **Napoleon** invaded. The paintings were removed in time but the buildings suffered badly not only under French occupation but in a subsequent serf uprising. In 1820 Arkhangelskoe was again damaged, this time by fire, but the paintings were saved yet again. After Yusupov's death in 1831 the estate stagnated but revived in the early 1900s under the Prince's descendants, the **Sumarokov-Elstons**. In 1916 the Moscow architect, Roman Klein, built the spectacular family mausoleum.

In the woods, left from the car park, is Yusupov's old **theatre**, one of the few surviving from the early 19th century. Of wood and stucco it was built in 1817 to the design of the Moscow architect, **Osip Bove**, and the Italian artist and landscape gardener, **Pietro Gonzago**. Long disused, in the 1920s some stage machinery, painted curtains, and a few of the Gonzago sets were discovered. In its heyday at a command of the libidinous Yusupov, the serf actresses would instantly disrobe to the delight of the mostly male audience.

Beyond the main gates are great iron **triumphal gates**, built by Stepan Melnikov in 1817, opening into the inner courtyard. Wings built in the late 18th century are linked by colonnades to the palace forming a **cour d'honneur**. The **palace**, with its many paintings and antique sculpture, was built in the 1790s to a plan by the French architect, **Charles de Guerne**, and is of two storeys each room opening onto the next. The exterior has remained much as it was under the Golitsyns but some of the interior rooms including the **Hubert Robert** and **Tiepolo** rooms were modified by the serf architect, Vasily Strizhakov, in 1816 under the supervision of Osip Bove. The architect **Yevgraf Tyurin** and artist **Nicholas de Courteille**, who painted many of the ceilings, completed the redecoration after the fire of 1820. Overlooking the park is a great **Oval Hall** ringed by Corinthian marble columns and dominated by the huge 1830s triple-tiered Russian chandelier.

The relatively unchanged carefully tended **grounds** between the house
and the river consist of the formal French garden and the more natural
English park. Where the garden abuts the sharp river escarpment are
two three-storey Stalin classical buildings of 1937 – a **sanatorium** for the
Ministry of Defence. Although lugubrious they are not unduly offensive
and offer fine views of the river and the Yusupov palace.

The palace faces the river from two splendid **terraces**; the larger lower
terrace with a fountain at the centre was laid out at the end of the 18th
century by the Italian, Giacomo Lombara. They are festooned with
copies of antique sculptures of which there are more than 200 in the
park, some from other estates. To the right and left on the carefully
tended grass are several pavilions and memorials. The first right, as you
face the river, is a brick temple to **Catherine II**, Yusupov's patron, built
by Tyurin in 1819. Within is a bronze statue of the Empress as Themis,
the goddess of justice, by the sculptor, Jacques Rachette.

Left of the terrace (facing the river) is the 1903 bust of **Pushkin** with
lines from his flattering poem about Prince Nikolai, *To a Grandee*. On
the avenue, right, a tall **column** bearing a bronze eagle commemorates
the visit of Nicholas I and his son, Grand Duke Michael, in the summer
of 1826, the year of his coronation. At the end of the avenue are two
park structures of the 18th century, the small **Caprice** palace built for
Golitsyn's wife, and the 18th century **Tea Pavilion**, containing Antokolsky's 1902 tomb of Princess Tatyana Yusupova. On the left side of the
lawn is the charming **Rose Pavilion**, a canopy with marble columns and
a wooden roof in the centre of which sits Cupid with a swan.

Follow the paved path left. On the right is the family **mausoleum**
perched dramatically on a steep ravine completed in 1916 by Roman
Klein only a year before the revolution and fated never to be used. The
church in appropriate classical style with columns, pediment and
rotunda is decorated with a frieze in bas-relief and is wonderfully
enhanced by the sweeping curve of the colonnade.

Over the ravine stands a picturesque **gate**, a store room of the late 18th
century with a passageway through the lower floor for a long disused
road to a ford. Farther on are the **Holy Gates**, modelled on a Roman
triumphal arch built in 1824 by Tyurin as the entrance to the traditional
Church of Michael the Archangel, perched on the high cliff of the
Moskva, refreshing to an eye by now sated with classical columns,
pediments and statuary. It was built of brick in 1667 by Boyar Yakov

Odoevsky probably by his serf master-builder, **Pavel Potekhin**, as a cube with gables clustering around the drum of the wooden cupola, a north chapel and a porch – the south chapel is later. The original iconostasis has gone but services are once again being held. Around the church are Yusupov family graves.

From Krasnogorsk on the Ilinsky Road, A-106, pass Arkhangelskoe and in 2 km at Glukhovo turn right 4 km under the Volokolamsk Highway M-9, then left and then right past a large rest house to Nikolskoe-Uryupino.

The peaceful scene at **NIKOLSKOE-URYUPINO** where two classical mansions, left, look across the pond to the seductive, 17th century Church of St Nicholas is deceptive for the army is in residence here. In the 17th century the village was owned by Prince Nikita Odoevsky, a powerful courtier, whose son Yakov, was the landlord of nearby Arkhangelskoe. After several changes of ownership, Nikolskoe-Uryupino and Arkhangelskoe were reunited under the same families in 1774 when Nikolai Golitsyn purchased Nikolskoe-Uryupino. In 1810 the two estates once again went their separate ways when Arkhangelskoe was acquired by the Yusupovs. The Golitsyns remained at Nikolskoe-Uryupino until 1917.

St Nicholas was built in 1664-5 for Nikita Odoevsky by his talented serf master-builder, **Pavel Potekhin**, probably also the builder of the more modest church at Arkhangelskoe for Nikita's son, Yakov, and the splendid church at Markovo, which shares features with St Nicholas. Its squat hunched shape is relieved by four tiers of gables around the central cupola. The design, as at Markovo, is of a cube supporting a central dome while four smaller chapels with domes mimic the main church on the four corners. Two of the chapels are ranged on either side of the central church, and two stand over the western open gallery, with the amusing 19th century belfry between them. It is a pity the red brick is now whitewashed, obliterating the traditional contrast of stone dressings against a red background. In the 1980s after decades as a grain store, it was cleared out and restoration work undertaken which revealed the delightful tiers of *kokoshniki* gables at roof level. Finally, St Nicholas was returned to the church in the early 1990s. Near the eastern apse and the war memorial are a few desolate graves of the Golitsyns including Prince Nikolai and his wife.

The gate through the fence to the **White House**, the older and more delightful of the two **mansions**, is usually locked but there is a convenient hole near the bus-stop for intrepid visitors. Intended as a hunting lodge, it was built in 1780 of one storey to the design sent from France of Charles de Guerne, the architect of the palace at Arkhangelskoe. The elegant facade combines Ionic and Corinthian columns and pilasters, small pediments and bas-reliefs on antique themes. The interior is exceptionally fine, an enfilade of rooms leading to the central Gold Room decorated with grisaille paintings by Boucher. At the back an exquisite loggia faces what was once a formal garden surrounded by a wilder park with much garden statuary. The caretaker can sometimes be persuaded to open the house to visitors.

The single-storey **Great House** next door built 1809-11 by one of the Golitsyn serf-architects served as the principal mansion. Its stark severity is enhanced by the heavy pediment that threatens to overburden the slim columns. After the revolution, the house became a museum but in 1929 was closed, and Nikolskoe-Uryupino was handed over to the army for **rocket development**. It was here in August, 1933 that the young scientist, **Sergei Korolev**, successfully launched the first liquid-fuelled Soviet rocket. To see the memorial, a tall white rocket, go along the pond past the main house and left along the path. Even these days the peace of the old estate can be suddenly shattered by a warning siren and a huge bang as a rocket is launched.

On the Ilinsky Road A-106, 7 km from Arkhangelskoe (or from Ruble-vskoe Shosse, turn left 10 km then right to the bridge across the Moskva, then left again) to Ilinskoe.

The estate of **ILINSKOE** was purchased in 1864 by **Empress, Mariya Alexandrovna**, wife of Alexander II, and in 1882 transferred to her son, **Grand Duke Sergei Alexandrovich**, uncle of Nicholas II and Governor-General of Moscow. Here his wife, **Elizaveta, Princess of Darmstadt**, wrote warm letters to her grandmother, Queen Victoria. In 1905 the deeply unpopular Grand Duke was assassinated by a terrorist and Eliza-veta, who had born the unhappy marriage uncomplainingly, devoted herself to charity. (In 1918 she died horribly at the hands of the Bolsheviks and has recently been canonised.) Ilinskoe passed to the nephew of Sergei Alexandrovich, **Grand Duke Dmitry Pavlovich**, in whose hands it remained until the establishment of Bolshevik power. The main house burnt down in 1917 and only the church and a classical pavilion survive.

The **Church of St Elijah**, *Ilii*, in the baroque style was built 1732-5 when Illinskoe was owned by the Streshnevs and is probably by Alexei

Yevlashev. With the addition in 1818 of two side chapels and, a decade later, the Empire bell tower, the church lost much of the baroque detailing although traces persist on the apse, the frieze, and on the surviving capitals. St Elijah was closed in 1937 and reopened in 1991 when much-needed repairs were set in train. The ochre-painted gate next door leads to a government dacha on the river where the grand ducal house once stood.

Continue through Alexandrovka to Petrovo-Dalnee, about 3 km from Ilinskoe.

Another summer home of the nobility stands by the Moskva at its confluence with the Istra. **Petrovskoe** was renamed **PETROVO-DALNEE** (the farther) in Soviet times to distinguish it from others of the same name.

On the left, opposite the signed right turn to the Mechnikov Biology Institute, are the walls and gates of Petrovskoe. The first gate once led to the Assumption Church, one of the earliest examples of the Moscow baroque style, which was demolished in the 1950s. On the right remnants of the stables and service buildings are on an axis with the main house. Now a holiday home run by the Ministry of Health tight security is in force but a polite request to the guardians of the gate should result in permission to look around.

Petrovskoe has a chequered princely history revolving around the **Golitsyn** family. In 1643 it was given as a dowry to Praskovya Likha-cheva on her marriage to Prince Ivan Prozorovsky. The unfortunate prince met an untimely death in 1670 when as Voevod (governor) of Astrakhan he was murdered together with one of his sons by the peasant insurgent, Stenka Razin. Another son, 9-year-old Boris, the future friend of Peter the Great, was strung up by the feet and only just survived, spending the rest of his life as a cripple. Prince Prozorovsky's strong-willed eccentric granddaughter, Anastasiya, married Prince Ivan Golitsyn thereby delivering Petrovskoe into the Golitsyn family. As a member of Peter's exclusive drinking club, Anastasiya attended the Tsar's feasts playing the part of the fool. In 1718 she was accused of supporting the Tsarevich Alexei and suffered public flogging and exile. When Catherine I came to the throne in 1725 Anastasiya was allowed to return to Moscow.

Fedor, Anastasia's son, was a favourite of the Empress Elizabeth who visited Petrovskoe in 1749 in the company of Ivan Shuvalov, the founder of Moscow University. Shuvalov's sister married Fedor's son, Nikolai, and inherited part of her brother's great library and art collection which was soon embellishing the rooms at Petrovskoe. It was her son, **Fedor Nikolaevich**, (1751-1827), one of the most educated men of his day, who between 1803 and 1807 rebuilt the main house in the form in which it survives.

In 1812 as the French army approached Petrovskoe, Prince Fedor hastily buried his valuables and made his escape. The French turned the elegant mansion with its recently completed interiors into a field hospital and used the doors for target practice. Petrovskoe then passed to Fedor's nephew, **Prince Vladimir Golitsyn**, 1847-1932, Moscow's *golova* or mayor, 1897-1905. The last owner before the revolution was Prince Alexander Golitsyn, a doctor, who built the local hospital.

Petrovskoe like so many other former noble estates became a refuge for homeless waifs, then a museum, then, in 1930, the **Mechnikov Institute for Infectious Diseases** which used the house as a laboratory for making vaccines. Only in the 1960s was the institute moved to more appropriate accommodation and the buildings repaired (even to the Golitsyn coat of arms in the pediment) and turned into a rest home.

Right of the gate is an attractive early 19th century house with columns and pediment. At right angles to it flanking the main courtyard is one of the two detached red and white **guest houses** built in the 1770s in the expressive Gothic style then in vogue. The **main house** with a loggia of four columns supporting the pediment with the Golitsyn crest sits on the brow of the cliff over the swollen Moskva River looking towards Znamenskoe. Within, the impressive hall and principal room, the *Krasnaya Gostinaya*, have been sensitively restored. At the back a fine Corinthian portico overlooks the river and vastly overgrown park and ponds.

Two **obelisks** which belonged to Petrovskoe stand where the road turns sharp right, forming the entrance to a government dacha given to **Khrushchev** after his forcible retirement in 1964.

From Ilinsky Road travel west over the Istra to **Dmitrovskoe** *where the red and white* **Church of Dmitry Solunsky** *built in 1689 by the conservative patriarch, Joachim, with its tent-shaped bell tower and fine north portal, makes a striking silhouette above the river. Turn left, west, following the high bank of the Moskva 3 km to an angled junction and make the* *awkward left turn to* **UBORY**. If the church at Dmitrovskoe built in 1689 represents conservative forces, the splendid Moscow baroque tower at Ubory, the **Church of the Saviour**, *Spasa*, begun only five years later for Petr Sheremetiev-Menshoi (the Younger), symbolises the forward-looking policies of Peter the Great.

The architect of the Ubory church is not only known, but his tribulations have been recorded. **Yakov Bukhvostov**, born a serf of the Tatishchev family, was freed to pursue his career as a master stone mason by his enlightened owner. He contracted to complete the Sheremetiev church in two years but work at Ubory was held up by delivery of materials and, more importantly, by Sheremetiev himself who suddenly decided to add a tall cube to support the octagonal tiers of the central tower. When Bukhvostov refused to demolish the partially completed building, Sheremetiev had him brought to court where he was sentenced to flailing by the knout. But Sheremetiev relented, the sentence was not carried out, and Bukhvostov completed the church in 1697 in the form desired by the client.

The glorious soaring **red brick tower** with contrasting stone lace-like ornamentation set on a promontory above the Moskva can be seen for miles around. The cube which supports the upper tiers rises out of the four petal-like symmetrical lobes which form the three entrances and the apse linked by a broad open terrace. Above the cube rise two receding octagonal towers – the upper containing the bells – bearing the drum and elegant, slim cupola with the tall cross. The tiers, windows and columns are richly embellished with elaborate stone carvings of vines and plants. The church, restored in the 1950s, has recently reopened for worship. Regrettably, the elaborate eight-tier iconostasis disappeared long ago.

A walk along the river bank by remnants of the ponds and park is soon interrupted by modern high-rise blocks behind a high fence closed to the public. This is another side of Ubory: a luxurious vacation establishment, a 'sanatorium', built in the 1970s for the Soviet elite and used by the new *nomenklatura*.

Continue west from Ubory rejoining the road from Dmitrovskoe which veers north through fields to avoid the sanatorium. Once, coming over a mound in the road, we were amazed to see in the shimmering sun a huge banner with the unmistakable visage of **Stalin** in the sky overhead. Our confusion was soon explained – amid the waving wheat was a clutch of people and cameras shooting the horrific ending of the film *Burnt by the Sun (Utomlennoe Solntsem)*. The director, Nikita Mikhalkov, used his own dacha in Nikolina-Gora (see below) as the setting for the film.

About 5 km from Ubory the road veers left and dips down to **NIKOLINA-GORA** where the road becomes Prokofiev Street and dachas with gardens and high wooden fences appear left and right. Nikolina-Gora, in a loop of the Moskva River, was formed in the late 1920s when the large wooden houses, many with exclusive access to the river front, were constructed. Among its first inhabitants were **Alexei Tolstoy**, the writer, and the notorious **Andrei Vyshinsky**, then rector of Moscow University. In the course of time they were joined by many other well-known members of the arts and sciences and it continues today to be a haven for their descendants.

At the T-junction of Prokofiev Street with the road to Zvenigorod and Uspenskoe, is the attractive ochre-coloured dacha, right, of the composer, **Sergei Prokofiev**, still used by his family. Across the Zvenigorod road a row of superior dachas front the Moskva River. **Andrei Vyshinsky**, the evil public prosecutor in the show trials, schemed to acquire the dacha with river frontage which then belonged to Leonid Serebryakov, the Central Committee secretary. Forced to act as a key witness in the 1937 Kamenev-Zinoviev trial, Serebryakov was himself tried and shot and his wife and daughter sent to concentration camps. Vyshinsky grabbed the Serebryakov dacha even before the trials were over, refurbished it at public expense, and entertained Stalin there. Now, more than 60 years later, the dacha is finally back in the hands of Serebryakov's elderly daughter, a survivor of 17 years in the gulag.

The dacha of the Nobel prize-winning physicist, **Peter Kapitsa**, lies right of the road by the river. A brilliant young Soviet physicist, Kapitsa worked for many years in Cambridge with Lord Rutherford. But in the 1930s during a return visit to his mother, he was virtually kidnapped and forced to remain in the Soviet Union. He managed to continue working in a new laboratory in Moscow using equipment kindly sent by Lord Rutherford but in 1945, when he refused to work on the atomic bomb, he came under serious threat from Beria and retreated for safety to his dacha at Nikolina-Gora. Here for the third time in his life he set up a new laboratory making most of the equipment himself. Visitors who book in advance will be shown his workplace and the beautiful hand-made apparatus.

From here it is 10 km to Zvenigorod through **Aksinino** *where the dilapi-*
dated red brick church has been repaired and reopened with the support
of film director Nikita Mikhalkov.

THE SOVIET ELITE ON THE RIGHT BANK:
USPENSKY ROAD A-105

In Soviet times the Moscow highway with the best surface was the
minor, immaculately paved Uspensky Road conspicuously guarded by
GAI posts. For ordinary motorists travel was unpleasant as sleek black
Zils and Chaikas, their lights flashing, travelled imperiously at high
speed in the middle of the road taking the leaders to and from their
country homes. Today this road still serves the heavily guarded dachas
for top government chiefs.

In Moscow on Rublevskoe Shosse travel 7 km to the intersection with the
MKAD. Veer left to join the Uspensky Road A-105 which runs parallel to
the Moskva River through wooded country, over the Usovo railway line to
Razdory and Barvikha station. Turn left (south) marked PODUSH-
KINSKOE SHOSSE 2 km.

BARVIKHA has not only an elite sanatorium but a romantic
mansion. Set well back, right, it resembles a forbidding Scottish castle
complete with turrets, crow-stepped gables and steeply pitched roofs.
It was built 1874-85 by Petr Boitsov, co-author with Roman Klein of
the Pushkin Museum, for the wealthy **Nadezhda Kazakova**.
Nadezhda, left a widow when her husband died at sea, chose as her
second husband the impoverished baron, **Bogdan Maiendorf**, who
brought his title and Baltic family connections to the marriage in
return for the fabulous castle and considerable wealth. Together they
amassed a fine collection of weapons and paintings and displayed
them in the luxuriously furnished house. One of their more original
ideas was to attach a valuable tapestry to the ceiling of the salon
which is still there after failed attempts by Tretyakov Gallery officials
to dislodge it. The Maiendorfs' splendid house became an orphanage,
then in the 1930s the elite **sanatorium** serving Soviet leaders. New
buildings appeared by the river including an interesting block with
glass bays designed 1929-34 by Boris Iofan, architect of the doomed
Palace of Soviets. Boris Yeltsin stayed there when recuperating from
his heart illnesses.

On request the genial caretaker will unlock the rooms of the darkly

Gothic interior. Although the furniture has long gone the wood panelling, the fine plasterwork ceilings and the carved wooden doors and
staircases remain. Besides the ceiling tapestry the salon (now the library)
has a huge fireplace with the monogram 'H X', House of Ikskul, the
ancient name of the Maiendorf family. The house, now a local children's
club, can be hired for receptions.

Return to the Uspensky Road and turn left 2 km for Zhukovka.

ZHUKOVKA is a strange place. It was created 1924-6 when the
frequently flooded village of **Lutskoe** across the Moskva River near
Ilinskoe, was transferred here. In the late 1920s Soviet leaders moved
into the old Zubalov summer houses nearby which meant that the area,
to the extreme discomfort of the Lutskoe villagers, was taken over by
the secret police under the dreaded **Nikolai Yezhov**. The Spanish
communist **Dolores Ibarruri**, Khrushchev's Minister of Culture
Yekaterina Furtseva, Stalin's Foreign Minister **Vyacheslav Molotov**, and
many other communist leaders had dachas here.

More recent Zhukovka dachas are by the river, right, past the petrol
station and shop. On the left lane the house (right side) with oriental
decoration belonged to **Tsedenbal**, former First Party Secretary of
Mongolia. Facing it on the left side was **Grishin's** dacha, Moscow's
long-reigning party secretary, replaced by Yeltsin in 1985. By the river
bank, right, is the dacha of the artist, **Ilya Glazunov**, who turned with
the times from painting sycophantic portraits of Soviet leaders to
patriotic and religious themes and is in charge of the frescoes in the
rebuilt Christ the Saviour Cathedral.

The comfortable dachas of the **Academicians' Village**, *Akademgorodok*,
left of the main road, were built at Zhukovka in the late 1940s for top
scientists, musicians, and other leading intellectuals of the Soviet Union.
Among the residents were the composer, **Dmitry Shostakovich**, dissident
and physicist **Andrei Sakharov**, and the cellist, **Mstislav Rostropovich**,
who gave refuge there to the writer, **Alexander Solzhenitsyn**, before his
expulsion from Russia.

*Continue on the Uspensky Road, ignoring the right turn to the bridge over
the Moskva, to* **USOVO** *which belonged before the revolution to the
grand ducal estate.* A small settlement called Ogarevo served the estate,
and it was here, at the so-called **Novo-Ogarevo Dacha**, that a series of
historic meetings took place in 1991 when Mikhail Gorbachev tried to

persuade the leaders of the Republics to conclude a new union treaty to prevent the break-up of the USSR.

Beyond Usovo station in the hamlet of **Kalchuga**, where the little river Medvenka flows into the Moskva, was the summer home of the Baku oil-rich Zubalovs. **Lev Zubalov** like Stalin seems to have suffered from persecution mania, for his dacha was surrounded by a high brick wall and within he built identical houses so that it would not be obvious which one he was living in. After the revolution the Zubalovs left and **Felix Dzerzhinsky**, head of the secret police, suggested the convenient Zubalov mansions would make good summer houses for Party leaders. **Stalin**, apparently, took Zubalovo 4 and other Party leaders, including Mikoyan and Voroshilov, occupied the rest. Stalin must have relished the irony of living in the summer home of the Baku and Batumi oilmen who in his youth he conspired to undermine. **Mikoyan**, according to Svetlana Stalin, carefully kept his dacha unchanged from the Zubalov days, even preserving the original furniture and garden statuary. Stalin, on the other hand, constantly altered his and after his wife committed suicide no longer went to Zubalovo. Mikoyan continued to use Zubalovo until his retirement in 1966 when he was unceremoniously evicted. These splendid summer houses continue to be government property closed to the public.

Return to the Uspensky Road and continue west to take the signed right turning to **ZNAMENSKOE**, *the village poised on the high bank of the Moskva.* Znamenskoe is part of the **Gorki-2 collective farm** founded in 1924 by Dzerzhinsky and the OGPU (secret police) to provide fresh produce for the Party bosses at Usovo and Barvikha. One of the earliest collective farms, it had access to the latest equipment and imported livestock. Needless to say its production figures were always high and it was constantly shown to visiting foreigners.

In 1742 Empress Elizabeth, daughter of Peter the Great, presented Znamenskoe to her favourite, **Alexei Razumovsky**. In 1769 Razumovsky built the **Church of the Sign**, *Ikony Bozhiei Materi 'Znamenie'*, in the baroque style associated with Elizabeth. Razumovsky's brother, Kirill, sold Znamenskoe to Elizabeth's second favourite, **Ivan Shuvalov**, and it was inherited by Shuvalov's sister, wife of Prince Nikolai Golitsyn of Petrovskoe (across the river near the large green sanatorium). The square-shaped church softened by rounded corners and lacking an extruding apse, has three identical facades comprising pediment, long elaborate baroque windows and identically decorated doors. On the fourth, west side the short bell tower with slim spire holds sway but the drum and cupola are rather small. The now functioning church which was used for many years as a granary suffered further from fire during the filming in the 1980s of Turgeniev's *Nest of Gentle Folk*.

Continue west on the Uspensky Road past the GAI post and traffic lights controlling the bridge to Nikolina-Gora to **USPENSKOE**. *Turn right at the war memorial and right again.* Here is another astonishing Scottish baronial pile, now an Academy of Sciences hospital, next to a delightful church overlooking the river. In the 1880s **Prince Boris Svyatopolk-Chetvertinsky** purchased Uspenskoe and built the palatial house with turrets and stepped gables to the design of the same Petr Boitsov of the even grander mansion at Barvikha. In 1892 Uspenskoe was purchased by **Sergei Morozov**, brother of Savva, the rich mill owner who had a dacha nearby. Sergei, who founded the Museum of Folk Art in Moscow, was patron of **Isaak Levitan**, the landscape artist, who came often to Uspenskoe. Once, in 1897, Levitan inveigled his close friend, **Anton Chekhov**, into joining him here. Chekhov, who had little respect for merchants, wrote scathingly that '*the house was like the Vatican, the lackeys were in pique waistcoats with gold chains on their stomachs, the furniture was tasteless, the wine from Levé's, the host had no expression on his face, and I ran away*'. After the revolution, it became a children's home, then the Horse Breeding Institute and finally the hospital.

Next door is the interesting **Church of the Assumption**, *Uspeniya*, now functioning again. It was built about 1730 for **Count Petr Apraxin**, whose sister, Martha, in 1682 married Tsar Fedor III. The style is old-fashioned especially the tent-shaped bell tower and the octagonal double drum but Petrine baroque has crept in in the semicircular arch which interrupts the roof and the attractive octagonal windows over the north and south doors. Unusually the interior has no wall paintings.

Continue 3 km beyond Uspenskoe to **GORKI 10**. The enigmatic Gorki 2 and Gorki 10 do not refer to the writer Maxim Gorky, whose name in Russian is spelt quite differently, but to 'little hill'. Nevertheless, **Maxim Gorky** does have strong associations with this place. Across the little river, Vyazemka, opposite a police station is a high fence with forbidding entry gates concealing highly prestigious government dachas. One of them, **Savva Morozov's** summer home, was presented to Maxim Gorky when he returned to the Soviet Union after years of self-imposed exile in Italy. Gorky died here in June 1936 possibly poisoned by order of Stalin for whom he was becoming an embarassment. The house, in classical style facing the Moskva (one of its residents was **General Grachev**, Yeltsin's Minister of Defence 1992-6), is surrounded by other dachas making a complex of government holiday homes within the heavily guarded compound.

Continue 2 km past the Gorki 10 stud farm to the right turn by the bus-stop for **Islavskoe** *reached in another 2 km where there is a droll figure of* **Lenin** so fat it is hard to believe its creator was not accused of treason. The impressive, rotunda **Church of the Saviour**, *Spasa*, was built in 1799 for General Ivan Arkharov whose unruly regiment was nicknamed Arkharovtsy, which now means ruffians. *Continue west towards the modern red brick sanatorium, Lesnye Dali and in 2 km by a bus-stop turn left onto a narrow road weaving down a hill 1 km to Dunino.*

DUNINO on the river has been a dacha village since the late 19th century. The fine house with the overhanging gazebo set in the hill against the woods, left, belonged to the writer, **Mikhail Prishvin**, from 1946 until his death in 1953. A trained agronomist, animal lover and passionate sportsman, he was a popular writer on nature even before the revolution, a subject that could be safely pursued in Soviet times. The charming house, built in the 1880s in the Finnish style, is now a museum cared for by a devoted secretary, Liliya Alexandrovna, who is engaged on publishing Prishvin's frank diaries (*10-4 closed Mondays*). She told us about the extraordinary change of atmosphere at Dunino in the 1980s when under Gorbachev's *glasnost* the villagers were finally able to speak frankly about their terrible sufferings in the long years of Soviet rule. Even this enchanting place hidden far from prying eyes, was paralysed by fear.

EN ROUTE TO THE RESURRECTION MONASTERY

From Moscow take the Volokolamskoe Shosse under the MKAD, veer left to the A-106 signed VOLOKOLAMSK 3 km, and turn right at traffic lights. **KRASNOGORSK**, population 91,000, formed in the 1930s from paper and textile villages on the River Banka, is a major holder of Russia's **film archive**. Apparently in Soviet times the archivists, ordered to destroy film of dissidents like the cellist, Mstislav Rostropovich, obstinately removed the labels and hid the canisters until, in recent times, they could be brought into the open.

Past modern blocks ranged oppressively either side of the road turn right at traffic lights to the estate of **Znamenskoe-Gubailovo** where the

church, the main house, two guest houses, the stable, a service building
and park still stand. In the 18th century **Prince Vasily Dolgorukov**
acquired the estate through marriage from the Volynskys. The Prince,
Commander of the Russian forces against the Turks in the Crimea,
decorated the gardens of his many estates including this one with the
stones scandalously looted from a Turkish cemetery. The Empress,
Catherine II, granted him the title *Krymsky* – of the Crimea – and
endowed him with the highest honours including Governor of Moscow
but, disappointed when she omitted to make him Field Marshal, he
retired to his estates.

In 1855 Znamenskoe was purchased by the textile merchants, brothers
Alexander and Nikolai Polyakov. Of Alexander's four sons Sergei
ardently supported the Symbolist poets – Valery Bryusov, Andrei Bely
and Konstantin Balmont (Sergei's brother, Yakov, and Konstantin
Balmont married two local sisters) – holding editorial meetings of their
journal, *Vesy* (Scales), at Znamenskoe. At Alexander Polyakov's death
his children commissioned a **mausoleum** in Art Nouveau style completed
in 1910 by the outstanding architect, Ilya Bondarenko. At the same time
the 17th century **Church of the Sign**, *Ikony Bozhiei Materi 'Znamenie'*,
was totally rebuilt, its new mundane form a striking contrast to Bondarenko's imaginative mausoleum. The church, once again holding services,
has been renovated while the abandoned mausoleum continues to
decline, its exotic luminous tiles fast disappearing.

The late 18th century **mansion** stands behind a small overgrown garden
with a rusticated ground floor and attractive two-storey loggia. The
mansion, for long a pioneer palace, continues in that role today as a
children's craft centre although dancing lessons had to be stopped to
preserve the fragile mouldings. There are fine walks in the wooded park
behind. The northern of the two brick guest houses/wings, which flank
the front garden is now the local law court. The dilapidated stable
stands behind it near the huge modern palace of culture. A wooden
service building, far right, accommodates the police whose black marble
bust of Felix Dzerzhinsky, first head of the Soviet secret police, is
almost hidden by foliage.

On the main road a short distance ahead by the hospital, right, is the
many-faceted pseudo-Russian **Church of the Assumption**, *Uspeniya*,
completed in 1897 by Nikolai Kokorin for the Polyakov mill workers
and now holding services again.

From Krasnogorsk continue 7 km west through Nakhabino (Moscow Country Club and golf course, right) and **Dedovsk** *where the 1911 Belgian-French textile mill was the most modern of any in the Moscow area. At Sadki the reopened* **Church of St John the Baptist**, *Ioanna Predtechi, built in 1741 is a rare example of the baroque of Anna's reign although the bell tower and spire are later. From Sadki it is a short distance to* **Lenino** *and the impressive war memorial, left, of a tank climbing a mound. It is from here that Soviet forces under Colonel Dokuchaev began the desperate offensive against the Germans.*

Continue on the Istra road to the GAI intersection and turn left onto the A-107. Cross over the first railway line and turn sharp right onto an unmarked, narrow road parallel with the railway which soon veers left and becomes a bumpy dirt road. In 4 km at the end of the Zelenaya Gorka pioneer camp turn right on a steadily worsening road 1 km to a junction of four dirt lanes by a well, left, with a cross. Take the right lane which rises through dense woods to **TROITSKOE**.

In the small square, left, is a war memorial dwarfed by an enormous church. The pseudo-Byzantine **Trinity**, *Troitsy*, was built 1904-13 by Mikhail Litvinov who seems to have been infected by the same grandiosity of the Christ the Saviour Cathedral in Moscow on which he also worked. A smaller, **wooden church**, also the Trinity, stands opposite in the shadow of its gigantic offspring. Protected by weatherboarding and looking handsome in fresh white and blue paint it was originally built in 1675 by Boyar R.F. Bobarykin and, although often repaired and modified, the apse and cube are said to be original. This very special church is used for important festivities like the blessing of the Easter cakes on Holy Saturday.

People sit companionably on benches chatting to one another outside the large church, which was never closed. What a strange place this village is, as if the long decades of Soviet power had passed it by. We definitely felt that we were in some kind of time warp at the unusual sight of a man with a horse stacking hay in neat bundles and his neighbour helping himself to some as though it was communal property. Even their speech sounded archaic. And yet Troitskoe is less than 60 km from Moscow on a frequent *elektrichka*. We were brought back to reality by the sight of palatial new *kottedzhi* lower down the slope.

From the Istra Road turn left at the GAI A-107 as for Troitskoe and cross over the narrow Istra River. Turn left to Krasnovidovo, a modern writers' holiday village – at tiny **Luzhki** *across the river the dilapidated* **Church of Sts Peter and Paul** *built 1730-5, has reopened. Continue east to Pavlovskaya Sloboda via* **Anosino** *where the* **Convent of Sts Boris and Gleb**, right, with the romantic corner towers, used as a garage for the collective farm has a ruined cathedral missing the upper part. The grounds have now been cleared of trucks and discarded oil drums, nuns have moved in and the gate church, St Dimitry, has reopened for services. Four km east of Anosino tucked into a bow on the Istra River is **PAVLOVSKAYA SLOBODA**.

Left, overlooking the river, is the remarkably powerful **Annunciation Church**, *Blagoveshcheniya*, built about 1625 for the **Boyar Boris Morozov**, courtier of Tsar Mikhail and tutor to the future Tsar Alexei. But Morozov's palace has long since disappeared along with his innovative iron foundry. In the early 19th century, Prince Yusupov of Arkhangelskoe established his **glass and crystal works** here only to see it destroyed by Napoleon's army. Today the grand church, for decades disfigured by broken cupolas and sagging walls, is the sole survivor.

The large brick cube resting on a high vaulted sub-basement is surmounted by five main cupolas and two lesser ones designating the side chapels. It is surrounded on three sides by a two-tier vaulted gallery, originally open, but enclosed in the 19th century to extend the *trapeza*. The porch and bell tower were dismantled in the last war by the Soviet army anxious to deny their use to the Germans. A sewing factory established in its spacious halls was removed only in 1995. Nevertheless, the church with its swelling line of five sumptuous apses, four-bayed facades and varied windows is one of the most interesting buildings of its era. In May, 1995 worship was reinstated in one of the chapels and a cross appeared on the one restored cupola. It must be helpful to the volunteers restoring the church that the priest, Father Vladislav, was trained as an architect.

Take the Volokolamsk Highway, M-9, 32 km to the exit signed ISTRA and join the A-107 or from the old Istra road turn right at the GAI post onto the A-107. In 3 km turn left to see the colourful pseudo-Russian church at Darna, the **Exaltation of the Cross**, *Vozdvizheniya, built in the 1890s by Sergei Shervud, son of the History Museum designer. 9 km from the old Istra road turn left signed P.L. TEMP and cross the bridge to the children's summer camp at* **KHOLMY**. *The octagonal-tower* **Church of the Sign**, *Ikony Bozhiei Materi 'Znamenie', on the left, missing windows and doors, was built in the Moscow baroque style in 1703-10 for*

Dmitry Golovin, a courtier in the reign of Peter the Great. Note the finely carved stone architraves on the triple apse and windows and the barley-sugar columns of the octagonal tier. The classical bell tower and the south chapel, now badly showing the ravages of time, were added 1825-30 for Princess Avdotiya Trubetskaya-Bove, probably by her husband, the Moscow architect, **Osip Bove**.

From Kholmy return south on the A-107 1 km and turn right 8 km to Andreevskoe, then turn sharp right 1 km to **POLEVSHINO**. The young **Chekhov**, newly graduated from medical school, and the artist **Isaak Levitan**, used to walk here from Babkino in the summers 1885-7. Nothing survives of the Babkino dacha or of the old estate at Polevshino except the ruined church which Chekhov used in two of his stories: *Vedma* (Witch) and *Nedobroe Delo* (An Awkward Business).

The **Church of the Kazan Virgin**, *Kazanskoi Ikony Bozhiei Materi*, was built in 1692-4 by the boyar Fedor Polevoi in the picturesque mid 17th century style, with traces of Moscow baroque. Orphaned by the age of 15, Fedor used the church for his family tomb but he too also died young and the estate passed to his descendants. In 1918 Polevshino was handed to Zvenigorod forestry officials and its furniture and furnishings taken by the Voskresensk Soviet of Deputies for their club. Its fortunes then rapidly declined; in 1935 it was closed and the Polevoi boyars' graves looted and destroyed. The church was then used as a pottery studio, grain storage and warehouse. Perhaps its strangest but most affecting role was as a shelter in the war for the Maximovka villagers hiding from the German army. Recently an Orthodox ecological society, Cherry Orchard, has taken it over and some repairs have been carried out. Nevertheless it stands lonely and sad, missing cupolas and drums, at the end of the road.

For **THE ISTRA RESERVOIR** take the right turn signed BUZHAROVO between the monastery and the river. In 8 km past Babkino/Mikhailovka where the road momentarily crosses to the left bank is **Buzharovo** and the **Transfiguration Church**, *Preobrazheniya*, built in 1859 in 17th century style. Cross the bridge to the right bank and take the right fork through the disorderly settlement serving the **Istra Dam**, built in 1935, originally called Kuibyshev after the Soviet leader. At **Lamishino** in 3 km is the intriguing, red brick **Church of the Kazan Virgin**, *Kazanskoi Ikony Bozhiei Materi*, which resembles early Serbian churches. It was built in 1902-5 by the Art Nouveau architect Alexander Galetsky, assistant to Fedor Shekhtel. At **Rozhdestveno** on the reservoir

21 km from Istra the elegant **Church of the Nativity of Christ**, *Rozhdestva Khristova*, built in 1828-30, is in use as the kitchen for the Moscow electricity department rest home. From Buzharovo take the road left 20 km through Kartsevo to **Ivanovskoe-Kozlovskoe** and the 18th century manor house of Prince Kozlovsky with delightful Art Nouveau towers and bays added in the early 1900s.

Take the old Istra Road through Krasnogorsk 56 km or the fast motorway, the M-9, and exit signed ISTRA/ZVENIGOROD.

ISTRA (formerly Voskresensk), population 35,000, is an industrial town of modern tower blocks, a centre for the rest houses and sanatoria that thickly populate the wooded valleys of the Istra and its tributaries. But its greatest asset is the splendid **New Jerusalem** Resurrection Monastery, *Voskresensky Monastyr 'Novy Ierusalim'*, on the Istra River. *Tickets can be purchased for the cathedral, the museum and the walk around the walls (closed Mondays and the last Friday of the month). There are reasonable toilets next to the ticket office.*

The ambitious **Patriarch Nikon** in 1656 chose this place for his powerful new monastery. It was modelled on Jerusalem even to the extent of renaming the Istra River the Jordan and the garden, Gethsemane. Unabashed by the harrowing schism in the Russian church he had unleashed in 1651 (see p.54), Nikon continued building his new monastery. Although **Tsar Alexei** applauded the project, he became disenchanted with Nikon's autocratic nature and in 1658 the offended Patriarch withdrew to Voskresensk. Eight years later Alexei finally ordered Nikon to return to Moscow but it was to a special court where he was removed from office, defrocked, and sent into exile at the northern Ferapontovo Monastery. In 1681 the new Tsar, Fedor, released him but the old man died on the long journey back and is buried in his singular cathedral.

When the monastery closed, a **museum** of the Moscow Oblast was established in the refectory. But in 1941 the **German army** occupied Istra and on December 11 retreated setting the town ablaze. In the monastery, the destruction was horrific: the towers and gate church were destroyed, the bell tower was totally wiped out, and the conical tower of the cathedral disintegrated into a mass of small fragments. The museum of the Moscow Oblast with its rich hoard of artifacts was completely annihilated. This terrible loss was somewhat mitigated by the heroism of museum employees who managed to evacuate most of the church treasures. Like the smashed imperial palaces around Leningrad, restoration of the monastery was undertaken as a matter of national pride and the leading Soviet architect, **Alexei Shchusev**, set to work as early as 1945.

Enter by the beautiful gate church appropriately named **Entry into Jerusalem**, *Vkhodoierusalimskaya*, a soaring white tower built 1694-7 by Yakov Bukhvostov, the master of Moscow baroque (see Ubory), in five receding tiers above the platform. The high pentagonal **walls** with seven towers and two gates were built 1690-4 also by Bukhvostov.

The strange cathedral constructed 1658-85 stands opposite the gate. The overblown gold cupola of the **Resurrection Cathedral**, *Voskreseniya*, puts in the shade the nearer only slightly smaller green cupola of the underground **Church of Sts Constantine and Helen**, while behind rises the richly decorated pyramid of the **Chapel of the Holy Sepulchre**, *Groba Gospodnya*. The cathedral is like no other church in Russia nor does it faintly resemble by its outward appearance the Church of the Holy Sepulchre in Jerusalem although the ground plans have similarities. All three churches are accessible from the main entrance – turn left for the cathedral and chapel and right, down some steps, to Sts Constantine and Helen. All that is left of the 7-tier tent-shaped bell tower, blown up in 1941, is a stump hidden under hoarding. The whole building inside and out was enlivened by the use of **tiled friezes** including the beautiful peacock's-eye design by the Belorussian, Petr Zaborsky.

In 1723 the heavy brick roof of the Holy Sepulchre suddenly collapsed. In 1749 it was rebuilt in lighter wood to the plans of **Bartolomeo Rastrelli**, Empress Elizabeth's baroque architect. It is Rastrelli who introduced the three tiers of lucarne windows into the conical roof, which allow light into the huge chamber, and who filled the interior with rich baroque plasterwork. **Matvei Kazakov**, the fine Moscow classical architect, was responsible for the impressive marble Chapel of Mary Magdalene, 1802, on the northeast of the cathedral. Outside, by Sts Constantine and Helen, are 74 graves of notables connected with the monastery including that of **Anna Tsurikova**, whose 1907 gravestone bears a fine mosaic by the artist, **Viktor Vasnetsov**.

Most of the sculptural ornament was lost in the explosion of 1941 which also severely damaged the vaulting and piers. As soon as it was feasible, the unbelievable mish-mash of rubble was carefully sifted for fragments. Happily, in the northern aisle two capitals remained intact to serve as models for those that were lost. Although the tent roof, now made of metal, is back in place, the vast interiors of the Resurrection Cathedral and Holy Sepulchre are still awaiting final restoration. Services are again being held in Sts Constantine and Helen, now restored to the rich baroque of the 18th century. The engraved copper gilded **iconostasis** of the 1750s commissioned by Count Alexei Razumovsky is also back in place.

Other buildings include the refectory by the west wall with the **Nativity of Christ**, *Rozhdestva Khristova*, built 1686-92, the gift of **TsarevnaTatiana Mikhailovna**, the great benefactress of the monastery. The Moscow Oblast museum has reopened here. The **infirmary** with its own small chapel is at the left while on the right are the **abbot's quarters** of 1750. Along the north wall are the **monks' cells** and at the centre the 17th century single-storey palata of the Tsarevna. Flanking the Holy Gate with its soaring church are far to the left the 1690s buildings of the **smithy, the malthouse and guardhouse** and, on the right, the **deputy abbot**.

Leave the monastery by the western Elizabeth Gate behind the refectory/museum for the **garden of Gethsemane**. On the right across a stream is Nikon's **hermitage**, the two-storey *skit*, built in 1658 as his residence during his self-imposed exile. Beyond is the Istra/Jordan River where Russians can often be seen being baptised. In the late 1970s a **museum of wooden architecture** opened here. In the centre is the exceptionally lovely **Church of the Epiphany**, *Bogoyavleniya*, from Semenovskoe, near Pushkino. It was built in 1730 using the *v oblo* or notch system, and *v lapu*, the tidier system for the apse where the log ends do not protrude. To the left is the small wooden **chapel** from Sokolniki near Chekhov which has been reconstructed here from old photographs. Other buildings include a large **peasant's house** from Vykhino in Lubertsy and a **windmill** from Tver Oblast.

On the old Volokolamsk Road beyond Istra turn right at Kholshcheviki, cross a railway line and continue 2 km through **GLEBOVO** *with its huge chicken farm. Descend towards the Maglusha River and just before the bridge turn left (west).* Here at **Brykovo** is the reopened **Church of the Epiphany**, *Bogoyavleniya* built in 1752-4 in baroque style for the Kvashin-Samarins. The modest church served as a lorry and tractor station for the poultry farms until 1988.

Continue west past depressing tower blocks and turn right at the T-junction beyond the poultry farm. In 2 km cross over the Maglusha to **Glebovo-Brusilovo**, where a great red and white church, the **Kazan**

Virgin, *Kazanskoi Ikony Bozhiei Materi*, rears up. In the pseudo-Russian style it is a large tent-shaped tower with miniature bell towers on all four corners. When we saw it, the top half was already painted but much remained to be done at ground level. Before the revolution Glebovo belonged to **General Alexei Brusilov**, the successful Tsarist First World War commander who threw in his lot with the Bolsheviks. Only fine Siberian silver firs and larches and this colourful church remain of the estate. At nearby Glebovo-Izbishche, now gone, Konstantin Shilovsky, the actor and playwright of the Maly Theatre, entertained his close friend, **Petr Tchaikovsky** in 1876 and 1877. Tchaikovsky was engaged on his greatest opera, *Yevgeny Onegin*, and Shilovsky helped him compose the libretto.

Continue from the church through woods 2 km to **Filatovo**. A charming wooden house with a portico beckons from the opposite bank of the Maglusha. Surrounded by overgrown limes and purple and yellow heart's ease, it is astonishing to find the *Zemstvo* school constructed in 1901 by the ubiquitous Savva Morozov, whose estate was at nearby Pokrovskoe-Rubtsovo. Now empty and derelict the romantic building painted dark brown with white columns and pediment and Venetian windows has a second storey at the back for teachers' flats. Encroaching on it from behind are modern school buildings which, ironically, have also fallen into decay. Beyond the school are the ruins of the 1750 **Nativity of Christ**, *Rozhdestva Khristova*, in the centre of a field surrounded on all sides by new dachas.

STATELY HOMES BETWEEN ISTRA AND RUZA

Ruza is the only town in the lightly populated country between Istra and the Mozhaisk Road, unencumbered by industry or even railway lines.

Take the Volokolamsk Highway, M-9, 64 km to the second exit for Istra. Follow the minor road 6 km towards Istra continuing ahead at the Kryuchkovo roundabout (ignore the right turning to Istra) to Pokrovskoe-Rubtsovo at Pionersk. Or from Istra travel west over the Istra River 2 km across a second bridge over the Maglusha, and take the first left signed D.O. CHEKHOVA to **POKROVSKOE-RUBTSOVO**.

The Nashchokins, owners from 1616 to 1770, built the church and laid out the formal gardens. In the late 18th century Rubtsovo was acquired by another family with ancient roots, the Golokhvastovs, who rebuilt the main house and planted the English, natural park. Dmitry Golokh-vastov, a cousin of Alexander Herzen, the influential democrat, played a major role in Alexander's life by persuading his father to allow him to enter university. In the 1890s Pokrovskoe-Rubtsovo was acquired by Savva Morozov, the wealthy mill owner, whose wife, Zinaida, kept the estate even after the revolution, perhaps because Lenin had sequestered her comfortable Gorki home.

The modestly baroque **Church of the Intercession**, *Pokrova*, right, which was not closed, was built in 1745 on a four-lobe central plan with heavy octagonal tier and dome. This is not immediately obvious because the long western extension with bell tower, cupola and spire, added in the 1770s as the winter church, destroys the symmetry. Within is the four-tier oak iconostasis of the early 1900s.

The classical **mansion** of brick and stucco stands across the road facing the park on one side and the wooded ravine of the Malaya Istra River on the other. It was built about 1830 by the Golokhvastovs as a small house of two storeys with mezzanine and portico of four Corinthian columns. But the modest house was transformed into a palace for the nouveau riche Morozovs by **Ivan Zholtovsky** who linked the free-standing wings, remodelled the facade, and skilfully added the end porti-coes of giant orders with verandahs. Nothing survives within, not even the layout and, now a hostel for refugees, it suffered from fire in 1999. As a curiosity, note the manhole covers around the mansion stamped Muir and Mirrielees, the popular Moscow department store before the revolution. Wooden dachas clutter the extensive park.

Opposite the Malaya Istra River, facing Pokrovskoe-Rubtsovo, is a heart sanatorium. Korpus No 1 was built 1911-13 as a **tuberculosis sanatorium** (renamed after Chekhov in the 1920s) by the notable Moscow architect, Ivan Rerberg. Zinaida Morozova donated the land and G.A. Korotaeva, for whom it was originally named, contributed the funds. The fine neo-classical building uses the Roman triumphal arch to good effect for the entrances to both the sanatorium and the chapel.

From the Volokolamsk Highway M-9 take the exit 65 km from Moscow marked MANSUROVO. At Mansurovo veer left signed RAKOVO passing the impressive church of the Nikolsky Pogost built in 1853 for P.I. Vyrubov by Nikolai Kozlovsky. Less than one km farther south, right, was the old Golokhvastov, later Vyrubov, estate, **Petrovo**, *of which only the two-storey wooden wing, park and cascading ponds remain.*

YURKINO lies 4 km south of Mansurovo towards Rakovo. Across a stream by a small lake, right, is an ancient church, the **Nativity of Christ**, *Rozhdestva Khristova*, built in the late 15th or early 16th century for the influential boyar, Yakov Golokhvastov of Petrovo. This small boyar's church, possibly by the Italian builders of the Moscow Kremlin under construction about that time, was the model for a whole group of 16th century churches including St Trifon in Moscow. It was one of the first to use the new device of groin-vaulting, probably originating at Pskov, which did away with the need for heavy piers in the narrow interior. Today, although the pilasters are still in place and the rounded side arches are discernible, it is hard to imagine the triple-bayed arches and strongly profiled cornice that united the three sides of the church with the forcefully protruding triple apse. But the tall slit windows on either side of the entrances are original as is the helmet-shaped single dome on the tall drum, presided over by the slim cross. On the west side are traces of the original terracotta frieze of acanthus leaves, perhaps a legacy of the Italian masters. The separately standing **bell tower** with the small spire was added in the 1820s. In 1948 the original appearance of the building was partially reinstated but since then, alas, it has been left to deteriorate.

For **NIKOLSKOE-GAGARINO** *take the old Volokolamsk Road to Novo-Petrovskoe, turn left onto the A-108 under the motorway, and take the left fork to Nikolskoe, about 12 km. Or at Mansurovo above turn right (west) to the T-junction at Alekseevka, turn left through Onufrievo past the large Trostenskoe Lake 4 km through quiet woods and turn right still following the lake. In 5 km at a T-junction turn right signed NIKOLSKOE to the ruined church and house, left.*

The abandoned **Church of St Nicholas** of the Gagarin estate is one of those where trees had sprouted making a bouquet of roof and walls. Yet, wonderfully situated overlooking Trostenskoe Lake, the ruins, now under restoration, are still beautiful. The centrally planned church was built in brick in 1777 by **Ivan Starov**, the fine St Petersburg architect. Its four lobes extrude cleverly from the square of the cube which supports a great rotunda, hemispherical dome, and tiny cupola. Opposite the Doric portico that denotes the western entrance stood the stunning round bell tower blown up by the Germans during heavy fighting in 1941 leaving only the foundations. The ruin of the church itself, however, is due to long decades of Soviet neglect.

The main house and other buildings of the estate also by Starov were built 1774–6 for **Prince Sergei Gagarin**, steward to the royal household, and remained in the Gagarin family until 1917. The elegant two-storey **main house** linked to wings by a curving wall is now the melancholy Children's Psychiatric Hospital No 16. If the courtyard facade seems severe the park side, where the house sits above the Ozerna River, is full of the lively contradictions of the baroque style counterposed with emerging classicism. Go through a gate, left, being careful in summer of stinging nettles in the untended garden to view the convex and concave curves, niches, columns and angled corner projections of the north facade.

On the courtyard side are the remnants of the formal gardens which give way to a more natural park designed by **Andrei Bolotov**, the Capability Brown of Russia. Two ancient oaks which stand either side of the courtyard define the space known as the green theatre where dancing and spectacles were staged.

ANNINO *is not easy to find. From Ruza take the northeast road towards Kolyubakino and in 11 km turn left towards Onufrievo and travel 5 km to the right turn to Annino. From Nikolskoe-Gagarino the best route is to turn right and then left to Safonikha, then turn right 10 km and left signed ANNINO 2 km on a good dirt road. The estate was owned in the 19th century by the Voeikov family one of whom was the outstanding climatologist after whom the observatory in Petersburg is named.*

The two-storey late 18th century mansion, a rest home, stands left. But it is overshadowed, right, by the **Church of the Sign**, *Ikony Bozhiei Materi 'Znamenie'*, built in 1690: two stunning tent-shaped towers standing close to each other like big and little sisters. Annino belonged to the **Boyar Ivan Miloslavsky**, the head of the Miloslavsky clan and a powerful figure at the court of Tsar Alexei. The Miloslavskys' power waned when Alexei married Natalya Naryshkina, then became prominent again in the reigns of Fedor and the regency of Sophia, only to be finally extinguished when the young Tsar Peter came to the throne.

As at Petrovskoe (see p.136) the feud between these opposing clans is reflected in their architecture: the traditional Miloslavskys preferred the old styles while the forward-looking Naryshkins sponsored the new Moscow baroque. The tent-shaped church completed by Ivan Miloslavsky's heir, Matvei Miloslavsky, at the beginning of Peter's reign (forty years after the Patriarch banned the style) is thus an expression of political dissent. The old church is made up of a cube with strongly protruding apse supporting the octagonal tier decorated with *kokoshniki* gables which in turn bear the soaring, slim tent-shaped roof, more than half the height of the building. The lesser tent-roofed bell tower, the foil to the taller pyramid, was added in the 18th century; the *trapeza* was widened in 1914.

From Annino travel south 18 km to Ruza and then take the road towards Ostashevo west. After 8 km turn right at Lenkovo (Linkovo) onto the unmarked road that leads to Volynshchina on the Ozerna Reservoir. A training ground for Olympic wrestlers it became a rest home in the post-Soviet period for the influential State Committee for Property. Modern buildings are tactfully disguised.

VOLYNSHCHINA-POLUEKTOVO is a refreshing example of a fine estate that is still virtually intact – house, wings, church, and obelisks. Park by the gates and walk down the avenue past the pair of **black obelisks** marking the boundary of the park. Through the pines a second pair of identical obelisks mark the inner courtyard framing a delightful mansion and four single-storey rusticated smaller houses or wings set at angles forming a cour d'honneur.

Poluekt Bobrok, who was decapitated battling the Tatars in 1436, gave his name to Poluektovo on the Ozerna River as did the new owners, the **Princes Volynsky**. In 1743 the land was inherited by the Volynsky relative, **Prince Vasily Dolgorukov** (also owner of Znamenskoe-Gubailovo in Krasnogorsk), famous for clinching the Russian victory at Perekop on July 14, 1771 against the much greater Turkish/Tatar forces. The poet Alexander Blok who visited Volynshchina in the early 1900s described in his memoirs the trophies of the Turkish wars in the house and grounds. The Dolgorukovs remained at Volynshchina until 1917, an unbroken tenure by the same family of five hundred years.

The design of this small estate is skilfully contrived, its layout from the first sighting of the obelisks suggesting the hand of a master architect, perhaps Matvei Kazakov whom the Dolgorukovs had employed in Moscow. The two-storey **main house** of the 1770s built of stuccoed brick with pediment and loggia is almost perfect, its symmetry only slightly marred by the early 19th century wooden staircase. Finely carved Ionic capitals and swaying garlands enhance the loggia and at either end semicircular niches indicate the doorways. Above, is the Dolgorukov coat of arms in bas-relief. On the river side panels of portraits in relief divide the pilasters whence an avenue of trees in former days led to the river. With the building of the reservoir water is now almost lapping at the walls.

The **Church of the Three Saints**, *Tryekh Svyatitelei*, now functioning, is situated off centre to the right of the courtyard. Of plain brick, with stone dressings it was built about 1780, almost at the same time as the house, to serve as Prince Vasily's burial place. It follows the petal design familiar in baroque churches, four major and four minor lobes, and is surmounted by an octagonal tier, a high roof, drum and cupola. This centralised design was marred by the *trapeza* and bell tower added in 1843.

From Annino travel 20 km south to Ruza or from the Minsk Highway (M-1) via Tuchkovo. **RUZA**, population 15,000, stands above the Ruza River, a tributary of the Moskva. An ancient town with a kremlin, it never attracted an independent prince but ricocheted between Zvenigorod, Volokolamsk, and Dmitrov until finally allying itself with Moscow. Although Ruza managed to repel the Polish attack of 1618, Polish forces returned a year later and razed it to the ground and the wooden kremlin and inner city were never rebuilt. Like Vereya to the south, it was bypassed by the railways and thus avoided industrial development not only of the late 19th century but also of Soviet times.

Timber from the richly wooded hinterland floated down the rivers to Ruza and even as late as the 1940s it was almost totally wooden except for a few masonry churches. The German army occupied the town from October 1941 to January 1942. Since the war, the leisure business serving the rest homes of the attractively wooded and watered countryside has become the main occupation. There are only a few buildings of architectural interest in the run-down main streets but its position high on the banks of the Ruza River gives unusually interesting contours to the town which, combined with abundant greenery and attractive wooden houses, endow the suburbs with great charm.

From whichever direction Ruza is approached, the roads lead to the unremarkable **centre** and the principal thoroughfare, Partizanskaya. The old Kremlin is a natural fortress surrounded on three sides by the high banks of the Gorodenka, Artyushka and Ruza Rivers and on the fourth by a ravine and earthworks. The **Cathedral of the Resurrection**, *Voskreseniya*, stands unhappily on the almost empty Kremlin square, minus its cupolas and drum and most of the bell tower. It was built in 1714 of brick in traditional form but was heavily altered in the pseudo-Russian style in the 19th century. An impressive memorial poignantly records the names of local victims of the Second World War.

A statue of Lenin dominates the junction of Partizanskaya with **Sotsia-listicheskaya Street**. In the distance, right, at No 58, is the terribly truncated **Church of Boris and Gleb** built in 1801, now a garage. At the opposite end of Sotsialisticheskaya Street, left, is its foil, the tall **Church of the Intercession**, *Pokrova*, now the town museum and in good order. It was built in 1781 in the baroque style, the usual octagonal on a cube with classical touches in the north and south pediments and tall bell tower.

From the west side of the Intercession Church take the winding paved lane over the Gorodenka River and up the opposite bank. Here, at the top of the hill on a pretty green with an old cemetery to one side, is **St Dimitry Solunsky**, *Dimitriya Solunskovo*, now returned to worship and repaired. St Dimitry was built in 1792 of brick with white stone detailing in the baroque style. The octagonal base (one side is the apse) supports a soaring central octagonal drum with bell apertures surrounded by four miniature, similarly pierced, octagonal drums bearing small domes. The complex facade has alternating heavily rusti-cated projecting sections with pediments and strong entablatures which contrasts with the open simplicity of the interior. Although two fat chapels with bell tower were grafted on to the western end in 1848, the overall delightful architecture, the high situation at the apex of the town, and the pretty wooden houses, make this the nicest corner of Ruza.

Leave Ruza by the Moscow Road, the A-108, from Partizanskaya Square. All along the wooded road are the sanatoria and rest homes of the Soviet elite. The **composers' House of Creativity** *lies to the right, deep in the woods, by the confluence of the Moskva and Ruza Rivers.* **Dmitry Shostakovich** composed many pieces here including the *24 Preludes and Fugues*. He spent December 1947 to January 1948 at the rest home in a particularly gloomy mood anticipating the Zhdanov decree attacking his music. A writers' rest home at Maleevka in the Soviet monumental style, also called the House of Creativity, is to the left, signed DOM TVORCHESTVA, before the turning to Staray Ruza. Among writers who have stayed here seeking the muse are Aitmatov and Akhmatova, Yevtushenko and Razgon. *Still on the A-108, cross over the Moskva and turn left past the cemetery to TUCHKOVO.*

Tuchkovo with belching chimneys and shabby tower blocks was named in 1912 after a hero of the Battle of Borodino. Turn right and left towards **KOLYUBAKINO** and in 2 km cross over the winding Moskva to **PORECHE** (there is another Poreche west of Mozhaisk). The large Gosplan rest home stands left while on the right is the engaging baroque **Church of the Kazan Virgin**, *Kazanskoi Ikony Bozhiei Materi*, built in 1763 amid little wooden houses nestled in the crook of the river.

At Poreche turn right onto an indifferently paved road signed VASILIEVSKOE. Within 3 km, past some vulgar houses of the nouveaux riches, is **VASILIEVSKOE,** *an enchanting place straddling the Moskva River*. The long uneven lane of small wooden houses faces the river with only the odd well or bench along the shore to break the view. Halfway along is a cottage with an outdoor shower ingeniously made from a spent artillery shell.

A striking, ruined, church stands guard at the far end surrounded by a brick wall with round corner towers. Built in 1705 by Yemelyan Ukraintsev, a leading diplomat in the reigns of Tsars Alexei and Peter the Great, the **Church of the Resurrection**, *Voskreseniya*, is based on both Moscow and Petrine baroque. Perhaps Ukraintsev, the old servant of the crown, preferred Moscow baroque, the modern style of his youth, but was obliged to show he was not backward in adopting the new, western style. The church is composed of an octagonal on a cube, a triple apse divided by pilasters, and elaborate melon-like portals. Rich stone cornices decorate every level. In a sharp engagement during the short German occupation of Vasilievskoe, Soviet troops on the right bank dislodged the enemy but in the process the German soldiers blew up the bell tower destroying it completely.

Vasilievskoe belonged in 1821 to Ivan Yakovlev, father of Alexander Herzen, the radical political philosopher. In 1828 his father built a new house across the water on the right bank and sold the left bank to a cousin, Dmitry Golokhvastov (see Pokrovskoe-Rubtsovo) thus dividing the village. A swaying suspension bridge takes pedestrians across the river to the wooded right bank and a path, left, leads via a pond and flower garden to a red brick pseudo-Gothic mansion. (Vasilievskoe can be approached on this side of the river via the Minsk Highway but to arrive from the left bank by the suspension bridge is infinitely more romantic.) In the 1880s Countess Alexandra Panina gave the estate to her nephew, Prince Alexander Shcherbatov, who commissioned Petr Boitsov to build this splendid, idiosyncratic 'castle' 1881-4 replete with

Gothic devices – tall chimneys, towers, pointed gables and even a moat (now empty).

In the 1920s Prince Shcherbatov's castle became a sanatorium for tuberculosis patients. After the Second World War, it was placed under the elite Fourth Section of the Ministry of Health which provided exclusive first-class treatment for Party bosses. The castle has therefore survived unusually well. Look inside to see the medieval hall with chandelier, large fireplace and minstrels' gallery. These days known as the Herzen Sanatorium, it provides services for those who can afford it.

Prince Shcherbatov also built St Panteleimon in pseudo-Russian style in 1900 to go with his country house. The huge drum was shorn of its cupola and for a long time served as the water tower for the sanatorium. The church is now functioning once more and is being restored.

VOLOKOLAMSK

Take the Volokolamsk Highway, M-9, 118 km and exit at DUBOSE-KOVO before the turning to Volokolamsk. Turn right and cross over the highway through Nelidovo 4 km to the war memorial. As the Germans converged on Moscow in the autumn of 1941 fierce battles broke out near Volokolamsk. The German Army had made its way with ease through the thousand miles of Belorussia and the Ukraine and had not expected to be stopped so near its goal. A remarkable war memorial of six monumental figures at **DUBOSEKOVO** near Volokolamsk commemorates one of these desperate battles.

On November 16, 1941 a German tank division was met by 28 Russian soldiers of the 316th Division of Major-General Panfilov. Attacked by tanks on the ground and bombing from the air, the soldiers managed to hold off the enemy for four hours destroying 14 of the 20 tanks in the first attack. When a second wave of 30 tanks came they armed themselves with grenades and Molotov cocktails and according to Soviet legend their officer, Klochkov, shouted 'Russia is vast but there is nowhere to retreat. Behind us is Moscow!' Whereupon he wrapped grenades around his body and threw himself under the nearest tank. Three more were similarly destroyed and the confused Germans withdrew leaving only five Russians alive but allowing sufficient time for Soviet reinforcements to arrive. The mass grave of the soldiers and a museum of the battle *(closed Mondays)* is at Nelidovo.

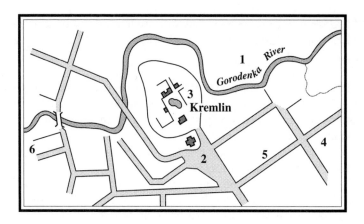

VOLOKOLAMSK   1. Gorodenka River, 2. Oktyabrskaya Square,
3. Kremlin, 4. Vozmishche, 5. Sovietskaya,
6. Dovatora

*Take the fast M-9 130 km to the exit signed VOLOKOLAMSK to the
centre via Panfilova Road. Or by the slower old road through Istra which
enters Volokolamsk via Sovietskaya Street.*

VOLOKOLAMSK, population 18,000, a hilly town founded in 1154 by
Yaroslav the Wise, is almost as old as Moscow. It is at the portage,
volok, where 12th century Novgorod traders carried their boats from the
Lama to the Voloshnya River to link up with the Oka and Volga
systems. By the 15th century the town was firmly in Moscow's orbit and
the Moscow Prince, Boris, brother of Ivan III, and then his son Fedor,
styled themselves Princes of Volotsk. From 1608 to 1611 Volokolamsk
was occupied by Polish troops but beat them off in 1613. The wooden
fortifications and walls of the Kremlin were destroyed in these events
and not rebuilt. By the 18th century, life in Volokolamsk was that of a
provincial town producing flax and linen. In 1781 an attempt was made
to straighten the tortuous lanes but its hilly topography allowed only a
few central streets to be forced into a grid pattern. Partisans in 1812
managed to save the town from French marauding parties but in 1941
Volokolamsk was occupied by the German Army from October until
December.

In 1905 the town was almost destroyed by fire but was soon rebuilt,
again mostly in wood. Modern building is confined to new districts and

small wooden and masonry houses still predominate. Volokolamsk has four handsome churches plus several others so mutilated they are no longer recognisable.

Whether the town is entered from the M-9 or from the old Moscow road, all routes lead to **Oktyabrskaya Square**. It is an elongated rectangle of pleasant two-storey shops closed by the Kremlin high on its mound at one end over the winding Gorodenka River, and at the other the 1913 wooden fire tower, the *kalancha*, behind the tank war memorial. Leave the car in the parking area and climb to the citadel. A salmon pink building on the left turns out to be the **Nativity of Christ**, *Rozhdestva Khristova*, built in the 1750s, now a clinic. The most striking of the Kremlin churches is the red brick **St Nicholas** in pseudo-Russian style built 1853-62 in the form of a Greek cross as a memorial to the Crimean War. Damaged in 1941, it was restored in the 1980s and now houses the town museum *(closed Mondays)*. (The left corner tower of the Kremlin houses a spotless toilet to which the museum staff have the key.) The most ancient building, which stands next to St Nicholas, is the **Cathedral of the Resurrection**, *Voskreseniya*, reckoned to have been built about 1490 during the reign of Prince Boris Volotsky. Like Moscow churches of the time, it is in white limestone with some brick built over a high basement and divided into three bays separated by pilasters. The only decorations are a three-part decorative frieze between the upper and lower windows and splendid portals of receding ogee arches embellished with 'melons'. The upper part of the church including the drum was rebuilt at the end of the 17th century when the gables were replaced by the pitched roof; it would probably have been surrounded on three sides by a gallery and porches. Inside are traces on one column of 15th century frescoes, possibly by Dionisy or one of his pupils; other fragments are from the 19th century. The helmet-shaped cupola on the high drum was reinstated in sensitive restoration by Soviet specialists in the 1960s. Nikolai Markov built the tall bell tower and clock in 1888 that rises five tiers, by far the tallest structure in the Kremlin. After the revolution the cathedral was closed and used for Kinoset, the cinema organisation; these days services have been reinstated for major festivals. The former church school stands between the cathedral and St Nicholas and behind the Kremlin, across the pond, are the early 19th century prison and former *prisutstvennye mesta* (now the hospital) in Empire style.

Not far from the Kremlin, on pleasant Komsomolskaya Street (right from Oktyabrskaya Square, the nearest lane to the Kremlin), a run-down furniture factory poised uncomfortably on a high spit of land surveying the surrounding country is a former church, a dire example of what happened to many in the Soviet period.

An ancient church 2 km east on the old Moscow Road in **Vozmishche**, now within Volokolamsk, can be reached from Oktyabrskaya Square by turning left (east) at traffic lights onto Sovietskaya Street. The **Nativity of the Virgin**, *Rozhdestva Bogoroditsy*, left, was built in 1535 as the cathedral of the Vozmishche Monastery which was closed under Catherine II. The severely plain walls are relieved by icon frames, a central cornice, and the fine 'melon' receding portals. Note the beautiful 17th century cross over the helmet-shaped dome. Alterations of 1792 transformed the segmental roof gables, still visible on the triple-bayed walls, into an ordinary hipped roof. The interior paintwork and iconostasis is of the 19th century but 16th century frescoes may still lie under the plaster in the altar and on the piers. The jarring bell tower of 1850 borrows motifs from Moscow baroque, the wrong style for this early church. Note the plaque in the wall left of the entrance recording the building in 1541 of a gate church and refectory, now long gone, by a master builder from Tver. In the grounds are the priest's attractive wooden house with a garden pavilion overlooking the Gorodenka Reservoir and a new icon painting school.

The white 17th century **Church of the Intercession**, *Pokrova*, which remained open in Soviet times, is the only survival of the monastery/ convents that once crowned Volokolamsk's hills. Because of the one-way system, follow the main road – Gorodskoi Val – past the Kremlin, across the Gorodenka River and immediately left onto a road that doubles back across the river. Keep turning right winding up the steep hill to reach the attractive church on Dovatora Street, No 9. It was built in 1695 by Natalya Naryshkina, the mother of Peter the Great, and served as the cathedral of the Convent of St Barbara until it was dissolved in 1764. A cube with a two-tier drum, onion-shaped cupola and plain walls it has window decorations of Moscow baroque obscured by the large south chapel added in 1806. The tall slim bell tower by I. Dmitriev was built in 1828. Within, the iconostasis and paintings are of the 19th century although some of the icons are older.

TO THE MONASTERY

Leave Volokolamsk via Gorodskoi Val on the west side of the Kremlin, cross the Gorodenka River and merge briefly with the bypass road then turn left signed VLADYCHINO and cross the Lama River 1 km to Ivanovskoe.

IVANOVSKOE (Bezobrazovo), left, on the Lama River, now the local technical college, was the estate of the ancient and numerous Bezobrazov family from the 18th century to 1917. The central courtyard is entered through grand gates with Tuscan columns and niches. Opposite, students pour cheerfully in and out of the late 18th century mansion. Two separate wings flank the main house making a square while extensive service buildings with Gothic overtones lie farther afield. Facing the estate, right, is the ruined but dignified **Church of the Sign**, *Ikony Bozhiei Materi 'Znamenie'*, built in 1783. The round, classical building has a fine western portico of four pairs of Doric columns flanked by twin bell towers. It remained open for services until 1941 when it was caught in the fighting between the German and Soviet armies.

Return to the main road and continue north passing through the Voloko-lamsk industrial suburbs 5 km to **KASHINO**. Kashino is famous for the first village electricity plant, generated by diesel oil, opened by Lenin and Krupskaya in 1920. The spread of electricity was a central plank in Lenin's economic platform introduced that same year at the 8th Party Congress. The generator is in a small building, left (rebuilt in 1970) where an obelisk stands with the famous slogan *Communism equals Soviet power plus electrification of the entire country.* Beside the obelisk an old-fashioned light bulb known as **Ilich's Lamp** (Ilich was Lenin's patronymic) was not functioning, perhaps symbolising that the light has gone out for Leninists. Two ladies on the street merrily eating the apples they were selling said the lamp had been broken by hooligans.

Continue to the crossroads and turn right to Teryaevo 26 km from Volokolamsk where the monastery is visible across a lake, left. Down a lane, right, is **Spirovo** *and the* **Church of the Ascension**, *Vozneseniya, built 1810–25.*

Situated on the low flat marshy lands of the meandering Sestra River, the strikingly beautiful **JOSEPH-VOLOKOLAMSK MONASTERY** *(Iosifo-Volokolamsky Monastyr)* is one of the foremost religious institu-tions in Russia. It was founded in 1479 by Joseph Volotsky, Abbot of the Pafnuty Monastery at Borovsk, who with his followers, the Josephites, favoured an active, worldly role for the church. Their opponents, the ascetic Hermits from Beyond the Volga led by Nil

Sorsky, advocated a contemplative life away from the world of politics and material wealth. The Josephites supported and were supported in turn by the powerful grand princes of Moscow which by 1462, the year of the coronation of Ivan III, had become the pre-eminent Russian town. After Constantinople fell in 1453 to the Turks, the Russian church demanded independence from Byzantium and claimed that Moscow had become the new centre of true christianity, the Third Rome. The founding of the monastery was thus emblematic of the new power of both the church and the Moscow rulers and marked the beginning of the decline of the reclusive hermits.

Close ties with the Moscow tsars meant royal visits and the frequent bestowal of gifts, and the Joseph Monastery became one of the richest in Russia. Like many monasteries, it was also used as a prison for heretics and reformers. Maxim the Greek, the priest from Athos, was incarcerated here in 1525 for opposing the divorce of Tsar Vasily from his barren wife, Salamonia, and only freed after the death of Vasily, fourteen years later.

The first stone **Cathedral of the Assumption**, *Uspeniya*, was built 1484-6 and Dionisy, the celebrated icon artist, painted the frescoes. In spite of the thick 16th century stone walls and towers, the monastery suffered such damage in the Polish siege of 1610 that Dionisy's frescoes were lost. The whole complex, including the cathedral, was completely rebuilt in the 1670s to the 1690s by the master builder, **Trofim Ignatiev**. With the advent of Soviet power, the monastery closed and it became a children's home and a museum. During the war with Germany, in autumn 1941 the octagonal 9-tiered **bell tower** was blown up by Soviet sappers, as elsewhere, to prevent the excellent observation post falling into the hands of the enemy. Restoration of the ruined buildings began in earnest in 1956 and ironically by 1989, when the monastery was handed back to the Orthodox Church, it was almost complete. The cathedral is now holding services again and German sponsors are assisting with further improvements.

Enter by the main or **Holy Gate** under the **Church of Sts Peter and Paul** built in 1679 and now open for services. Erected by Trofim Ignatiev it is magnificently garbed in the bright colours and ornamentation of the 17th century. Using the main arch as support for the gallery it rises only one more tier to the three rows of ogee gables which in turn support the drums and five cupolas. Against the white background the contrasting deep pink of the details, and green of the tiles add colour while above, the closely packed gold cupolas with their intricate crosses complete the radiant picture. For pilgrims this joyous church gives a splendid welcome and provides a delicious contrast to the more ascetic cathedral. The abbot's residence built in 1797 is right of the gate, the treasury to the left.

The brick **refectory** left of the cathedral is the oldest building in the monastery. The early 16th century building survives in the grand eating hall supported by a single pier like Moscow's Faceted Palace. Also like its prototype, the walls and vaulted ceiling are entirely covered with religious scenes painted in 1904 to the designs of Ivan Kuznetsov. The windows and upper part of the **Church of the Epiphany**, *Bogoyavleniya*, at the northeast corner were rebuilt in 1682 by Trofim Ignatiev in the lavish style of the gate church. The church is whitewashed on its upper parts, the rest left in bare red brick to demonstrate the earlier period.

The magnificent **Cathedral of the Assumption** was built 1688 to 1692. The high standing of the monastery is evident from the generous donations of the tsars and the engagement of the Moscow Kremlin masons under master builder, **Kondraty Mymrin**. The tall brick church over a high stone basement surmounted by five cupolas on long drums with elaborate gold crosses is in the traditional form of an inscribed cross with four piers and extruding apse. Surrounded on three sides by an open gallery which serves both basement level and the first floor, it has a traditional triple-bayed facade finished in *zakomary* roof gables. Although the overall form of the cathedral relates to the 16th century, there are some Moscow baroque innovations in the sculptured window frames and capitals. Brightly coloured tiles in the blue peacock's-eye design executed by the master tile maker, **Stepan Polubes**, are everywhere, giving colour to the porches and galleries, underlining the string course and the apse, circling the building below the arched gables and under the cupolas of the drums. The octagonal stump of the bell tower is left of the entrance.

Of the **frescoes** completed in 1696 by the Potapov brothers only those on the columns survive but they are in remarkably good condition. In 1904 the wall frescoes were repainted by **Nikolai Safonov**, the Palekh artist, also to designs by Ivan Kuznetsov. The original carved baroque iconostasis 1740-57 of five tiers is still in place, its swirling columns of twisted vines flanking the royal doors.

The 16th century **walls** suffered badly in the Polish siege and were mostly rebuilt in the late 17th century to the design of Ivan Neverov.

Neverov was inspired by the Simonov monastery in Moscow, especially in the use of conical towers which give the monastery such a fine silhouette. Other 18th and 19th century buildings are the school, monks' cells, poorhouse, choristers' buildings and hostel.

A NEST OF GENTLE REBELS

Many of the sons of the noble estates around Volokolamsk found themselves at the heart of the traumatic Decembrist rebellion of 1825, the conspiracy of officers against the monarchy of Nicholas I. These defiant young men often married the sisters of their fellow conspirators in neighbouring estates and became tied to each other by blood as well as belief. After the uprising failed, most received sentences of hard labour in Siberia or reduction to the ranks.

From Volokolamsk travel north through Kashino and turn left at the T-junction past Suvorovo and the richly decorated red brick Church of the Nativity of the Virgin, right, completed in the 1890s by Sergei Borodin. In 3 km turn right signed YAROPOLETS, past the square with the curious busts of Lenin and Krupskaya, rarely depicted together, and turn right to the Goncharov property, left.

YAROPOLETS (named after the 12th century Prince Yaropolk) on the tortuous Lama River was divided early on into two large estates, Yaropolets-Goncharov and Yaropolets-Chernyshev.

The colourful **Goncharov estate** was inherited in 1823 by Natalya Ivanovna Goncharova, whose daughter, Natalya, was to become the wife of **Alexander Pushkin**, Russia's great poet. Pushkin incurred the opprobrium of Tsar Nicholas I for his audacious poems and was suspected, quite rightly, of sympathy for the Decembrists. Unlike Pushkin the Goncharovs were not in the highest echelons of society – they had entered the ranks of the nobility through the Kaluga merchant, Afanasy Goncharov, sailmaker for Peter the Great. Natalya, only 16 when he first proposed, was not a match for him intellectually or emotionally but her remarkable beauty won him over and the disastrous marriage, which was to bring about his downfall, was concluded in 1831. Although Pushkin came to Yaropolets only twice in his life, in 1833 on his way to Moscow when he raided his mother-in-law's library, and briefly in 1834, the room he occupied has been reverently kept as Pushkin's room. The estate remained in the hands of the Goncharovs until the revolution.

Without for once having to exercise the imagination over a pile of ruins, Goncharov demonstrates how a stately country house of the 1780s looked. A hospital in the 1930s, today it is the rest house of the Moscow Aviation Institute. Remarkably, only the theatre and the orangerie were totally destroyed in the war and the damaged buildings were masterfully restored in the 1960s. They are executed in the classical manner with columns and pediments but there are Gothic overtones and the strong colours, white details against dark red brick, are more like the potent tones of Moscow baroque than the gentle shades of classicism. Some suggest the architect may have been Ivan Yegotov.

Through round crenellated entrance towers, the **Church of St Catherine** gleams white with an unusual gold ball on its octagonal dome and a spire over the bell tower. It was built in 1755, the familiar octagonal on the cube, but in the early 19th century the two side chapels with classical pediments and Doric porticoes were added. It was returned to the church in 1992 and regular services are now held. Opposite, to the right, is the interesting V-shaped estate **manager's house**. Two **weavers' workshops** by the grand entrance, right, are a reminder that these estates were largely self-sufficient.

From the church through a second gate is the large grassed courtyard with a splendid old larch in the centre, sometimes used to tether riding horses. To the left is the long curve of the low **house** looking east flanked by two-storey wings attached by enclosed galleries. The un-stuccoed red brick is opposed throughout by white stone pilasters, architraves and the Corinthian portico with its red and white pediment and recessed bay. Within, the ceiling paintings and decorations of the main halls including the Pushkin room were destroyed by fire during the war. To visit the renewed Pushkin room ask at the library where a librarian is happy to show visitors the attractive salon with columns.

Farther on the same road the formerly magnificent estate of the **Cherny-shevs**, fabulously rich grandees from St Petersburg, is in a pitiful condition compared to the Goncharovs'. The property remained in the Chernyshev family from 1717 until the debacle of 1917.

The house and church were built in the 1760s under Field Marshal **Count Zakhar Chernyshev**, the Moscow Governor-General whose house (rebuilt) on Tverskaya is now the offices of the Moscow mayor. In his youth, suspected of harbouring an affection for Grand Duchess Catherine (later Catherine II) the Count was hurriedly sent on a diplomatic mission. In 1825 the Field Marshal's grandson, also called Zakhar, became involved in another kind of scandal when he took part in the **Decembrist uprising** and was sentenced to hard labour in Siberia. One of his sisters, Alexandrine (Annie), was the wife of one of the principal Decembrist leaders, Nikita Muraviev. Although forced to leave her child behind, she bravely chose to follow her husband to the remote wilds of Chita and had the distinction of carrying Pushkin's famous poem which has cheered other doomed convicts ever since:

In the depths of the Siberian mines,
Keep that proud patience.
The heavy chains will fall,
The prison gates will open wide.
Outside, freedom awaits you.

The Chernyshevs did not, like many aristocratic families, turn against their children but sent generous allowances and gifts to both Annie and Zakhar in the depths of Siberia where there was not even a sewing needle to be had. Convicted Decembrists were deprived of their titles and property rights and in 1832 at the death of their father these were granted to Zakhar's sister Sophia, whose husband, a Kruglikov, thus became **Count Chernyshev-Kruglikov**. In 1834, having served his time in Siberia, Zakhar was exiled to Yaropolets, now belonging to his sister and her husband. Although in the general amnesty of 1856 the title and the estate were returned to him, he died in Rome without heirs and Yaropolets reverted to the Chernyshev-Kruglikovs.

The **palace**, possibly by the architect Petr Nikitin, lies to the left behind a high fence. Of two storeys with an attic floor it extends via galleries on either side to two vast square buildings at right angles to the central house forming a huge courtyard. The facade was decorated in stucco with garlands, cornices, mouldings and window surrounds. The interior was likewise handsomely appointed especially the Blue Room with its marble medallions of portraits of the Chernyshev family. The grounds with three terraces and plantings of limes were once filled with park statuary and pavilions and even a strange mosque but these were lost in the Second World War. Only the obelisk, erected in honour of Catherine II's visit in 1775 stands on the third terrace. The house suffered badly from artillery fire, both German and Soviet, and has further deteriorated. New brickwork and a new roof in the 1990s were a brief sign of improvement.

On the right side of the road opposite the palace is the remarkable
Church of the Kazan Virgin, *Kazanskoi Ikony Bozhiei Materi*. Built
in 1798 possibly by Matvei Kazakov, it is a carefully balanced composition of two parts with two separate domes and apses on east and west
linked at the centre by porticoes giving the impression of a great ship.
The eastern section was the church and the western the family mausoleum which contains the tomb of the Field Marshal in the form of a
truncated marble pyramid, possibly by Fedot Shubin. (The marble
reliefs are now in Moscow's Museum of Architecture.) Sadly this magnificent church, which survived the depredations of time and war,
was closed in 1962 in Khrushchev's anti-religious campaign. The
unbecoming pseudo-Russian bell tower erected in 1871 continues to be
used as a water tower.

A little farther is the small dam and early **hydroelectric power station**
opened in 1921 by the Yaropolets peasants in answer to Lenin's call for
electrification. The station was equipped to serve 13 villages. When the
lights finally went on, the villagers, like those at Kashino, called them
'Ilich's lamps' (no doubt a term devised by Kremlin spin-doctors). The
station was destroyed in 1941 but rebuilt two years later and still
functions.

Turn right on leaving Yaropolets 4 km, after crossing the Lama River, to
Fedorovskoe, right.

FEDOROVSKOE built in the late 18th century for Prince Alexei
Shakhovskoy stands abandoned and alone, untarnished by later
additions, in the quiet green valley of the Kolpyana, a tributary of the
Lama. It consists of the main house built in the 1790s but without its
portico, two of the four separate wings, church and barn.

The semi-ruined **Church of the Consolation of All Sorrows**, *Vsekh*
Skorbyashchikh Radosti, to one side of the main house has a most
original design. It was constructed for Prince Shakhovskoy in 1768 in
Ukrainian baroque style. The octagon, crowned by a sloping roof and a
second octagonal drum and dome, rose like a pillar from the centre of
four clover-shaped cusps all crowned with conical roofs on which tiny
cupolas rested. Unhappily in 1882 the west cusp was removed to
construct the *trapeza* and since then the other three have also disappeared leaving only the central octagon. The tall bell tower built in 1894
by the popular Sergei Rodionov discreetly reflects the style of the
church. The wooden granary stands near the church.

On the M-9 beyond Volokolamsk (where it ceases to be a motorway) travel 20 km and turn right (north) 8 km via Koptyazino and Zatesovo to **BELAYA KOLP***, right. Or from Fedorovskoe travel via village roads through Khanevo.*

In 1533 **Grand Duke Vasily III**, while hunting in the local forests, fell suddenly ill and had to be carried back to his lodge at Belaya Kolp. He died soon after, leaving his vulnerable 3-year-old son, the future Ivan the Terrible, to the mercy of the Kremlin's intriguing boyars. In 1658 Belaya Kolp passed to **Prince Stepan Shakhovskoy** and remained in the Shakhovskoy family until 1917. In the early 1820s young Prince Valentin Shakhovskoy, a pupil at the famous cavalry school in Moscow run by Nikolai Muraviev of nearby Ostashevo, became involved in the dissident officers' movement that led to the Decembrists' uprising.

The Prince was married to Elizaveta Mukhanova, a sister of his close friend, Petr Mukhanov, who was sentenced to hard labour in Siberia for his role in the Decembrists' uprising. Mukhanov fell in love in turn with Prince Valentin's sister, Varvara, who joined him in Siberia, ostensibly to help the convicts. Marriage to one's sister-in-law is prohibited in the Orthodox Church and the unhappy lovers were refused permission to marry. Nevertheless Princess Varvara and Petr Mukhanov remained true to one another throughout their lives. Two of Prince Shakhovskoy's other eight sisters married, successively, the leading Decembrist, Alexander Muraviev, of nearby Ostashevo (the prohibition did not prevent a sister from marrying her brother-in-law if the other sister had died).

Belaya Kolp was thoroughly rebuilt in the early 19th century by Prince Mikhail, father of Valentin. The main house, which stood at the centre of the ensemble, was destroyed during the revolution and the most impressive of the surviving buildings is the **Church of St Andrew**. It was built in 1807 in the classical style, a cube with extruding apse, two rows of windows and Doric entablature, mounted by a large round drum and tall spherical dome. The linking refectory is of the same period but the three-tier bell tower was added later, still in the classical form agreeing with the style of the church.

Leave Volokolamsk south by Panfilova Road, cross the railway line at Privokzalny 18 km to Ostashevo. En route at **Spass** *is the newly white-*

washed **Church of the Transfiguration**, *Spasa Preobrazheniya*, built in 1791 which remained open.

At **OSTASHEVO** an expressive war memorial stands on the square, a reminder of the ferocious battle in October, 1941 when the Germans captured Ostashevo only to be thrown back a month later. But the once noble estate is in a sorry state. It was laid out at the end of the 18th century by Prince Alexander Urusov who willed it in 1813 to his step-son, **Major-General Nikolai Muraviev**. The Major-General, a veteran and hero of the 1812 war, was director of the cavalry school in Moscow for young officers, which was influential in encouraging the secret societies – 22 of the graduates became active members of the Decembrist movement. From 1816 the school moved to Ostashevo in the summers and meetings of the secret societies took place here attended by the Chernyshev and Shakhovskoy families and the Sheremetievs from Pokrovskoe.

The Major-General's own sons – he had five – were not immune to the attractions of conspiracy. **Alexander Muraviev**, a founder member of the Union of Welfare, was the most notable of the brothers to take up the liberal cause. He was arrested at his estate at Botovo north of Volokolamsk and sent to Siberia in 1826 followed by his determined wife, Princess Praskoviya Shakhovskaya, sister of Prince Shakhovskoy. When Praskoviya died, Alexander married her sister, Princess Marfa. Alexander's brother, Mikhail, was also a founder member although after his marriage to a Sheremetiev, he foreswore further involvement and firmly declared loyalty to the Tsar.

After these exciting years, the estate was purchased by a leading agricul-tural reformer, **Nikolai Shipov**, who also bought Botovo perhaps in payment for Alexander Muraviev's many debts. His son, Dmitry, was a distinguished leader of the *Zemstvo* movement.

In the late 19th century the estate again changed hands when it was acquired by **Grand Duke Konstantin**, a grandson of Nicholas I. Unusually for a Romanov, he was a romantic poet who wrote poems under the pseudonym K.R. some of which were set to music by Tchai-kovsky. His fourth son, Oleg, seemed to have a talent for writing and the Grand Duke hoped he would follow him in his literary pursuits. But when the First World War broke out Oleg was one of the first Russian casualties. Oleg's body was buried at Ostashevo in the specially built memorial church and the heartbroken Grand Duke died shortly afterwards. But the family tragedy was not yet played out. In July, 1918 at Alapayevsk the Bolsheviks murdered three more of the Grand Duke's sons – Ioann, Konstantin and Igor – throwing them down a mineshaft together with the Grand Duchess Elizaveta Fedorovna. Of his eight children, four with their mother managed to escape abroad. After the revolution, the splendid house and other buildings were left to decay until in 1929 the local authorities took it over as offices.

Although shabby and neglected it is remarkable that a large part of the Grand Duke's estate has survived at all. The obelisks still point the way to the main house, the stables are still in use, and much remains of the picturesque walls and towers. Far to the right are the old cattle barns but it is the **stable** for horses and carriages, left, that strikes the eye. Built in the mid 19th century they are fronted by a grand four-tier brick Gothic tower and clock. It is replete with pinnacles, merlons, blind arcading, and a splendid ogee-shaped arched entrance repeated above in the main window.

Ahead is the main courtyard flanked by two Gothic towers in brick and contrasting white stone. To the left and right are the L-shaped estate offices and the manager's house. Round corner towers mark the inner courtyard. What seems to be the main house, a two-storey heavy classical building, was only built in the 1950s on the site of the house. It now accommodates a local museum, with exhibits on the history of the estate, which observes erratic hours (*closed on Mondays*). Two 18th century modest wings stand either side; the galleries connecting them to the house are in a perilous state.

To the right on the edge of the woods overlooking the river are the ruins of the once fine Art Nouveau **mausoleum-church** where Prince Oleg and the Grand Duke were buried. It was built by the Petersburg architect, Marian Peretyatkovich, in 1915 employing medieval Pskov and Novgorod features – a cube with four piers, a single cupola and a bell tower attached to the south wall. The muted decoration girdling the drum, apse and church is in the medieval *begunets* and *porebrik* patterns. Because of war, revolution and Soviet power, it was only consecrated in 1995. There are hopes it will be restored but the huge holes in the fabric make this a daunting task.

Across the Ruza River and left at **Brazhnikovo** *is the soaring Moscow baroque* **Church of the Annunciation**, *Blagoveshcheniya, built 1713-15 in three receding tiers.*

DEEP IN THE COUNTRYSIDE

*Take the M-9, 150 km to Shakhovskaya, then north 16 km to Ramenye,
then 5 km towards Lotoshino then left through Streshnevy Gory to
Kornevskoe and* **MARKOVO**.

The farming village of Markovo, part of Prince Meshchersky's land in
Lotoshino, lies west of Volokolamsk and Lotoshino, on the edge of the
Moscow Oblast. Here an astonishing event took place in the heady days
of the first revolution in 1905. A local group of peasants, who were
actively following the political unrest of those days through their
reading club, began to meet under the leadership of local teachers and
the peasant writer and Tolstoyan, Sergei Semenov. They decided to
form a political party, the **Peasant Union** and sent a list of demands to
the newspapers in Moscow including: elections to a properly constituted
parliament; no arrests without the approval of a court; all children to be
entitled to education; and the right to hold public meetings. On 31
October, 1905 they declared themselves the **Republic of Markovo**, a
president was elected, and they took over all local administration
including schools. Recruitment for the Russian army in the Markovo
district ceased. The Republic grew in fame, its influence spread to other
villages and a professor from Chicago arrived to lend his assistance. But
after the disturbances of 1905 had been overcome, the forces of the law
descended and in July, 1906 all the Markovo leaders were arrested and
imprisoned. Semenov was released after a few months and went abroad
returning to his native Andreevskoe, near Bukholovo, in 1908. Here he
struggled to introduce modern farming methods and literacy but his
leadership was resented by the elders and in 1922 he was murdered.

*Take the M-9, 150 km to Shakhovskaya, turn left, south, on the R-90 for
20 km then turn left 6 km to Repotino, then right 2 km to the tall church
visible across open fields at* **PESKI**. *(It can also be approached from
Poreche and the Minsk Highway.)*

The rare **Church of the Purification**, *Sreteniya*, stands on a knoll in the
middle of water meadows like a forgotten jewel from another era. It is
not only a particularly fine example of a rare wooden 18th century
church, it has somehow survived whole and undisturbed throughout the
Soviet period never having been closed or desecrated. It even escaped
the fighting in 1941. The only upheaval occurred in 1858 when it was
transferred to Peski from the village of Sereda in order to make way for
a new church there. The Sereda church was destroyed in the 1930s.

The church on a brick foundation is made of logs protected by weatherboard in the northern Russia manner. It consists of two towers, one for the church and the other for bells, linked by a low steeply roofed *trapeza*. The church, which has two pentagonal apses, rises from the cube base in three octagonal receding tiers culminating in the hemispherical faceted dome and cupola. The even taller bell tower has a two-tier cube base with one strikingly tall octagonal tier and above, under the roof, an open grill for the bells. The towers are painted black with red trim while the cupolas are light blue decorated with stars. The interior walls of the church, unlike the plastered *trapeza*, are hung with canvas in the traditional manner and painted with biblical scenes. The iconostasis of the early 1900s contains some 17th century icons from the Old Believer Church of the Trinity in Moscow given to the Peski church in 1857, the same year in which the *Yedinovertsy* Old Believers (including those at the Trinity church) attached themselves by special agreement to the Orthodox Church. Another great treasure is a remarkable 18th century wooden sculpture of the Russian saint, Nil Stolobensky. His aged, humped figure on the left in the *trapeza* just before the church proper is sometimes carefully draped with a shawl.

Services are held every morning but beware, for after 1 p.m. it is locked. A special festival is held on St Elijah's day, 2 August, attracting many local people and pilgims.

As we walked up to the church the priest came forward warily. He was suspicious of strangers in this remote place, for the church had been robbed, although the thief had been caught and sent to prison and the icons returned. A few years ago when there was no road connecting the church with the outside world he and the few parishioners had to struggle through the water meadows in high boots to reach it; in spring and autumn it could be completely cut off. We began to appreciate how it was that the church had survived the Soviet period so well and even to be grateful for that Russian scourge, *besputitsa* – absence of roads.

INDEX

Dates are given for architects and designers where available.